C++ Programmer's Companion

Designing, Testing, and Debugging

Stephen R. Davis

Addison-Wesley Publishing Company

Reading, Massachusetts   Menlo Park, California   New York
Don Mills, Ontario   Wokingham, England   Amsterdam   Bonn
Sydney   Singapore   Tokyo   Madrid   San Juan
Paris   Seoul   Milan   Mexico City   Taipei

Many of the designations used by manufacturers and sellers to distinguish their products are claimed as trademarks. Where those designations appear in this book and Addison-Wesley was aware of a trademark claim, the designations have been printed in initial capital letters.

The authors and publishers have taken care in preparation of this book, but make no expressed or implied warranty of any kind and assume no responsibility for errors or omissions. No liability is assumed for incidental or consequential damages in connection with or arising out of the use of the information or programs contained herein.

Library of Congress Cataloging-in-Publication Data

Davis, Stephen R.,   1956-
    C++ programmer's companion : designing, testing, and debugging / Stephen R. Davis.
       p.   cm.
    Includes index.
    ISBN 0-201-60829-4
    1. C++   (Computer program language)   I. Title.
QA76.73.C153D37   1993
005.4'3 – – dc20   92-28198
                                              CIP
                                            r 92

Sponsoring Editor: Julie Stillman
Project Management: Elizabeth Rogalin and Claire Horne
Production Coordinator: Kathy Traynor
Cover Design: Mary Reed/ImageSet Design
Set in 11-point Times by Benchmark Productions

2 3 4 5 6–MA–96959493
Second printing, May 1993

Contents

Acknowledgments

Bringing a book to the public is never a solitary effort. I would like to acknowledge the assistance of Bob Bourbonnais, whose technical reviews and suggestions have resulted in a much–improved book. I would also like to thank E-Systems, Inc., for its support and encouragement. I am also indebted to Claire Horne, Elizabeth Rogalin, Julie Stillman, Camilla Ayers, Kathy Traynor, and numerous others without whose efforts this book would never have seen the light of day. But, of course, my deepest thanks go to my son, Kinsey, and wife, Jenny, who have been willing to share Dad with that infernal machine these long months.

Introduction

The demands of an ever-changing marketplace have led to the emergence of a new generation of programming languages. The flagship object-oriented programming language is C++, a hybrid based on ANSI standard C. C++ melds the power of the object-oriented paradigm with C, the existing standard for software development on the PC.

In my years of working with C++ and teaching it to others, I've learned how tricky C++ can be. As a hybrid, C++ blends features of different programming styles in occasionally inconsistent ways.

This book results from years of frustration for me and my students. My intent was to create a book that can serve as a complete "one-stop shopping" guide to writing error-free software. The *C++ Programmer's Companion* shows you how to conceive, design, implement, test, and debug high quality C++ programs in minimum time. It also alerts you to a series of pitfalls that the C++ programmer must learn to avoid.

Everyone from the advanced beginner to the experienced C/C++ programmer, from the hobbyist to the professional software engineer, should find valuable information on good C++ programming style in the *C++ Programmer's Companion*. I presume a knowledge of C.

What This Book Covers

C++ Programmer's Companion is divided into two sections, the first being devoted to creating, testing, and debugging a C++ program. The second part of the book, the Error Message Desk Reference, includes a list of all significant C++ compile time errors for both the Borland and Microsoft compilers.

Chapter 1 provides an overview of the C++ language for those familiar with C but not completely at ease with the syntax of C++. This chapter also explains the object-oriented programming paradigm on which the C++ extensions are based.

It is easier to avoid software errors through careful design, development, and testing, than it is to remove errors through debugging. Chapter 2 discusses the rationale for using error prevention techniques early in the development cycle, rather than error repair techniques later.

A quality program is based on a good design written to satisfy well-established requirements. A consistent, loosely coupled coding style that makes efficient use of encapsulated class hierarchies helps produce a program that is easy to understand, debug, and maintain. Rigorous reviews at each step of the process ensure that these principles are being adhered to, thus avoiding surprises during integration. Chapters 3 and 4 discuss the requirements, design, and coding phases of a project.

To provide help during the coding phase, Chapters 5 and 6 present a comprehensive list of C++ traps and pitfalls, offering examples and explanations of each. Special attention is given to pointer problems, including those stemming from 80x86 segmentation.

Despite the programmer's vigilance during design and coding, some errors will slip into the program. Chapter 7 covers the testing techniques currently used to find those errors in a systematic way.

Chapters 8 and 9 wrap up the first part of the book with a discussion of debugging tools and methods, and a step-by-step sample debugging session of a program containing many of the errors mentioned in Chapters 5 and 6. Some unique debugger problems are presented as well.

The Error Message Desk Reference contains a listing of over 125 of the most common C++ compile time errors. Each error entry contains an explanation of the error and sample code containing that error. The sample code is then corrected to show how to solve this type of problem. The compiler messages generated by both the Borland and Microsoft C++ compilers are presented with each entry. The accompanying error index provides the programmer with quick and easy access to the Borland or Microsoft error message, making this section a handy desktop assistant for the C++ programmer.

Why You Need This Book

As software applications become increasingly complex, the cost and effort required to develop these applications continues to rise. Today's programmer must learn and adapt to new methodologies to keep the software development process manageable. I think you'll find that the *C++ Programmer's Companion* delivers the techniques you need to develop high quality C++ programs in less time. I welcome your comments and can be reached at my MCI Mail address of SDavis, or via Internet at RD4738.ETSUV2.ETSU.EDU.

Part 1

Development

Chapter 1

Review of C++

This chapter is an overview of the C++ language and the object-oriented paradigm. It assumes knowledge of C. Programmers already familiar with both of these topics may turn to Chapter 2. However, many programmers who have just begun to dabble with C++ treat it as simply "a better C" and are confused by some of the concepts behind the language. I encourage such readers to refresh their understanding of object-oriented programming and C++ before undertaking the task of learning to write and debug C++ programs.

A more detailed explanation is presented in *The C++ Primer* by Stanley Lippman. The current standard reference for C++ is *The Annotated C++ Reference Manual* by Ellis and Stroustrup.

What is Object-Oriented Programming?

The programming community has seen different programming techniques come and go in its 40-year life span. As with art, architecture, automobile design, and other areas of human endeavor, different methods of programming were not originally recognized as anything more than variances in personal styles. Slowly, however, differing approaches were recognized as developmental philosophies or **paradigms**.

Programmers came to realize that the paradigms they use greatly influence the cost and quality of the final product. A good paradigm leads to a better quality product at a lower price.

The most recent programming paradigm, the one adopted by C++ and the one advanced by this book, is **object-oriented programming**, or **OOP**.

The History of C++

The object-oriented paradigm was first introduced in the late 1960s with the language Simula67. It was further developed during the '70s especially with the language Smalltalk-80. The popularity of OOP grew considerably during the '80s with the introduction of object-oriented versions of most conventional languages.

C++ is the result of adding object-oriented programming capabilities to the base C language. It is not, however, the only possible result of this fusion: the Objective C language used with the Next machine is another.

C++ started with the addition of simple classes to C. The result, known as **C with Classes**, was first described by Bjarne Stroustrup in 1982. This language was expanded and refined until it was renamed **C++ Version 1.0** and was introduced to the world in *The C++ Programming Language* by Bjarne Stroustrup in 1986. While this book has historical interest, it is no longer recommended to beginning programmers because C++ has evolved with each new revision. The definitive version of the language as of this writing is *The Annotated C++ Reference* by Ellis and Stroustrup, which describes Version 2.1.

Some C++ implementations are interpreters that convert C++ input modules into C output modules; the output modules are then compiled and linked in the standard way using conventional C tools. Although these interpreters are extremely portable (C compilers exist for almost all machines), the extra interpret step slows compilation and makes debugging somewhat more difficult. (AT&T's `cfront` is such an interpreter.)

C++ began to catch on in the PC world with the introduction of true C++ compilers, first from Zortech and one year later from Borland. These packages offered all of the advantages of C++ with the convenience of C. The attraction of C++ was enhanced by the fact that programmers could purchase either package, which included a C compiler, at only a small premium over the C-only version.

The History of Programming Paradigms

What is the object-oriented paradigm? Webster's Collegiate Dictionary defines *paradigm* as an example or pattern. A paradigm is merely a way of thinking, an approach to solving a problem. Different programming paradigms have dominated over the years. The earliest of these styles is best described as **chaos programming**.

The hallmark of the chaos style of programming is a carefree, anything-goes approach in which all thought is directed at solving the problem with no thought given to the method. Chaos programs have little organization, either physically or logically, with `jump` and `go to` commands sprinkled liberally throughout. Chaos is best typified by early versions of BASIC.

In the earliest days of programming, chaos worked reasonably well: memory restrictions so limited the size of programs that programmers were able mentally to keep track of all of the logic paths within a program. This was important since each path represented a potential error that must be tested. As program size grew, however, the number of different paths through a program grew exponentially under chaos.

A program consists of a series of statements, each of which, when viewed from the outside, appears as an independent agent. We can model the lines within a program with schoolchildren in a room. The flow of control within the program passes from one line to another, much as a note might pass from one schoolchild to the next. Without any restrictions on the way the children can interact, the number of different paths the note can take becomes bewildering.

Even if we make the restriction that no student may receive the note twice, the number of paths grows dramatically with the number of students in the room. The number of different paths through N points is equal to the sum of $i = 1$ to N of $N!/(N-i)!$. Even if the number of paths is limited only to those paths that include all children, we still see a factorial rate of increase in the number of paths. This progression is as follows:

# of nodes	# of paths	# of paths that include all nodes
1	1	1
2	4	2
3	15	6
4	64	24
5	325	120
6	1956	720
7	13,699	5040
8	109,600	40,320
9	986,409	366,880
10	9,864,100	3,628,800

Without any restrictions on itself, the chaos program becomes virtually impossible to test and debug as its size increases. Too many different paths exist with too many different interactions for the programmer to follow.

The first major improvement over the chaos paradigm came with the introduction of **functional programming**. Originally introduced as a way to reuse common code, functions developed into basic building blocks. A programmer could divide the problem at hand into several smaller problems, each to be solved separately by its own function. The problems could be further subdivided recursively, resulting in a multilevel, function hierarchy. Although chaos reigned within the functions, the resulting functional programs were easier to complete. The most popular functional programming languages are FORTRAN and COBOL.

A program that requires 100 lines to solve has some 10^{158} possible paths running through it using the chaos approach. If we assume 5 extra lines per function as overhead, the same program divided into four separate functions would be 120 lines long. However, the resulting functional program has 10^{33} potential paths, calculated as follows:

2.6 E32   paths through a 30-line function
* 4

1.1 E33   paths through a functional program

Functional programming can significantly reduce the number of interactions. As the functions become smaller, a point of diminishing returns is reached. First, the overhead of dividing up the program increases with the number of functions, partially cancelling the benefit. Second, the number of interactions between functions increases with the number of functions.

The next major programming paradigm, **structured programming**, reduced the number of interactions within the functions themselves by restricting what the programmer could do. Gone were the chaotic jumps back and forth within the function. Programmers were constrained to neat loops and `if . . . then . . . else` clauses with single entry and single exit points. The classic structured programming languages are C and Pascal.

These smaller blocks offered many of the advantages of functions without as much overhead. Neither did they allow for as many different paths.

Reconsider the preceding hypothetical program using structured programming. The program contains the same four functions, but these have been internally divided into five smaller blocks of six lines apiece. Because of the restrictions of structured programming, only ten different paths exist through these blocks within the functions. The additional overhead of structured programming, however, has increased the program length to 150 lines.

```
   720  number of paths through six lines
*    5  number of blocks
   ----
  3600
+   10  number of interactions between blocks
   ----
  3610
*    4  number of functions
   ----
14,440  paths through structured program
```

The number of paths through the program has been reduced to the order of 10^4.

Structured programming eased the debugging task in another way as well. Functional (and, of course, chaotic) languages had poor data structures. Although programmers were supposed to pass all data into and out of functions via arguments, without powerful data structures this was often not possible. Functions were forced to refer large blocks of common memory. Almost no data modularity was possible. When data became corrupted, it was very difficult to determine which function was to blame.

By contrast, the structured programmer could bundle data elements together into more easily identified structures (Pascal calls these RECORDS; C calls them `structs`). This made it more likely that functions could restrict themselves to passed arguments and avoid access to common memory.

The Object-Oriented Paradigm

As programmers gained experience with structured programming languages and techniques, they realized that additional gains in programming efficiency would not be made by further restricting program code interactions. To make further improvements, programmers focused on the data structures.

To understand this move, we must examine how programs are written. All problems exist in some world known as the **problem domain**. Once the requirements of the system are understood, the analyst builds a model of the problem. This model must capture the essential features of the problem while abstracting away the confusing details. The designer then sets about writing a design that solves the problem, works entirely within the analyst's model, and fulfills the customer requirements.

Programs exist in the internal world of computers, known as the **program domain**. The programmer must write the instructions and build the data structures to port the design from the problem domain into the program domain.

Consider a program designed to control the air-conditioning system of a large building. The programmer starts by modeling the relevant building activities: A building has doors that let in heat; the doors are opened more often during the day, especially at 8:00 A.M., noon, and 5:00 P.M.; the external temperature varies, hitting a peak around 3:00 P.M.; electricity is cheaper at night than during the day, and so on. Once the model is understood and known to be accurate (testing of real buildings is necessary to ensure an accurate model), the programmers set about writing functions and data structures for each aspect of the model.

Programmers realized that the more program domain structures could be made to resemble their real-world analogs, the easier would be the job of porting from one stage to the next. Pascal records and C structures allow the program to model some aspects of real-world objects accurately, but they fall short in other respects. These structures only allow the programmer to assign passive properties — those that can be assigned a value — and not any active properties that the object might possess, such as what the object does when you turn it on, or throw it, or sit on it. In addition, the taxonomic relationships among objects cannot be expressed. For example, there is no way to define a structure `EasyChair` in terms of an existing structure `Chair`.

The object-oriented paradigm attempts to address these shortcomings. It is characterized by the properties of data abstraction, encapsulation, inheritance, and polymorphism.

Data abstraction refers to the ability to build a data structure to define an object and then to use it within a program without having to pay attention to its internal details, much as a person might manipulate a real-world object — such as a microwave oven, a writing pen, or a household pet — without seeing its internals. Data abstraction simplifies the programmer's task by reducing the number of details to be dealt with at any given time.

Encapsulation provides the enforcement necessary to make sure that only functions immediately associated with the data structure are allowed access to its internal details. Without encapsulation, data abstraction is merely a convention, a rule of convenience, that a function might break at any time. With encapsulation, functions cannot reach into the data structure any more than you can reach into the internals of your microwave.

The **inheritance property** allows the programmer to describe new objects in terms of previously defined objects. For example, the programmer may describe a new type of object `Sedan` in terms of an existing base type `Automobile`. This serves two purposes. First, it saves effort because it is easier to describe only the properties unique to a `Sedan` than to define all of its properties. Second, inheritance expresses a relationship between `Automobile` and `Sedan` that is not expressible in purely structured languages. This is known as an **IS A relationship:** that is, a `Sedan` is an `Automobile`. Logically, wherever an `Automobile` is called for, a `Sedan` should do, even if a `Sedan` performs a particular operation slightly differently than the general `Automobile`. The reverse may not be true, however, as an `Automobile` is not a `Sedan`. The ability to stand in for a base type is **polymorphism**.

To write a program using the object-oriented paradigm, the programmer finds the essential classes of objects in the problem domain and identifies the taxonomy between them. In small programs, this is straightforward. In larger programs, the base classes and those derived from them may not be so obvious. An incorrect choice results in an inaccurate model, which rapidly complicates the job of porting the solution.

Various techniques have developed to help properly identify and connect the base objects. These techniques, collectively known as object-oriented analysis and object-oriented design, will be covered in Chapter 3.

C++ Syntax

C++ is the next step in the evolution of the C language. The original C, introduced by Kernighan and Ritchie, is commonly known as K&R or Classic C. This version was replaced by the ANSI Standard version, known as Standard C, in the late 1980s.

Work began on C++ in the early 1980s. Development of the ANSI Standard for C++ is well underway as of this writing. Only minor differences exist between implementations.

Evolution of C++

C++ is a hybrid language created by adding object-oriented concepts to a base C language. C++ has adapted with and, in many cases, lead the development of Standard C. C++ is almost a superset of ANSI C: that is, a well-written ANSI C program (one that does not generate warnings when compiled with all warnings enabled) will almost surely compile without problems under a C++ compiler. Adherence to C compatibility was intended to simplify the transition from C to C++, thereby enhancing its acceptability.

The extensions that C++ provides over ANSIC fall into essentially two categories: those that are related to the object-oriented paradigm and those that are not.

A Better C

As a language, Classic C has many problems. Its syntax is concise, but obtruse in the extreme. Its type checking is almost nonexistent. Many of the details concerning evaluation of mixed expressions were not spelled out, leaving compiler writers to draw different conclusions.

In creating Standard C, the X3J11 American National Standard Committee addressed many of these issues. However, because the committee's intent was to create a new version of the same language — not a new language — their flexibility was limited in many areas. The X3J11 committee considered its job to be as much clearing up matters left dangling by the K&R definition as adding new features. When new features were added, they were added without changing the philosophy of the Classic C language.

Although C++ is still essentially a compatible superset of Standard C, it is a distinct language. Therefore, the inventors of C++ had considerably more freedom to add features suggested by their experience.

The New Comment Style   In addition to the standard /* */ comment style of C, C++ allows a comment to begin with a // and end at the end of the line. A single-line comment is functionally equivalent, but slightly easier to type, and avoids the common error of forgetting to close the comment properly.

Other than preprocessor constructs, this is the only statement in C++ that is sensitive to the end of the line. In addition, a /* */ comment appearing within a // comment is not recognized, and vice versa. In the early days of C++ this fact was used at compilation to determine whether the compiler was C or C++ based on the following:

```
int _CPP_ = 1 //*  */ 2
          ;
```

A C compiler parses the preceding into

```
int _CPP_ = 1 / 2
          ;
```

resulting in a _CPP_ value of 0, while the C++ compiler sees it as

```
int _CPP_ = 1
          ;
```

resulting in a value of 1. This does not work with C compilers such as Borland C that accept the `//` comments. (The Borland C compiler provides a `__cplusplus` intrinsic that is defined when in C++ mode. Other compilers provide similar intrinsics.)

Function Prototyping   C++ enforces a higher level of type checking. Where all pointer types once might have been considered equal, a pointer to an integer is not assignment compatible with a pointer to a character in C++ (at least not without a warning being generated).

Similarly, the type of functions must be more strictly defined as well. A function declared as follows:

```
int fn(int a, char b);
```

is no longer simply the function `fn()`. It is now a function `fn()` taking an integer and a character and returning an integer. This is written `int fn(int,char)`.

All functions must be prototyped to establish their type. This is done in three ways:

1. The function is defined before it is used. In this way, the definition itself forms the prototype. This appears as follows:

```
int square(int x) {
    return x*x;
}
int mainFunc() {
    int y;

    y = square(5);
}
```

2. A prototype declaration before the function is used. This appears as follows:

```
int square(int x);        //prototype declaration
void mainFunc() {
    int y;
```

```
        y = square(5);
}
int square(int x) {
    return x*x;
}
```

3. If a function is referenced without a prototype, C++ invents one from the way in which the function is called (often called a Miranda prototype). Although this feature may seem like a labor-saving device, it is dangerous and can introduce bugs that are difficult to track down. (We will revisit this issue in Chapter 5.)

A function may be declared as taking no arguments either by leaving the argument list blank (`fn()`) or by specifying the argument as void (`fn(void)`). A function may be declared to take any number of any type of arguments by using an ellipsis as the argument (`fn(...)`).

In addition, a function may be assigned default arguments as in the following prototype declaration:

```
int fn(int a, int b = 10);

fn(1,  2);              //call 1
fn(3, 10);              //call 2
fn(3);                  //call 3
```

Here the function requires two integer arguments, the second of which defaults to 10. The second and third call have identical effects, resulting in an initial argument of 3 and a second argument of 10 in both cases. Multiple arguments may be defaulted, but they must be assigned from right to left.

Function Overloading Since C++ requires a function to have a prototype, C++ can rely on the prototype to be part of the function's identification. For example, C++ can differentiate between a function `fn(int)` and a function `fn(char*)` both by the way it is declared and the way it is used.

```
void fn(int i) {
    printf("integer = %d", i);
}
void fn(char* pC) {
    printf("character string = %s", pC);
}


void otherFunc() {
    int i = 5;
    char *c = "a string";

    fn(i);              //invokes the first function
    fn(c);              //invokes the second function
```

Function overloading should not be confused with polymorphism. In function overloading, the decision of which function to call is made at compile time on the basis of the static (that is, declared) type of the arguments. Polymorphism is a run-time decision based upon the object's actual type.

Function overloading reduces **namespace clutter** resulting from the requirement in C that all procedures have a different name regardless of the similarity between their functions.

Consider the function sqrt() designed to take the square root of a number. We can limit ourselves to taking the square root of integers, floats, and doubles. C, however, would require three different functions with three different names, say sqrtInt(), sqrtFloat(), and sqrtDouble(). C++ requires three functions, but they may all carry the name sqrt() (actually their full names are sqrt(int), sqrt(float), and sqrt(double)).

Function overloading also can allow the programmer increased efficiency. In the preceding example, we might have coded a single sqrt() function as a single sqrt(double). Since C++ can convert either an int or a float into a double, this single function represents a least common denominator. However, this function involves considerable overhead when invoked for an integer. The sqrt(int) and sqrt(float) versions can be added later without touching the different calls to avoid this overhead.

Finally, overloaded functions allow programmers to add new data types to existing programs. For example, assume that the programmer needed to add a `Complex` data type. Using function overloading, the programmer is able to add a `sqrt(Complex)` to handle square root functions as well.

Overloaded functions must differ sufficiently in their arguments so that C++ can differentiate which function is intended with each call. For example, C++ can differentiate between the following functions:

```
void fn(int);              //initial function
void fn(float);            //different type argument
void fn(int*);             //pointer is different too
void fn(struct MyClass*);  //different type of pointer
void fn(unsigned int);     //unsigned vs. signed above
void fn(int, int);         //two args vs. one above
```

Functions cannot be differentiated by return type because a function's return type is not always obvious in use. The call in the following example does not necessarily refer to the `void fn(int)` function, since the results of an `int` function may be discarded without comment.

```
void fn(int);
int  fn(int);          //error: can't differentiate
                       //by return type
void myFunc() {
    fn(10);            //call int fn() or void fn()?
}
```

In addition, C++ cannot differentiate functions by their default arguments.

```
void fn(int a);
void fn(int a, int b = 0);
void myFunc() {
    fn(1, 2);          //clearly refers to second fn()
    fn(1);             //to which does this refer?
}
```

Function declarations containing ellipses cause overloading problems when overlaps exist with other functions. Consider the following three declarations:

```
void fn(int    a,   ...);          //function #1
void fn(char *pA, ...);            //function #2
void fn(int    a, int b);          //function #3

void myFunc() {
    fn(1);              //refers to function #1
    fn("my name");   //refers to function #2
    fn(1, "myname");//refers to function #1
    fn(1, 2);         //refers to function #1 or #3?
}
```

Referential Variables   C++ allows a variable to be declared refer-ential as follows:

```
int i;
int *pI = &i;        //declare a pointer to i
int &rI = i;         //declare a reference to i

 i   = 10;           //all three statements...
*pI = 10;            //...have the exact same...
 rI = 10;            //...affect
```

Here the variable `rI` is a reference to `i`: that is, any reference to `rI` is treated exactly as a reference to `i`. Since `rI` is an alias for `i`, it is of the exact same type. Reference is not part of the type. The reference must be established at definition — any subsequent use of `rI` refers to its alias.

Referential variables are used mostly as arguments to or return values from functions. For example, in the code segment that follows the value of `i` after returning from the function `fn1()` is still 0, since C always passes by value.

The conventional solution to this problem is to pass the address of the variable and allow the function to store a value into this address, as shown in function `fn2()`. Thus, after the call to `fn2()` the value of `i` in `mainFunc()` is 2.

Declaring the argument referential has the same effect. The reference of the variable `rI` is established when the function is called as `i` so that the value of `i` after returning from `fn3()` is 3.

```
void fn1(int i) {
    i = 1;
}
void fn2(int* pI) {
   *pI = 2;
}
void fn3(int &rI) {
    rI = 3;
}
void mainFunc() {
    int i = 0;
    fn1(i);            //i = 0 upon return
    fn2(&i);           //    2 upon return
    fn3(i);            //    3 upon return
}
```

Since the reference is not part of the type of an object, the following two function declarations are ambiguous.

```
void fn(int  arg);
void fn(int& rArg);

void myFunc() {
    int a;
    fn(a);             //call function #1 by value or
                       //function #2 by reference?
}
```

Declarations within Blocks   C++ allows variables to be declared almost anywhere within a block, not just prior to all executable statements. For example, the following declaration is legal.

```
for (int i = 0; i < 10; i++)...
```

There are a few places where variables cannot be declared, for example, within the conditional clause of a `for`, `while`, or `do . . . while` loop. The space for the variable is allocated at the beginning of the block, irrespective of where the variable is declared within the block; however, the program may not refer to the variable until after its declaration.

Inline Functions   One of the most abused aspects of C and a major source of errors is its macro definitions. In use macros appear like functions; unlike functions, however, they are expanded in place. Using macros, small services could be performed without the overhead of performing a function call and return. The following examples show some of the problems of macros.

```
#define square(x) x * x

int a, b, c;

a = square(2);      //expands to a = 2 * 2
b = square(2 + 3);  //expands to b = 2 + 3 * 2+ 3
c = square(a++);    //expands to c = a++ * a++
```

In the first call the variable a is assigned the value 4 as expected. In the second expression, b is assigned the value 11 instead of the expected 25 because multiplication has a higher precedence than addition. This problem can be solved by being more circumspect in the macro definition as follows:

```
#define square (x) ((x) * (x))

b = square(2 + 3)    //expands to ((2 + 3) * (2 + 3))
```

The third assignment is more difficult to solve. Here a is incremented twice and c is assigned the value 20 rather than the expected 16. In general, it is incorrect to invoke a macro with an expression that has side-effects. (Here the expression a++ has the side-effect that the value of a is incremented.)

Unfortunately, macro definitions appear like function calls, and it is not generally obvious which calls are to functions and which to macros. In addition, since expansion of the macro is not normally visible to the programmer, expansion problems are very difficult for inexperienced programmers to track down.

To solve these problems, C++ replaces macro definitions with **inline functions**. Functions declared with the `inline` descriptor are expanded wherever they are called by the compiler. Inline functions offer the same efficiencies as macros, but without the dangers. Thus, in the following example, the same three assignments result in the expected values of 4, 25, and 16 (with a incremented only once).

```
inline int square(int x) { return x * x;}

int a, b, c;

a = square(2);          //expands to a = 2 * 2
b = square(2 + 3);      //expands to b = (2 + 3) * (2+ 3)
c = square(a++);        //expands to c = a * a; a++
```

The time required to perform a function call is usually short. It does not make sense to declare a large function inline because the time to perform the call itself becomes insignificant relative to the time it takes to perform the function statements. However, inline functions can represent a significant savings for very small functions that are called repeatedly. The break-even point is about three C++ statements. If any more than three statements are required, the function should probably not be declared inline.

Certain things force a function outline. Functions that contain a loop, as in the following example, are automatically outlined.

```
inline int loop(int a) {
    for (int i = 1; --a;)
        i *= a;
    return i;
}
```

Attempting to take the address of an inline function results both an inline version and an outline version. Direct calls are expanded inline, whereas calls made through the pointer refer to the outline version. Consider the following:

```
inline int max(int a, int b) {
    return (a > b) ? a : b;
```

```
}

void myFunc() {
    int i = 1, j = 2, k;
    k = max(i,j);    //refers to inline version

    int (*pFun)(int, int) = max;  //forces creation
                                  //of outline version
    k = (*pFun)(i, j);  //refers to outline version
```

Here the first call is expanded inline, whereas the second call — through the pointer `pFun` — is made to an outline version of the same function. Recursive functions declared `inline` are handled similarly.

Due to this schizophrenic behavior, functions invoked indirectly through pointers, as well as recursive functions, should not be declared inline.

The `volatile` and `const` Storage Classes   Declaring a variable to be `volatile` indicates to the compiler that its value is subject to change by forces external to the program. That is, the compiler should make no attempt to cache its value in a register to reduce the number of times it is loaded from memory.

The use of `volatile` can best be explained with an example. In lower memory, the PC BIOS retains the current time in units of clock ticks since midnight. Roughly 18.2 times per second, the Programmable Interval Timer chip of the PC generates an interrupt. This interrupt is fielded by the BIOS, which increments this location.

A DOS program can delay by sitting in a tight loop while waiting for the counter to reach a specified value, as follows:

```
unsigned *pTimer = 0x0040006CL; //addr of tick counter
unsigned targetVal;

//wait one second (18 timer ticks from now)
targetVal = *pTimer + 18;
while (targetVal != *pTimer);
```

However, this program segment may not work as planned. An optimizing compiler might cache the value of `*pTimer` in a register to avoid accessing the memory location every time through the loop. Normally this would be valid, since nowhere in the loop is `*pTimer` modified. In this case, however, the value of `*pTimer` is being changed by the interrupt, which is not visible to the program. Declaring `pTimer` as follows solves the problem.

```
volatile unsigned *pTimer = 0x0040006CL;
```

Since the compiler now knows that external forces are at work (namely the timer hardware), it will no longer attempt any optimizations and will read the timer value each time through the loop as intended.

The `const` storage class is almost the reverse. A `const` variable is not subject to change by the program. That is, a `const` variable may not appear on the left-hand side of an assignment. Thus, a `const` variable may be used wherever a constant is allowed — for example, in an array declaration. A `const` variable must be explicitly initialized at declaration because it cannot be changed later. The difference between a `const` variable and a constant is that a `const` variable has an address.

In compound declarations, the `volatile`-ness or `const`-ness may be applied separately. The following declaration:

```
volatile unsigned const *pTimer = 0x0040006CL;
```

declares a constant pointer to a volatile unsigned: that is, the pointer may not be changed, but the location pointed at may be changed at any time.

Scope Resolution Operator

A local variable declaration masks any global variable of the same name. In the following code segment, the global variable `var` was not accessible from within the `fn()` in C. C++ allows the use of the global resolution operator `::` to explicitly refer to the scope of the variable. Thus, `var` refers to the local version while `::var` refers to the global. The scope resolution operator may also be used to refer to members of structures that have been overloaded by members of the same name in derived structures.

```
int var;
void fn() {
    int var;
```

```
    var = 1;           //refers to the   local variable
  ::var = 2;           //refers to the global variable
}
```

Anonymous Unions   C++ includes support for unions that carry neither a class nor object name, hence the designation anonymous. These unions are often used to examine an object in a byte-wise fashion as in the following example:

```
void displayBytes(float value) {
    union {
        float x;
        unsigned long 1;
    };
    x = value;
    printf("value = %f,(%lx)", x, 1);
}
```

An anonymous union can also be used to save space within a structure that contains two mutually exclusive sets of data, as in the following:

```
struct VehicleTaxData {
    char modelName[40];   //vehicle's model name
    char manName[40];     //name of manufacturer
    unsigned displacement; //for motorcycles
    unsigned weight;       //for cars and trucks
};
```

In this example, state road taxes are calculated based upon how much wear the vehicle inflicts on the road surface. For motorcycles, which have a very high horsepower-to-weight ratio, the state uses the engine displacement. For large vehicles, which damage roads through the pressure they apply, taxes are based on weight. Notice, however, that no single record requires both displacement and weight. Thus, memory space can be saved by allowing both elements to occupy the same location in memory via the anonymous union.

```
struct VehicleTaxData {
    char modelName[40];   //vehicle's model name
```

```
    char manName[40];      //name of manufacturer
    union {
        unsigned displacement; //for motorcycles
        unsigned weight;       //for cars and trucks
    };
};
```

This second use of anonymous unions is usually a bad idea. Anonymous unions are a source of many software defects. For example, a maintenance programmer may forget (or never realize) that the displacement and weight fields are mutually exclusive. Unless the number of records is large and the duplicated space great, the amount of memory saved does not warrant the dangers of using an anonymous union.

C with Classes

Despite the additions and improvements to the language mentioned so far, it is the class construct that enables C++ to implement data hiding, data abstraction, inheritance, and polymorphism — the features that make C++ an object-oriented language. Classes, and all that they bring with them, make C++ more than just an improved dialect of C.

Class Construct   The class construct is based upon the C structure (`struct`). C structures allow programmers to design data objects that closely describe "real-world" objects.

Consider, for example, a structure `Address` that might be used to hold personal addresses in a database. Having created such a structure, the careful programmer would then write a series of functions for accessing the data within this structure. The structure definition would be placed in an `include` file as follows:

```
/*Define the structure for an address*/
struct Address {
    unsigned   streetNumber;
    char*      streetName;
    char*      cityName;
    char       state[3];
```

```
    char      zipCode[6];
};
typedef unsigned long ulong;

//prototype declarations for access functions
void  initAddress(struct Address* addressPtr,
                  unsigned sNumber, char* sName,
                  char* cName,      char* stateName,
                  char* zipC);
void  deleteAddress(struct Address *addressPtr);
void  streetAddress(struct Address* addressPtr,
                    char* name);
void  cityAddress(struct Address* addressPtr,
                  char* name);
ulong zipCodeAddress(struct Address* addressPtr);
```

The implementation of these functions is then written in a C++ source file.

```
#include <string.h>
#include <stdlib.h>
#include "address.hpp"            //defines struct Address

/*initAddress - create an address*/
void initAddress(Address*   addressPtr,
                 unsigned sNumber, char* sName,
                 char*    cName,   char* stateName,
                 char* zipC) {
    int length;

    addressPtr->streetNumber = sNumber;

    length = strlen(sName) + 1;
    if (addressPtr->streetName = (char*)malloc(length))
        strcpy(addressPtr-> streetName, sName);
    length = strlen(cName) + 1;
    if (addressPtr->cityName = (char*)malloc(length))
        strcpy(addressPtr->cityName, cName);
    strncpy(addressPtr->state, stateName, 2);
```

```
        addressPtr->state[2] = '\0';

        strncpy(addressPtr->zipCode, zipC, 5);
        addressPtr->zipCode[5] = '\0';
    }


    /*deleteAddress - delete an address*/
    void deleteAddress(Address *addressPtr) {
       if (addressPtr->streetName)
          free(addressPtr->streetName);
       if (addressPtr->cityName)
          free(addressPtr->cityName);
    }


    /*streetAddress - fetch the street address as an ASCII
                      string (with a space between number
                      and street)*/
    void streetAddress(Address* addressPtr,
                       char*           name) {
       itoa(addressPtr->streetNumber, name, 10);
       strcat(name, " ");
       strcat(name, addressPtr->streetName);
    }


    /*cityAddress - fetch the city address as a string*/
    void cityAddress(Address* addressPtr,
                     char*           name){
        *name = '\0';
        strcat(name, addressPtr->cityName);
        strcat(name, ", ");
        strcat(name, addressPtr->state);
        strcat(name, "  ");
        strcat(name, addressPtr->zipCode);
    }


    /*zipCodeAddress - return zip code as a single long*/
    ulong zipCodeAddress(Address* addressPtr){
        return atol(addressPtr->zipCode);
    }
```

A small program that uses the `Address` structure, including a few of its access functions, follows:

```
#include "address.h"

void main() {
    Address address;
    char buffer[80];

    initAddress(&address, 107, "Rockcrest",
                "Mesquite", "Tx", "75401");
    streetAddress(&address, buffer);
    cityAddress(&address, buffer);
    deleteAddress(&address);
}
```

As we can see, the function `initAddress()` is used to initialize an `Address` object. The street address is called into `buffer` using the function `streetAddress()`, while the city address is retrieved using `cityAddress()`. When the function is finished with the object, it is deactivated by using the `deleteAddress()` function. The keyword `struct` is not necessary in C++ when declaring an object as in the declaration `Address address`. The structure name is sufficient.

The tendency to define all of these functions in a single module and to give them names containing the word *Address* is an attempt to achieve some level of data encapsulation. As long as all functions access the `Address` structure through these functions, only they must be modified to accommodate minor changes to the `Address`. In addition, any errors found in an `Address` object are traceable to one of the access functions. Unfortunately, C does not provide any means to enforce this regulation, and without enforcement, some function invariably breaks the rule and accesses the structure internals directly. Thus, when an `Address` object appears corrupted, the programmer may have difficulty finding the source of the error.

C++ handles this issue by allowing the access functions to be declared as members of the structure. These **member functions**, also called **methods**, become a part of the structure just like the data members. A structure `Address` with member functions appears as follows:

```
struct Address {
    unsigned  streetNumber;
    char*     streetName;
    char*     cityName;
    char      state[3];
    char      zipCode[6];

    void initAddress(unsigned sNumber,
                     char*     sName,  char* cName,
                     char*     stateN, char* zipC);
    void deleteAddress();
    void streetAddress(char* name);
    void cityAddress(char* name);
};
```

The definition for one of the access functions is as follows:

```
/*streetAddress - fetch the street address as an ASCII
                  string (with a space between number
                  and street)*/
void Address::streetAddress(char* name) {
    itoa(streetNumber, name, 10);
    strcat(name, " ");
    strcat(name, streetName);
}
```

Notice how similar this function is to its C cousin. However, the name of the function includes the name of the structure as well. The function is no longer `streetAddress(char*)`, but `Address::streetAddress(char*)`. (The scope resolution operator divides the structure name from the function name.) The function must be invoked with an object of type `Address`. Not only does the type of the object determine which `streetAddress()` function is invoked, but it becomes the current object upon which the function operates.

The references within the function to `streetNumber` and `streetName` refer to the members of the current object, which is pointed to by the reserved name `this`. Thus, referring to `streetName` within a member function is equivalent to `this->streetName`. An explicit argument pointing to the `Address` object is no longer nececcessary.

```
#include "address.hpp"

void main() {
    Address address;
    char buffer[80];

    address.initAddress(107, "Rockcrest",
                        "Mesquite", "Tx", "75401");
    address.streetAddress((char*)buffer);
    address.cityAddress((char*)buffer);
    address.deleteAddress();
}
```

Each call refers to the object `address`. Thus, `address.street-Address()` returns the street address contained within the object `address`. This is similar to the C example, except that the syntax resembles that of a data member.

Although we have made the access functions members of the structure, we have done nothing to hinder other functions from making direct access to the data members of `Address`. C++ provides for this control with the `private` and `public` keywords. Members declared within a private section of a structure are accessible only to other members of the structure; those declared within a public section are accessible to anyone.

Thus, for greater protection we might have defined our `Address` structure as follows:

```
struct Address {
  private:
    unsigned streetNumber;
    char*    streetName;
```

```
    char*      cityName;
    char       state[3];
    char       zipCode[6];

public:
    void initAddress(unsigned  sNumber,
                    char*      sName,  char* cName,
                    char*      stateN, char* zipC);
    void deleteAddress();
    void streetAddress(char* name);
    void cityAddress(char* name);
};
```

The four access functions are declared public. All of the data members in this example are declared private. Since the access functions are members of the structure, they continue to have access to the private data members; however, no non-member functions may now access them directly.

Well-built structures leave most data members (the critical ones, at least) private while providing public member functions for controlled access. Since the overhead of providing a separate function for each data member and of making a function call each time that member is accessed might be a deterent to using access methods, C++ allows member functions to be defined within the structure itself, as follows:

```
struct MyStruct {
  private:
    int data;

  public:
    int value() { return data; }
};
```

A member function defined within the structure definition is assumed to be an inline function. Accessing the member `data` via the inline member function `MyStruct::value()` does not introduce any additional overhead, but it does ensure that the caller will not inadvertently modify `data`.

In C++ **class** is another name for a structure whose members default to private: (A `struct` defaults members to public, whereas a `class` defaults to private. There is no other difference.) Thus, the following definition has the identical effect as the preceding.

```
//class version of MyStruct
class MyStruct {
    int data;

  public:
    int value() { return data; }
};
```

It is considered good programming style always to supply the `private` and `public` declarations explicitly. As long as these declarations are present, the `class` and `struct` keywords may be used interchangeably. Common practice is to reserve `struct` for C structures that do not implement data hiding or inheritance (such structures are called **aggregate classes**) and to use `class` elsewhere. The same rules apply to use of the terms *structure* and *class* in speech.

Occasionally a non-member function must be granted access to a private member. To avoid forcing the data member public, C++ allows the class to grant access privileges to a non-member function by declaring it a **friend**. Declaring a class to be a friend has the effect of declaring all of its member functions as friends.

```
class MyStruct {
    friend void anotherFunc(MyStruct* pMS)
    friend class AnotherClass;
  private:
    int data;

  public:
    int value() { return data; }
};

void anotherFunc(MyStruct* pMS) {
    int value = pMS->data;//this fn has direct access
                          //because it is a friend
}
```

Constructors and Destructors   When class objects are created, they must be initialized before they can be used. In fact, uninitialized objects are usually dangerous in the sense that their nonsensical values may prove fatal to some member functions. In the foregoing address example, an initialization method was provided: `initAddress()`. This is such a common requirement, however, that C++ provides for the declaration of special functions, called **constructors**, that initialize an object when it is created.

A constructor always bears the name of the class and has no return type (not even `void`). To ensure that every object is initialized before it is used, the constructor for an object is called automatically when that object is created.

A constructor may be overloaded with other constructors that have different arguments. The rules for overloading constructors are the same as for overloading any other function.

Similar to the constructor is the **destructor** that is invoked whenever an object is destroyed. The destructor carries the same name as the class but is preceded by a tilde. The destructor has no arguments and, therefore, cannot be overloaded.

The new class `Address` and the sample program that uses it appears as follows:

```
class Address {
  private:
    unsigned  streetNumber;
    char*     streetName;
    char*     cityName;
    char      state[3];
    char      zipCode[6];

  public:
    Address(unsigned sNumber,
            char*     sName,   char* cName,
            char*     stateN,  char* zipC);
    ~Address();
    void streetAddress(char* name);
    void cityAddress(char* name);
};
```

```
void main() {
    Address address(107, "Rockcrest",
                        "Mesquite", "Tx", "75401");
    char buffer[80];

    address.streetAddress(buffer);
    address.cityAddress(buffer);
}                               //destructor called at this point
```

Two constructors are of particular note: the constructor that takes no arguments, called the **default constructor**, and the constructor that takes a reference to an object of its own type, the **copy-initializer** or **c-i constructor**.

For the Address example, these might appear as follows:

```
#include <stdlib.h>
#include <string.h>

class Address {
  private:
    unsigned streetNumber;
    char*    streetName;
    char*    cityName;
    char     state[3];
    char     zipCode[6];
    void     initAddress(unsigned sNumber,
                    char*    sName,   char* cName,
                    char*    stateN,  char* zipC);

  public:
    Address(unsigned sNumber,
            char*    sName,   char* cName,
            char*    stateN,  char* zipC);
    Address();
    Address(Address& oldAdd);
    ~Address();
    void streetAddress(char name[]);
    void cityAddress(  char name[]);
```

```
};
//initAddress - private method to create an address
void Address::initAddress(unsigned sNumber,
                          char* sName,      char* cName,
                          char* stateName, char* zipC) {
    int length;

    streetNumber = sNumber;

    length = strlen(sName) + 1;
    if (streetName = (char*)malloc(length))
        strcpy(streetName, sName);

    length = strlen(cName) + 1;
    if (cityName = (char*)malloc(length))
        strcpy(cityName, cName);

    strncpy(state, stateName, 2);
    state[2] = '\0';

    strncpy(zipCode, zipC, 5);
    zipCode[5] = '\0';
}


//now the constructors
Address::Address(unsigned sNumber, char* sName,
                 char*     cName,    char* stateName,
                 char* zipC) {
    initAddress(sNumber, sName, cName, stateName,
zipC);
}
Address::Address() {
    streetNumber = 0;
    streetName   = (char*)0;
    cityName     = (char*)0;
    state[0] = state[1] = state[2] = '\0';
    for (int i = 0; i < 6; i++)
```

```
        zipCode[i] = '\0';
}
Address::Address(Address& oldObj) {
    initAddress(oldObj.streetNumber, oldObj.streetName,
                oldObj.cityName,     oldObj.state,
                oldObj.zipCode);
}
```

In use, the constructors appear as follows:

```
#include "address.hpp"

void main() {
    Address address1(107, "Rockcrest",
                    "Mesquite", "Tx", "75401");
    Address address2;
    Address address3(address1);
}                        //destructor called at this point
```

The object address2 is initialized with null values. The address3 object is initialized with the same values as address1. It is not a reference, but an independent object whose initial values are the same.

The new and delete Operators   A problem arises with constructing objects that are allocated off of the heap. Consider the following example:

```
void fn() {
    MyClass localObj(10, 10);
    MyClass *pHeapObj = (MyClass*)malloc(sizeof
MyClass);
    //...
}
```

The MyClass(int, int) constructor is called automatically to initialize the object localObj when the variable goes into scope. However, no constructor is called for the object allocated using the malloc() call. One could not even imagine an extension to the syntax of malloc() to cover this problem. The problem is that `malloc()` is a standard library function that accepts only the size of the object to allocate. The object it returns is of type `void*`. The programmer cannot instruct `malloc()` as to which constructor to call.

To remedy this problem, C++ replaces `malloc()` with an operator that does know the class of the object it is creating. The previous example becomes the following:

```
void fn() {
    MyClass localObj(10, 10);
    MyClass *pHeapObj =  new MyClass(20, 20);
    MyClass &heapObj  = *new MyClass(30, 30);
    //...
    delete pHeapObj;
    delete &heapObj;
}
```

The `new` operator allocates space off of the heap, like `malloc()`, and then calls the proper constructor for that class. The return value from `new` is a pointer to a constructed object of the proper type. Therefore, the cast is no longer necessary.

Objects are not destructed when pointers or references to them go out of scope. Thus, for heap objects, it is necessary to destruct them and return them to the heap manually. Since the `free()` standard library function in C has the same problems as `malloc()`, the `delete` operator is used.

Overloading Operators   Another important part of the object-oriented paradigm is data abstraction. Once a new class has been defined, C++ allows the programmer to use it without concern for its internal details. This allows the programmer to abstract away the details.

Defining member functions is an important part of data abstraction. The programmer who uses a class needs only to deal with the interface functions. The specifics of the class internals are masked by making them private and, hence, are inaccessible to the outside world. Another part of the abstraction is the ability to overload the existing operators for objects of a new class.

The classic example is the class Complex. C++ comes with the common arithmetic operators — such as +, -, =, and so on — defined for integer and

floating point classes; however, C++ does not include a type for complex
numbers. A complex number consists of two parts: a real part and an
imaginary part. (An imaginary number is a number that when multiplied
by itself is negative. It is expressed as a real number times the square root
of negative one.) A class `Complex` appears as follows:

```
class Complex {
  private:
    float real;
    float imaginary;

  public:
    Complex() {
              real = imaginary = 0;
          }
    Complex(float r, float i = 0.0) {
              real = r;
              imaginary = i;
          }
    Complex(Complex& c) {
              real      = c.real;
              imaginary = c.imaginary;
          }
    float Real() { return real; }
    float Imag() { return imaginary; }
};
```

One can imagine a series of different member functions that have no
equivalent in real numbers — such as taking the magnitude or the complex conjugate. However, normal arithmetic operations have meaning on
complex numbers.

To see how operators are overloaded for a class, first think of an operator as a special case of a function call. In such a view

```
float a, b, c;

a = b + c;
```

can alternately be expressed as

```
a = +(b, c);
```

or, to use the C++ syntax,

```
a = operator+(b, c);
```

Thus, for a class `Complex` we might define a function as follows:

```
Complex operator+(Complex& a, Complex& b) {
    float realPart = a.real + b.real;
    float imagPart = a.imaginary + b.imaginary;
    return Complex(realPart, imagPart);
}
```

Since the data members of `Complex` are private, such a function would have to be declared a friend of `Complex`. Alternatively, an operator can be declared a member function of the class of the left-hand object. In this example, this appears as follows:

```
class Complex {
  private:
    float real;
    float imaginary;

  public:
    Complex() {
            real = imaginary = 0;
        }
    Complex(float r, float i = 0.0) {
            real = r;
            imaginary = i;
        }
    Complex(Complex& c) {
            real      = c.real;
            imaginary = c.imaginary;
        }
```

```
float Real() { return real; }
float Imag() { return imaginary; }

Complex operator+(Complex& b) {
    float realPart = real + b.real;
    float imagPart = imaginary + b.imaginary;
    return Complex(realPart, imagPart);
}
};
```

All of the operators may be overloaded except ., ?:, .*, .->, and ::. New operators may not be invented. In addition, the programmer cannot change an operator's precedence or binding. (See Chapter 5 for a discussion of precedence and binding.)

Inheriting Classes   When you begin to view the world as a collection of objects of different classes, you notice that many of these classes are similar in some respect. For example, all automobiles share certain common characteristics many, but not all, of which are shared by other vehicles.

Given this relationship, an automobile can be described by first describing a vehicle and then describing in what ways an automobile differs from a vehicle. This is more trouble than it is worth for a single class, but when other classes are added to this taxonomy — as in Figure 1–1 — the savings are substantial. Describing every class individually would result in considerable redundancy.

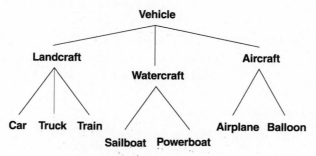

Figure 1–1. A taxonomy of vehicles

C++ allows a programmer to define a class in terms of a previously defined class through the mechanism of inheritance. Consider the class `Vehicle`, which describes things that can carry people or goods from one place to another. The example contains three distinctly different types of vehicles: `Landcraft`, `Watercraft`, and `Aircraft`. Each vehicle type is further subdivided. This process of specialization could be continued down to individual makes and models of cars, airplanes, and sailboats. (Of course, this is not the only possible result. Other, equally reasonable, breakdowns are possible.)

This relationship can be described in C++ as follows:

```
typedef unsigned uint;

class Vehicle {
  private:
    uint weight;
    uint xVel, yVel;
    uint maxSpeed;

  public:
    Vehicle(uint w, uint maxS) {
        weight   = w;
        maxSpeed = maxS;
        xVel = yVel = 0;      //start out stopped
    }

    //move() starts the vehicle out in the specified
    //x and y velocities, or as close as the vehicle can
    //get without exceeding 'maxSpeed'
    virtual void move(uint xV, uint yV);
};

class Landcraft : public Vehicle {
  private:
    uint noWheels;
    uint licenseType;

  public:
```

```
        Landcraft(uint noW, uint licenseT,
                  uint w, uint maxS) : Vehicle(w, maxS) {
            noWheels    = noW;
            licenseType = licenseT;
        }
        void move(uint xV, uint yV);
    };


class Watercraft : public Vehicle {
  private:
    uint maxWinds;

  public:
    Watercraft(uint maxW, uint w, uint maxS)
                  : Vehicle(w, maxS) {
        maxWinds     = maxW;
    }
    void move(uint xV, uint yV);
};


class Aircraft : public Vehicle {
  private:
    uint maxAltitude;
    uint inAir;

  public:
    Aircraft(uint maxA, uint w, uint maxS)
                  : Vehicle(w, maxS) {
        maxAltitude = maxA;
        inAir       = 0;    //start out on the ground
    }
    void move(uint xV, uint yV);
};
```

In this example all vehicles share the properties of weight, maximum speed, and current velocity. To indicate these shared features, each class inherits the class `Vehicle`. This designation is indicated in the declaration of the three derived classes; for example, `class Aircraft :`

`public``Vehicle` is read "class `Aircraft` inherits the class `Vehicle`." Class `Vehicle` is called a **base class** of `Aircraft` while `Aircraft` is a **subclass**, or **derived class**, of `Vehicle`. In addition, each subclass of `Vehicle` has its own properties that it does not share with `Vehicle`, but that it does share with all of its own subclasses. These are the members defined within the class itself.

A subclass need not have intimate knowledge of the internals of a base class. For example, the constructors for each subclass automatically invoke the base class constructor to initialize the base class members.

Class Polymorphism   In addition to saving programmer effort, the previous hierarchy expresses a relationship between different types of vehicles. A car is a type of landcraft, and all landcraft are a type of vehicle. That is, anywhere a vehicle might be called for, a car will do. A car shares all of the properties of a vehicle. This is the is__a relationship; that is, a car is a vehicle.

(The reverse is not true. A car has properties that are not shared by all vehicles — in our example, wheels. An application that requires wheels cannot make do with a watercraft.)

A problem can arise, however, when invoking the member functions of a vehicle. Consider the following function:

```
void stopVehicle(Vehicle& vehicle) {
    vehicle.move(0, 0);
}
```

Here the function `stopVehicle()` accepts a reference to vehicle and then sets its velocity to 0. Since the method `Vehicle::move()` is defined, there appears to be no problem. However, a similar method `move()` is defined in each of the three subclasses. This is to be expected since the process of getting a landcraft moving differs considerably from the process of getting a watercraft underway, not to mention that of getting an aircraft airborne!

So what should happen in an example like the following?

```
void main() {
    Aircraft ac(10000, 2000, 240);
    stopVehicle(ac);
}
```

It seems clear that `stopVehicle()` should invoke the method `Aircraft::move()` and not `Vehicle::move()`. However, such a decision cannot be made at compile time, it must be deferred to run-time when the actual type of the vehicle object — not just its declared type — can be ascertained. This process is called **late binding**.

Late binding exacts a slight performance penalty, as the CPU must determine which method to invoke. Since most methods are not overloaded by methods in subclasses, this penalty is unnecessary in roughly 90 percent of method calls. To avoid this penalty, the default in cases such as `stopVehicle()` is to call the method in the base class without regard to whether that method is overloaded in a subclass. This is known as **early binding** because the decision is made earlier in the process — at compile time.

To enable late binding in C++ a method must be declared with the `virtual` keyword. In the preceding example, `Vehicle::move()` is declared virtual.

Occasionally insufficient information exists in a base class to implement a method properly. For example, it may be impossible to write a method to `move()` a generic vehicle. This usually happens only when all members of the base class rightfully fit into one of the subclasses: that is, there are no vehicles that are not landcraft, watercraft, or aircraft (ignoring spacecraft for the moment). In these cases the function can be defined as follows:

```
class Vehicle {
  private:
    uint weight;
    uint xVel, yVel;
    uint maxSpeed;

  public:
    Vehicle(uint w, uint maxS);

    //move() starts the vehicle out in the specified
    //x and y velocities, or as close as the vehicle can
    //get without exceeding 'maxSpeed'
    virtual void move(uint xV, uint yV) = 0;
};
```

This is called a **pure virtual** method, and the class is a pure virtual class. It is not possible to instantiate a pure virtual class. That is, no object of class `Vehicle` can be created as long as it is pure virtual. A subclass may inherit a pure virtual class. The subclass ceases to be pure virtual as soon as all of the pure virtual methods are overloaded with real methods. The classes `Landcraft`, `Watercraft`, and `Aircraft` are all non-pure virtual classes.

Stream I/O   One of the benefits of C is the fact that the Input/Output process is handled by functions out of the C library and not by primitives of the language. This gives programmers the flexibility to adapt the I/O library to specific applications and enhances the ability to port the language to new machines.

Unfortunately, the `printf()` and `scanf()` mechanisms, while flexible, are not type safe. Since instructions about the number and type of arguments are buried within a control character string, the compiler cannot check argument types as with other functions. This leads to a significant number of errors in C programs, particularly `scanf()` problems like the following:

```
int    i;
float  f;
double d;

scanf("%i",   i);  //forgot to pass &i; this writes into
                   //random memory location
scanf("%d",  &d);  //'d' refers to decimal; use 'lf'
                   //instead
scanf("%lf", &f);  //'lf' reads double; this will
                   // overwrite the
                   //word following the float f
```

To combat these problems, C++ includes a new I/O mechanism known as **streams**. Streams are based upon the two classes `istream` and `ostream` defined with the include file `iostream.h`. This include file also defines four default streams as follows:

Stream Name	Standard C equivalent
cin	stdin
cout	stdout
cerr	stderr //is not buffered
clog	stderr //is buffered

The constructors for `istream` and `ostream` allow stream objects to be opened on other files as well.

```
ostream   outObj("C:\\MYFILE.TXT");
istream   inObj("C:\\URFILE.TXT");
```

Output is handled by overloading `operator<<(ostream&,...)` for each of the intrinsic types. When overloaded, this operator is called an **inserter**, for example, `operator<<(ostream&,int)` is the integer inserter. Input is handled by `operator>>(istream&,...)` which is called the **extractor**.

```
int i;

cout << "enter i:";
cin  >> i;

cout << "i = ";      //invoke the char* inserter
                     //operator<<(ostream&,char*)
cout << i;           //            int    inserter
cout << '\n';        //            char   inserter
```

The `iostream.h` include file defines special constants that can be used to control the stream, for example, set the output precision or flush the output buffer.

```
cout << endl;      //insert a NewLine and flush buffer
```

Since all inserters return the `ostream` object they are passed, they may be strung together on a line.

```
int i, j, k;

cout << "i = " << i << "j = " << j << "k = " << k << endl;
```

operator<< binds from left to right so the first expression to be evaluated here is cout << "i = ". This returns the object cout. The next expression then becomes cout << i, which also returns cout, and so on.

Custom inserters can be written for user-defined classes as well as in the following example Complex class.

```
#include <iostream.h>

class Complex {
  private:
    float real;
    float imag;

  public:
    Complex() {
        real = imag = 0;
    }
    Complex(float r, float i = 0.0) {
        real = r;
        imag = i;
    }
    float realPart() { return real; }
    float imagPart() { return imag; }
};

ostream& operator<<(ostream& os, Complex& c) {
    os << '(' << c.realPart() << ','
            << c.imagPart() << "i)";
    return os;
};
```

The inserter outputs the real and imaginary portions of the Complex number surrounded by parentheses and separated by a comma. It is very important that the inserter return the ostream passed it; otherwise, it would not be possible to chain this inserter with others on a single line.

Notice that the inserter cannot be written as a member of the class, because it would have to be a member of the class `ostream`, the left-hand argument, to which the programmer has no access. In use, the custom insert appears like those for the intrinsic classes.

```
void main() {
   Complex a;
   Complex b(10);
   Complex c(05, 10);

   cout << "a = " << a << endl;
   cout << "b = " << b << endl;
   cout << "c = " << c << endl;
}
```

Writing extractors is similar except that error checking must be added.

Templates   A problem arises when building generalized utility classes such as queues, linked lists, and so on. In general, these classes are intended to maintain lists of objects, irrespective of what the objects might be. The problem arises because strong typing rules preclude a class containing a pointer to "whatever."

Techniques used to address this problem invariably involve void pointers and casts to the appropriate class where needed. However, these solutions are limited and clumsy.

A better approach is to define a proto-class that can be instantiated into a new class for each class type upon which it operates. This is handled by the **template**.

A template describes a family of closely related classes. The following defines a template class `Vector`.

```
template <class T> class Vector {
   private:
      T*   pT;
      int size;

   public:
      Vector(int length);
      T& operator[](int index) { return pT[index]; }
};
```

This template class may be instantiated into objects as follows:

```
Vector<int> vIntegers(20);
Vector<Complex> vComplex(10);
```

The first declaration creates a class `Vector<int>` and then generates an object of that class using the `Vector<int>(int)` constructor. The second declaration defines a `Vector<Complex>` class and object.

Functions may also be declared templates as in the following example:

```
template <class T> T max(T a, T b) {
    return (a > b) ? a : b;
}
```

Function templates do not generate any code until they are instantiated. They may be instantiated either explicitly as follows:

```
void fn() {
    int max(int, int);
    int a, b;

    a = max(a, b);
}
```

or implicitly in use:

```
void fn() {
    int  a, b;
    char c, d;

    a = max(a, b);  //instances int max(int, int)
    c = max(c, d);  //instances char max(char, char)
}
```

Exception Handling   A separate problem arises with the handling of exceptions. Standard C defines a set of conditions called **signals**. A signal is raised, using the standard library function `raise()`, whenever a problem is detected. Signals exist for problems such as divide overflow, illegal

instruction, or illegal address. Using the standard library function sig-
nal(), the programmer can define a local function to handle a signal.
Whenever that signal is raised, the user-defined function is invoked. If no
user function is defined for a given signal, a default handler is invoked.

A signal handler has three courses of action open to it when a signal is
raised: It can terminate the program with a suitable error message, it can
generate an error message and then return to the point of the error, or it
can longjmp() to a predefined safe location. The latter action is the most
common.

This solution presents several problems for C++. First, the long jump
mechanism is not safe. Errors introduced by long jumps are difficult to
find. In addition, a long jump from within a function to a function several
layers above does not properly destruct the objects declared within those
functions.

C++ exception handling provides a safer signaling mechanism that
takes care of any objects created between the point of the exception handler and the exception handler. The mechanism is based upon the **try
block**, the **catch handler**, and the **throw expression**. In outline, the mechanism appears as follows:

```
void fn() {
    try {
        //...        //any number of statements
        anotherFn(0.0);
        //...
    }
    catch (char* pString) {
        cout << "Exception:" << pString;
    }
    catch (Overflow& oflow) {
        //handle using an object of class Overflow
    }
    catch(...) {
        //this catch catches all exceptions
    }
}
```

The keyword `try` followed by an open parenthesis begins the try block. Immediately following the closed parenthesis appear any number of catch handlers. Catch handlers are unary operators of type void. They may be overloaded as in the example.

An exception is raised when an expression is thrown, as in the following:

```
void anotherFn(float denominator) {
    MyClass anObject;

    if (denominator == 0.0) {
        Overflow object("Divide by zero",
                        __LINE__,__FILE__);
        throw object;
    }
    //...              //function continues
}
```

The function `anotherFn()` checks to see if its argument `denomina-tor` is 0. If so, it throws an object of class `Overflow`. This matches the argument of the second catch handler and so control branches to that point. Before control leaves `anotherFn()`, however, the object `anObject` is destructed.

This can be very useful for the management of resources in the presence of exceptions, as in the following:

```
class Lock {
  private:
    unsigned lock;              //# of lock allocated

  public:
    Lock(unsigned whichLock); //allocate lock
    ~Lock();                    //release lock
};

void fn() {
    //...
    Lock myLock(0x0001);        //allocate lock
```

```
//...
if (somecondition)
    throw "a problem";
//...
}                               //function may return
normally
```

This function allocates a lock, presumably to protect a critical region. If an exception occurs in the middle of the function, the lock must be released. Associating the lock with a local object ensures that it will be released properly. The constructor for the object grants the lock, whereas the destructor — which is called no matter how control leaves the function — releases the lock.

Conclusion

This chapter has reviewed the object-oriented paradigm and how it differs from those that preceded it. The four tenants of OOP — data hiding, data abstraction, inheritance, and polymorphism — have been discussed. The C++ syntax was reviewed by comparing it with Standard C upon which it is based.

The following chapters will examine how bugs are created and how programs can be written to avoid generating errors. You will see how proper style and technique contribute to defect avoidance. Many of the syntactical features reviewed in this chapter can be used to detect bugs early in the debugging process. However, many of these same features can create problems for the unwary or careless programmer.

The Economics of Debugging

A sufficiently patient and determined programmer should be able to produce a reasonably bug-free program using any technique given sufficient time and money. (It is virtually impossible to prove the absence of all software defects. A reasonably bug-free program is one that causes the user no consternation.)

Of course, programmers do not have an infinite supply of time or money. Every program has an anticipated worth, and at each point in the program's development, there is a cost to complete the program. If at any time the cost to complete exceeds the program's anticipated value, the program should be scrapped. This is true whether the program is being produced for a company or for personal use.

Not all programs are financial disasters. Even large projects can be produced on time on budget, and with a minimum of pain to the programmers. Good programming techniques minimize the cost to develop quality software. The next five chapters will discuss some of these techniques, but first I will review why these techniques are so important.

Correcting Software Defects

Software costs can be measured in either dollars or hours. In a corporate environment, one is directly converted into the other — the cost of a programmer hour ranges from $40 to $90, including overhead. For the independent programmer the relationship is just as direct, if not quite as obvious.

Although there is a wide variance, the average cost to repair a software defect is a function of the phase of development in which the fix is attempted. Figure 2–1 graphically displays this relationship.

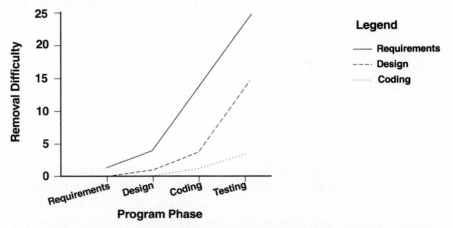

Figure 2–1. The relationship between the difficulty of correcting a bug and the software phase in which the correction is made.

If requirements errors found during the requirements phase are assigned a relative difficulty to correct of 1, the same error rates a difficulty of 4 during design, implying that it takes four times as long to fix the same problem at this stage. During the coding phase, a requirements error rates a 15 and during final testing a 25. (In *Software Engineering Economics*, Barry Boehm, a noted software economist and father of the COCOMO software cost estimation model, suggests these values are conservative. His studies indicate the actual ratios may be much higher.)

In similar fashion, a design error is assigned a difficulty factor of 1 during the design phase, a 4 during the coding phase, and a 15 during final testing. Coding errors are assigned a factor of 1 during coding and 4 during final testing.

This relationship has a profound effect on the approach the programmer should adopt to debugging. For example, let us compare two identical programs developed with different methodologies. In the first case, the programmer developed a thumbnail design and proceeded to begin coding at the terminal. In this **ad hoc methodology**, the majority of errors remain to be found during the testing phase. Few errors are identified during coding and none during the design phase. With this approach, 10 requirements errors, 20 design errors, and 60 coding errors occurred. The cost (in some unspecified units) to correct each error is equal to the difficulty factor of the phase in which the error was detected. The overall cost to correct all of the errors found in this program is as follows:

Error Type		*Error Discovered in This Phase*				
	Reqrmnts	*Design*	*Coding*	*Testing*	*Total*	*Cost*
Requirements	0	0	5	5	10	200
Design		0	10	10	20	190
Coding			20	40	60	180

Total						570

In the second case, the programmer used a more careful, controlled methodology that tends to reveal software errors earlier in the program. This is an **error avoidance methodology (EAM)**. The cost of this program is as follows:

Error Type		*Error Discovered in This Phase*				
	Reqrmnt	*Design*	*Coding*	*Testing*	*Total*	*Cost*
Requirements	3	3	2	2	10	95
Design		10	5	5	20	105
Coding			40	20	60	120

Total						320

In these examples, the cost to fix software errors using an EAM is roughly half that of an ad hoc methodology. To be fair, writing software using an EAM does take slightly longer. However, fewer errors are generated with an EAM than with an ad hoc methodology.

Programmers and their employers worry about the cost of defect prevention. While this is a valid concern, studies of areas other than software have shown that the cost of defect prevention is more than made up by the savings in defect removal. In fact, in *Quality is Free* P. B. Crosby concluded that the cost savings were so great that "quality is free."

This estimate of relative cost fits with the results of metric data accumulated on numerous real-world software projects in the field. Boehm reports that programs using ad hoc programming practices on average are 2.3 times as expensive as similar programs using modern programming practices ("modern" being defined as the state of the art in 1981). This number rises dramatically as the size and complexity of the program increase.

The cost to fix an error rises dramatically over time for many reasons.

1. To correct a design problem found during debugging, many functions must be rewritten or deleted. The effort spent writing and entering these functions is lost. Correcting the same error during testing also wastes the time spent unit testing and debugging these functions. Even functions that are only slightly modified require further debugging and testing. One radar software project measured effort losses of 318 percent due to continuous changes in requirements late in the program (that is, 138,000 instructions had to be written and tested to produce the 33,000 instructions delivered to the customer).

2. New functions are based upon software functions that already exist. Each layer of software is built upon the layer below it. Changes made to correct software errors in one layer can affect all subsequent layers. Changes are less apt to affect preceding software layers since they existed first. The longer a function exists in a system, the more other functions come to depend on it and the greater the cost becomes to change it.

3. One bug can mask other bugs. For example, if a program cannot output floating point values properly, the remaining floating point algorithms cannot be tested properly either. Once the floating point output problem is fixed, the programmer might find that these routines have problems as well.

4. Test teams may be distracted by volumes of trivial errors, causing them to overlook serious problems. In *Managing the Software Process* Watts Humphries reports that when a software development company instituted more careful error avoidance methodologies, they noticed a 50 percent reduction in the number of bugs found during testing. They also noted a 78 percent reduction in the number of bugs that made it into the field. By producing half as many errors during

development, they reduced the number of delivered errors by three-fourths. Other studies also show that the rate of reduction in shipped errors drops faster than the rate of errors produced during development. Apparently giving the testing people fewer problems to track allows them to do a better job of looking for the remaining bugs.

5. The number or people working on a project increases over time. In the early stages a relatively small team ascertains the customer requirements and assembles the initial program design. During the design phase the team grows slightly to handle the increasingly detailed design. During coding the number of people involved swells considerably. This is shown graphically in Figure 2–2. A major design error found during the early design phase may impact only a few individuals. Schedules can be slipped and staffing plans delayed with little impact to the budget. The same problem found during early testing may delay a large number of programmers while the design is reconsidered resulting in significant cost overruns.

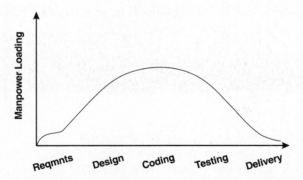

Figure 2–2. Number of people involved on a large software program as a function of time

Managers are generally less forgiving of defects isolated late in the program. By that time most of the budget and schedule have been consumed, and options are limited. Working hours may have to be increased, resulting in decreased efficiency and programmer morale, or the schedule and budget may have to be slipped.

Avoiding Software Defects

The cost to remove a software defect rises almost exponentially the later the problem is detected. The function can be extrapolated in the opposite direction as well. Consider the cost of avoiding the software defect in the first place.

The cost of an error that never occurs is the amount of effort the programmer expended avoiding the error. Comparing this cost with the cost of debugging and error removal involves probabilities.

If all coding errors were caught during the debugging phase, we would not need to invest much, if anything, in avoiding their occurrence (because the cost to fix an error at this phase is very low). However, since we know that many coding errors do slip through debugging, some remain after testing, and a few even make it into the delivered product, it is worth considerable effort to avoid their production in the first place.

Depending upon the cost to fix the problems and the quality of our testing, we might be willing to spend quite a lot in error avoidance. Consider, for example, the preceding debugging cost figures for an ad hoc and an EAM program. The cost breakdown by phase for a medium-sized program is somewhat as follows:

Phase of Program	*Percentage of Cost*
Requirements	6
Design	34
Coding	15
Testing (including unit testing & debugging)	45

(These numbers are adapted from Boehm's *Software Engineering Economics* for a medium-sized, well-managed program. An ad hoc program would likely have a longer debugging and testing phase.)

If we assume that at least half of the debugging/testing effort is spent correcting software errors, then we could spend as much as an extra 50 percent during the requirements, design, and coding phases to achieve our software error reduction, and we would still come out ahead.

NASA goes to great extremes to avoid software defects. NASA hires independent contractors to write the same program separately. During space missions the different versions are run simultaneously on separate computers on the assumption that independently created programs will not have the same defects.

In addition to learning ways to avoid introducing bugs, programmers can follow techniques that make software defects easier to find. Electronic circuits contain internal test points and settings to facilitate the job of testing them prior to shipping. Good software is developed the same way. Programmers build test points into unit interfaces to allow data values to be checked easily during testing.

Accurate program status is a beneficial side effect of improved software methodologies early in the program. With the ad hoc approach, initial progress appears quite rapid, but the debugging and testing phases invariably drag on past the deadline, resulting in reported progress similar to that shown in Figure 2–3.

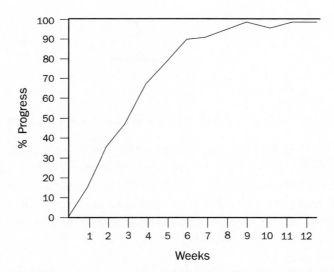

Figure 2–3. Typical progress reported by the ad hoc programmer

Why is this so? First, this is another expression of the axiom that the cost to fix a bug increases the later it is discovered. Even though 95 percent of the software might, in fact, be completed, a problem found late in development will take a long time to fix because of its ripple effect on other modules and the amount of retesting that must be performed.

Failure to develop software carefully and methodically may lead to a false sense of progress. Coding may appear to be going rapidly with the programmer reporting progress optimistically without knowing how many errors have been introduced into the program or where they reside. Such a programmer has not learned the difference between speed and progress.

Using an EAM, reported progress resembles that shown in Figure 2–4.

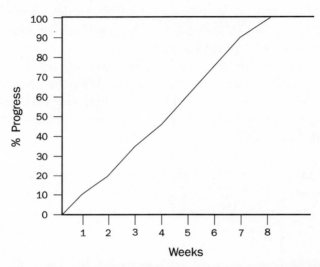

Figure 2–4. Typical progress reported by an EAM programmer

Although initial progress appears slightly slower, gone is the schedule-robbing, asymptotic approach to completion. The programmer knows more accurately the true progress of the software at each point during its development. The EAM programmer completed the module in eight weeks, which could have been predicted by extrapolating early progress, rather than the twelve weeks required by the ad hoc programmer. In addition, once this module is ready for integration with the rest of the system, the programmer's supervisor can be reasonably certain that it will work as advertised.

Aids in Avoiding Software Defects

Programming languages can be a help or a hindrance in writing defect-free software. Early languages designed for batch mode operation attempted to save programmer effort and needless compilation cycles by attempting to make sense out of whatever source code the programmer might submit.

FORTRAN, for example, does not require that variables be declared. In a prepass, the compiler scans for the different variable names. The type of a variable is presumed from its first letter. Variables beginning with the letters I, J, K, L, M, or N are assumed to be integers. All other variables are assumed to be floating point.

The result of this is obvious in hindsight. A misspelled variable is not flagged as a simple compile-time error but creates a new variable. The resulting bug is left for the programmer to find manually during debugging. Perhaps worse, freed of the need to declare variables, the programmer almost never comments their purpose. The number and purpose of variables quickly become lost, and determining whether a particular variable name has already been used becomes more difficult.

PL/1 went even further in this regard. Although variables must be declared in PL/1, the Checkout compiler attempts to make sense out of almost anything the programmer throws at it. The problem with this approach is that the compiler is almost always wrong. (At least PL/1 informs the programmer via warning messages of anything suspicious that it finds.)

While FORTRAN and PL/1 relieve the programmer of some bother during the coding phase, they create much more trouble during the debugging phase both by misinterpreting the programmer's intent and by encouraging haphazard programming techniques. The overall effect is increased costs and decreased quality.

Pascal takes the opposite approach. Type checking in Pascal is quite strict. Any construct that is the least bit questionable is challenged with a compilation error. The programmer is required to demonstrate that the code accurately conveys the programmer's intent. In this way, obvious software errors are not left by the compiler for the programmer to find manually.

Classic C resembles FORTRAN in its approach to error checking. Type checking is weak with functions having only a return type. Mixed-mode expressions are allowed with all pointer types considered essentially equivalent. Standard C tightened up the type checking rules as far as possible without defining a new language. Full function prototypes, tighter type checking, and distinction between pointer types catch some programmer errors early. C++ tightens these rules further.

However, C++ is still mediocre in its error checking. The grammar is terse and cryptic with little redundancy to allow for cross checking. Consider the following common error:

```
int a;

if (a = 5) {
    //...
```

Here it is clear that the programmer intended a == 5, however, a = 5 is a valid expression. This and a host of other traps introduced by C++ syntax are discussed in Chapter 5.

Fortunately, modern compilers help somewhat in this regard, allowing warnings to be issued for some of the most common C++ pitfalls. (All of the popular PC compilers can generate a warning for the above if() error, for example.) Enabling these warnings and taking notice of them weeds out many simple errors early.

Some languages go much further in helping to detect programming errors early. Although Pascal is quite strict in its parsing, it can only find syntactic errors such as a variable used incorrectly or an array indexed beyond its range. The Eiffel language allows the programmer to surround functions with what Bertrand Myer in *Object-Oriented Software Construction* calls **contracts**. A function may specify its prerequisites and its promises. If the function's prerequisites are met, it promises to produce certain results. During debugging, Eiffel verifies a function's prerequisites upon entry and its promises upon exit. If either is found to be lacking, Eiffel halts the program with a suitable error message.

Programming and Self-Discipline

The error avoidance methodologies presented in this book decrease the number of software errors. Cohesive modules containing loosely coupled functions help in avoiding obscure problems. They also reduce the amount of software that must be modified and retested when errors occur. These techniques are discussed in detail in subsequent chapters.

Programmers can also help their case by enabling all of the warning messages available with their compilers. Even if a suspicious construct is not an error, it does not hurt to have it pointed out as a possible problem. Even when compiler warnings are not extensive, static analysis tools — such as lint for C — can find questionable constructs.

All of this notwithstanding, most programmers do none of these things. Given the cost to find and remove bugs, it is difficult to understand why the warning messages available in most compilers are optional. In fact, for most compilers, the default is no warning messages at all.

One problem is the lack of apparent progress during the coding phase. Error avoidance requires a careful, methodical approach. The programmer cannot generate the same volume of output as with the more lackadaisical ad hoc methodologies. Faced with no initial code output, uneducated supervisors grow concerned. The programmer might grow anxious as well.

Remember, ad hoc code generation is not real progress. In *Managing the Software Process* Humphries observes, "Most drivers starting on a new journey will, regardless of their hurry, pause to consult a map. They have learned the difference between speed and progress." Programmers who are not careful about the quality of their output merely overstate their progress.

Programmers also find error avoidance programming to be less sexy. Programmers are often considered somehow apart from the rest of the engineering community. Programmers themselves actually encourage this perception. (Who has not seen the "Real Programmers Don't Eat Quiche" lists that make their way around?)

However, programmers must shed this view and begin to see themselves as engineers. Humphries notes, "With modern, large-scale programs we have passed the point where the lone genius can personally support an undocumented creation." Programming must become less of an art form and more of an engineering science.

Many programmers are hampered by the lack of positive programming experience. These programmers feel that "debugging past midnight a few weeks" is the way programs are supposed to be developed. Without examples to the contrary, they continue to use techniques that guarantee that marathon sessions will be necessary, and the product suffers as a consequence.

One final reason for failure to learn from mistakes involves the extremely long development cycles of large programs. People react best to correction when it is immediately tied to the transgression. Unfortunately, programming style is a decision made very early in a program and the effects of an incorrect choice may not be felt for months. By the time a program is in trouble — either behind schedule, over budget, or both — the individuals involved may not be able to remember back to the beginning of the program to determine where the problems might lie. Remember, the importance of a decision on the financial success of the program is inversely proportional to its distance from the program's start.

This problem is exacerbated by large organizations that don't involve programmers in the testing of the program and thereby deny them feedback on the quality of their work. Without feedback, the same error may be repeated over and over again. While the test teams improve at finding this recurring error, doing so distracts them from other problems that may not be as common.

In addition, without feedback the programmer has little reason to maintain a high quality of work. Perhaps feeling like an automaton on an assembly line, the programmer experiences no apparent difference in status, feeling of accomplishment, or paycheck bonus for having taken the time or made the effort to produce a quality product.

As James Coggins put it in his "Designing C++ Libraries" presentation to USENIX90, "We want to learn from experience rather than from study. . . . Unfortunately, experience is an effective but inefficient teacher. Newton said he saw farther because he stood on the shoulders of giants. Computer programmers stand on each other's toes."

This situation is a bit like the hiker who, being lost in the woods takes great pains to find the way out, without ever asking how the way was lost in the first place. Could not measures have been taken prior to setting off that, if not avoiding getting off the trail altogether, would have at least facilitated the job of finding the trail again?

Conclusion

Studies have shown that people in every industry want to do a good job. Programmers want to produce a high quality, error-free product. However, it is not enough simply to tell oneself, "Today I will do a better job." To improve the product, the development process must be improved.

Error avoidance methodologies cannot be boiled down to a single, cure-all approach that, when followed religiously, will detect and correct software errors at the earliest possible chance. As Brooks says, "There is no silver bullet." Instead, the EAMs presented in the remainder of this book form a set of good programming and debugging techniques, many of which use the object-oriented nature of C++ to minimize the cost of software defects.

In conclusion, it should be noted that there is no absolute economic proof that a careful software development methodology is cost effective. To produce such proof, one would need to develop the same set of large, expensive programs using different programmers and different methodologies. No one has yet been willing to foot the bill.

The volume of circumstantial evidence is extensive, however. Costs to repair problems detected in the field range from 2 to 20 times greater than the costs to fix the same problems back in the office. This does not include the costs of customer dissatisfaction, bad press reviews, and ill will generated by a poor quality product.

The automobile industry faced a similar quality and customer dissatisfaction crisis during the '70s and early '80s, but waited until one-third of their market share had eroded before responding. Hopefully, the computer industry will be quicker to respond.

The next two chapters examine the process of developing and designing quality software. The traps and pitfalls of C++ are explored in Chapters 5 and 6. By studying and becoming aware of these problems, the reader may be better able to avoid them.

Chapter 3

Designing C++ Programs

This chapter will examine how to design programs to minimize the number of software errors that will have to be dealt with in later phases. A good C++ program is the result of an understanding of the requirements, followed by a design that has been carefully implemented using structured, modular coding techniques.

Of course, requirements, designs, and coding phases have been the lifeblood of the structured programmer since the 1970s. The rules of good requirements, design, and modularity are as applicable to C++ development as they were in COBOL or FORTRAN. Object-Oriented Programming does not relieve the programmer from this methodical approach to development. Although Object-Oriented Analysis and Design slightly changes the analysis and design process, it does not change their importance.

Developing a C++ Program

A program goes through the following five distinct phases over its life span:

- requirements phase
- design phase
- coding phase

- test
- maintenance

The design phase can be subdivided into high-level and detailed design. The test phase can be subdivided as well. The next sections discuss these phases in more detail. The remainder of this chapter examines the requirements and design phases in depth.

The Phases of Program Development

A program goes through several distinct phases between concept and reality. The first phase of development is the **requirements phase**. During this phase, the programmer discusses and contemplates the problem with the customer. It is important that the programmer attempt to visualize the problem from the user's standpoint. The requirements phase results in a requirements specification. This takes the form of a document in which the requirements of the system are clearly spelled out. The specification should refrain, however, from discussing how the system will achieve its goals.

If the programmer learns something of the user's vocabulary during the requirements phase, communication will be smoother throughout the development of the program. Further, a requirements document written in computerese is not very enlightening to the user and may lead to misunderstandings that will not become obvious until the user sees the product. Remember that changes at the end of the process are quite expensive.

The **high-level design** stage follows the requirements phase. High-level design divides the program into its highest level building blocks and defines the roles of each of the blocks as well as their interface to each other and the outside world. Messages and data structures shared between blocks are identified and their formats are defined in a general way, but their structural details are left vague at this point.

The output of the high-level design phase is generally some type of **Program Design Language (PDL)**. PDL may take the form of a structured English or a loosely structured programming language. In practice, PDL generally takes some of the features of both.

The next phase, **low-level design**, further defines each block identified during the high-level design stage. The low-level design should generate a PDL with adequate detail to allow coding without reference to other sources. It should also define the detailed format of all messages and data structures shared between modules.

Work should descend evenly through the design phases. That is, the high-level design for the majority of modules within the system should be complete before beginning the low-level design phase for any but the most basic modules. To do otherwise risks the possibility that low-level design work will be wasted if problems found in the high-level design of a module cause major modifications in an already completed module.

The next step, the final stage in the actual writing of the program, is the **coding phase**. Coding consists of converting the detailed design into a machine-readable form, such as C++. By nailing down design decisions early, the programmer is free at this point to concentrate on style issues. Coding style may not seem important to the midnight hacker, but it affects the testability and reusability of the resulting program.

The next two phases — testing and integration — are not strictly part of program writing and will be covered in Chapter 7 along with the maintenance phase.

Even programmers working individually on small- to medium-sized programs should follow each of these development steps. Of course, the amount of effort expended on each phase should be commensurate with the size of the program: A small program need not generate a bound requirements document with table of contents and index — a simple white paper will suffice. A larger program, especially one involving multiple programmers, will require more formal documentation.

Programmers working in groups can benefit immensely by adopting a review process in which the output of each step is reviewed by others in the group before the programmer proceeds to the next phase. Reviews serve two purposes. First, the programmer is more likely to devote the required attention to the requirements and design stages if this work is to be seen and critiqued by others. Generating good high-level and detailed designs in the absence of such peer pressure requires more self-discipline than most programmers have. Second, others can often see logic errors or design problems that the inventor does not see. Spotting these errors early more than makes up for the time spent in the review process itself. I believe that instituting rigorous reviews is the single most important contribution to quality code. The details of conducting such reviews are covered in Chapter 7.

Scheduling the Development

Once the phases of development have been identified, they must be scheduled to make efficient use of developers', programmers', and customers' time. Today, two main scheduling styles are used: the Waterfall Method and the Recursive Method. The Waterfall Method is the older method, the one with which most readers are likely to be familiar. Later in this chapter we will examine the Recursive Method and contrast the two.

Waterfall scheduling   The most popular method for scheduling development phases is the **Waterfall Method**. This method foresees an orderly, unidirectional progression, as shown in Figure 3–1.

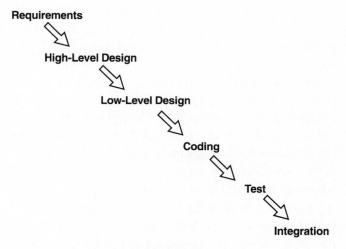

Figure 3–1. Waterfall development method

In each case the output of one phase of the program flows smoothly downstream into the next. In a pure waterfall approach, no flow occurs in the opposite direction. Work does not begin on phase N until phase N-1 is completed and corrected. Of course, there must be some communication upstream. Frequently problems during one stage necessitate changes to the previous phase. Therefore, some small communication path must exist in the reverse direction to allow corrections to be fed back into previous steps. These corrections may, in turn, force-feed back into even earlier steps. The resulting **Modified Waterfall Method** is shown in Figure 3–2.

Even in the modified waterfall method, however, the majority of information flows downstream.

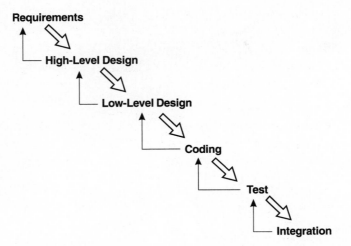

Figure 3–2. Modified waterfall method with feedback

Both forms of the waterfall method demonstrate serious inflexibility with respect to changing requirements. That is, a waterfall project in the detailed design phase cannot respond well to a change in the requirements. Historically the response among software managers (to whom the predictability of the waterfall model has such great appeal) has been to outlaw such changes. The customer is required to sign off on the completed requirements analysis. Work on the detailed design is delayed until the customer has agreed on the requirements and later changes to the requirements are either impossible or extremely expensive. While this may appeal to software engineers and managers, it ignores human nature.

First, both the customer and the programmer learn more as a project progresses. The customer has time to reconsider the implications of decisions made earlier. The programmers may think of problems that were not previously considered. Further, external conditions may simply change. Any of these events may affect the requirements of the system, necessitating basic design changes.

Second, the act of solving a problem changes it. The customer gets a chance to experience the program in action, which invariably leads to suggestions for improvement.

Recursive scheduling   In response to these realities, many developers use the **Recursive Method** depicted in Figure 3–3.

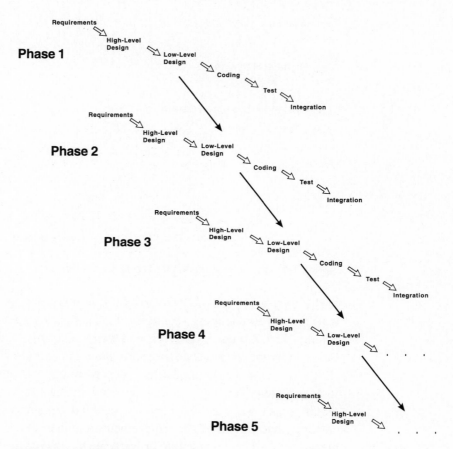

Figure 3–3. Recursive method

In this methodology, the program is developed in a stepwise fashion. A more or less normal waterfall process is used to implement a bare-bones, phase 1 version of the program. This version contains only the most basic features, just enough to run. Once experience is gained with this prototype, the development team designs a more sophisticated phase 2 version. The second version is also missing features, but is considerably more advanced than its predecessor. The programmers continue developing smaller mini-programs, each one based upon its predecessor. The final product is usually the phase 4 or phase 5 product.

The recursive methodology generates a better product than the waterfall approach. Things that don't work quite as expected can be isolated in the phase 1 or phase 2 products and fixed before the final version is produced. The recursive approach is also more efficient than the waterfall method in cases where neither the programmer nor the customer has much experience with the problem.

Commercial developers have always used a form of recursive development: early beta versions of programs generated with subsets of the basic capabilities. Eventually a Version 1.0 is created and brought to market. Even before Version 1.0 begins shipping, however, requirements and design work is begun on Version 2.0. As the product matures through revisions, capabilities are added and features that did not work out as expected are replaced.

Recursive development is an attractive alternative to the restrictive waterfall method. However, recursive development does not mean ad hoc development. The designers must generate a set of requirements for each phase. It is not necessary to wait until development of phase 1 is complete before working on the requirements for phase 2 — many of the lessons gleaned from phase 1 will be obvious before the software is completed. However, the coding of each phase must be preceded by a description of the requirements, a high-level design, and a low-level design.

Obtaining a clear statement of the project goals is even more important in recursive development. The developer must be assured that the program will end when the requirements have been satisfied. If the customer wishes to retain maximum flexibility, it is possible to bid and pay for each phase independently.

Program Requirements

The most important prerequisite to a good design is an understanding of the problem the customer wants solved. This may seem obvious, but it is amazing how often a beginning programmer sets out busily writing and debugging a program that the user does not want. If the program being written does not address the problem, it makes little difference how well it executes. "All paths are equally good if you don't know where you are going."

Establishing the customer's requirements is not always as simple as it may seem. Generally, the programmer lacks expertise in the customer's domain, and the customer almost certainly lacks computer expertise. The user and the programmer come to the table with differing prejudices and assumptions about the nature of the problem and its solution and speaking a different language. This can lead to software systems that solve a problem, just not the problem.

Without evaluation criteria stemming from a set of well-understood requirements, it is impossible to test the final product adequately. How can the programmer determine if a program generates the proper results if there is no agreement as to what the proper results are? For small programs, what constitutes correct output may be obvious. In addition, all parties may agree on how the program should respond in the absence of input errors. However, for programs of even moderate size disagreement will arise as to how the program should respond to situations such as boundary and error conditions.

Finally, the requirements document forces the customer to seriously consider what the system is to do. Without a written requirements document the programmer can solve a problem only to have the customer add additional features. This can lead to a never-ending project.

A Case Study

(The following case study was presented by Barry Boehm in *Software Engineering Economics*.) In the late 1960s *Scientific American* magazine had been using a manual process for registering new subscribers. As a result of a rapid increase in the number of subscribers, the manual system was becoming overburdened and inefficient. Subscribers were complaining at an alarming rate. What was needed was an automated subscription handling process.

To address this need, the management for *Scientific American* contracted with a software house to develop a computerized system tailored to its needs. Typical of programmers new to a problem, the software company approached the problem from a programming perspective. They formulated the problem ("registering new subscribers to the magazine") and devised and implemented a software solution.

Once the subscription personnel had been trained and the new system installed,

- costs went up
- reliability and quality went down
- more personnel were required
- employee morale decreased and turnover increased

An analysis of the system revealed the source of the problem. The software house — unfamiliar with the vagaries of the magazine subscription business — had devised a system that worked well, perhaps even optimally, as long as subscription requests were submitted with no missing data and without mistakes, including data entry errors. Unfortunately, this was not what *Scientific American* wanted or thought that they had purchased.

Subscription cards were entered by keypunch operators and accumulated into batches for processing. In the presence of even trivial input errors, the program would reject the entire batch. Since little error reporting and no error correction was built into the system, it was left to the user to laboriously search the entire batch for the error, often with little indication of what caused the problem.

At first *Scientific American* attempted to change its data entry procedures to avoid the types of errors that caused the program so much grief. Eventually, however, the magazine hired a new consultant, one willing to spend more time analyzing the problem.

The second consultant began by determining the problem the magazine was attempting to satisfy: "Increase subscription fulfillment speed and reliability at the same or less cost as the original manual system." Stating the problem this way turned the attention of the designers to the sources of delay, error, and cost in processing subscriptions and not just to the problem of writing a program to process a subscription form.

A total system solution including the requirements for a new, more fault-tolerant software package was devised. In addition, the consultant drew up a set of criteria to be used to evaluate proposals from software vendors. Armed with this new information, *Scientific American* was able to request proposals for a new subscription program and to evaluate and select the design that best fit their needs.

A Scanner: the Requirements

Let us examine a brief example of a system requirements specification. Our customer has contracted us to provide a simple scanning receiver controller system similar to that provided by citizens' band or police band scanners. The receiver and terminal are to be provided by the customer. The following is a partial requirements specification for the receiver controller system:

The system shall consist of a customer-provided serial terminal, microcomputer with sufficient internal memory and external disk space, and serial receiver. A block diagram of the system is shown in Figure 3-4.

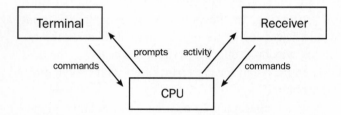

Figure 3–4. Block diagram of the scanning receiver system

The operator shall be allowed to input commands to control the system via the terminal. The operator shall have the following commands with the given meaning:

Tffff	tune to frequency ffff and hold
Affff	add frequency ffff to the scan list
Rffff	remove frequency ffff from the scan list
C	reset scan list
S	(re)start receiver scanning through the list
H	stop scanning through the list

It shall not be necessary to stop the system from scanning before tuning the receiver. The system shall maintain a scan list of frequencies entered by the user. During scan, the system shall tune the receiver to the next frequency in the scan list. The system shall hold on this frequency as long as the receiver indicates activity on this channel. When the receiver indicates no activity, the system shall continue to the next frequency in the scan list.

```
All input from the terminal is in ASCII and must be verified for correctness.
Incorrect input shall be flagged with a descriptive error message. All output to
the terminal is ASCII. If scanning is enabled, the system shall continue to scan
during operator input.
Output to the receiver shall consist of one of the following ASCII strings:
```

`R`	reset receiver
`Tffff`	tune to specified frequency
`E`	enquire as to activity

```
The response from the receiver to the enquire command shall consist of one of the
following ASCII strings.
```

`A`	activity detected
`I`	inactivity detected

Notice that these requirements are incomplete. They do not specify how much memory the host microprocessor has, how fast the receiver should be able to tune, the frequency range of the receiver, and so on. Since the customer is providing the hardware, we have assumed that sufficient hardware is being provided to satisfy the need. Things will become difficult, however, if this turns out not to be so. On what grounds will the programmer be able to request more memory if the program does not fit into the RAM available on the host CPU? Is the programmer at fault for wasting RAM or did the customer not provide enough? Modern languages have trouble producing "Hello world" executables smaller than 100K, while the customer may consider 64K to be more than adequate.

In addition, these requirements do not specify any minimum or maximum capabilities. For example, how many frequencies must the system be able to hold in the scan list in order to satisfy the need? How fast must the system be able to search them? These limits are best spelled out even when they are "reasonable." A vague requirement cannot be satisfied.

Command Languages

The design of any program that handles input defines, either implicitly or explicitly, a command language. The preceding example defined two input languages: one for commands input from the user terminal and a second for commands going to the receiver. Often the language is constrained by external devices over which the programmer has no control, such as the case with the receiver command language.

In other cases, however, the designer is free to define whatever language seems to fit best. Unfortunately, in most cases the designer leaves the command language implicit in the specification. Either it isn't perceived as being a language or it just doesn't seem that complex.

Leaving the command language implicit robs the designer of the opportunity to examine and rationalize its design. Consider the following modification to the foregoing requirements:

```
Frequencies can be added to the scan list by first
entering a four-digit frequency (units are MHz).
Without waiting for a return, the system will
immediately prompt for an action to which the operator
may enter an A for add or an R for remove. The scan
list can be cleared by entering C followed by a
return. The operator starts the system scanning from
the beginning of the scan list by entering an S.
Scanning may be temporarily held by entering an H. The
operator may restart scanning from where it was held
by entering an R. The operator shall be able to tune
the receiver to any frequency by entering T followed
by a nine-digit frequency in units of Hz.
```

These requirements implicitly define a command language for manipulating the program. A moment's reflection reveals that the language is not a very good one, however. The following problems surface:

- The R command is used twice for different purposes.
- Some commands specifically require a return and others do not; most don't specify.
- The A and R commands specify frequency as a four-digit number in units of MHz while the T command uses a nine-digit, Hz format.
- The A and R commands call for the frequency to be entered first, while the T command expects the frequency to be entered after the command.

This may seem an extreme example only because of its small size. Inconsistencies as glaring as these do arise in large programs.

It is best to specify most command languages by listing in tabular form all of the commands available along with the arguments that they expect. This was the course followed in the original receiver specification. The tabular specification of the preceding language appears as follows:

```
ffff A          add a frequency to tune list
ffff R          remove a frequency from tune list
C               clear scan list
S               start scanning from beginning
H               hold (that is, stop) scanning
R               restart scanning from where held
T ffffffff      tune receiver to a specific frequency
```

A tabular description of the command language is more approachable than the verbal description and easier to read. From this list the problems noted earlier become clear. Whenever possible the tabular format for defining an interface language is preferred over the wordy, paragraph description format. (A paragraph may accompany the table to explain the terms; however, the table should be considered the design guideline.)

A tabular description is fine for simple languages, but a problem arises when commands must be entered in a particular order or when some commands accept only certain subranges of data. Consider if we add the restriction implied in the preceeding specifications concerning the ordering of S, H, and R commands. For example, a Restart command cannot be entered until after scanning has been Held at least once; that is, it doesn't make sense to restart if you never started. Further, a Hold command makes no sense if scanning is not underway. The table provides no way to state these time-ordered requirements. A textual explanation of these restrictions would have to be added. Unfortunately, textual footnotes can be easily lost or overlooked.

A more powerful command language description tool is the **Backus-Naur Form** (or **BNF**). In this description you begin by defining low-level concepts, then work your way up. Consider the following partial description.

```
command ::= argument_command | non_argument_command
non_argument_command ::= 'C' | 'S' | 'H' | 'R'
```

```
argument_command ::= freq_first_command |
                     freq_last_command
freq_first_command ::= frequency1 {'A' | 'R'}
frequency1 ::= digit digit digit digit
digit ::= 0 - 9
```

Here a valid command is defined as either an `argument_command` or a `non_argument_command`, reflecting the dichotomy in command formats (`::=` is read "is defined as"). A `non_argument_command` is either the letter C, S, H, or R. The `argument_command`s are broken into the frequency first and the frequency last camps, reflecting the second (unfortunate) dichotomy. A `freq_first_command` consists of a type 1 frequency followed by either an A or an R. You could continue in this fashion to define the entire command language, including any temporal relationships or restrictions.

BNF representations of a command language can be extremely rigorous. They are great aids in building the command parser and in test generation. Both the programmer and the test generator know which inputs are allowed and which should be rejected. This type of description also forces the programmer to carefully consider exactly what types of input should be allowed. In their rigorousness, BNF representations can seem a bit unapproachable to the average programmer, however. An overly harsh BNF description may obscure problems in the command language rather than highlight them. BNF is most often used to define complex languages, such as programming languages.

For the average application with a simpler command grammar than that of a programming language, a relaxed syntax description can be employed. My personal favorite is the following:

```
{ffff {A|R}}
{C}
{S}[{H}{S|R}]*
{T ffffffff}
```

Here are four different command chains that are completely independent; that is, they can be entered in any order. Anything within a pair of braces is a required entry. Thus, the first command type specifies a four-digit frequency followed by a mandatory character that must be either an A or an R.

The third command type is the most interesting of the four. This command string must start with an S (start). Having entered an S, only the command H (stop) makes sense. The H can then be followed by either an S (start) or an R (restart), which returns us to the state where only H is allowed.

The trailing * indicates that this cycle of {H}{S|R} can be repeated any number of times, including zero. The symbol $^+$ indicates repetition of one or more times, while the format $^{n/m}$ is used to indicate n as the maximum number of times with m the minimum.

Notice that we have explicitly stated that R must be preceded by an H command, which, in turn, must be initiated by an S command.

While not as rigorous as BNF, this format gives the customer and programmer a clear overview of the syntax, like the tabular view, but adds some indication of the ordering of commands. It is just as clear, if not more so, that the formats of the A, R, and T commands should be changed to fall in line with one another.

A command language can be implemented in a decentralized fashion. For example, allowing the functions responsible for handling the tune, add and remove commands to read and parse the frequency from the command stream independently. This approach runs counter to the concept of levels of abstraction and good modular cohesion, however. It is preferable to write a single command parser responsible for comparing command input against the description of what constitutes legal input, in whatever format it takes.

The best command parsers are table driven. Such tables include information on the number and type of arguments and the address of the function to handle the command input. For example, the following simplistic parser handles the foregoing commands (with the A and R commands converted to the post command frequency format).

```
#include   <stdio.h>

//DataStruct - structure to hold the input arguments
//             to be passed to the processing functions
struct DataStruct {
    char      command;
    unsigned  argument;
};
```

```
//prototypes for the command processing functions
int addFreq(DataStruct*p);
int rmvFreq(DataStruct*p);
int tuneRcvr(DataStruct*p);
int clrTable(DataStruct*p);
int startScan(DataStruct*p);
int stopScan(DataStruct*p);

//commandTable - list of legal commands along with the
//               associated processing functions
const int numberOfCommands = 6;
struct {
    char  command;
    char  numArguments;
    int (*pFunction)(DataStruct*);
} commandTable[numberOfCommands] = {{'A', 1, addFreq},
                                    {'R', 1, rmvFreq},
                                    {'F', 1, tuneRcvr},
                                    {'C', 0, clrTable},
                                    {'S', 0, startScan},
                                    {'H', 0, stopScan}};
// parse() - compare the input command (the first letter
//           of the input buffer against the recognized
//           commands listed in the commandTable[]. Return
//           a nonzero if not found.
int parse(char* buffer) {
    DataStruct s;

    sscanf(buffer, "%c", &s.command);
    for (int index; index< numberOfCommands; index++)
        if (s.command == commandTable[index].command) {
            if (commandTable[index].numArguments == 1)
                sscanf(buffer, "%c%d",
                        &s.command, &s.argument);
            return (*commandTable[index].pFunction)(&s);
        }
    return 1;
}
```

```
//main() - sample of how the parse() function is used
void main() {
    char buffer[80];
    for (;;) {
        printf("Enter command:");
        gets(buffer);
        if (parse(buffer))
            printf("Illegal command\n");
        else
            printf("Ok\n");
    }
}
```

Of course, the preceding parser is simplistic. Provisions could be added for commands that accept more than one argument or arguments of different types (for example, ASCII strings). In addition, this parser does not check to ensure that only four digits of frequency are entered; however, adding these embellishments to parser() is straightforward.

Languages in which a given command always has the same meaning (it may or may not be allowed, but its meaning does not change) are called **context insensitive**, because the meaning of a command is not sensitive to the context in which it is used. The alternatives are called **context sensitive** languages.

For example, in the previous specifications the definition of two R commands is not an error. The remove frequency R command is preceded by a frequency. When entered first on a line, an R must mean Restart. Thus, if the understanding of an R entered from the terminal is based on whether it is preceded by a frequency, a parser could be generated to those specifications.

Context sensitive languages are much more difficult to parse than context insensitive languages. The program cannot simply run through a list of expected command tokens and compare them with what was entered. The table must contain duplicate command types along with extra state information to be used in resolving ambiguities. Context sensitive grammars are needed in such complex applications as programming languages but they should be avoided in simple program interfaces.

With modern Graphical User Interfaces (GUI), operators do not enter commands the way they might have in the past. Therefore defining a command language is not as critical as it once was, but the programmer should write down interface rules such as the following:

- frequencies will be in five-digit format with units of MHz
- the Control speed keys will be used for editing (then list the speed keys)
- the Alternate speed keys will be used for commands

The GUI almost invariably comes with a set of guidelines from the vendor — such as Apple's guidelines for the Macintosh, CUA for Windows and OS/2, and the OSF guidelines for Motif applications. While these guidelines are generally intended to make life easier for the user by providing a consistent interface across applications, they can also help the programmer by stipulating some of these variables. Often GUI interface guidelines are hard-coded into the interface software; however, the guidelines that are voluntary should be followed as consistently as possible. Vendors spend a lot of time and money researching these guidelines. It is naive to think you can improve on their effort in a few days time.

Program Design

Let us consider the steps that a programmer must go through to generate a program to solve a problem. Figure 3–5 depicts the process of analyzing a problem, creating a design, and producing a program from that design.

The requirements specify the problem to be solved. The problem exists in its own world, the problem domain. The domain of our sample problem is that of radios and user interfaces. The requirements describe the problem in the terms of the problem domain. The requirements say nothing about how the problem is to be solved.

The analysis phase must create a model that represents the programmer's understanding of the problem with unimportant details removed. This type of analysis is the way in which humans analyze problems. We build a model that incorporates the essential features of a problem. We then solve the problem in this model and map the solution back into the real world.

During the design phase, the programmer generates a design from the analysis model. Like the analysis model, the design is intended to be read solely by humans; however, unlike the analysis model, the design captures the details of the eventual program solution. Coding consists of converting the human-readable design model into a machine-readable source program.

Each of these steps involves translating from one model to the next. Each translation introduces errors into the system. (In *Managing Software Reliability*, M.G. Walker uses the RF analogy of noise introduced at junctures in a circuit. The number of software errors is proportional to the amount of noise in the system. Noise is introduced most easily at the translation points since these are sources of impedance mismatch. Reducing the impedance mismatch at the translation points reduces the noise. It is an interesting analogy to those familiar with electronics.)

Errors introduced during early translations become errors in the final system (unless caught by a review along the way). The number of errors increases with the difficulty of the translation. Thus, a complete design that results in a simple one-to-one mapping from the design model into the software solution substantially reduces the number of errors in the final system.

The **Structure Analysis/Structured Design** (**SASD**) approach described by Yourdan, Constantine and others proposed a rigorous methodology for creating a design from the analysis model. This design often consisted of low-level PDL or flowcharts that were easily mappable into FORTRAN, Pascal, or C source code. The problem with SASD, from an object-oriented point of view, is that the design bore little resemblance to the analysis model. Given an object in the analysis model, it was difficult, if not impossible, to find its corresponding object in the design.

Object-Oriented Analysis (**OOA**) and **Object-Oriented Design** (**OOD**) keep the translations small during each step. OOA creates a model based upon objects taken directly from the problem. OOD maps these objects directly into C++ classes. A solution discovered in the analysis model maps directly into the design. C++ allows the design classes to be coded directly into a machine-readable C++ program.

The challenge to the C++ programmer is to understand and practice good object-oriented analysis and design without losing sight of the fundamentals of structured analysis and design.

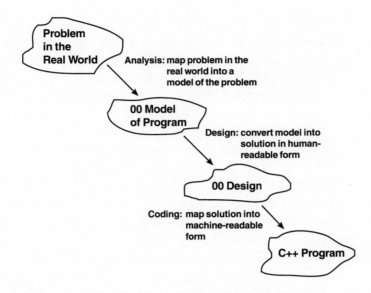

Figure 3–5. The analysis, design, and coding process

Structured Design

Programmers are all familiar with the classical top-down structured approach to program design. A large problem may involve hundreds, if not thousands, of factors that must be taken into consideration in the program design. Work by experimental psychologists during the 1950s, most notably G. Miller writing in *The Psychological Review* in March 1956, suggest that the human mind can only consider seven objects simultaneously, plus or minus two. This limitation seems to be related to the size of the brain's short-term (dare I say "cache") memory.

The design of even a simple program is beyond the ability of a human programmer to solve in a single step. Thus, the programmer divides the problem into several smaller problems, each of which can be solved independently. The solution to the larger problem is reduced to combining the solutions of the smaller problems.

Of course, the smaller problems may be too large to solve as well, so they may be further subdivided. This process continues until the problems become sufficiently small that they can be solved in a structured language, such as C.

Solving the Scanner Problem: the Structured Approach

The scanner problem presented earlier can be solved using a classical top-down, structured approach. Of course, this is not the only structured solution one might imagine.

A high-level description of the main program comes first. I will use modified English as my PDL.

```
// main task
Clear terminal
Reset scan list to empty                    (clearList())
Start receiver tune task
Loop
    Write user prompt to terminal           (writeTerminal())
    Read terminal input                     (readTerminal())
    Select command from
        T: Hold receiver tuning             (holdTune())
           Tune receiver                    (tuneReceiver())
        A: Add frequency to list            (addFreq())
        R: Remove frequency from list       (removeFreq())
        S: Start receiver tuning            (startTune())
        C: Clear scan list                  (clearList())
        H: Hold receiver tuning             (holdTune())
```

A separate tune task is required, since scanning is to proceed independently of user input. The PDL for the tune task appears as follows:

```
Reset receiver
Loop
    If receiver tuning enabled
        Tune receiver to next frequency     (tuneReceiver())
        Do
            Enquire as to activity          (enqReceiver())
        While receiver returns Active
```

Where possible, large functional blocks have been identified and given a name. Presumably each of these functions will be implemented by C++ functions in other modules. The next iteration of the high-level design would decompose each of these functions in turn, providing a similar high-level design for each. The detailed design would specify the error-handling paths, the arguments to each of the identified functions, and the content of any messages between the main task and the receiver tune task.

Object-Oriented Design

If we reflect upon the preceding design, we might notice how verb-oriented it is. Each line of PDL begins with a verb stating what is to be done. Structured analysis is a verb-oriented methodology — it strives to describe the process, the flow of data, with less regard for what is being manipulated. Decomposition is based upon the nodes of a flow chart.

Object-oriented design is based on the idea that solutions are first mapped out in the problem domain and then transformed into the solution domain of the working program. Modeling the problem domain requires accurate abstractions of the objects found there, and abstractions are best described by nouns. To utilize abstractions most effectively, programmers must be able to describe their designs primarily in terms of objects.

In *Object-Oriented Software Construction*, Bertrand Myer suggests the following steps:

- find the objects
- describe the objects
- describe the relations between the objects
- use the objects to structure the program

Finding the objects is mostly a matter of experience. The programmer begins with a list of candidate objects and then considers which of these are fundamental and which are derivative or misleading. As reported by Booch, Shlaer, and Mellor, candidate objects can be found in the following:

- tangible things — cars, radios, terminals
- roles — mother, student, teacher
- events — landing, tuning, steering
- interactions — loan, meeting, intersection

Another fruitful approach to developing candidates is found in domain analysis. Domain analysis looks for the candidate objects that are common to all applications within a given domain. The programmer becomes immersed in the concepts, vocabulary, and viewpoint of the problem domain. By looking at other applications, one can discern quickly what experts in the field consider to be fundamental.

Moore and Bailin suggest the following steps:

- Construct a strawman generic model of the domain by consulting with domain experts
- Examine existing systems within the domain and represent this understanding in a common format
- Identify similarities and differences between the systems by consulting with domain experts
- Refine the generic model to accommodate existing systems

Finding a domain expert is generally just a matter of speaking with your customer. When no concrete customer exists, seek out the expected users of the program. Examine other systems, both computer-based and not, that these users already employ. Look for their common abstractions and attempt to determine which abstractions work well and which do not. These abstractions are the most fruitful source of candidate objects.

An alternative to domain analysis is to underline the nouns and verbs in the requirements document. The nouns represent candidate objects and the verbs their candidate methods. This process has the advantage of simplicity but it requires considerable knowledge and skill on the part of the designer. The list of candidates can become quite large, and it falls to the designer to weed out unlikely candidates and build on the powerful abstractions.

Once the objects have been determined, the designer must look for commonalities among them. These commonalities make up the candidate classes. Given a set of objects, often several sets of classes are possible. Only consideration of the problem suggests which of the possible classes is most advantageous.

For example, consider the following object list:

Airplane
Bicycle
Balloon

Car

Jet

Sailboat

Ship

Truck

The most obvious class grouping is that shown in Figure 3–6.

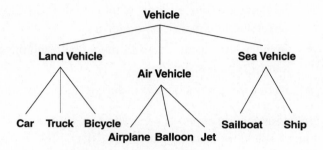

Figure 3–6. A possible grouping of classes

Suppose, however, that the fundamental distinction between these objects is the mode of power employed. This would suggest a completely different class hierarchy as shown in Figure 3–7.

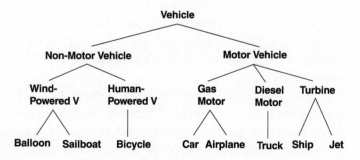

Figure 3–7. An alternate grouping of the same classes

Either grouping is valid, depending upon the nature of the problem to be solved.

Once the candidate classes have been chosen, the designer must describe the relationships between the classes and use the resulting classes to structure the program. Most of the methods proposed for performing this synthesis have been designed with automation in mind. Clearly the major CASE tools will be ported to OOA&D. Cadre has been one of the pioneers in this regard. However, the **Class-Responsibilities-Collaborators**, or **CRC, Method** for organizing classes — proposed by Ward Cunningham and described in "Think Like an Object" by Kent Beck in the October 1991 *UNIX Review* — is attractive because of its simplicity and because it can be performed easily with simple index cards.

The CRC Method characterizes classes along three dimensions listed below:

- Class name. Pick base classes using one of the foregoing techniques. Choose the names carefully to clearly delineate the borders of the class.

- Responsibilities. Each class fulfills a purpose in the design. Describe each class in a short phrase using active verbs. Refine the verbs chosen to describe succinctly and clearly the limits of the class's responsibilities.

- Collaborators. Each class relies on other classes to implement the complete design. Noting the collaborators both highlights the interclass dependencies and refines the designer's understanding of how responsibilities are being distributed over the classes.

To use the CRC Method, the designer begins by noting each of the design classes in the upper left corner of an index card. Below this, the designer lists the initial responsibilities of the class. Along the right-hand side, the designer notes the collaborator classes upon which the class depends to carry out its responsibilities.

The class names, responsibilities, and collaborator lists are jockeyed back and forth until the designer has achieved a set of clearly delineated classes that do not depend too tightly on each other or on too many different classes.

Beck suggests that using index cards offers the following advantages:

- Approachable. Designers can focus on the design effort without worrying about the details of using a new tool or of getting the output formatted properly.

- Physical. Holding an index card allows the designer to hold the class itself. This can help the designer think "like an object," ignoring information not written down on the card (remember, the class knows only what is written on the card).

- Portable. The index cards can be moved easily and port easily from one CPU instruction set to another.

Beck suggests several criteria for evaluating CRC class descriptions. First, use consistent names taken from a physical metaphor. This will help the designers and programmers imagine the role the class plays in the scheme of things. Second, use terse, strongly worded responsibilities. Use the same verb in different classes for the same operation. For example, a class `Terminal` and a class `Printer` might both have a method `write()`, though the implementation of the method might be different. Third, a single class should not have too many collaborators nor should any one class appear on too many different collaborator lists. Classes that are referenced by almost every class in the system are a sure sign of procedural thinking.

Classes that have no responsibilities should be deleted, as they obviously don't do anything.

Solving the Scanner Problem:
The Object-oriented Approach

Let us now develop an object-oriented design to solve the scanner problem. To identify an initial candidate list for object classes, we can begin with the system block diagram: Terminal, CPU, Receiver. Clearly a `class Terminal` and a `class Receiver` have merit. Since the CPU is not called out specifically in the requirements, a `class CPU` seems unnecessary and is dropped. (In the detailed implementation, it might be worth creating a `class SerialPort` to encapsulate the communication hardware of the microprocessor.) An examination of the capabilities of each class leads to the following suggestion for class methods:

```
class Receiver {
  public:
    Receiver();            //initialize the receiver
    void tune(char* freq); //tune to a given frequency
    int  activity();       //returns 1 if receiver
```

```
                                        //detects activity; else 0
};

class Terminal {
  public:
    Terminal();                 //clear the screen
    void read(char cmd, char* args);//prompt then read
                                //command and arguments
    void error(char* s);        //display error string
    int  validate(char cmd, char* args);//validate
                                //command
};
```

The function `Terminal::validate()` examines the entered command to make sure that it is correct. One of the things it must validate, of course, is the entered frequency. If the user enters a frequency that is out of range of the receiver, an error message must be generated. Upon reflection it is clear that receiver details, such as frequency range, should not be included in the `Terminal` class. Thus, we need a `Receiver::validate()` to validate the user-entered frequency.

Notice also that a receiver command might fail (return a `Nak` to a tune or initialize command, or other than an `A` or `I` to an inquiry). In C++ programmers frequently retain an internal error status that can be queried and reset from outside the class. Common practice is to define 0 as "no error," allowing a nonzero value to indicate the nature of the problem. As long as the error status is nonzero, tune and activity requests are ignored. This allows a high-level function to detect and analyze an error even if it occurs within a function many layers removed from the high-level function. Once detected, the error must be acknowledged by resetting the value to 0.

The expanded `Receiver` class appears as follows:

```
class Receiver {
  public:
    Receiver();                 //initialize the receiver
    void tune(char* freq);      //tune to a given frequency
    int  activity();            //returns 1 if receiver
                                //detects activity; else 0
    int  validate(char* freq);//returns 1 if legal
                                //frequency
```

```
    int  rdState();          //read error state
    void clear(int val = 0); //clear (set) error state
};
```

Examination of the structured high-level design suggests two further classes: class `TuneList` and class `TuneTask`.

Class `TuneList` encapsulates the tune list entries. It can be implemented from scratch or it can inherit from one of the library list classes. This class must allow frequencies to be added and removed from the list, and it must allow sequencing from one frequency to the next. Thus, the class is provided with the following public definition:

```
class TuneList {
  public:
    TuneList();                //create an empty tune list
    int    add(char* pFreq);   //add a frequency to list
    int    remove(char *pFreq);//remove a frequency
                               //from list
    char* nextFreq();          //return next frequency
    void   clear();            //clear frequency list
};
```

The class `TuneTask` describes the receiver tuning task to the main program's execution thread. This task stems from the requirement that the scanning of frequencies proceed independently of user input. Assigning execution threads to class objects to implement their interface is a powerful metaphor. Some object-oriented languages, most notably the actor-based languages, support this process directly. This allows the interface between execution threads to be controlled by the public/private class controls. In addition, execution threads can be abstracted in the same way that functional blocks are abstracted.

Even though multithreading is not supported directly in C++, nothing precludes a separate execution thread from being spawned with a static method of an encapsulating class the same way it is spawned with a function (assuming, of course, that the operating system supports multithreading). A candidate public interface for `TuneTask` is as follows:

```
class TuneTask {
  public:
```

```
    TuneTask();                     //start execution thread
    static void thread();           //thread starts with
                                    //this fn
    void start();                   //start tuning through list
    void hold();                    //stop tuning through list
};
```

Figure 3–8 shows how these proposed classes interact.

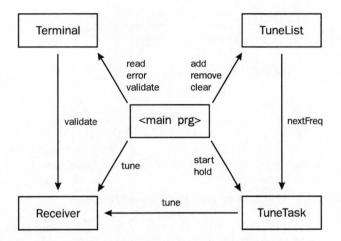

Figure 3–8. Interclass dependencies in OO solution to scanner problem

Keeping in mind that TuneTask represents a separate execution thread, a potential problem exists with the Receiver::tune() method. Both the main thread and the TuneTask thread appear able to tune the receiver at the same time. This may result in two tune commands garbling each other.

If the main thread only accesses the tune method via the TuneTask class, the access can be controlled and the problem averted. The new TuneTask class description is as follows:

```
class TuneTask {
  public:
    TuneTask();                     //start execution thread
    static void thread();           //thread starts with
                                    //this fn
    void start();                   //start tuning through list
```

```
    void hold();              //stop tuning through list
    void tune(char* pFreq);   //tune to freq and hold
};
```

The new class interaction description appears in Figure 3–9.

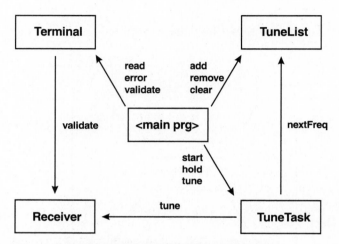

Figure 3–9. Improved interclass dependencies

A similar problem might exist with simultaneous access to the `Tune-List` class. That is, `TuneTask` may attempt to access the `nextFreq()` method at the same instant that the list is being updated with either the `add()`, `remove()`, or `clear()` methods. The conventional approach to this problem is to code these functions carefully to avoid any reentrancy problem, perhaps by using operating system semaphores. A more object-oriented approach would be to make these methods private to the `Tune-List` class to preclude access from other tasks. You would then make `TuneTask` a friend of `TuneList` and give it public methods `add()`, `remove()`, and `clear()` to provide the outside world with controlled access to these functions.

The CRC cards for this design are shown in Figure 3–10.

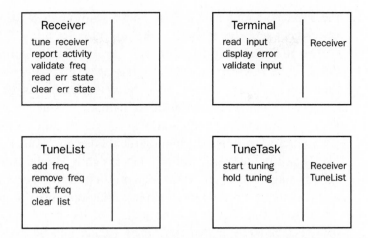

Figure 3–10. CRC cards for the object-oriented scanner solution

Other techniques could have been used for finding candidate classes and essentially the same results would have been achieved. For example, an analysis of the requirements specification reveals the following non-trivial nouns:

channel	receiver
input	scan list
operator	system
output	terminal

The `operator` entry can be dropped since the program does not attempt to model the operator's activity (that is, the role of the operator object will be played by the human operator). Of the remaining eight candidates, three were implemented in the foregoing design. The fourth class (`TuneTask`) would have come to light by analyzing the requirement that the system continue to tune the receiver during operator input.

Interface Control Document

A portion of any design is the **Interface Control Document**, or **ICD**. The ICD describes the system's software interfaces: that is, the layout and meaning of each field of data interchanged between programming units in the program. Just as it is difficult to keep the design decisions straight over the life of the program, it is virtually impossible to remember which messages contain what data and how it was to be stored. The ICD is to the data what the design is to the code.

The ICD should grow with the design as well. During the high-level design, it is sufficient to identify messages in a vague way. For example, the high-level design might say, "Send the tune message to the receiver." Clearly this command will need to include a frequency and possibly other data, such as mode, bandwidth, and so on, but it is not necessary to detail the format of this data during high-level design. Thus, the high-level ICD would call out a tune command and assign it a name for future reference. At this stage coordinating the different messages, their purpose, and general content, is more important than nailing down the bit patterns.

An ICD should contain the names of the functions that produce the data, as well as those that consume the data. This information is necessary when the message format must be changed — as it invariably will be as the design progresses.

As the design develops, the ICD should be expanded to define the exact format of the messages. Data formats are basically defined in two ways: either pictorially or with C++ constructs.

Figure 3–11 shows a hypothetical tune command sent to a receiver. The message has been broken into sixteen-bit words with the most significant bit on the left. The bits have been numbered as well. The numbering of bits establishes the standard to be used throughout the documentation. The names of the fields are written into their bit positions within the message.

A C++ structure can also be used. For example, the following code segment defines the same hypothetical tune command.

```
//RTM - the Receiver Tune Message
struct TuneMsg {
    char command;      //this is always a 'T'
    float freq;        //frequency [MHz]
    uint mode:2;       //0 -> CW, 1 -> FM, 2 -> AM, 3 -> USB
    uint hiPower:1;    //1 -> high power mode
};
```

This format is clear to the C++ programmer and self-documenting, as the same definition can be used in the actual code. However, this definition does not unambiguously specify what the message looks like in memory, where it counts.

Consider the bit field `mode`. The C standard does not specify how bit fields are packed into memory. Leaving this question open was intended to allow compilers to choose the most efficient packing algorithm for the base machine. Without a standard, it is impossible to specify exactly how bit fields will appear in memory. Thus, the compiler might choose one of several different packings for `mode` and `hiPower`. Some of these are shown in Figure 3–11.

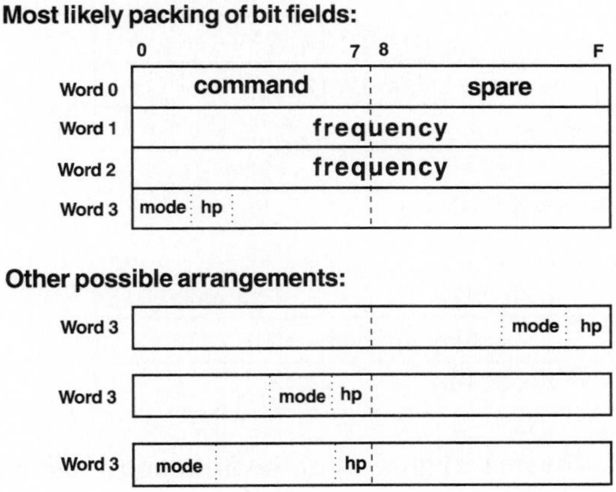

Most likely packing of bit fields:

	0	7 8	F
Word 0	**command**	**spare**	
Word 1	**frequency**		
Word 2	**frequency**		
Word 3	mode : hp		

Other possible arrangements:

		mode : hp
Word 3		mode hp

Word 3	mode hp	

Word 3	mode	hp

Figure 3–11. Possible packing arrangement of two-bit fields in a structure

What about the frequency? Does it start on an odd boundary? Some compilers would store the frequency in the word after the command character while other compilers would pack the frequency immediately after the command to save space. In fact, most C++ compilers for the PC allow the programmer to select either alternative with a compilation switch. Figure 3–12 on the following page shows two possible alignments of the frequency field in a structure.

This moving about of fields is acceptable as long as it is handled identically in both the sender and receiver. If the sender and receiver are compiled with the same compiler using the same settings, there should be no problem. However, if the two are not compiled with the same C++ compiler, or if the message format is fixed, as would be the case with an off-the-shelf receiver, the two might get out of synch, resulting in confusion.

In general there is no problem with using C++ structure based format definitions if and only if

1. bit fields specify all 32 bits in a word. This limits the flexibility the compiler has in placing the bits.
2. bit fields do not attempt to extend over a 16-bit boundary.
3. word length values are always placed on word boundaries.
4. double-word length values always place on double-word boundaries.

Frequency could be on even boundary:

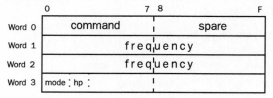

Or on odd boundary:

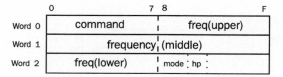

Figure 3–12. Possible alignment of the frequency field in a structure

ICDs can also be used to describe database entries. Applications that use external databases are extremely dependent upon the format of the data. Since the database represents a communication path much like messages, the ICD is the logical place to capture these design decisions.

Object-oriented ICDs   As with other classes, C++ classes that describe messages may be assigned methods. These methods should be limited to packing and unpacking the data in the message, as the message does not belong to the logic of either sender or receiver.

After adding access methods, the full definition of the sample tune command message becomes the following:

```
//RTM - the Receiver Tune Message
struct TuneMsg {
    enum modeSetting {modeCW  = 0,
                      modeFM  = 1,
                      modeAM  = 2,
                      modeUSB = 3};
```

```
            enum powerSetting {powerLow = 0,
                               powerHi  = 1};

      private:
        char command;    //this is always a 'T'
        float freq;      //frequency [MHz]
        uint rMode:2;    //0 -> CW, 1 -> FM, 2 -> AM, 3 -> USB
        uint hiPower:1;  //1 -> high power mode

      public:
        TuneMsg(float f, modeSetting m, powerSetting power);
        float frequency();         //return frequency...
        modeSetting mode();        //...mode...
        powerSetting power();      //...or power setting
    };
```

In addition, similarities in command formats can also be captured via inheritance.

While to the programmer command formats are part of the message definition, they may not belong in the ICD. Using methods of a `TuneMsg` class to pack and unpack data fields is a design decision of the code. It provides a clean encapsulation of the details of the tune message, but is not a property of the data itself. If, for example, the sender of the message were written in a language other than C++, this extra information would be of little use to the programmer.

If both the sender and receiver are to be written in C++ on the same machine, the distinction is not important. In this case, the designers may choose to include the method definitions in the ICD.

Program Modularity

Both the structured and object-oriented design techniques simplified the job of solving a problem by decomposing it into smaller problems. The programmer is able to solve large, complex problems by using the tools provided by the already solved smaller problems. A working function provides an abstraction that the programmer can use later without giving thought to how it accomplishes its task.

For example, the structured design broke out the routine `writeTerminal()`. When viewed from the perspective of the problem at hand, this is a simple routine: write a string out to the terminal. However, anyone who has dealt with the programming of Input/Output hardware such as the Universal Asynchronous Receiver Transmitter (UART) chips typically used to communicate with serial terminals knows that this type routine is far from simple. It involves programming interrupt controllers, initializing communication channels, and handling interrupts from the chip. Nevertheless, the programmer working on the main problem will use `writeTerminal()` as a simple tool, no more thinking about its internals than a carpenter worries about the inner workings of a drill.

(This, of course, assumes that one of the standard C library routines, such as `printf()`, is not available or is not applicable. In fact, the functions that make up the standard C library are a good example of such function abstraction. Few programmers ever examine the source code of `printf()` even though they used it routinely. And how many programmers have ever looked at the format of a `FILE` structure even though they use `FILE*` with all of the C stream I/O functions?)

By the same token, the job of writing `writeTerminal()` is simplified by being spared knowledge of the overall problem. All the programmer needs to know is that `writeTerminal()` is being passed a character string and the nature of the hardware interface.

An implicit assumption in this argument is that these smaller functions work only through the communication channels described. Suppose that in addition to the character string argument to display, `writeTerminal()` read an error indication flag out of a global variable somewhere. If the global variable is set, `writeTerminal()` outputs an error message rather than the indicated string.

This complicates `writeTerminal()` in at least two ways. First, the `writeTerminal()` logic is mixed with that of its parent. Its programmer is no longer isolated from decisions made about the parent function. Second, a communication path is opened that, unless carefully documented, is not obvious to the reader who might justifiably assume that `writeTerminal("Enter:")` should put up a prompt on the display, irrespective of the value of a global flag somewhere. Both of these factors damage the abstraction that modular programming is attempting to achieve.

Thus, abstraction is based upon three concepts important to good program modularity: **cohesion**, **coupling**, and **normalization**.

Cohesion refers to a consistency of purpose that makes the result easier to understand. A function that exhibits poor internal cohesion is difficult to assign any single role and, hence, difficult to abstract. Strong cohesion is better than weak cohesion.

Coupling refers to the type of communications interface that exists between a function and the other functions that make up the system ("the outside world"). Functions that communicate strictly through well-defined interfaces are said to have loose or weak coupling since the function is easily "unhooked" from the system for use in some other application. A function that is tightly bound to its system through mysterious, undocumented paths is said to have tight or strong coupling. Loose coupling is preferable to tight coupling. Coupling applies only to functions.

Normalization implies that an abstraction will be made once and then reused as appropriate. Normalization avoids solving the same problem more than once — wasting effort as the two solutions are debugged, tested, and maintained separately.

Cohesion

Cohesion deals with the content of a function. It takes the different elements that comprise the function, such as the individual C++ statements, and asks, "How well does this element relate to the other elements of this function?" Remember that the goal of our design was to produce functions that represent lines of PDL or steps in our design at some level, as in the following:

```
//...
write to the terminal (writeTerminal())
read terminal input (readTerminal())
//...
```

The function `writeTerminal()` serves as an abstraction for the steps necessary to output an ASCII string to the remote serial terminal. If `writeTerminal()` performs other, obscure operations as well, it becomes a poor synonym for the PDL line "write to the terminal" that it was created to represent.

In addition, poor cohesion has maintenance implications. Functions that contain closely related elements are easier to follow than functions that do not; that is, a function is easier to follow when it attempts to accomplish only one goal.

Even though I will be discussing cohesion only with respect to functions, cohesion can be applied in some sense to modules. (I am using the term **module** to refer to a source .CPP or .CXX file containing C++ functions. A **function** is a single entry point that is called, performs some operation, and returns.) A module may contain many different functions. A module that contains closely related functions is easier to understand when viewed externally. Modules that act as a repository for a random set of functions appear confused and muddled.

The levels of cohesion (order from most cohesive to least cohesive) are as follows:

- functional
- sequential
- communication
- procedural
- temporal
- logical
- coincidental

Functions that demonstrate only coincidental cohesion are always unacceptable. Those that demonstrate procedural, temporal, or logical cohesion are generally considered difficult to maintain and are considered unacceptable for the majority of applications.

Functional Cohesion   A functionally cohesive function is one in which all elements contribute directly to the execution of one, and only one, task. If the purpose of the function can be described in one sentence without the appearance of an *if*, *and*, or *but*, then the function demonstrates functional cohesion. For example, "the purpose of `writeTerminal()` is to output a string to the terminal." A functionally cohesive function may perform multiple steps as long as they are all directed at the same single purpose.

Sequential Cohesion   A sequentially cohesive function performs several functionally cohesive operations in a row. One would expect the purpose of a sequentially cohesive to resemble that of a functionally cohesive function except for the inclusion of "and" statements. For example, "the purpose of this function is to reset the receiver, tune the receiver, and then determine activity."

Communicational Cohesion   A communicationally cohesive function is one in which all the operations performed relate to the same input or output. This type of function is closely related to a sequentially cohesive function except that the connection between the steps is slightly more tenuous. For example, "The purpose of `getInput()` is to read input from the terminal and validate it." Here the only connection between the "read from terminal" and the "validate input" operations is the fact that they both involve input data.

Procedural Cohesion   Procedural cohesion occurs when different and possibly unrelated operations are being performed, depending on the values contained in the data arguments. The most obvious example of a function with procedural cohesion is `printf()` from the standard C library. The first argument to `printf()` is a string, possibly containing %-type format controls. Every %-type control relates to the next argument to the function. The actual letter after the % sign determines how that argument is interpreted. Consider the following example:

```
char *s;
int   i;
float j;

printf("Integer i = %d\n", i);
printf("Float   j = %f\n", j);

printf("S = %s, i = %d, j = %f\n", s, i, j);
```

The steps taken to convert a floating point number into its ASCII representation are completely different from those taken to convert an integer. Therefore, the conversion functions invoked by the second `printf()` call are totally different from those invoked by the first call and, yet, the only difference is in the %f versus %d. Further, the third `printf()` call converts three different types due to the presence of three different %- operators.

Temporal Cohesion   Temporal cohesion occurs when the only relationship between the functional elements is that they need to occur at the
same time or in some temporal sequence.

The most common temporal functions are initialization functions called
at program start-up to initialize variables, open files, and so on, as in the
following example:

```
void initProgram() {
    //first reset the terminal
    resetTerminal();

    //and clear the screen
    writeTerminal(CLEAR_SEQUENCE);

    //keep track of row and column number
    col = row = 0;

    //put out the first prompt
    writeTerminal("Enter:");

    //go ahead and reset the Receiver while we're here
    resetReceiver();
    tuneReceiver("00901");       //90.1 MHz, my favorite
}
```

Temporal functions often reference large numbers of global variables or
have large argument lists, which negatively impacts their coupling (as we
will see later).

In structural programming languages, temporal initialization and termination functions were difficult, if not impossible, to avoid. However, C++
constructors allow each class to initialize itself, making temporal functions
largely unnecessary. (All of the operations in the preceding `initTermi-
nal()` function could have been handled by the constructors for `Termi-
nal` and `Receiver`.) A constructor that might perform several operations
to initialize an object is not temporal if all of the objects it references are
dedicated to a single purpose.

Logical Cohesion   A function has logical strength when some tenuous logical relationship exists between the operations performed by
the function. For example, a function that performs all operations on a
terminal might have logical cohesion. Such a function would resemble
the following:

```
//
//  handleTerminal - perform the RESET, INPUT, OUTPUT and
//                   SCROLL operations
//
int handleTerminal(int operation, char* pString) {
    int noLines;
    int retValue = 0;

    //perform a reset on RESET and prior to INPUT
    //or if specifically requested
    if (operation == RESET || operation == INPUT) {
        retValue = resetTerminal;
        if (retValue) {                 //on error,...
            if (operation == INPUT)//...if there is a
                *pString = '\0';    //...string, clear it;
            return retValue;            //...now return
        }

     //now perform the OUTPUT or INPUT operation
     switch (operation) {
        case OUTPUT: retValue = writeTerminal(string);
                     break;
        case INPUT:  retValue = readTerminal(string);
    }
    if (retValue)
       return retValue;

    //on OUTPUT or REQUEST, scroll terminal up one line
    if (operation == OUTPUT || operation == SCROLL)
        retValue = scrollTerminal();
    return retValue;
}
```

Here the four different terminal operations have been combined. Often
the incentive for logical cohesion is to save a few lines of C++ code. In the
preceding example a reset is performed as a result of either a RESET or a
READ request. Similarly, a scroll operation is performed as part of a
SCROLL or a WRITE request. This is misguided. The logic involved in the
four operations is intertwined, leading to a larger number of paths and a
greater complexity than is necessary. The result is more difficult to test
and maintain. In addition, the result actually executes slower due to the
additional if statements that must be included.

The following function — which also demonstrates logical strength, but
with much less intertwining — is less objectionable.

```
//
// handleTerminal - perform the RESET, INPUT, OUTPUT and
//                  SCROLL operations
//
int handleTerminal(int operation, char* pString) {
    int noLines;
    int retValue = 0;

    //perform the indicated operation
    switch (operation) {
        //on RESET, simply reset the terminal
        case RESET:  retValue = resetTerminal();
                     break;

        //to INPUT, first reset terminal then read
        case INPUT:  if (retValue = resetTerminal())
                         retValue = readTerminal();
                     break;

        //to OUTPUT, output string and then scroll up one
        case OUTPUT: retValue = writeTerminal(string);
                     scrollTerminal();
                     break;

        //to SCROLL, perform scroll operation
        case SCROLL: scrollTerminal();
```

```
    }
    return retValue;
}
```

Logical cohesion resembles temporal cohesion in that the function involves different but related operations. The main difference is that no sequence is implied in logical cohesion (it is not obvious from looking at the `handleTerminal()` function in what order the four operations will be performed).

Coincidental Cohesion   The weakest form of cohesion is coincidental cohesion. In this form, instructions or functions are thrown together for no obvious reason. This can occur in various ways. Suppose a programmer is asked to break a single function or module into pieces to fulfill some maximum size criteria. If the programmer decides to divide the function every twenty-five lines, the resulting functions likely would not show any more than coincidental cohesion.

Coincidental cohesion in functions can also arise when the programmer notices a sequence of instructions that recurs frequently. For example, assume the following instruction sequence occurred often:

```
    resetReceiver();
    printf("Enter:");
    scanf("%s", globalBuffer); //globalBuffer is static
    globalVal = 2 * strtol(globalBuffer, 0, 10);
```

A beginning programmer might replace every occurrence of this sequence with a call to the following coincidental function.

```
void coincidentalFn(void) {
    extern char globalBuffer[];
    extern int globalVal;

    resetReceiver();
    printf("Enter:");
    scanf("%s", globalBuffer);
    globalVal = 2 * strtol(globalBuffer, 0, 10);
}
```

This practice should be actively discouraged. Raising coincidental strings of instructions to the level of a function obscures their serendipitous nature. The reader is likely to be mislead into thinking that there is some significance to the grouping of the four instructions. Further, any one of these sequences might need to be changed in the future.

Notice that the name of the example function does not describe what it does. In fact, it is generally difficult to descriptively name a coincidental function since it doesn't do any one thing. The description of purpose for a coincidental function is likely to contain unrelated phrases.

Compare the preceding coincidental function with the following related function that shows strong cohesion:

```
void getTermInput(char *pBuffer) {
    printf("Enter:");
    scanf("%s", pBuffer);
}
```

Here the function restricts itself to those instructions relevant to the job of "getting terminal input," as the name of the function implies.

Coupling

While cohesion refers to the function, coupling refers to how the function interfaces with the functions around it. Remember that `writeTerminal()` formed a useful, easily understood abstraction only as long as its interface to the remainder of the design was readily apparent. The more `writeTerminal()`'s internal logic became intertwined with that of the remainder of the system, the more difficult it was to view it as an independent agent.

Like cohesion, coupling has important maintenance implications as well. The more tightly bound a function is to the code that surrounds it, the more likely that changes in the environment will break the function, causing it to no longer operate properly.

Finally, reuse suffers when coupling rules are not followed. The interface a function represents to the outside world becomes that function's surface area. Each communication path is another bump on that surface that must be accommodated if the function is to be reused in a different application. A loosely coupled function resembles a regular geometric figure with relatively few recesses or protrusions. A tightly coupled function, by contrast, represents a jigsaw puzzle piece with nooks and crannies that must be satisfied if the function is to be fitted into or replaced in a future program.

There are five levels of coupling, arranged from best to worst:

- data/stamp
- control
- hybrid
- common
- pathological

Here the goal is to achieve the loosest possible coupling between the function and its environment. The fewer assumptions each makes about the other, the less likely that one of those assumptions will be violated.

The coupling factors that influence error generation and maintenance are, in decreasing order of importance, as follows:

- type of coupling. Functions with Data/Stamp and, to a lesser extent, Control coupling have good programming style. Hybrid and commonly coupled functions may be defensible depending on the application. Pathological coupling is always poor style and should be avoided.
- the type of information passed. Data items have less negative effect than control items. Therefore, Data/Stamp coupling is rated higher than Control coupling.
- the volume of information. The more data passed to the function, the more difficult it is to maintain. However, this represents a trade-off between efficiency and reliability if the missing data must be recreated by the function.
- direction of control flow. Passing control variables downward from calling function to called function is worse than passing error returns upward.

Data/Stamp Coupling   The classic definition of data coupling holds that two functions are data coupled if they communicate by passing data elements through parameter lists only. The following function demonstrates data coupling:

```
void tuneReceiver(int freq, int amFm, int bandWidth);
```

The frequency, AM/FM, and bandwidth settings to which to tune are individually specified as arguments. (We are assuming that the function requires no other data from the program.)

Functions are stamp coupled if they refer to the same compound data structure. The following function demonstrates stamp coupling:

```
struct TuneParams {
    int frequency;
    int amFm;
    int bandWidth;
};
void tuneReceiver(TuneParams& newParams);
```

Here the caller stores data into the `TuneParams` structure and then passes a reference to the object to the function where the data is unpacked. Because structures are so important in C, C programmers tend to generate more stamp-coupled than data-coupled functions.

In object-oriented languages, however, some confusion arises. C++ raises the importance of user-defined types to a level almost equal to that of intrinsic types such as `int`, `char`, and `float`. Thus, what constitutes "elementary data types" is not necessarily clear. Consider the following modified example:

```
class TuneParams {
  private:
    int frequency;
    int amFm;
    int bandWidth;

  public:
    TuneParams();
    tuneReceiver();
```

```
};
void anotherFunc(TuneParams&);
```

Here `anotherFunc()` accepts a reference to a user-defined class, just as before. Although not quite as obvious, so does the member function `tuneReceiver()`. (Remember, all non-static member functions receive a pointer to the current object as a hidden first argument.)

Programmers could probably accept that most functions in C++ demonstrate, at best, stamp coupling; however, by allowing user-defined types the privileges of intrinsic types, C++ collapses data and stamp coupling into a single case.

Control Coupling   Functions are control coupled when one passes information intended to control the logic flow of the other. For example, the following function has a control coupled interface:

```
void tuneReceiver(int freq, int forceReset) {
    int resetFlag = forceReset;

    //loop until no error on tune
    do {
        //if reset flag set, reset the receiver
        if (resetFlag) {
            output(resetCommand);
            resetFlag = 0;
        }

        //tune receiver
        output(freq);             //tune to freq

        input(error);             //check for error
        resetFlag = error;        //on error, reset next time
    } while(!error);
}
```

Here, the function tunes the receiver and then checks for an error. If an error occurs, the function retries by first resetting the receiver and then retuning. The `forceReset` argument is passed in from the outside to cause a reset to be performed even before the first tune, thus influencing the function's internal flow.

Control flow can be in either direction. In fact, the most common direction is from the called function to the calling function, as in the following example:

```
int writeTerminal(char*);

void myFunc() {
    for(;;) {
        if (writeTerminal("Enter:")) {
            resetTerminal();   //on error, reset and retry
            continue;
        }
        //...
    }
}
```

Here, the function `writeTerminal()` returns an error indication that the calling function uses to determine whether to reset the terminal and try again. This upward form of coupling is considered less harmful for two reasons: (1) it does not violate cohesion rules, and (2) it is difficult to avoid.

Hybrid Coupling   Hybrid coupling is similar to control coupling, but instead of using a separate control variable, the hybrid coupled function uses an otherwise unacceptable range for values for a data variable. For example, in the following:

```
void tuneFreq(int freq) {
    //if passed a frequency of -1, reset to default
    //values
    if (freq= =-1) {
        tuneFreq(defaultFreq);
        return;
    }
    //...
}
```

`tuneFreq()` understands a frequency of -1, which is out of range, to be a control indicator to tune the receiver to the default frequency.

Hybrid coupling is worse than control coupling for two reasons. First, not only does the calling function directly influence the called function, but now it must have knowledge of the acceptable ranges of the arguments.

Second, the reader may not always know what does and does not constitute an acceptable range of values. Further, future expandability of the system can be severely restricted. Consider, for example, an inventory application in which the upper two bits of an eight-bit part number are used for control information. The number of different inventory items is reduced from 256 to 64. Worse, future expandability is complicated because the maintenance programmer can no longer simply increase the word size to accommodate more items — the control bits must be moved as well.

Common Coupling Functions are common coupled when they refer to the same global data area. In C++ this common area takes the form of a global variable. This is not the same as stamp coupling in which the functions share a common class.

Common coupling in a function is not difficult to detect. Consider the following:

```cpp
extern int notOk;

void writeReceiver(void* command) {

    //first check the global semaphore
    while (notOk) {
        reschedule();
    }
    notOk = 1;
    //...
}
```

The function uses the global variable `notOk` as a semaphore. Presumably other functions that access the receiver directly are doing the same. However, the maintenance programmer has no idea what other functions these might be.

Functions are not commonly coupled when they access external data through a class. For example, the iostream classes maintain an error state flag that, when nonzero, indicates an I/O error has occurred. Every subsequent iostream access is denied until the I/O error flag has been cleared. This does not represent common coupling since the flag is maintained within the object and is only accessible via methods of the class.

Pathological Coupling   Pathologically coupled functions directly access each other's internals, for example, jumping directly into the middle of a function or overwriting its machine instructions. This is not generally a problem in C++ since the language does not support most of these features. From a maintenance standpoint, it is too dangerous to be allowed. Pathological coupling is always considered bad style.

Normalization

The third major stylistic factor is functional normalization. The goal of functional normalization is to reduce the amount of duplication of functionality to a minimum. Consider the `getTermInput()` example function used previously:

```
void getTermInput(char *pBuffer) {
    printf("Enter:");
    scanf("%s", pBuffer);
}
```

This function seems so simple that some might wonder that it is called out as a function at all. In the interest of efficiency, why not place the `printf()` and `scanf()` calls wherever the function is required?

Normalization implies the creation of new abstractions that result in the simplification of the calling functions. Simplification allows more attention to be paid to the problem at hand with the result of fewer software defects.

Further, normalization allows the programmer to debug a particular code sequence once. For example, the foregoing `getTermInput()` function contains a software error. Since the size of the buffer is not specified and is not known to the function, it can be easily overflowed in the `scanf()` call, resulting in unpredictable behavior. A second argument is needed to indicate the size of the buffer. The second argument can be used to limit the number of characters to be scanf()ed into the buffer. A corrected version of getTermInput() is as follows:

```
void getTermInput(char *pBuffer, int buffSize) {
    char inFormat[10];

    //display prompt
    printf("Enter:");

    //create format %Ns where N comes from buffSize
    sprintf(&inFormat[0], "%%%ds", buffSize);

    //use the format to scanf() in argument
    scanf(&inFormat[0], pBuffer);
}
```

In the normalized case, getTermInput() must be corrected and retested. The programmer will probably use a small test program designed specifically to debug this function since it may not work properly the first time. This is especially important if more than one programmer is involved since it allows the other programmers to continue working with the original program unhindered. Once working, getTermInput() may be dropped into the program and retested with a reasonably good chance of causing no problems.

In the nonnormalized case, the programmer has little choice but to change every occurrence of the prompt code sequence. If it does not work the first time, then every occurrence must be changed again until eventually it does work.

Normalization also allows the program to be modified more easily. Suppose that, once deployed, the customer wants the interface changed to place the input command prompt in a particular row and column. In the normalized solution, a call to position the cursor must be added to the getTermInput() function immediately prior to displaying the prompt.

```
void getTermInput(char *pBuffer, int buffSize) {
    char inFormat[10];
```

```
//position cursor and display prompt
positionXY(PROMPTCOL, PROMPTROW);
printf("Enter:");

//create format %Ns where N comes from buffSize
sprintf(&inFormat[0], "%%%ds", buffSize);

//use the format to scanf() in argument
scanf(&inFormat[0], pBuffer);
}
```

In the nonnormal program, the programmer must scan each `printf()` call and make the necessary addition only to those that display the prompt. In this case, that may not be too difficult, but as the complexity of the functionality increases the difficulty of finding it buried within the program increases as well (and no two incarnations of the same functionality will be coded identically).

Normalization can also aid in performance enhancement. A loosely coupled, normalized function enables the programmer to reexamine a function that might be too slow to increase its performance with little danger of breaking the system. Consider the following code that determines whether a point (x,y) is within the radius R of a circle drawn around the origin. R is #defined in the module header.

```
//given a Point p and a radius R, calculate whether p is
//within R of origin
r   = sqrt(p.x * p.x + p.y * p.y);
if (R > r) {
    //...function continues...
```

Since this function is used throughout the program, the careful programmer makes this into a separate function as follows:

```
//withinRadius - calculate whether a Point p is within R
//                of origin
int withinRadius(Point& p) {
    float r;
    r   = sqrt(p.x * p.x + p.y * p.y);
```

```
    return R > r;
}
```

When the program is not quite fast enough, the programmers are asked to see where performance improvements can be made. One alert programmer notices that since R is #defined it would be easy to also #define an RSQUARED, which is calculated at compile time, and save performing the sqrt() function in real time, a very time-consuming function without a math coprocessor. Since r is local to the function and is used in only the one place, the programmer is justified in assuming that it does not need to be calculated — only the eventual within radius determination is important. The optimized function appears as follows:

```
inline int withinRadius(Point& p) {
    return RSQUARED > (p.x * p.x + p.y * p.y);
}
```

In the non-optimized case, replacing the square root with the optimized version is somewhat more difficult. First, of course, the calculation must be found everywhere it occurs within the program. Further, the modifying programmer must make sure that r is not used somewhere else within the function before the square root calculation can be avoided.

Normalize abstractions, not C++ statements. Programmers should never throw unrelated C++ statements together into a function to normalize them. This results in functions with coincidental cohesion, the worst sort. In the preceding example, it was the act of determining whether a point was within a circle that was normalized, not the actual C++ statements that are involved in this calculation.

Data Leveling   In a well-normalized program, you can see levels of abstractions, each built upon its predecessors. One level of drivers interfaces directly with the I/O hardware of the host machine. The next level uses this layer to send and/or receive messages from the other machine. A further layer atop this one performs intelligent communication, and so it goes.

A well-normalized program does not modify a given data object at different levels of abstraction. Making sure that this is so is called **data leveling**.

It is not difficult to see why this should be so. If the abstraction boundaries have been drawn correctly, one level will not need access to the variables of another level. For example, what does a low-level UART driver need with a variable indicating the tuned frequency of the receiver? It certainly has no business modifying it.

Programs that do not follow this rule can be exceedingly difficult to debug. As the programmer steps through a program, it is natural to focus attention solely on the current level of abstraction. Variables that are set in a function are assumed to retain their value across calls to lower level functions. When this is not the case and the variable is set incorrectly, it will take some time for the programmer to discover where to look. Further, performing operations on the same variable at different levels complicates the job of setting up the conditions necessary to test the different cases.

When making all modifications to an object at a given level is not possible, the next best solution is to perform complementary operations at the same level. For example, an object might be created and destroyed at one level but used at a different level. Thus, the following code segment:

```
void level1Fn(int arg) {
    Object *pObj = new Object(arg);
    //...pObj is not modified in level1Fn()
    level2Fn(pObj);
}
void level2Fn(Object *pObj) {
    //...use pObj here
    delete pObj;
}
```

should be replaced by the data leveled version:

```
void level1Fn(int arg) {
    Object *pObj = new Object(arg);
    //...pObj is not modifed in level1Fn()
    level2Fn(pObj);
    delete pObj;
}
void level2Fn(Object *pObj) {
    //...use pObj here
}
```

The rules of coupling imply, but do not require, data leveling. In both of the preceding examples, the functions `level1Fn()` and `level2Fn()` demonstrate the same coupling.

Modularity of Classes

Improving coupling and cohesion is as desirable a goal in an object-oriented program as it is in a structured program. Member functions follow the same cohesion rules as conventional, nonmember functions. They follow the same coupling rules as well, with the caveat that nonstatic data members of the class are not global data.

The C++ programmer has another consideration as well: improving intraclass and interclass coupling and cohesion.

Intraclass Cohesion

Intraclass cohesion refers to how well a class describes a single abstraction in a clear, concise manner. In *Object-Oriented Design with Applications,* Grady Booch writes that classes demonstrate good intraclass cohesion when they are sufficient, primitive, and complete.

A class is **sufficient** if it "captures enough characteristics of the abstraction to permit meaningful and efficient interaction." That is, the class must provide the capabilities of the abstraction that the class is attempting to mimic. If some important facility is missing, another class or external function will need to reach into the class to provide that ability.

A class is **primitive** if it cannot be easily divided into separate classes. A primitive class represents a single concept. Thinking about a primitive class brings forth a clear and easily defined mental image.

If a class can be subdivided into two or more mutually private classes without adding serious overhead, then it represents more than a single abstraction and is not primitive. (A class is mutually private with respect to another class if it does not make reference to the other class's private members.)

Dividing a nonprimitive class breaks up the multiple intertwined abstractions, resulting in more but simpler class definitions. This will generally lead to a clearer concept of the problem.

If a primitive class is subdivided, however, it no longer contains sufficient information to represent an abstraction completely. Rather than a class `Car`, for example, the programmer ends up with two classes, `FrontOfACar` and `BackOfACar`. Each class must continuously reference the private members of the other. The complexity of the member functions and the level of coupling between the classes rises drastically.

Thus, the programmer should continue to subdivide class definitions into simpler and simpler concepts until it becomes difficult to conceive of or implement the abstraction that the new, proposed class represents.

Often classes are nonprimitive because the designer is simply confused as to what the fundamental abstractions truly are. Other times, a hierarchical relationship may exist between classes. In these cases, the class definitions may be made primitive through a process known as **factoring**. In factoring the programmer uses inheritance to break out the primitive class definitions and yet retain their relationship.

Given a particular problem, the analyst may have decided to define a class `Vehicle` to describe both cars and trucks. Although this abstraction is fine for some purposes, certain properties are difficult to assign since they are not shared by all vehicle types (for example, cargo bed size or trunk space are not shared by both trucks and passenger cars). By factoring, the programmer creates two primitive subclasses `Car` and `Truck`, both derived from the base class `Vehicle`. The resulting class hierarchy is considered primitive since it accurately reflects a set of abstractions and their relationships to the detail required by the problem.

Finally, a class is **complete** if its public interface provides a sufficiently complete set of operations to be usable. A complete class is easy for other functions to use since all of the needed operations that others must perform on the class are provided.

Completeness is a relative concept. A minimalist programmer may be satisfied with a limited number of basic operations. Another programmer may choose the opposite tack, providing a smorgasbord of different interface functions.

When a class is created, the property of sufficiency will dictate that certain public operations be present. Generally, the programmer will want to start with these public methods. As other functions begin to use the class, the need for additional operations will arise. The programmer may then choose to add these new methods to the interface to make them part of the class.

Intraclass module cohesion is improved by defining all of the member functions of a class within a single C++ source module. Generally, the declaration of the class and the definitions of any inline methods are placed in an include file bearing the name of the class and either the extension `.H`, `.HPP`, or `.HXX`. Source files that use the class reference this include file. The source file is given the name of the class with a `.CPP` or `.CXX` extension, depending upon the compiler.

Interclass Coupling

Interclass coupling refers to how loosely the methods of a class couple with functions external to the class, be they members of other classes or nonmember functions.

Ideally, one would like to provide the external interface description of the designed class along with any constraints and leave the implementation details up to the programmer. The class can be developed independently but in parallel with the remainder of the system. Not only does this provide maximum efficiency in terms of programmer resources, but it minimizes the coupling between the class and the system.

Minimizing the interclass coupling offers the same advantages as minimizing coupling between nonmember functions: functions that are easier to write, easier to debug and test, and easier to maintain.

Through the mechanism of data hiding, classes can hide their internal structures. The parts that a class leaves visible to external functions is known as the **class surface area**. The public members of a class make up its surface area. Classes minimize their surface area for the same reasons that functions minimize their level of coupling.

Minimizing the surface area of a class makes the system less dependent upon the implementation details of the class. When any function can reach in and access any member of a class, the maintenance programmer is severely restricted in what types of changes can be made to the class to fix other problems without undergoing a complete retest of the system. New members may be safely added, but every old member must remain largely unchanged. This makes the system very sensitive to changes in the class.

In addition, decreased surface area makes the class less vulnerable to changes in the system. This, in turn, makes the class more reusable, as it is more likely to be applicable to completely different programs.

The programmer minimizes surface area by reducing the number of public members to only what is needed to remain complete. Member functions that are needed by other member functions should be moved into the private section (much as a function is declared static when it is not needed outside of a module). In addition, data members should almost never be made public, for to do so invites uncontrolled access. Often programmers provide access methods to allow external functions to read the value of internal variables, as in the following example:

```
class SSRecord {
  private:
    char *pName;
    long   ssNumber;
    int    elig;

  public:
    SSRecord(char* pN, long ssN, int e);
    char* name (char*pBuffer) {
        strcpy (pBuffer, pName);
      return pBuffer;
    };
    long number() {
      return ssNumber,
    };
    int eligible() {
      return elig;
  };
};
```

As long as these methods return by value, external functions are precluded from modifying the class objects data members. However, it is difficult to return compound members, such as the name ASCII string in the foregoing example: presumably, the function name() returns a pointer to the same name pointed at by pName. In any case, access methods still provide the external world with a view into the class's internals, albeit a controlled view. As you will see, the number of these access methods can be reduced to further limit the class's surface area.

Policing the Class Surface Area   Once a class has been written and debugged in situ, it must be installed into the system. The debugging task is simplified if the programmer can rapidly determine on which side of the class surface a problem exists, when one arises. Did the error occur outside of the class or inside of the class?

A class has control over its internals. Careful class programmers are jealous about letting this type of internal information out for fear that it might be corrupted by some function beyond their control.

However, a class does not have control over goings on outside of its own borders. Therefore, many class programmers build "customs checks" at the class's public interfaces to check for illegal imports. For example, in the following function, the argument is assumed to be a pointer to a string containing a nine-digit Social Security number. Rather than accept this blindly, however, the function first counts the number of characters and checks for dashes in the proper places.

```cpp
class Address {
  private:
    long ssNum;
    //other data

  public:
    //other methods
    //storeSSNum - store the social security number;
    //              return a 0 if successful;
    //              a SS number must have the format:
    //                123-45-6789
    int storeSSNum(char *pString) {
        //first check to make sure its legal
        if (pString[3] != '-')
            return 1;
        if (pString[6] != '-')
            return 1;
        if (strlen(pString) != 11)
            return 2;

        //okay to copy it
        long temp;
        sscanf(pString, "%ld", &temp);
        ssNum = temp;
        return 0;
    }
};
```

If dashes are missing or if the overall length of the string is incorrect, the function returns a nonzero value. If the checks pass, the function is satisfied that the string is a Social Security number and control passes "beyond customs" where it is converted into a `long` and stored in the object.

The checks in this case are coded in such a way as to remain in the final deliverable system. Sometimes the interface checks need be enabled only during the coding and debugging phases. These checks are removed in the final deliverable product to improve performance.

Such checks are most easily implemented using the `#assert` macro defined in the include file `assert.h`. This macro accepts a condition. When the macro is encountered, if the condition is true, `#assert` takes no action. If the condition is not true, the program is halted after outputting an error message that includes the C++ module name and line number.

Recoding the same code fragment with `#asserts` results in the following:

```
#include <assert.h>

class Address {
  private:
    long ssNum;
    //other data

  public:
    //other methods
    //storeSSNum - store the social security number;
    //             a SS number must have the format:
    //                 123-45-6789
    void storeSSNum(char *pString) {
        //first check to make sure its legal
        assert(pString[3] == '-');
        assert(pString[6] == '-');
        assert(strlen(pString) == 11);
```

```
                //okay to copy it
                long temp;
                sscanf(pString,"%ld", &temp);
                ssNum = temp;
        }
};
```

Defining the symbol NDEBUG during compilation converts all #asserts within a module into null statements.

Notice that the function no longer returns an error indication — if the Social Security number is faulty the program will be terminated. Thus, #asserts are only useful as internal sanity checks — they should not be used to check for illegal user input.

Customs requirements may be established upon exit as well. Consider, for example, the following class designed to manipulate the location of a point on the earth in both spherical and Cartesian coordinates.

```
struct XYZLoc {
    float x, y, z;
};


class Location {
  private:
    float latitude;
    float longitude;
  public:
    Location(float lat, float long) {
        //first check values for legal range
        assert(lat <=   90.0 && lat  >=   -90.0);
        assert(long <= 180.0 && long >= -180.0);

        //they look okay, store them
        latitude  = lat * degreeToRad; //[rad]
        longitude = long* degreeToRad; //[rad]
    }
    int convertToXYZ(XYZLoc& result) {
        //perform radial to Cartesian coordinate
        //conversion
        double x, y, z;          //local storage for x,y,z
```

```
    x = earthRadius * cos(longitude) * cos(latitude);
    y = earthRadius * sin(longitude) * cos(latitude);
    z = earthRadius * sin(latitude);

    //now make sure that the sum x**2, y**2 and z**2
    //is roughly equal to the radius of the earth
    double sum = x * x + y * y + z * z;
    double delta = earthRadius * earthRadius - sum;
    if (delta < 0.0)
        delta = -delta;
    assert(delta < epsilon);

    //data is okay, store it and return
    result.x = x;
    result.y = y;
    result.z = z;
    }
};
```

The constructor for class `Location` makes sure that the supplied latitude and longitude figures are within range and then saves them. The method `convertToXYZ()` converts the spherical coordinates into Cartesian coordinates. Before it returns the calculated values, it checks the x, y, and z coordinates. It uses the fact that the square root of the sum of their squares must be equal to the radius of the Earth (for a point on the Earth's surface, as we have assumed). If this does not check out, the method has done something wrong and it terminates without returning. Since the latitude and longitude data was checked on entry, the programmer may assume that a software defect lies inside the class.

Rather than the analogy of a customs agent, Bertrand Myer uses that of a contract. The public interface that the class projects represents a set of promises or a **software contract** that the class makes to the outside world. (For example, `convertToXYZ()` promises to return a point [x,y,z] on the surface of the Earth.) However, the class may set prerequisites. (In this case, that the latitude and longitude provided are legal.) If the prerequisites are not met, then the class cannot be held to the contract.

The checks on input data that were added in the previous examples test to determine that the class prerequisites are met. The checks of the output data ascertain that the class promises are kept.

Software contracts are a useful aid in building reliable, reusable classes. As we have noted, the technique tends to isolate software defects to the class or the application. In addition, these extra checks find software defects early before they become hidden by subsequent calculations.

Even more important, however, is the mental attitude the concept of software contracts engenders. The class programmer begins to feel primarily like a builder of a tool. This, in turn, leads to classes that have very loose coupling with the external application.

The Law of Demeter In 1988, Lieberherr, Holland, and Riel presented a paper called "Object-Oriented Programming: An Objective Sense of Style" in which they proposed a set of rules they called **The Law of Demeter** for analyzing interclass coupling. (Demeter was the name of the project upon which they had been working when they devised these rules). The Law of Demeter defined a set of rules that a programmer could use to analyze the strength of interclass coupling within a given program. Rather than generate a quantitative "strength value," the law was presented as a set of progressively less desirable options with which to compare two different possible class definitions (much like the cohesion and coupling rules for functions).

Unfortunately, Lieberherr, Holland, and Riel were primarily Smalltalk programmers (Demeter was a Smalltalk system). Although they presented a C++ version of the rule, it was criticized as being flawed. A more considered C++ version of the Law was formulated by Markku Sakkinen in *SIGPLAN Notices*. The class version of the C++ law according to Sakkinen is as follows:

For any class C, and for any member function M of C, every class object that M directly accesses or references in any way must belong to one of the following classes, in order of decreasing preference:

1. the class C itself
2. the classes of the arguments and result of M
3. the data member classes of C
4. the classes explicitly declared to be known to C

5. the data member classes of the classes covered by rule 2
6. This access or reference must not directly specify any data member, class or nonclass, of the object concerned unless the object is an instance of one of the classes covered by rule 1 or rule 2
7. For any function M that is not a function of any class, the above rules shall hold with the addition that classes can be explicitly declared known to M.

Here a "class object of C" is an object of class C including any of its members. "Directly accesses or references" means accesses via either the . or -> operators.

Rule 1 implies that a member function may access any other members of the same class, whether private or public, as in the following:

```
class Port {
  private:
    unsigned address;              //hardware port address
    void send(char*);              //send string to port

  public:
    Port(unsigned addr);           //constructor

    void init() {                  //send init string to port
          const char* initSequence = \"0x1BR"; //<C>R
        if (address)               //if valid port address...
            send(initSequence); //...reset hardware;
                                   //...both rule 1 accesses
    }
};
```

The function `Port::init()` accesses both the data member `address` and the member function `send()` directly. The fact that this rule comes first implies that this is the most desirable form of coupling.

Rule 2 covers objects that are arguments to functions as in the following:

```
class ExtDevice {
  public:
```

```
        void init(Port& port) {
            port.init();          //rule 2 access
        }
};
```

The function `ExtDevice::init()` accesses the function `Port::init()` via the object `port`, which is one of its arguments. Of course, `Port::init()` is only accessible because it is a public member of `Port`.

Rewriting the `ExtDevice` class slightly demonstrates Rule 3, coupling through data members:

```
class ExtDevice {
  private:
    Port* pPort;
  public:
    ExtDevice(Port& port) {
        pPort = &port;
    }
    void init() {
        pPort->init();          //rule 3 access
    }
};
```

This type of coupling is considered slightly worse than Rule 2 coupling since it is less modular.

Rewriting this case again demonstrates Rule 4 covering acquaintances of a class:

```
class Port {
  private:
    //...same as before...
} serialPort(0x0800);

class ExtDevice {
  public:
    void init() {
        serialPort.init(); //rule 4 access
    }
};
```

Since the class `Port` is declared within the same module as the definition of `ExtDevice::init()`, its public members are known. Further, since variable `serialPort` has global scope, it too is known to the class `ExtDevice` and all of its methods. (Actually, what Sakkinen had in mind was a bit more stringent than this. He proposed that a new keyword `acquaintance` be added to C++ with a syntax similar to `friend` and that classes not declared acquainted not be accessible; however, this suggestion has found little resonance in the C++ community.)

A method declared to be a friend of a class is implicitly acquainted with that class. This coupling is considerably stronger and less desirable than access strictly through the public interface.

In the following example, the class `ExtDevice` has been named a friend of the class `Port`. This form of coupling goes beyond what is considered good programming style.

```
class Port {
    friend class ExtDevice;
  private:
    //...same as before...
} serialPort(0x0800);

class ExtDevice {
  public:
    void init() {
        serialPort.send("+++ATH"); //rule 4 access
    }
};
```

Rule 6 specifies that the data members of a class should be accessible only to the member functions of that class and no other. In addition, adding an access function is discouraged, but not strictly ruled out, by the law. Consider the following extreme example:

```
class Port {
  private:
    unsigned addrss;

  public:
    Port(unsigned initAdd) { addrss = initAdd;}
```

```
        unsigned& address() { return addrss;}
};

//externalFunction - send a message to a port p
void externalFunction(Port p, char* message) {
    unsigned portAdd = p.address();   //get port address
    send(portAdd, message);           //send the message
}
```

Clearly defining the function `Port::address()` has done nothing to encapsulate the data member `addrss`. In returning a reference to `addrss`, the calling function is empowered to change its value without control. Redefining the `address()` function to return type `unsigned` instead of `unsigned&` to prevent modification of the data member helps slightly:

```
class Port {
    //...same as before...
    unsigned address() { return addrss;}
};
```

This still gives the outside world knowledge of the internals of the class `Port`. Upon reflection it is clear that the class `Port` must be incomplete. If it were complete, external functions would have no need for the port address.

Coupling is reduced if the class `Port` can anticipate what extra functions the external world requires; that is, why does `externalFunction()` need the port address? Cannot the class `Port` provide this function instead of allowing this inside information out of the class? Rewriting the preceding example to provide the needed capability results in the following:

```
class Port {
  private:
    unsigned addrss;

  public:
    Port(unsigned initAdd) { addrss = initAdd;}
    void send(char* msg);      //send msg to port 'addrss'
```

```
    char* read();              //read from port 'addrss'
};


//externalFunction - send a message to a port p
void externalFunction(Port p, char* message) {
    p.send(message);
}
```

externalFunction() no longer has any knowledge of the internal workings of a Port.

I am not familiar with any work that has attempted to correlate the Law of Demeter with the maintainability of the resulting class. However, work is continuing with the law and other measures of interclass coupling to allow just such correlations to be made.

Interclass Coupling and Inheritance   As we have seen, inheritance is a powerful tool in describing the relationships between classes of objects. In addition, inheritance allows reuse of class definitions without modification. Further, inheritance can increase class cohesion by allowing class definitions to be factored into their most primitive form.

Inheritance is a dual-edged sword when it comes to interclass coupling, however. A subclass often references the private members of its base class, leading to a strong coupling between classes. Further, a deep inheritance tree adds complexity as each call to a virtual method must be resolved into one of any number of possible classes. Inheritance may add bulk to the final program by including the object code for base classes that are never instanced with an object.

Inheritance is justified when it is used to express an is_a relationship between the base class and the derived class. That is, a class should be derived from another class when the object represented by the class is a special case of the object represented by the general class. When this is not the case, the relationship is known as a **client** or a **has_a** relationship. As Meyer states, for two classes A and B, "Inheritance is appropriate if every instance of B may also be viewed as an instance of A. The client relationship is appropriate when every instance of B simply poses one or more attributes of A."

For example, it is conceivable that a class `Car` could inherit a class `Motor` as follows:

```
class Motor {
  private:
    int noPistons;

  public:
    Motor(int pistons) {noPistons = pistons;}
    void start();
    void accelerate(int howMuch);
    void stop();
};

class Car : public Motor {
  public:
    Car(int pistons) : Motor(pistons) {}
    void startCar() { start();}
};
```

The attributes of the motor — such as horsepower, number of pistons, and so on — may be viewed as attributes of the car that contains it as well. In addition, this gives `Car` access to the methods of `Motor` that it needs. However, it does not properly express the relationship between a `Car` and a `Motor`: a car is not a special case of a motor. Rather, a car has a motor. Most models of cars are available with multiple engine options, often with different numbers of pistons. The car–motor relationship should be expressed as follows:

```
class Car {
  private:
    Motor motor;

  public:
    Car(int pistons) : motor(pistons) {}
    void startCar() { motor.start();}
};
```

Expressing the incorrect relationship between classes should be detected during the design, as it does not clarify the relationship between the abstractions involved.

One question that arises when applying the Law of Demeter to inherited classes is, Should the data members of the base class be considered members of the derived class? If they are, then according to Rule 1 any member function of the derived class may access any data member of the base class directly. If not, however, this access is precluded by Rule 6.

There are logical arguments on both sides of the issue. On the one hand, many programmers view a derived class and its base class as a single logical entity. Others argue that each class should be considered independent.

To accommodate these two views, two different interpretations of the Law of Demeter have arisen. The so-called **Weak Law of Demeter** says that the protected and public members of a base class should also be considered members of the derived class. The **Strong Law** says they should not.

C++ endorses both views. Public inheritance views the subclass as an extension of the base class; members of the base class remain accessible in the subclass. Private inheritance views the derived class as a separate entity; the members are not accessible. A privately derived class that follows the Strong Law of Demeter demonstrates considerably weaker coupling than a subclass that answers only to the Weak Law. However, designing such classes to operate efficiently is often difficult.

Class Normalization

There are two aspects to normalizing a class. One is a mapping of the functional notion of normalization onto the class concept: avoid creating classes that overlap in responsibilities, create a class to describe a valid abstraction when possible, avoid redundant methods within a class. The benefits of this type of class normalization are the same as those noted before — easier to create and maintain and simplification of the higher level functions.

Another aspect of normalization within classes involves allowing members to float to their proper level of abstraction within a class hierarchy. When a property of a base class is incorrectly ascribed to a lower level, it will be duplicated in all of the subclasses.

As an example, consider the following class relationships adapted from Lieberherr:

```
struct Basket {
    Fruit f;
};

struct Fruit {
};

struct Apple : public Fruit {
    Weight weight;
};

struct Orange : public Fruit {
    Weight weight;
};

struct Weight {
    int value;
};
```

To display graphically the relationships between the preceding classes, Lieberherr uses the symbology shown in Figure 3–13.

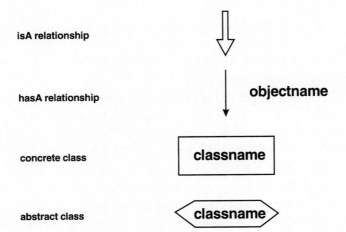

isA relationship

hasA relationship   **objectname**

concrete class   **classname**

abstract class   **classname**

Figure 3–13. Graphic notation for depicting class relationships

Applying these symbols to the sample problem results in the inheritance graph shown in Figure 3–14.

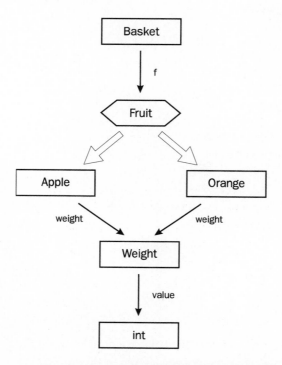

Figure 3–14. Graphic representation of nonnormalized Fruit

`Basket` contains the single element `f` of abstract class `Fruit`. A `Fruit` can be either an `Apple` or an `Orange` (that is, both `Apple` and `Orange` are subclasses of `Fruit`). Both `Apple` and `Orange` contain a member `weight` of class `Weight`.

This last aspect of the graph reveals the error. Both `Apple` and `Orange` contain an element of class `Weight`. Thus, weight is a property of all fruits. Moving the property `Weight` up into `Fruit` as shown in Figure 3-15 normalizes the class hierarchy.

Leaving a class inheritance graph unnormalized not only obscures the true relationships between the abstractions, but also complicates the coding. Functions receiving an object of class `Fruit` will not be able to ask that object its weight without first casting the object into one of its subclasses.

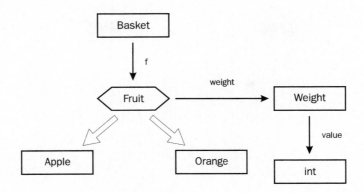

Figure 3–15. Graphic representation of normalized Fruit

Conclusion

A quality program is based upon a sound analysis of customer requirements that are written down and discussed with the programmers and customers. The requirements should not anticipate the design. Requirements should not be construed by the programmers as cast in stone, but should be viewed as a best effort estimate of the true requirements. Requirements will change and programmers' attitudes and methodologies should reflect this.

Once the requirements are understood and have been discussed, the programmers turn their attention to the high-level design. The primary goal of the high-level design is to create appropriate abstractions to simplify the job of later design and implementation. The high-level design should be reviewed by peer groups, looking for holes that might cause trouble later.

The detailed design phase begins to examine how these classes are to be implemented. Questions to be answered during this phase center around class issues, such as completeness, and modularity issues, such as coupling, cohesion, and normality.

Once the detailed design is complete, including an understanding of the public interface of the identified classes, it is time to set about the work of coding. Techniques to reduce the number of software defects will be examined in Chapter 4.

Chapter 4

Writing C++ Programs

Once a good design has been established and reviewed by peers, it is time to set about the task of actually coding something. Not surprisingly, techniques used during the coding stage have a profound effect on the number of software defects to be fixed during debugging and testing. This chapter will examine general style issues. Specific C++ traps and pitfalls will be covered in Chapters 5 and 6.

Coding Style

Coding style is critical to creating solid applications in a timely fashion. A careless, haphazard style tends to hide software errors, leaving them to be found and fixed at greater expense during later phases. A clear, consistent style allows the programmer to concentrate more on the program logic and less on the syntactical details of the program.

Consider the following sample function that reduces a positive fraction less than 1 to the lowest common denominator.

```
void fn(int*pNumerator, int *pDivisor) {
    int quotient, common, i;

    quotient=*pNumerator/*pDivisor;
    *pNumerator-=quotient**pDivisor;
```

```
for (common = 1, i=2; i<=*pNumerator; i++)
   if (*pNumerator%i==0 && *pDivisor%i==0)
      common=i;
*pNumerator/=common;*pDivisor/=common;
}
```

This program generates numerous mysterious compiler errors because the line `*pNumerator/*pDivisor` is interpreted as `*pNumerator /* pDivisor` by the C++ parser. Reformatting the code properly, as follows, removes the error.

```
void fn(int *pNumerator, int *pDivisor) {
   int quotient, common, i;

   quotient      = *pNumerator / *pDivisor;
   *pNumerator -= quotient     * *pDivisor;

   common = 1;
   for (i = 2; i <= *pNumerator; i++)
     if ((*pNumerator % i) == 0 && (*pDivisor % i) == 0)
         common = i;
   *pNumerator /= common;
   *pDivisor   /= common;
}
```

There are two approaches to generating well-formatted source code. One is simply to adopt a formal style and stick to it. Once comfortable with the language, most programmers quickly settle into a personal coding style that changes only slowly over time. Establishing a formal style is only a matter of writing down the rules that the programmer finds work the best, generating the clearest, most readable source code.

These rules are enforced as part of the source code review during which the submitted source module is compared with the coding style guidelines in search of violations.

A coding style should include items such as the following:

- the formatting of blocks of code; for example, "an `if` statement is followed by an opening brace on the same line. The closing brace lines up with the `if`. The enclosed block is indented 3 spaces."

- the naming of objects; for example, "variable names start with a lower-case but may contain uppercase letters at the beginnings of words (for example, `smallObject`). Pointer objects begin with a `p`."
- the naming of classes; for example, "classes are named like objects except they begin with an uppercase letter."
- the naming of macros; for example, "#define names appear in all uppercase."
- the rules for commenting, including the commenting of function headers, function arguments, and block comments within functions.

(The preceding examples come from my own style guide adopted from Borland's proposal for standardized object naming throughout the C++ world.)

Another naming standard is the Hungarian notation used by Microsoft. These names use the following prefixes:

c	char
i	int
n	short
by	unsigned char
b	boolean
w	unsigned int
l	long
dw	unsigned long
fn	function
sz	NULL terminated string

Any naming convention can be used as long as it is applied uniformly and consistently.

In addition, a good coding style includes a naming convention for modules and the functions they contain. Suppose that a database program consisted of three basic components: the human interface, the command parser, and the database engine. The names of modules that deal principally with the interface could begin with an `I`, those that parse commands with a `P`, and those that make up the database engine with a `D`. In this way, the programmer knows at a glance that the module `DINTRFC.CPP` is part of the database portion of the program and not part of the external interface, as one might assume from the remainder of the name. A similar convention for function names allows the programmer to identify their roles immediately as well.

An alternative to source code formatting is to use a commercial source code reformatting tool. With such tools, the programmer writes C++ modules using whatever style desired. Once written, the modules are submitted to a reformatter that cleans up the code using a consistent set of rules, such as those listed earlier.

Although the manual approach gives better results in general, reformatters have two advantages. First, they are consistent. The formatting of modules from several programmers appears consistent after being run through a reformatter even if they were coded originally with different styles. Second, reformatters are very good at catching indention problems such as the following:

```
float logAbsValue(float a) {
    if (a >= 0)
        if (a != 0)
            return log(a);
    else
        return log(-a);
    return 0;
}
```

Here the casual reader might assume that `logAbsValue()` returns a 0 in the event that `a` is 0. However, reformatting the program correctly reveals that this is not true.

```
float logAbsValue(float a) {
    if (a >= 0)
        if (a != 0)
            return log(a);
        else                    //this else goes with second if
            return log(-a);
    return 0;
}
```

Some software houses use a combination of the two approaches. First, they adopt a coding style guideline that their programmers are obliged to follow. They then write a format-checking tool to enforce this guideline.

(The software department in which I work uses this approach.) In this way, they reap the advantages of both methods.

Function Complexity

A part of any good style guide should be a limit to the size of a function. As you have seen, a cohesive function limits itself to solving a single problem. Large functions are usually large because they try to solve several problems at once. Dividing large functions into a number of smaller, better focused functions increases their cohesiveness, making the result easier to read.

Large functions almost always offer a large number of logic paths. Each of these paths must be tested at least once before the programmer can determine with any certainty that the function does what it is intended to do. Smaller, simpler functions provide a fewer number of paths to debug. When combined with other debugged functions, their internal complexity is largely abstracted away.

Measuring Complexity   Of course, in order to limit the complexity of a function, there must be some agreement as to what *complexity* means when applied to something as amorphous as a C++ function. (The term software *size* is often used, more or less synonymously, as well.) Exactly "how much stuff" does a particular function represent?

Determining proper metrics is a problem common to all areas of human endeavor in their infancy. Before quantitative progress can be made, some agreement must be achieved as to what the fundamental properties are and how they should be measured. Good metrics allow researchers to devise empirical relationships that appear to hold universally. Examination of empirical relationships eventually reveals the underlying law. Discovering and studying laws expands our understanding of science. In addition, armed with laws and the metrics upon which they are based, practitioners can predict how systems will act before they are built.

The first science to arrive at a good set of metrics was physics. It may be hard to appreciate that originally much confusion existed over what constituted fundamental physical metrics. Considering Newton's Laws of Motion from today's perspective, we may overlook the importance of declaring Mass to be the essential measure of "how much stuff" an object represented over Weight — which had been the commonly held measure of stuff up to that time.

A good software metric should allow the programmer to predict with some certainty (allowing for human and random variation) the number of hours it will take to code, debug, and test a software function and the statistical number of errors that function will carry with it into test.

Any software metric can only tell us so much. Weinwurm, Zagorski, and Nelson, as reported by Boris Beizer in *Software Testing Techniques,* show that software cost is heavily influenced by external parameters such as the number of meetings attended, the number of items in the database, the relative state of the hardware, and the documentation requirements. The COCOMO and Price-S parametric software cost prediction models include these and other seemingly unrelated factors in their software bid models.

(One curious factor that figures rather highly in both COCOMO and Price-S is the number of years since the programming language was introduced — the maturity of the language is taken as an indication of the number of problems that the programmers will encounter with the environment. These bidding tools have yet to include "object-orientedness" as a costing factor, however.)

What, then, are the desirable properties of a software complexity metric? A useful complexity metric should satisfy the following:

1. Be easily, objectively calculable. Independent observers should be able to calculate the same value for a given function. Reproducibility is a cornerstone of modern science and engineering. A subjective metric would be of questionable use.
2. Retain its complexity. Adding something to a program should never reduce its complexity.
3. Be uncheatable. It should not be possible to reduce the software complexity by making trivial, cosmetic changes to the function — such as putting several statements on one line, reducing or increasing the length of variable names, and so on.
4. Show a high correlation with programming, debugging, and testing efforts required by that module or the number of software defects contained in that module. Metrics that do not fulfill this criteria are useless.

Software complexity metrics are not required for functions that change themselves dynamically. Determining the complexity of a function after it has modified its own code may be quite difficult. How much complexity is added by the fact that the code is in a state of flux? In addition, some programs write other programs. Artificially created programs may not be measurable by conventional metrics, and these types of programs are not covered in this discussion.

With these guidelines in mind, consider the following three common software complexity metrics.

The LOC Metric The most obvious, and historically the first, measure of software complexity is the line count, usually abbreviated **LOC** (lines of code) or **KLOC** (thousand lines of code).

The primary attraction of this metric is the ease with which it is calculated (fulfilling Rule 1). Most compilers generate some type of line count as a part of their output. In any case, programs to count statements within a source module are easy to write. Even in their absence, programmers can quickly count the number of pages of listing. (Listings also can be weighed on a scale: a high correlation exists between software size in LOC and listing weight in pounds or kilograms.)

At first only executable lines were counted in the LOC metric, because it was thought that only they could produce software errors. More recently, programmers have tended to include all lines for two reasons: the representation of data has come to be seen as just as important as the code, and counting all lines removes any interpretation that might cause differences to arise.

The LOC metric fulfills Rule 2, but fails miserably on Rule 3. Programmers can (and do) skimp on comments or gang several C++ statements together on a single line to avoid going over a two-page limit. A slight modification to the LOC metric, the Statement metric addresses this problem by counting the number of independently executable statements. Thus, the following `for` loop counts as two lines but five statements:

```
for (sum = i = 0; i < 10; i++)
    sum += array[i];
```

Neither the LOC nor the Statement metric fulfills Rule 4 well either. Even a short function may be quite complex. In fact, a 50-line FORTRAN program consisting of 25 `IF...THEN` statements could offer up to 33 million distinct logic paths!

Further, the LOC metric adds no penalty for confusing compound constructs such as the following:

```
for(fn(val = otherV++ * 10); val ; val--, otherV++)
```

Studies have shown that results in correlating reliability to LOC are mixed. As reported in Boris Beizer's *Software Testing Techniques*, Thayer, Lipow, and Nelson show error rates varying between 0.04 percent and 7 percent for programs with similar LOC values, a variability of almost 200 to 1. This makes inferring an error rate from an LOC measure difficult. LOC is probably a reasonably good measure of the complexity of small functions, but it is overly optimistic for programs of more than 100 lines.

The Halstead Metrics   A more reliable set of measures of software complexity are the **Halstead metrics**. Like the LOC metric, all of the Halstead figures are **linguistic metrics**. Linguistic metrics are based upon properties of the program that do not require interpreting the text. In these metrics, all operators count the same and all operands the same (though they may differ from each other).

The first, known as the **Halstead Length**, is given by the sum of the total number of operators and operands in the program. Halstead reasoned that a count of the number of operators and operands might give a reasonable assessment of "how much is going on" within the function. A sample of the Halstead Length is as follows:

```
N = N₁ + N₂

where
  N₁ total number of operators in the function
  N₂ total number of operands in the function
```

In the following copy-initializer constructor there are six operators and three operands, resulting in a Halstead Length of nine.

```
struct Vector {
    int length;
    Vector(Vector&);
    void copyVector(Vector&);
    //...other members
};

Vector::Vector(Vector& sv) {
    length = 0;
    copyVector(sv);
};
```

The operands are {}, =, ;, () and ; plus the implicit -> operator applied to `length` (as in `this->length = 0;`). The operands are `length`, 0, and `sv`.

In his work Halstead discovered that the Halstead Length of a function could be predicted with reasonable accuracy even before the function was written. The predicted Halstead Length that follows tracks closely the actual Halstead Length for most programs.

$$N^\wedge = n_1 \log_2 n_1 + n_2 \log_2 n_2$$

`where`

    n_1 `number of unique operators in the function`
    n_2 `number of unique operands in the function`

Suppose, for example, that a particular programmer typically uses roughly 50 different operators for programs of any length and that the detailed design reveals that some 20 different operands will be necessary. In this case, $N^\wedge$ equals 369.

This formula works quite well for functions larger than 5 to 10 lines. Correlation values for $N^\wedge$ to N seldom drop below 0.8 for programs of any size. $N^\wedge$ tracks N so well, in fact, that the ratio $N^\wedge/N$ has been given the name **Halstead Purity Ratio** and is used as a stylistic guide by some. Functions with purity ratios outside of the range 0.5 to 2.0 are called into question.

From the Halstead Length, Halstead derived the **Halstead Volume** shown by the following formula:

$$V = (N_1 + N_2) \log_2(n_1 + n_2)$$

where

   n_1 number of unique operators in the function
   n_2 number of unique operands in the function
   N_1 total number of operators in the function
   N_2 total number of operands in the function

If the preceding example program used its 50 unique operators in 300 different places and its 20 unique operands in 300 places, then the Halstead Volume would be 3678.

Halstead suggested this as an alternate measure of program complexity since, unlike the Halstead Length, it tends to penalize programs with a large number of unique operands and operators.

One interpretation of the Halstead Volume is that it measures the number of mental lookups a programmer must make to read and fully understand the entire program using the most efficient search algorithms known. Since people tend to make a mistake every E0 mental comparisons, the average number of bugs in such a program is given by the following formula. The constant E0 has been empirically determined to be in the range 3000 to 3200.

$$B^\wedge = V / E0$$

where

   $B^\wedge$ is the predicted number of software errors
   V is the Halstead Volume
   E0 is between 3000 and 3200

Thus, the small sample program we are using should have 1.2 post-compilation software bugs.

How well do Halstead's metrics, particularly the Volume metric, stand up to our evaluation criteria? Clearly all of the Halstead metrics pass Rules 2 and 3.

Not so clear is how well these metrics stand up to Rule 1. For example, exactly what counts as an operator and an operand is left to the individual's opinion. Consider that Halstead's work was performed primarily on FORTRAN, although APL and Pascal were considered. In particular, C++ did not exist at the time. However, studies reported by SET Laboratories show that as long as the Halstead metrics are used to compare functions and are not used as absolute values, minor differences in the counting rules have little effect if they are applied consistently. (Of course, the constant E0 may have to be empirically redetermined for different counting rules.)

Once determined, the rules can be applied mechanically. This allows computerization of what is otherwise a laborious and error-prone task. For example, the tool **PC-Metric** from SET Laboratories (P.O. Box 868, Mulino, OR 97042) processes C++ modules, generating the Halstead metrics, the McCabe complexity to be studied next, and others for each function in the program and for the overall program. The analysis for the following sample class `Vector` is shown in Figure 4–1 on page 153.

```
class Vector {
  private:
    unsigned length;
    int      *pData;
    void      copyVector(Vector& s);

  public:
    //constructors and destructor
    Vector();
    Vector(int initVal, int length = 1);
    Vector(Vector& sV) {length = 0;
                        copyVector(sv);}
    ~Vector();

    //access methods
    int size() { return length;}
    void print();

    //operators
    Vector& operator+(Vector& v2);
    int&    operator[](int offset);
};


//code for the member functions
```

```
Vector::Vector() {
    printf("Creating vector of zero length\n");
    length = 0;
    pData  = 0;
}
Vector::Vector(int iVal, int l) {
    printf("Creating vector of length %d\n", l);
    length = 0;
    if (pData = new int[l]) {
        length = l;
        for (int i = 0; i < l; i++)
            pData[i] = iVal;
    }
}


Vector::~Vector() {
    printf("Destructing vector of length %d\n", length);
    if (length)
        delete(pData);
    length = 0;
}


//copyVector() - given a new source vector, copy the new
//               data into the current object
void Vector::copyVector(Vector& sv) {
    printf("Copying vector of length %d\n", sv.length);

    //if the size is different, delete the data block
    //and get a new one
    if (length != sv.length) {
        //delete the old data
        if (length) {
            length = 0;
            delete pData;
        }

        //now get a new block
        if (sv.length)
```

```
                    if (pData = new int[sv.length])
                        length = sv.length;
        }
    }


    //print() - print the contents of the vector
    void Vector::print() {
        printf("(");
        int i;
        int max = length;
        if (max)
            for (i = 0;;) {
                printf(" %d", pData[i]);
                 if (++i >= max)
                    break;
                printf(",");
            }
        printf(")");
    }
    //operator+() - add each member of the vectors together
    Vector Vector::operator+(Vector& v2) {
        //if vectors are of the same arity, no problem
        Vector& v1 = *this;
        if (v1.length == v2.length) {
            Vector t(0, length);
            int i;
            for (i = 0; i < length; i++)
                t.pData[i] = v1.pData[i] + v2.pData[i];
            return t;
        }


        //otherwise, one of the other must be of arity 1
        int scalar;
        Vector* pS = 0;
        if (v1.length == 1) {
            scalar = v1.pData[0];
            pS      =&v2;
        }
```

```
        if (v2.length == 1) {
            scalar = v2.pData[0];
             pS     =&v1;
        }


        if (pS) {
            Vector t(0, pS->length);
            int i;
            for (i = 0; i < pS->length; i++)
                t.pData[i] = pS->pData[i] + scalar;
            return t;
        }


        //if nothing matches, return a null vector
        Vector t;
        return t;
    }


//operator[]() - index an element of a vector
int dummy = 0;
int& Vector::operator[](int offset) {
    if (offset > length)
        return dummy;
    return pData[offset];
}
```

Allowed ranges can be established for each metric. Functions that fall outside these ranges are marked in a separate exceptions file.

Analysis programs of this sort are a necessity for anyone intending to make serious use of the Halstead metrics.

How well does the Halstead metric correlate with actual bug rates? Lipow reports agreement between predicted and actual bug count of plus or minus 8 percent for programs from 300 to 12,000 executable statements (more than 115,000 LOC were included in this study). Other studies have shown similarly high correlation rates.

Function	FT	n1	n2	N1	N2	N	N^	P/R	V	E	VG1	VG2	LOC	BLK	CMT	<;>	SP	VL
Vector::Vector(Vector)	PB	5	3	6	3	9	16	1.82	27	68	1	1	2	0	0	2	0	4
Vector::size()	PB	3	1	3	1	4	5	1.19	8	12	1	1	1	0	0	1	0	6
Vector::operator=(Vector)	PB	7	1	8	1	9	20	2.18	27	95	1	1	2	0	0	2	0	1
Vector::Vector()		5	4	8	5	13	20	1.51	41	129	1	1	5	0	0	3	0	6
Vector::Vector(int, int)		13	7	25	16	41	68	1.65	177	2633	3	3	9	0	0	6	2	3
Vector::~Vector()		10	4	12	6	18	41	2.29	69	514	2	2	6	0	0	3	1	6
Vector::copyVector(Vector)		16	6	46	30	76	80	1.50	339	13557	7	7	25	3	5	8	6	4
Vector::print()		13	9	32	14	46	77	1.67	205	2074	4	4	13	0	0	9	2	3
Vector::operator+()		19	9	93	58	151	109	0.72	726	44442	7	7	35	3	3	20	9	3
Vector::operator[]()		7	4	9	5	14	28	1.98	48	212	2	2	5	0	0	2	1	6

Headings:
```
 FT = function type
 n1 = unique operators
 n2 = unique operands
 N1 = total operators
 N2 = total operands
 N  = Halstead length
 N^ = estimated Halstead length
 P/R= purity ratio (estimated / actual Halstead)
 V  = Halstead Volume
 E  = Halstead Effort
 VG1= McCabe Cyclomatic Complexity
 VG2= extended McCabe Cyclomatic Complexity
 LOC= lines of code
 BLK= no. of blank lines
 CMT= no. of comment lines
 <;>= no. of executable semicolons
 SP = average maximum span of variables
 VL = average variable name length
```

Figure 4–1. Sample output from PC-Metric for a class `Vector`

McCabe Cyclomatic Complexity

As well known as the Halstead metrics is the **McCabe Cyclomatic Complexity Metric**. Unlike the linguistic Halstead, McCabe is a **structured metric**. Structured metrics analyze the meaning of the C++ statements in a program. In particular, the McCabe complexity counts the number of different logical paths through a function. The idea is that the chances of a software logic error are much greater at a decision point (a branch of some type) than in the middle of straight line code. A series of straight line code, with no branches, has no effect on the McCabe number. Thus, McCabe complexity is unaffected by function bulk. The formula for the McCabe metric is as follows:

```
V = e - n + 2p
where
```

```
e = number of edges (paths)
n = number of nodes
p = number of components
```

Figure 4–2 shows the logical paths drawn out for several different functions along with the resulting McCabe complexity for each.

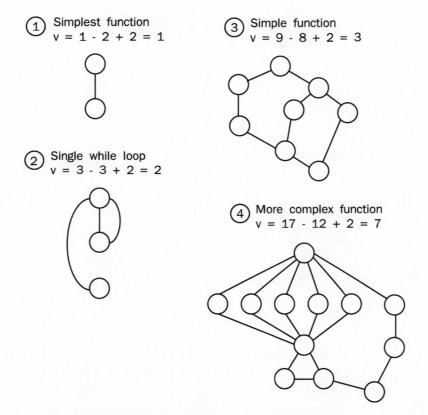

① Simplest function
v = 1 - 2 + 2 = 1

③ Simple function
v = 9 - 8 + 2 = 3

② Single while loop
v = 3 - 3 + 2 = 2

④ More complex function
v = 17 - 12 + 2 = 7

Figure 4–2. McCabe Cyclomatic Complexity for different modules

The McCabe metric cannot generate a value of less than 1, even for the most trivial function. As the number of branches increases, the number rises linearly by integer values. This provides a short-cut means of calculating the McCabe value: simply add up the number of branch statements (that is, if, while, for, and so on) and add one.

The McCabe metric is relatively insensitive to loops, treating a for loop the same as a single logical if branch. McCabe considered this an advantage, but subsequently many consider this a disadvantage since a loop is more prone to error than a simple branch.

How well does the McCabe metric stand up to our evaluation criteria? First, the McCabe metric is easily calculated. PC-Metric and other analytical tools can calculate V automatically. Unlike the Halstead metric, calculating McCabe by hand is not particularly laborious. Second, adding things cannot reduce the McCabe metric.

However, the McCabe metric is subject to cheating in one way. A compound `if` statement is obviously more complicated than a simple `if`. In the following code segment, the first `if` is more complicated than the second.

```
if (a < b && c < d) {          //first if
   ...
}
if (a < c) {                   //second if
   ...
}
```

The original McCabe metric counts them both as a single node. This allows programmers to combine `if` statements, reducing the apparent complexity of the resulting code. To address this, Myers has suggested counting not the number of branching statements, but the number of predicates. Myers, then, views the first `if` as two statements, as follows:

```
if (a < b)                     //first predicate
   if (c < d) {                //second predicate
      ...
   }
```

This modified metric is sometimes called the **Extended McCabe Cyclomatic Complexity**.

Researchers have been able to show a high correlation between the V measurement of a function and the likelihood that that function will contain an error. In one field study reported by Markham, McCall, and Walters in the *IEEE Conference Proceedings*, a correlation coefficient of 0.88 was observed between V and reported problems in more than 40 large modules.

T. J. Walsh's work, as reported by Boris Beizer, cites a military software program consisting of 276 procedures to which the metric was applied. They found that 23 percent of the functions with V greater than 10 accounted for 53 percent of the bugs. Walsh goes on to say that routines with V greater than 10 had 21 percent more errors per LOC than those with values less than 10.

McCabe himself reported considerable luck at tying troublesome programs to high cyclomatic complexity. In particular, McCabe reported a set of 24 FORTRAN graphics routines with complexities ranging between 16 and 64. When he confronted the source of these routines as to why the numbers were so high, McCabe was told that those subroutines had been provided for study precisely because they broke so often. Further investigation revealed that the higher complexity routines were the most troublesome of the group (the worst of the worst, as it were).

McCabe also reports that all programmers demonstrate a characteristic complexity range in which they feel comfortable. A particular programmer might generate functions in the 3 to 7 complexity range almost without regard to the type of problem being solved, while another programmer routinely exceeds 40 to 50.

Using Complexity Metrics   Many companies establish complexity limits for functions as part of their coding guidelines. Usually these are voluntary, but occasionally they are dictated as part of the contract by the customer. In such cases, some upper limit is set for the complexity of a function. Functions that exceed this limit are rejected unless they have been given some type of special dispensation from the project manager.

The idea behind these rules, of course, is to induce programmers to produce small, modular functions that are easy to debug and maintain. Rules of this sort are, in general, a very good idea, but they cannot be enforced blindly. Some functions resist simplification. Subdividing a function solely to comply with an arbitrary complexity metric is worse than leaving the function alone. One cohesive large function is easier to debug than two uncohesive, strongly coupled small functions.

Often complexity limits are based on the LOC metric. A function may be limited to 50 C++ statements or two pages of listings (including comments), for example. These two standards are roughly equivalent, depending upon coding style. Although LOC is not the best metric in the world, it is reasonably accurate for small functions when good coding style is enforced. Thus, the 50-statement rule is probably reasonable.

The Halstead metrics make a better set of stylistic guidelines. As with the LOC metric, a limiting value for the Halstead Length or Volume is established and enforced by automatic tools such as PC-Metric. Functions whose size exceeds these limits are flagged by the tool and must be corrected or the rule must be waived.

The McCabe Cyclomatic Complexity Metric is a useful style guideline at the function level, in light of the high correlation between this metric and the probability of an error. The McCabe metric also has the advantage over the Halstead metrics of being easy to determine by hand. During coding, the programmer is aware of how each statement contributes to the complexity. McCabe himself proposed a threshold of 10, and most organizations have adopted this suggestion. However, this number is arbitrary and can be adjusted up or down to fit the organization.

Since they measure different things, both the Halstead and the McCabe metrics can be used as coding guidelines. Functions that exceed the Halstead Volume but not the McCabe metric, for example, are logically simple but contain too much "stuff." Functions that remain within the Halstead Volume limit but exceed McCabe are small but have overly complex control flow. This type of information is useful when rewriting functions.

The complexity of a function can be reduced by factoring out the complexity into subroutines. For example, Figure 4–3 on the following page shows how the McCabe complexity of a function may be reduced.

In the first step, the right-most `if` statement is removed by placing it into a function of its own. Calling a function does not add to the McCabe complexity of a function because it is not a conditional branch. (A function call does add to the Halstead Volume, but it probably does not add as much as the code that it replaces.) This process can be repeated until the function complexity is reduced to 1.

Notice that factoring out the McCabe complexity of a function does NOT reduce the complexity of the overall program, however. In fact, the overall complexity of the program increases by 1 for every function that is factored out.

Metrics have other uses in addition to serving as coding guidelines. First, metrics can be used to guide the testing phase.

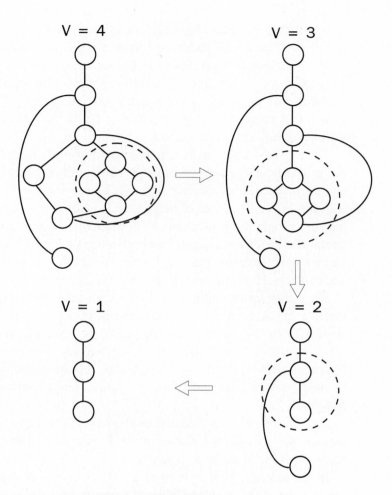

Figure 4–3. Factoring out McCabe complexity

The Halstead predicted bug count is often used during testing. The predicted number of bugs combined with the rate at which bugs are being discovered should give the programmer some idea of how long to expend on testing. (Remember, however, that the rate at which bugs are detected and fixed will decrease as testing progresses since the bugs become more difficult.) In addition, the predicted bug count is used to help direct testing. More time and effort should be exerted in those parts of the program where the estimated bug count is higher.

In addition, the McCabe metric is sometimes used as a lower limit to the number of test cases. If the number of test cases in a function is less than the McCabe complexity, then it is likely that either

- test coverage is not complete — one or more paths is left untested, or
- the function can be simplified — several paths are strongly tied together, so that taking one branch early in the program implies that a subsequent branch later in the program will always be taken.

Other than serving as a minimum, the McCabe metric is not a good guideline for determining the proper number of test cases. Further discussion of test cases occurs in Chapter 7.

Another use of metrics is the area of **preemptive rewriting**. As a program enters the integration phase and the various pieces come together, problems inevitably arise. Typically, these problems are not uniformly distributed over software modules. Once it becomes apparent that a particular module is producing more than the average number of bugs, the software task leader will wonder whether the module should be rewritten.

Rewriting a module makes sense for several reasons. Knowledge during integration is more complete than it was during development. (Do not fool yourself into thinking that it is complete, however.) Programmers generally have a much deeper understanding of the problem and the environment.

In addition, modules that have shown themselves to be difficult are usually assigned to the most capable programmers, who may not have been available during the development phase.

Finally, every patch to fix a bug adds to the complexity of the module. This tendency is known as **software entropy**. (The Law of Software Entropy says that without the application of a large amount of programmer energy, a function will tend to its natural state of complete randomness and confusion.) While the original module may have passed complexity guidelines, modules that have been regularly patched almost certainly do not and will be difficult to maintain.

Thus, a software task leader may use either the Halstead or McCabe metrics to determine whether a module requires rewriting. If the majority of functions remain below the McCabe guidelines then the logic is still reasonably simple. If the Halstead numbers are within range, none of the functions has swelled beyond tolerance. If not, then the module should be considered for rewrite.

Applying Complexity Metrics to Classes   The   complexity metrics considered thus far answer the question, How complex is this function or module? Work is just beginning on the answer to, How complex is this class?

In a paper titled "Towards a Metric Suite for Object-Oriented Design," Shyam R. Chidamber and Chris F. Kemerer proposed the following candidates for class metrics:

1. Weighted Methods per Class (WMC) — calculate the complexity of each method of the class individually, then sum them all up.
2. Depth of Inheritance Tree (DIT) — count the deepest extent of the inheritance tree.
3. Number of Children (NOC) — count the number of immediate subclasses.
4. Coupling Between Objects (CBO) — count the number of noninheritance relationships between the class and other classes.
5. Response for a Class (RFC) — count the number of methods of the class plus the number of methods called by those methods.
6. Lack of Cohesion in Methods (LCOM) — construct a set of the instance variables used by each method. LCOM is the number of disjoint sets formed by intersecting those sets.

The WMC is a straightforward extension of the non-object-oriented complexity measures. That is, the amount of "stuff" in a class should be the sum of the "stuff" in all of its methods. Which of the functional metrics is used is a matter of taste.

The DIT and NOC measures refer to the need for a good inheritance tree to be balanced — neither too wide and shallow, nor deep and narrow. Time may prove some ratio of NOC to DIT to be a better guide. The CBO and RFC metrics attempt to measure the lack of encapsulation. That is, how sensitive one class is to changes in other classes.

The LCOM metric requires further explanation. Consider the following class:

```
class MyClass {
  private:
    int a;
    int b;
    int c;

  public:
    void fn1() {
        //uses a & b & c
    }
    void fn2() {
        //uses a & b
    }
    void fn3() {
        //uses b & c
    }
    void fn4() {
        //uses a
    }
};
```

The sets of members accessed by the functions are $I_1 = \{a,b,c\}$, $I_2 = \{a, b\}$, $I_3 = \{b,c\}$, and $I_4 = \{a\}$. The different intersection sets are $\{a,b\}$, $\{b,c\}$, $\{a\}$, $\{b\}$, and $\{\}$, for an LCOM of 5.

Another technique used in structured languages may apply to object-oriented environments: **function checkpointing**. In function checkpointing, weighting values are assigned to different types of constructs that may appear in a function. These constructs are known as checkpoints. The overall value of the function is the sum of the weights of all the checkpoints that appear in the function.

Function checkpointing is in many ways a generalization of the metrics discussed so far. For example, if the only construct recognized is a line of code and if it is assigned the value one, then the results are identical with the LOC metric. If, on the other hand, a weighting of one is used for each branch statement and zero for all other statement types, the results resemble those of the McCabe Complexity Metric. A set of functional checkpoint values can be devised for most other metrics, as well.

In "Function Points in an Ada Object-Oriented Design," Ernie Rains proposed a checkpoint system for Ada, an object-based language, that

includes a weight for each attribute, operation, exception, "with" statement, constant, and "used by" statement. The weights for a class are then
totaled — including all of its methods — to arrive at a size for each class.
Such checkpointing can and will be generalized to C++ classes in the near
future.

Although each of these metrics has theoretical justifications, insufficient time has passed for anyone to conclude that one of these metrics is
clearly superior to the others. Only time will tell.

Using Multiple Compilers   Coding style can be improved somewhat by employing more than one compiler. In some applications, multiple compilers are a necessity. Developing a program on the target
environment may not be practical. Especially during the early stages of
module debugging, it may be more practical to compile and execute programs on the development environment, switching over to the target environment at a later stage.

Even when not required, using several C++ compilers to check a program results in increased portability. Programmers may not be aware of
what features are part of the language and what ones are extensions in a
particular implementation. In addition, some compilers may be better at
catching different errors. A good scrubbing by two or more C++ compilers, each with all warnings enabled, should wring out all of the possible
compile-time errors.

Invariably, incompatibilities arise between C++ compilers, especially
because C++ is a growing, evolving language. To support multiple compilers, programmers often resort to conditional compilation statements. To
facilitate the use of conditional compilation statements, most compilers
predefine labels indicating the compiler type. Borland's compilers define
the label `__TURBOC__` with the current version number, Microsoft
defines the label `_MSC_VER` and Zortech defines the label `__ZTC__`, to
name a few. This allows the following construct to be made:

```
#ifdef _TURBOC_
    //...compile this only on Borland compiler
#endif
```

Conditional compilations to work around compiler peculiarities should
be avoided if possible and, when not possible, limited to only what is

absolutely necessary. Conditional compilation changes the code being executed between different environments. Thus, no matter how much module testing was performed on the development machine under Compiler A, modules containing conditional compilation must be retested when the module is compiled for the target machine with Compiler B. Otherwise a software error lurking in the "Compiler B only" code will slip into integration or the final product.

If conditional compilation involves more than a single label, testing must be performed on every combination of labels. If a module has three independent #defines, each of which has two values, the module has eight configurations, each of which must be tested (and retested whenever the module changes).

Many compiler or machine dependencies can be worked around without resorting to conditional compilation. One technique is to use typedefs within #defines to encapsulate machine details. Suppose an int is 16 bits on the development machine, but 32 bits on the target machine. The following pair of definitions allows the remainder of the program to refer to a single type (WORD) of the same size on both machines.

```
#ifdef _HOST_

//within HOST.H
typedef unsigned long WORD;    //a 32-bit word

#else

//within TARGET.H
typedef unsigned int WORD;     //a 32-bit word
#endif
```

The size of the different variable types is a source of incompatibility between environments, as these are not specified in the ANSI definition. The characteristics of the integer data types are specified in the limits.h include file, those for the floating point types are specified in float.h. When moving between compilers on the same processor, most of the incompatibilities can be avoided by simply specifying short or long since the size of an int is most freely interpreted.

Compiler peculiarities can be handled in a similar fashion. The directive to force a function to use C calling rules, even when Pascal rules are the default, is called `_cdecl` on Microsoft and Zortech compilers and `cdecl` on Borland compilers. The following coding allows the universal use of `_cdecl` on all compiler types.

```
#ifdef _TURBOC_
#define _cdecl cdecl
#endif
_cdecl int myFunc(void);
//...and so on
```

The preceding type of conditional compilation is not as likely to mask errors as the following alternative style:

```
#ifdef _TURBOC_
cdecl int myFunc(void);
//...and so on
#elseif
_cdecl int myFunc(void);
//...declarations repeated here
#endif
//...non-conditional statements here
```

This extends to missing functions, as well. For example, the Watcom C compiler utilizes a POSIX compliant `opendir()` function to search a directory for a file rather than the PC standard `findfirst()`/`findnext()`. To avoid this problem, programs that must support both environments usually include a `findfirst()`/`findnext()` in a compatibility source file. Within `.H` file, the prototype is provided as follows:

```
#ifdef __WATCOMC__
int findfirst(const char* path, struct ffblk *pFB,
              int attr);
int findnext(struct ffblk *pFB);
#endif
```

Within the source file `COMPAT.CPP` is the source file for these functions. (This function must access the DOS `0x4E` service call directly or use the available `opendir()` function.)

The particulars that cannot be handled in this fashion should be kept with a single source module as much as possible. Although this may result in a single module containing disparate functions, the disadvantages of poor module cohesion are outweighed by the fact that only one module need be completely retested for each possible setting of the conditional labels.

Using the Features of C++

The C language offers many tools a programmer needs to manage and reduce software complexity: the function call mechanism, a good set of flow control structures, and a powerful data structure. C++ adds further features that can be used to reduce software complexity and enhance reliability: inheritance, constructors and destructors, and operator overloading.

Using Inheritance

Inheritance promotes software quality by allowing working, tested classes to be reused in new applications. New programs can inherit some existing methods while extending and enhancing other methods, all without modifying the original base class. This extensibility is the core of the object-oriented paradigm.

Using Inheritance to Promote Class Reuse   A class that has been debugged — especially if that includes time in the field as part of a working application — represents a valuable asset, one that should not be taken lightly. Debugged classes should not be modified, if at all possible, since the costs of doing so are very high.

As long as an existing class can be taken in total and dropped into a new application, the programmer may begin by assuming that the class works as advertised — especially if the class contains "customs code" to check the values going across the surface in both directions. The application will need to be thoroughly tested, including all possible input to the class, but this testing can remain external to the class if the class was properly tested in the previous project.

However, once the class has been opened up and modified internally, the programmer can no longer be sure that the class works as intended. Then the class must be completely retested, beginning with the internal tests.

This limits the usefulness of C structures even when they are only accessed via access functions because existing structures can rarely be found to fit the new requirement exactly. Invariably some modifications to the structure or the access functions will be required and this will force a complete retest.

However, a program can modify an inherited base class by overlaying one or more methods without having to open up the class and subject it to the risk of a software bug infection. Although the subclass must be thoroughly tested, it is apt to be much smaller than the base class, because it contains only the code that modifies the base class's behavior.

Consider the following example. A Receiver control class has been successfully used on a previous program. It provides the following methods:

```
class Receiver {
  private:
    int   output(int command); //output a command to rcvr

  public:
    Receiver(long portAddress);//start receiver
    Receiver(Receiver&);       //start second rcvr object
    Receiver();                //start using default adrss
    void tune(float freq);     //tune the receiver
    void mode(int amFm);       //set the mode selector
    void bandWidth(int bwSetting); //set the band width
    int   validate(float f, int amFm, int bwSetting);
    void reset();              //reset after an error

    ~Receiver();               //turn the receiver off
};
```

The foregoing public methods are provided to tune the receiver, set the mode selector, and select the band width. The `validate()` function checks the input parameters to make sure that they are legal — this function is called by the `tune()`, `mode()`, and `bandWidth()` methods, but may be called from external functions as well. Other methods are provided to reset the receiver in the event of a failure, to start the receiver at program initialization, and to turn the receiver off when the program terminates. All of these methods use the private method output() to perform the actual command send to the receiver.

Two problems arise when we try to use this class in a new project with a similar, but not identical, receiver from the same manufacturer. First, let us say the new receiver has a narrower AM frequency range than the previous, more expensive receiver. Because not all frequencies that were legal before remain so now, a modification is required to validate(). Since all other methods use the validate() method to determine whether the command parameters are legal, this is the only function that should be affected.

Second, the new receiver uses a different command format and a LAN-type interface instead of a serial connection. All output to the receiver is via the private method output(), so that should be the only method that has to be changed to implement the new command format. Since the LAN interface requires a node address as well as a port address, more information must be added to the class.

Rather than modify the tested class Receiver, you can use inheritance to overload the changes into a new class NewReceiver as follows.

```cpp
class NewReceiver : public Receiver {
  private:
    unsigned nodeAddress;      //node address on lan

    int  output(int command); //output a command to rcvr

  public:
    NewReceiver(unsigned nodeAddr, long portAddress) :
            Receiver(portAddress) {
                    nodeAddress = nodeAddr;
            }
    NewReceiver() : Receiver() {
                    nodeAddress = 0;
            }

    int  validate(float f, int amFm, int bwSetting);
};
```

The subclass is considerably smaller and simpler than the base class `Receiver`.

The remaining methods are either adapted or borrowed from the base class. The constructors for `NewReceiver` are trivial, relying on the `Receiver` constructor to reset and initialize the receiver. A copy-initializer constructor is not needed since the default c-i constructor is sufficient to copy the one data item unique to `NewReceiver`. `NewReceiver` relies on `~Receiver()` to disable the receiver when the program terminates.

The method `NewReceiver::validate()` is implemented by borrowing heavily from the base method, `Receiver::validate()`, as follows:

```
int NewReceiver::validate(float f, int amFm, int
bwSetting) {
    int result;

    //first check params using "old rules"; on failure
    //return failure indication immediately
    result = Receiver::validate(f, amFm, bwSetting);
    if (!result)
        return result;

    //now check the frequency range in AM mode
    if (amFm == AM)
        result = f >= MINAMFREQ && f <= MAXAMFREQ;
    return result;
}
```

If the function `Receiver::validate()` reports that the parameters are illegal for the previous receiver with its wider range, then they are illegal for the new set as well. If, however, the parameters pass the previous validation and the new mode is AM, you must reexamine the frequency. Still, this single test is far simpler than the `Receiver::validate()` method.

Only the method `output()` is a complete rewrite. With the command formats being dissimilar and the hardware interface different, sufficient similarities between `Receiver::output()` and `NewReceiver::-output()` to warrant reuse in this case.

Using Inheritance to Ease Extensions to Existing

Classes Inheritance can also be used to allow an existing application to be extended to cover unforeseen but related problems. Consider a class hierarchy describing the various types of video adapters available for the IBM PC and its family of compatible machines. Figure 4–4 shows one possible taxonomy of such adapters.

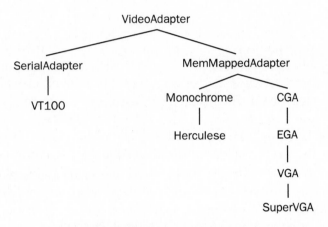

Figure 4–4. Taxonomy of video adapters for the PC

Terminals are divided into two different groups: serial devices (`SerialAdapter`) and memory-mapped devices (`MemMappedAdapter`). A PC requires at least one memory-mapped terminal, but some applications support extra serial terminals even though the BIOS does not. Only one standard serial terminal type is envisioned (`VT100`) although others certainly are possible. The memory-mapped video adapters fall into two camps: the monochrome adapter (`Monochrome`) and its derivatives and the color graphics adapter (`CGA`) and its followers (`EGA`, `VGA`, and `SuperVGA`).

To support the application, the base class offers the following methods:

```
class VideoAdapter {
  public:
    VideoAdapter();            //save screen and clear
    ~VideoAdapter();           //restore contents of screen

    virtual void print(char*, Font&) = 0;
    virtual void position(int x, int y) = 0;
    virtual void drawObject(int x, int y, Object&) = 0;
};
```

The methods print() and position() are used to facilitate ASCII output. The drawObject() method is used to draw an object of class Object, which is defined somewhere else. In all cases, x and y refer to the location on the display. The classes VideoAdapter, SerialAdapter, and MemMappedAdapter are all virtual because they are too general to be able to implement the output methods — they lack sufficient details. These methods are overloaded in the non-virtual subclasses.

Given the foregoing classes, the application is completed and deployed. Some time later a new video adapter is introduced for the PC. This adapter has on-board intelligence, a video processor, and higher resolution than the EGA and VGA cards that rely on the host CPU to perform most operations.

Most new video adapters provide some backwards compatibility mode and this new card is no exception: it can be treated like a color graphics adapter, but at significantly lower resolution and without gaining any performance benefit from the presence of the on-board video processor. Rather than treat this new card as an overpriced CGA, the maintenance programmer can add a new class defined as follows:

```
class SmartAdapter : public CGA {
  public:
    SmartAdapter();            //save screen and clear
    ~SmartAdapter();           //restore contents of screen

    virtual void print(char*, Font&);
    virtual void position(int x, int y);
    virtual void drawObject(int x, int y, Object&);
};
```

The output methods have been reimplemented for the new video adapter. Existing functions containing statements such as:

```
void myFunc(VideoAdapter& va) {
    char respBuffer[80];        //response buffer

    va.position(0,0);           //position in upper left
    va.print("Enter command:", Courier12); //prompt

    cin >> setw(80) >> respBuffer; //get response

    //... and so on
}
```

automatically use the on-board video processor as soon as the class `SmartAdapter` is installed and the system is recompiled.

Using Inheritance to Replace Switch Statements

In the non-inheritance implementation of the preceding video adapter problem, separate functions exist for each class of video adapter. A single structure contains the data needed for all video types, plus an extra field to indicate the actual adapter type.

At each point where output to the video card is to be made, a `switch` statement is needed to call the appropriate output function. For example, the earlier `myFunc()` would appear as follows:

```
void myFunc(VideoAdapter *pVa) {

    switch(pVa->adapterType) {
    case VT100: positionVT100(0, 0);
                printVT100("Enter command:", Courier12);
                break;
    case MONO:  positionMono(0, 0);
                printMono("Enter command:", Courier12);
                break;
    case CGA:   positionCGA(0, 0);
                printCGA("Enter command:", Courier12);
                break;
```

```
    case EGA:    positionEGA(0, 0);
                 printEGA("Enter command:", Courier12);
                 break;
    case VGA:    positionVGA(0, 0);
                 printVGA("Enter command:", Courier12);
                 break;
}


//...and so on
```

Although it is fairly easy to add the following case to handle the smart adapter, doing so would violate the "don't touch it if it works" rule.

```
    case SMART: positionSmart(0, 0);
                printSmart("Enter command:", Courier12);
                break;
```

The maintenance programmer must find all of the places where this addition will be necessary and add the required edits. Each edit opens the possibility of a software defect being introduced. Missing a `switch` statement hidden within the program is likely to introduce a defect as well.

The problem with a `switch` statement is that it is not extensible. It can only handle the cases foreseen at the time it is programmed. Adding a new case necessitates changing the code. Late binding is extensible. A new subclass can be added to describe the new case. This class can overload any methods that must be expanded or modified in the new class. The remainder of the program automatically handles the new case without modification.

Consider the example of a bank that maintains multiple types of checking accounts: a normal account requires no minimum balance, a preferred checking account requires a $500 balance, and an extra preferred account requires a $1,000 balance. Accounts are automatically transitioned from one type to another as the balance rises above or falls below the balance minimums. (This example is adapted from S. R. Davis, "Objects Which Change Their Type," *Journal of Object-Oriented Programming*.)

Several differences exist between the accounts as well, but consider just the check-processing charge aspect for now. Normal accounts charge a processing fee of 25 cents per check, preferred accounts 10 cents, extra preferred accounts have no fee. The function to assess the check charge using structured techniques would look like the following:

```cpp
float checkCharge(CheckingAccount& acc) {
    switch(acc.type) {
      case NONPREFERRED:  return 0.25;
      case PREFERRED:     return 0.10;
      case EXTRAPREFERRED:return 0.00;
    }
    cerr << "Illegal account type\n";
    return 0.25;
}
```

The late bound approach utilizes different subclasses of the class CheckingAccount to assess the different check processing rates as follows:

```cpp
class CheckingAccount {
  private:
    //...other private members...
  public:
    virtual float minBalance() = 0;
    virtual float charge() = 0;
    //...other public methods...
};

class NormalAccount : public CheckingAccount {
  public:
    float minBalance();
    float charge();
};
float NormalAccount::minBalance() {
    return 0.00;
}
float NormalAccount::charge() {
    return 0.25;
}

class PreferredAccount : public CheckingAccount {
  public:
```

```
     float minBalance();
     float charge();
};
float PreferredAccount::minBalance() {
     return 500.00;
}
float PreferredAccount::charge() {
     return 0.10;
}


class ExtraPreferredAccount : public CheckingAccount {
  public:
     float minBalance();
     float charge();
};
float ExtraPreferredAccount::minBalance() {
     return 1000.00;
}
float ExtraPreferredAccount::charge() {
     return 0.00;
}
```

Ideally other virtual methods would be devised to handle the other disparities between the account types. These various methods would then be combined into a single source module for each class, such as NRMACNT.CPP, PREFACNT.CPP, and EPRFACNT.CPP.

The program is written and deployed into the field. After some time, the bank changes its policy regarding checking privileges. The bank decides to add a new balance level and change the pricing structure. Now the bank managers would like the following account types and balance requirements:

Type	Balance	Check Charge
Normal	$ 0.00	$0.35
Special	$ 350.00	$0.20
Preferred	$ 750.00	$0.10
Extra Preferred	$ 1250.00	$0.00

The maintenance programmers are asked to add this new type and to make the necessary changes while keeping the changes to the existing software to a minimum. (Bank systems are very critical and must undergo a lot of testing. Retesting extensive changes to bank software is quite expensive.)

In the case of the structured solution, the function `checkCharge()` must be modified. If this were the only function that made such a decision, the situation would not be so bad. Unfortunately, these sorts of decisions about the account type are likely to be distributed throughout the system. (Remember, the account types have other differences as well — we are only examining the processing charge aspect.)

In the case of the object-oriented solution, the maintenance programmer need only add a new subclass `SpecialAccount()` and modify the `minBalance()` and `charge()` methods of the existing classes to reflect the new policy. Changes to the remainder of the program are not required.

It has always been a temptation to assign a type field to classes, allowing the programmer to ask questions such as, What type are you? Several proposals to this end have been put forward including the addition of an `is__a` operator to return an object's class at run time. The C++ community has resisted such suggestions since a type field invites the use of `switch()` statements.

Using Inheritance to Enhance Maintainability

Besides saving development effort, reusing base classes via inheritance eases future maintenance. Let us reexamine the receiver problem presented earlier to see why.

With the non-inheritance approach, the old receiver software must be modified to work with the new receiver. This modification breaks the connection between the two software sets, since the new receiver software no longer works with the old receiver.

Assume that after both programs are deployed, a serious error is found in the old receiver software. The problem is isolated and fixed. Since the new receiver software was copied from the old software set, the problem probably exists in the new program as well. Fixing the problem in the old receiver software does not automatically fix the problem in the new receiver software.

A test case that revealed the problem in the old receiver program must be run against the new receiver program, perhaps with changes to accommodate receiver differences. Once it is revealed that the problem does exist, the changes must be independently reintroduced into the new software set. Since making these changes involves extra work, it very often does not happen. "Wait until the new receiver users complain about the problem. If they never complain, then there must not be a problem," is the argument one hears.

The same applies to improvements instituted in different software sets. Suppose that the new receiver program institutes an optimization algorithm to search channels with recent activity more often than channels that have not shown activity for some time. This algorithmic improvement could be retrofitted into the old receiver set software since it is not impacted by either the format of the tune commands or the hardware interface. However, without a strong impetus to do so, the programmer does not generally follow through. As problem fixes and improvements accumulate independently in the two software sets, the programs begin to look less and less alike.

The inheritance solution does not share this problem. The subclass is still based upon the original base class and not a modified copy of it. If a bug is found in one of the base class methods, the fix can be dropped into the new receiver program. In addition, future improvements in a base class can be carried from either program to the other without requiring modification to the class. (Of course, both programs will need some retesting with the new class installed.)

Case Studies   The independent evolution of software sets was documented by Cadre Technologies, maker of the Teamwork series of CASE tools, by Wybolt in the 1990 *Proceedings of the USENIX C++ Conference*. Cadre had been adding features, including several editors, to their CASE tools for several years. Originally, each editor was created by making a copy of the existing editor that most closely resembled what was desired and then making the necessary modifications. This added some 25,000 to 67,000 lines of C code per editor. Unfortunately, it also copied any bugs inherent in the existing editor. Even when programmers were conscientious, bug fixes had to be made in multiple places, increasing their cost. Without specific protocols, many programmers were not so conscientious, leaving bugs to be found and fixed independently in the different editors. New and improved features added to editors often were not carried over into editor clones, leading to inconsistencies in both the code and the user interface. This further complicated the task of propagating bug fixes in the different editors.

To address this problem, Cadre switched to a C++ implementation using subclassing to create new editors. This reduced the amount of code added per editor to 3,000 to 10,000 lines of C++, roughly a 7 to 1 reduction in the number of lines of code per editor. It was found to be considerably easier to maintain consistency, as improvements and bug fixes were automatically propagated to all relevant editors.

In "A Study of the Impact of C++ on Software Maintenance," Denis Manel and William Havanas report similar, albeit not so spectacular, savings at Bell Laboratories. Bell Labs has a product called CXR. The initial release of this product consisted of some 63KLOC of C and C++ code. Some of the subsystems were built using a conventional structured design while other subsystems used an object-oriented, inheritance-based design. At the time of the report, CXR had gone through five revisions, labeled CXR1 through CXR5. Manel and Havanas reported the following comparisons between the object-oriented and the conventional subsystems.

First, within the object-oriented subsystem, approximately 37 percent of the classes were derived from other classes. Due to class libraries, this led to a reuse savings of some 33.6 percent by CXR5. By CXR5 the line count had increased to 132 KLOC overall, with some 67 KLOC of class code reused one or more times.

Further, Manel and Havanas noted that while CXR5 had grown by some 40 percent over CXR3, without the extra reuse of classes offered by inheritance the increase would have been some 93 percent.

Reusing Classes

As Cox points out in "Object-Oriented Programming: An Evolutionary Approach," hardware designers rarely build a new chip to satisfy a particular application. Building a chip is an expensive, time-consuming process. Instead, boards are designed with a knowledge of what chips are available. The resulting design is implementable with existing hardware. Even chip designers do not often design at the gate level, selecting instead from libraries of standard gate arrays or standard cells.

Software manufacturers generally take the opposite approach. The programmer designs an application oblivious to what software components may be available. Once the design is complete, the programmer may cast about to see if any existing classes fulfill the design requirements. Not surprisingly, they rarely do.

I say *may*, because programmers often do not even try. A recent informal search of Purdue University's library system, reported by Edward H. Bersoff and Alan M. Davis in *Impacts of Life Cycle Models on Software Configuration Management*, revealed more than fifty different sorting programs, a dozen of which used the identical algorithm.

This is unfortunate since reusing software offers the same benefits as reusing hardware: (1) greatly reduced development time, (2) greatly reduced development costs, and (3) increased reliability because the reused components have already been shaken down.

Smalltalk programmers are the reuse leaders of the programming world. Smalltalk encourages a programming style based upon reusing existing classes. The *Journal of Object-Oriented Programming* notes that benefits of reuse are clear: "Smalltalk programmers often tell stories of how they built a complicated application in a few days. These experiences can occur only because the programmers are able to reuse so many software components and abstract designs. Building reusable components and designs takes much more time. However, it is time that pays off handsomely in the long run."

C++ software is not reused for several reasons —

- Not enough is known about recognizing potentially useful software components.
- Not enough is known about cataloging components so that they can be found by others.
- Not enough is known about how to design software with existing components.
- Not enough is known about how to motivate programmers or organizations to use existing components.
- Fear of copyright infringement.

These problems must be solved before software reuse is to become commonplace. Many people feel that centering reuse around extensible classes will help solve many of these problems (except for the motivational issue). This is why Cox suggests building classes to achieve some commonly required purpose and then packaging these as Software Integrated

Circuits. Software ICs should be designed and tested to be "rock solid," probably with substantial use of customs control software at the input and exit points of all public methods. Limitations and assumptions of the Software IC are noted and documented. This, along with a revision history, is written up in specification sheets like those maintained for common hardware ICs. These specification sheets are updated as new revisions of the class are issued (revisions are necessary to fix bugs or to add new capabilities).

Reuse should not be limited to C++ source code, however. Reuse should begin at the design level, starting with class abstractions. Reusing class designs saves design time and effort while ensuring that the class code will find a place in the overall application. In addition, abstractions that worked well can be designed back into future applications while those that did not can be avoided.

Class libraries may originate from sources that are purchased or written natively. The next two sections compare these two alternatives, their advantages and disadvantages.

Purchasing Class Libraries   The primary advantage of commercial class libraries is cost. The class vendor can amortize the development cost over many customers, so that the purchase price of a class library represents only a small fraction of the cost to develop such a library in-house. The purchase price is not the only cost involved in using a commercial library, however. Much more is spent in learning to use the library.

Weighed against this cost advantage is the fact that the application programmer becomes dependent upon the class vendor. If the class library is misrepresented or of low quality, the program will suffer. The best way of defending yourself against this threat is to purchase several competing libraries. Rather than attempting to make a decision based upon some claims in an advertisement or discussions with the vendor, purchase several candidates and evaluate them in-house. A few evaluation criteria follow:

- availability of source code. Without source code, the application's programmer is too dependent upon the vendor.
- reliability. Any class library, whether purchased or written in-house, contains software errors; however, a commercial library should be reasonably free of defects. Particularly obvious defects

indicate a lack of careful testing on the part of the vendor and throw the entire package into question.

- good style. If the source code lacks a careful, clear style, it is unlikely that good techniques were followed in the library's construction and it probably contains more than its share of software defects.
- approach. The application programmer must accept the approach taken in the class library. If this approach is not optimum for the application, the resulting program will suffer.
- royalty arrangement. If you plan to sell the program you create, be sure that you are not required to pay a royalty to the class library vendor for each package sold.

In order to justify the cost, both in terms of dollars and programmer time, a library must perform some significant tasks. Libraries consisting of a lot of fairly small classes are not worth the trouble. Small encapsulations provide little benefit: the surface area of such classes is large compared to their volume. Thus, the programmer has a lot to learn (surface area) for little gain (volume).

Gigantic inheritance hierarchies, such as that offered by the public domain National Institutes of Health (NIH) library, are worse. The programmer must learn not only the interfaces to the different classes, but also the deep, often confusing inheritance relationships between them. In addition, the application gains too much bulk in the form of unused classes.

The ideal class library is one designed to cover a particular niche application and cover it well. One might purchase a Matrix class containing all of the common matrix operations or a Fast Fourier Transform (FFT) class with optimized algorithms to achieve good performance on very large data sets. The best commercial libraries are probably those aimed at limited, well-defined markets.

Building Your Own Class Libraries The alternative to purchasing a commercial library is to build one yourself. This has the downside of cost: a good, generic class library represents an extraordinary investment in time and care. A reusable class must be held to a higher standard of documentation. Others will be reusing this class, perhaps over an extended period. The specifications sheets proposed by Cox are a good starting place for deciding what type of documentation to use.

Reusable classes should be as generally applicable as possible. This may result in slightly slower performance as the performance/generality trade-off is tilted towards generality. The class must make no unnecessary assumptions about the surrounding application, and the assumptions it does make must be documented. Reusable classes must be written with good coherence, weak coupling, and a small, regular surface area.

However, custom classes offer advantages as well. Custom classes originate from existing applications. Almost completed programs should be scoured for classes that reflect reusable abstractions particularly well. These classes will be most profitable when reused in subsequent projects. Like a diamond in the rough, the bulk of the class is already present. What is required is to polish the documentation and comments, cut the class surface to make it more regular, and smooth and harden the interface to make the class less sensitive to external elements.

Custom classes are likely to fit the originator's requirements. Companies, as well as individuals, tend to specialize in solving particular types of software problems. As such, they tend to run into the same challenges repeatedly. A class built for one project is more likely to be adaptable to future programs than a commercial class developed by an outside firm.

Reinstalling a polished class in its original location invariably improves the original application as well. The coupling between the class and the application is reduced and the application is forced to deal with a more generic abstraction.

Constructors and Destructors

Like inheritance and software reuse, the proper use of constructors and destructors is a powerful tool in producing reliable, defect-free code.

Programmers put checks in the methods of a class to make sure that a class object never enters an illegal state. The constructor initializes the object into a legal state when it is created. Values are initialized, pointers zeroed out, and whatever other means are needed are taken to ensure that the methods of the class will not be confused when dealing with the resulting object.

In languages that do not support constructors, the programmer must write an initialization function that is called as soon as the program begins in order to initialize the system. This function typically stores values into a host of global variables, opens files, allocates blocks of memory, and carries out any number of other housekeeping chores. This type of function shows only temporal cohesion since the various housekeeping steps are not related in any logical way. Making sure that an initialization step has not been overlooked is difficult. Further, each addition of an object or file requires an edit to the initialization function.

Constructors allow the initializing of a class object to be combined with the object declaration. The initialization code can be compared with the structure declaration and method definitions that surround it in the module. The resulting system has higher cohesion without the possibility of forgetting to initialize an object before use.

The different constructors involved in the class of an inheritance hierarchy must be allowed responsibility for their own areas. Consider, for example, the following simple class hierarchy:

```
#define NULL (int (*)[10])0

class BaseClass {
  protected:
    int data;                 //simple data member
    int (*pBlock)[10];        //pointer to a block of data

  public:
    BaseClass() {
            data = 0;         //initialize to zero
            pBlock = NULL;
            }
    BaseClass(int i) {
            data = i;
            pBlock = NULL;
            }
};

class SubClass : public BaseClass {
  protected:
    int otherData;
```

```
public:
   SubClass() : BaseClass() {
           pBlock = NULL;
           otherData = 0;
        }
   SubClass(int i, int j) : BaseClass(i) {
           pBlock = NULL;
           otherData = j;
        }
};
```

Here the constructor for SubClass goes a little too far in initializing not only its own data member, otherData, but also the pointer BaseClass::pBlock. Of course pBlock is accessible to the subclass and one could argue that you can't be too careful, but this does not show proper division of labor. Suppose, for example, that the base class is modified so that pBlock is initialized not to 0, but to point to a block of memory off of the heap, as follows:

```
class BaseClass {
  protected:
    int data;               //simple data member
    int (*pBlock)[10];      //pointer to a block of data

  public:
    BaseClass() {
            data = 0;        //initialize to zero
            pBlock = new int[10];
        }
    BaseClass(int i) {
            data = i;
            pBlock = new int[10];
        }
};
```

Although one would expect BaseClass and SubClass to continue to work together in harmony, they do not. No sooner does the constructor for BaseClass set pBlock to point to the block of heap memory and return than the constructor for `SubClass` takes over and zeroes it, losing the block of memory and confusing `BaseClass` in the bargain.

`SubClass` should restrict itself to initializing its own data members, even when it has access to the data members of its base class, as follows:

```
class SubClass : public BaseClass {
  protected:
    int otherData;

  public:
    SubClass() : BaseClass() {
            otherData = 0;
          }
    SubClass(int i, int j) : BaseClass(i) {
            otherData = j;
          }
};
```

Constructors can be used to perform more than just variable initialization, however. A variable declared globally is constructed before `main()` is executed and destructed when the program terminates. The programmer may use this fact by assigning a class to a particular piece of hardware, database, or file with the idea of instantiating the class once, globally. The constructor for the class can then initialize the hardware, open the data, or create the file as desired. This is particularly appropriate when the remainder of the class acts as an abstraction for the external resource by providing access methods and the like.

For example, a program that outputs data over a serial port might contain the following class definition to make sure that the UART is set properly at program start-up. The destructor restores the UART to its previous state when the program terminates.

```
#define PORTADDRESS 0x8020
#define BAUD 9600
#define PARITY NONE

class SerialPort {
  private:
    int prevBaud;    //previous state
```

```
        int prevParity;

   public:
     SerialPort();     //initialize UART at PORTADDRESS to
                       //BAUD rate and PARITY
    ~SerialPort();     //restore UART
} theSerialPort;

void output(char* pString) {
   //...output to the port...

};
```

Even in the cases where only a single asset is being described by the class, the programmer should assign an object to the hardware and continue to use that object throughout the program. This helps keep the abstractions straight — `theSerialPort` is a software representation of the serial port in every case, not just during initialization.

```
#define PORTADDRESS 0x8020
#define BAUD 9600
#define PARITY NONE

class SerialPort {
  private:
    int prevBaud;
    int prevParity;
  public:
    SerialPort(unsigned portAddr,
              int baud, int parity);//initialize UART
   ~SerialPort();                   //restore UART

    void output(char*);         //output string
} aSerialPort(PORTADDRESS, BAUD, PARITY);

void myFunc(SerialPort& p, char* pString) {
   //Output to the port...
   p.output(pString);

   //...other stuff...
```

This also enhances extensibility of the program. Suppose that the boss decides that the preceding program should be moved to a machine with several I/O ports. A faster CPU gives the new machine sufficient speed to keep several ports running at full speed. You are asked to make the necessary program modifications.

Modifying the first program will be difficult since there is no concept of the serial port simply as **an** object — rather it has been treated as the port. Modifying the second version will be considerably easier. A separate object can be defined for each port as follows:

```
SerialPort port1(PORT1ADDRESS, BAUD, PARITY);
SerialPort port2(PORT2ADDRESS, BAUD, PARITY);
SerialPort port3(PORT3ADDRESS, BAUD, PARITY);
//...and so on
```

A few high-level functions undoubtedly will require slight modifications to create the multiple port objects, but the majority of functions should not, and the `SerialPort` class will not, be changed.

Operator Overloading

C++ added to C the ability to identify existing operators as user-defined types. This feature, known as operator overloading, allows the programmer to define what + might mean when applied to a newly created `Complex` class, for example. When properly used, operator overloading results in code that is easier to read.

```
Complex c1, c2, c3;
//...other stuff
c1 = c2 + c3;                   //using operator overloading
c1 = add(c2, c3);               //nonoverloaded alternative
```

Operator overloading is a contentious issue, however. Some claim that it may do as much harm as good by masking the actual complexity involved in something as innocuous looking as an operator. Programmers with this outlook prefer explicit functions that, though more clumsy in appearance, clearly identify themselves as function calls. They prefer `Complex add(Complex&, Complex&)` to an overloaded operator.

When carefully applied, operator overloading can simplify the application software by extending the abstractions presented by the user-defined class. In the following code segment:

```
Complex c1, c2, c3;


c1 = (c2 + c3) / 2;
```

it is clear that `c1` is the average of `c2` and `c3`. Being accustomed to the symbols + and /, the reader does not think about what these operators might mean when applied to a `Complex` type or how they might be implemented. If `operator+(Complex&, Complex&)` and `operator/(Complex&, Complex&)` have been implemented correctly and efficiently, the result is ideal simplicity. Of course, if they have not been properly implemented, it may take the programmer some time to consider the + and / operators as the source of the problem.

Virtual Arrays via Operator[]   Overloaded operators may be quite complex, performing behind the scenes manipulations to perform their tasks. A good example of this is using `operator[]`, the index operator, to implement a virtual array.

Normal arrays remain completely resident in RAM waiting to be accessed by the program. Big arrays consume large blocks of RAM, depriving the application. In architectures that support demand-accessed paged memory, the logical memory block containing the array may, in fact, be paged out to disk, freeing the hardware RAM for other uses. In systems that do not support demand paging, such as DOS, Windows, and Macintosh, the program must either leave the entire array in RAM or handle the paging of blocks of array to and from disk on its own.

This manual paging of array blocks to and from disk can be hidden from the application by implementing it in the `operator[]` as shown in the following class `FileArray`:

```
#include <stdlib.h>
#include <io.h>
#include <fcntl.h>
```

```
#include <sys\stat.h>
#include <iostream.h>

typedef unsigned int uint;

//DataBlock - the user may modify this to add any type of
//            data desired; however, it cannot be a virtual
//            subclass: its size must be known at compile
//            time
struct DataBlock {
    int sampleData;
};


//FileArray - implement a virtual array by overloading
//            the index operator. Provide a cache to
//            improve access performance.
class FileArray {
  private:
    int         fileHandle;    //handle for data file

    uint        noBlocks;      //number of cached elements
    DataBlock *pCache;         //cache up so many blocks
    uint        *pCacheIndexes;//indexes of the cached blocks
    static uint tlIndex;

    void  flush(uint index); //flush a block to disk
    void  readBlk(uint index, uint blockNo); //read
                                //block from disk

  public:
    FileArray(char* fName, uint noBlks);
    DataBlock& operator[] (uint x);
   ~FileArray();
};
//FileArray() - allocate sufficient cache space and open
//              the specified file
```

```
FileArray::FileArray(char* fName, uint noBlks) {
    //open the file
    _fmode = O_BINARY;
   fileHandle = creat(fName, S_IREAD | S_IWRITE);

  //now allocate memory
  noBlocks = noBlks;

  //allocate room for both the cache and the indexes
    pCache = new DataBlock[noBlocks];
    pCacheIndexes = new uint[noBlocks];

  //now clear out the cache indexes (nothing in cache now)
    for (uint index = 0; index < noBlocks; index++)
        pCacheIndexes[index] = 0xffff;
}


//~FileArray - flush any remaining data blocks
FileArray::~FileArray() {
    uint index;

    for (index = 0; index < noBlocks; index++)
        if ((pCacheIndexes[index] & 0x7fff) != 0x7fff)
            flush(index);
}


//operator[]() - fetch the address of the specified block
//               in cache; if it is not in cache, then read
//               it into cache first
DataBlock& FileArray::operator[] (uint x) {
    //looked for index of block in the cache; return
    //address of cached block to the caller
    for (uint index = 0; index < noBlocks; index++)
        if ((pCacheIndexes[index] & 0x7fff) == x) {
            pCacheIndexes[index] &= 0x7fff;
            return pCache[index];
        }
```

```
//block is not in the cache; find a space for it, read it up
    //and return that location
  for (;;) {
      if (pCacheIndexes[tlIndex] & 0x8000) {
          readBlk(tlIndex, x);
          return pCache[tlIndex];
      }

      //mark the current index and move the translation
        //lookaside pointer over one
        pCacheIndexes[tlIndex] |= 0x8000;
        if (++tlIndex >= noBlocks)
          tlIndex = 0;
    }
  }


//flush() - flush a cache block out to disk
void FileArray::flush(uint index) {
    uint blockNo = pCacheIndexes[index];
    long fileOffset = blockNo * sizeof(DataBlock);
    lseek(fileHandle, fileOffset, SEEK_SET);
    void *pTarget = (char*)(&pCache[index]);
    if (write(fileHandle, pTarget, sizeof(DataBlock))
          == -1)
        cout << "Error on write of block #"
              << blockNo << endl;

    //clear out the index
    pCacheIndexes[index] = 0xffff;
}


//readBlk() - read a block from file into the specified
//            cache block
void FileArray::readBlk(uint index, uint blockNo) {
    //if the specified block has data, flush it first
    if (pCacheIndexes[index] != 0xffff)
        flush(index);

    //now read data up into the block
```

```
long fileOffset = blockNo * sizeof(DataBlock);
lseek(fileHandle, fileOffset, SEEK_SET);
void *pTarget = (char*)(&pCache[index]);
 if (read(fileHandle, pTarget, sizeof(DataBlock))
     == -1)
    cout << "Error on read of block #"
         << blockNo << endl;

//store the data block number in the index array
pCacheIndexes[index] = blockNo;
}
```

The user defines a class `DataBlock` to contain whatever data is desired. The class `FileArray` implements a virtual array of `DataBlock`s. The constructor must be provided with the name of the file to be used as out-of-RAM storage. `DataBlock`s are written out to this file to regain space and are read back when needed. The application program also provides the constructor with the number of blocks to be cached into RAM.

Accessing a disk file is much slower than accessing RAM. To achieve acceptable performance, therefore, virtual array schemes must cache the most recently accessed data blocks into RAM. When a block is needed, the class first checks its cache. If the block is in the cache, the class does not need to go out to disk for the data.

Caches work amazingly well due to a principle known as **locality of reference**. This principle says that if a program accesses a block of data N, the probability that the next block to be accessed will be block N is higher than for some other block chosen at random. Further, the probability of N being accessed drops slowly for each subsequent non-N reference.

In the previously defined class, the method `operator[]()` searches the cache for the desired block index. If it is found (this is called a **cache hit**), a reference to the block is returned. If it is not found, then the method looks for the least recently used block into which to read the desired data.

Once found, `operator[]()` calls the method `readBlk()` to read the data. This function first checks to see if the cache block is empty (index == 0xffff). If it is not, it writes the block out to disk via the method `flush()`. It then reads the data block into the cache block and returns its address.

The destructor for `FileArray()` flushes any remaining cache blocks
out to the data file. (The data in virtual arrays is retained from one invocation of the program to the next. This makes them convenient for database
applications as well.)

A `FileArray` virtual array is accessed like any other array, as the following example shows:

```
void main() {
    //create an array with 10 cache blocks
    FileArray x("data", 10);
    //now store data into the first 20 elements
    for (int i = 0; i < 20; i++)
        x[i].sampleData = i*i;

    //read the data back
    for (i = 0; i < 20; i++)
        cout << "x[" << i << "] = " << x[i].sampleData
             << endl;
}
```

There is one restriction on the use of `FileArray` virtual arrays, however. Be careful not to take the address of a `DataBlock` and hold it too
long or it may get flushed out to disk as in the following:

```
FileArray x("data", 10);

DataBlock *pDB;
//...
pDB = &x[i];            //this is okay, so far
pDB->sampleData = 5;    //we are assured that pDB is okay
                        //because we have not accessed any
                        //other elements of x yet
//...
fn(x[j]);               //accessing x[j] may cause x[i]
                        //to be purged
pDB->sampleData = 10;   //pDB may not point to x[i]
                        //anymore
```

Accessing `x[j]` may cause the block represented by `x[i]` to be flushed, thereby causing the pointer `pDB` to be invalid. (One could overload `DataBlock::operator->()` to check for this occurrence.)

Overloading Operators to Provide Error Checking   Another common use for operator overloading is to provide range checking of arguments. Here again, a good example is provided by `operator[]()`.

Normally C++ provides no boundary checking of a supplied index. However, by overloading the indexing operator, the programmer can create a boundary check, as in the following example:

```
//MyClass.h
#include <iostream.h>

typedef unsigned int uint;

//MyClass - this class overloads operator[] to provide range
//       checking of index. Out of range values are flagged
//       and the erroneous value stored off for later
//       examination
class MyClass {
  private:
    uint noElements;
    uint errorIndex;   //contains last invalid index
    uint errorValue;   //contains last invalid reference
    uint *pDataArray;

  public:
    MyClass(uint size);
    uint& operator[](uint index);
};

//MyClass.cpp
MyClass::MyClass(uint size) {
    noElements = 0;
    if (pDataArray = new uint[size])
        noElements = size;
```

```
    }
uint& MyClass::operator[](uint index) {
    if (index >= noElements) {
        cerr << "Index " << index <<
                " beyond the final element" << endl;
        errorIndex = index;
        return errorValue;
    }
    return pDataArray[index];
}
```

The constructor for `MyClass` allocates the specified number of elements and saves this value. The `MyClass` object can then be referenced like an array via an index. The index is checked against the size of the array, and if it is found to be out of bounds, an error is flagged. For example, the following function generates an error on the final reference, because it is beyond the end of the array.

```
#include "MyClass.h"    //must also link with MyClass.c

void main() {
MyClass mc(10);         //allocates space for 10 objects
    int i = 0;

    for (;;) {
        //...other stuff
        if (i > 10) break; //this test should be i >= 10
        mc[i] = i * i;    //access the i'th element
        i++;
    }
}
```

Once the program has been tested, the overhead involved with performing the range checks can be avoided by removing the checks from `MyClass` without modifying the application code. The run-time version of `operator[]()` is as follows:

```
class MyClass {
    //...other class definition unchanged
```

```
    //implement operator inline to avoid overhead
    uint& operator[](uint index) {
        return pDataArray[index];
    }
};
```

Although this inline version performs no error checking, it also adds little or no overhead to the program. The maintenance programmer can easily reenable the debug version of `MyClass` to help find bugs as they appear.

Overloading Operators and Signature Fields   Checking the index to make sure that it is not out of range will reveal a large percentage of array-related addressing problems. However, no index exists for linked list elements. These elements are simply pointed at by other elements. If any one of the pointers in a linked list becomes corrupted, the program is almost certain to crash. Finding such problems is not easy, however, as the crash tends to occur some distance from the point of derailment.

A technique known as **signature checking** can be used to isolate all manner of addressing problems. In this process, each class of object is assigned a unique "signature." This signature is queried at key points to ascertain that an address points to a valid object. This is demonstrated in the following example:

```
#include <iostream.h>

#define MyClassSignature 0x1234
typedef unsigned int uint;

class MyClass {
  private:
    uint signature;
    //...other elements

  public:
    MyClass() {
        signature = MyClassSignature;
    }
```

```
     void sigCheck() {
         if (signature != MyClassSignature) {
            cerr << "Bad pointer " << (void*)this << endl;
            abort();
         }
     }
     //...other methods
};
```

A function `fn(MyClass* pMC)` can check `pMC` to make sure that it points to a valid `MyClass` object as follows:

```
void fn(MyClass* pMC) {
    pMC->sigCheck();              //make sure pMC is valid
    //...
 }
```

The checking of pointers can be made invisible to the application program by overloading `operator->()` as in the following example:

```
#include <iostream.h>
#include <process.h>

#define MyClassSignature 0x1234
typedef unsigned int uint;

class MyClassPtr {
  private:
    uint signature;

  public:
    uint data;

    MyClassPtr(uint d) {
        signature = MyClassSignature;
        data = d;
    }
    void sigCheck() {
        if (signature != MyClassSignature) {
```

```
              cerr << "Bad pointer " << (void*)this << endl;
              abort();
          }
      }
      MyClassPtr* operator->() {
          sigCheck();
          return this;
      }
};
```

In practice, its use looks something like the following:

```
void fn(MyClassPtr pMC) {
    cout << "pMC->data = " << pMC->data << endl;
}


void main() {
    MyClassPtr pMC = 5;

    fn(pMC);
};
```

Care must be taken in overloading `operator->()`, as the argument to the operator is not a pointer to a `MyClassPtr`, but rather an object of class `MyClassPtr`.

Signature fields will be examined again in Chapter 6 when linked lists and their problems will be discussed in some depth. It should be noted here that `sigCheck()` must not be a virtual function for reasons that will be covered in Chapter 6.

Functionoids   C++ allows functions to pass more than pointers to data between functions. The original Kernighan and Ritchie definition of C provided an example of a `sort()` function that accepted as its arguments the address of a function to compare two elements and another function to swap two elements. When these pointers are in error, the program is certain to crash.

Since the programmer has no direct control over what the compiler stores in a function, it is not practical to place a signature field at the beginning of each function. By overloading the call operator (`operator()()`), the pointer to the function can be wrapped with a data structure and adorned with a signature field. Since objects of this class look and act much like functions, they are commonly called **functionoids**.

This is demonstrated in the following segment:

```
#include <iostream.h>
#include <process.h>

typedef unsigned int uint;

struct Functionoid {
  private:
    #define FUNCSIG 0x1234
    uint signature;
    int   (*pFunc)(char*);
  public:
    Functionoid(int (*p_f)(char*)){
        signature = FUNCSIG;
        pFunc = p_f;
    }
    int operator()(char* pC) {
       if (signature != FUNCSIG) {
           cout << "Functionoid address wrong" << endl;
           abort();
       }
       return (*pFunc)(pC);
    }
};
```

Here the class `Functionoid` contains two data elements: the signature field and a pointer to a function that accepts a `char*` and returns an int. The constructor for `Functionoid` does nothing more than initialize the two data members. The function call operator checks the signature field before invoking the function indirectly. If the field is invalid, the program is aborted with an appropriate error message as before. If not, the function pointed at by `pFunc` is invoked, and the return value is returned to the caller.

In use, functionoids look like functions except that they are constructed as in the following example:

```
#include <fnctnoid.h>
extern "C" {
  int printf(char*,...);
}

//define a trivial user function
int printFn(char* s) {
  return printf(s);
}

//here is a function that accepts a functionoid argument
void otherFn(Functionoid& fnoid, char* s) {
  fnoid(s);
}

void main() {
  Functionoid print(printFn);     //declare functionoid
  print("print out some string\n"); //now call it

  otherFn(print, "a different string");
}
```

The functionoid `print` is initialized with the trivial function `printFn`. The functionoid is then invoked both directly and indirectly through the sample function `otherFn()`.

An even safer functionoid can be constructed by relying upon the fact that the first few bytes of every function of the same type are the same. These initial instructions set up the stack and lay the groundwork for the remainder of the function. Thus, any pointer that proclaims to be a pointer to a function must point to the same two or three bytes. By checking that this is true, we can verify not only that the functionoid object is valid but that the pointer it contains points to a valid function as well.

```
struct Functionoid {
  private:
    #define FUNCSIG 0x1234
    uint signature;
    int   (*pFunc)(char*);
```

```
//the first two bytes of two functions of the same
//type are identical under most architectures
//(the following _cs is needed for 80x86 processors)
int checkPreamble() {
    uint _cs * p1, _cs * p2;

    p1 = (unsigned _cs *)printf; //pick sample function
    p2 = (unsigned _cs *)pFunc; //compare to our own
    return (*p1 != *p2);          //return 0 if okay
}


public:
 Functionoid(int (*p_f)(char*)){
    signature = FUNCSIG;
    pFunc = p_f;
    if (checkPreamble()) {
        cout << "Functionoid passed wrong address"
             << endl;
        abort();
    }
 }
 int operator()(char* pC) {
    if ((signature != FUNCSIG) || checkPreamble()) {
        cout << "Functionoid address wrong" << endl;
        abort();
    }
    return (*pFunc)(pC);
 }
};
```

The function `checkPreamble()` compares the preamble of the function pointed at by `pFunc` with the preamble of a similar function. If they are different, the function returns a nonzero. The `_cs` pointer type is needed for 80x86 architectures since the pointers point into the code segment.

This check may not work for all environments. In addition, unlike functions cannot be compared. For example, under Windows a nonexportable function should not be compared to an exportable function because their preambles differ.

Functionoids provide a much safer means of saving the address of a function in a table or passing to another function. As with the previous overloaded examples, the overhead of the checks can be removed prior to final testing and delivery by replacing the `operator()()` function with an inline version that performs no check.

Conclusion

This chapter has reviewed the elements of good C++ coding style. The lessons of cohesiveness, coupling, and normalization have been applied to C++ programming. The meaning of complexity when applied to something as amorphous as software has been examined. Finally, the object-oriented features of C++ that offer unique opportunities for reducing the density of software errors during the writing and initial debugging phases have been reviewed.

Even so, C++ is a difficult programming language. The programming flexibility of C++ gives the programmer innumerable ways to trip up. Although no panacea, a working knowledge of the most common pitfalls might help the reader recognize them when they occur. Chapter 5 is devoted to a discussion of these problem areas. Since pitfalls involving pointers are so common, they are given their own discussion in Chapter 6.

Chapter 5

C++ Traps and Pitfalls

During the coding phase the programmer must deal with another rich source of errors — C++ traps and pitfalls. The coding difficulties introduced by the C/C++ syntax will be considered first. By becoming aware of these common problems, the reader may be able to avoid them. The discussion moves on to the problems presented by functions, in particular the standard C library functions that C++ programs are compelled to use. Finally, the idiosyncratic problems presented by the grafting of the object-oriented paradigm onto the structured C language are examined.

The most common and perplexing set of software problems — those dealing with pointer variables — is such a thorny issue that it warrants its own chapter, Chapter 6.

C++ Syntax

The syntax of C++ is a funny thing. To the beginning C++ programmer, it seems obscure. Its OO features confuse the structured programmer while its structured heritage confuses the OO programmer. After a few months, however, the semantic rules of C++ seem all but obvious. It seems like art: Maybe I can't explain it, but I know it when I see it.

A deeper analysis reveals that plenty of nets are afloat in the C++ waters waiting to trap the unsuspecting programmer, both beginning and experienced. Knowledge of these traps can help programmers avoid the snares or, at least, help them realize when they have wandered into one.

Tokenizing Rules

C++ inherits a very free syntax from C. C++ syntax is position independent except for the `//` comment and the preprocessor commands (the latter is not technically a part of the language). Statements may appear on any column and may be spread over multiple rows if desired. The part of the C++ compiler that reads your .CPP or .CXX source program is known as the **lexical analyzer**.

The lexical analyzer parses through the source code, breaking it up into tokens. A **token** is one or more characters that the compiler reads as a unique symbol. For example, `+` is a token; however, `++` is a different token as is `+=`. That is, the character `+` is a part of three different tokens.

The lexical analyzer searches for tokens in a strictly left-to-right, top-to-bottom fashion. Tokens may be separated from one another by white space (space, newline, tab, vertical tab, or formfeed). A token may not contain white space.

For example, the following simple function:

```
int max(int a, int b) {
    return (a > b) ? a : b;
}
```

actually appears to the analyzer as:

```
int
max
(
int
a
,
int
b
)
{
//...and so on
```

When a predefined token is detected, C++ assumes that it knows the token's meaning. For example, a variable cannot be declared `for`, since that token is already defined by the language. Tokens that consist solely of letters are also known as **keywords**.

(As an aside, it is interesting to note that FORTRAN takes exactly the opposite view. First, FORTRAN is column dependent; second, white space is completely ignored even in tokens; and, third, keywords are not reserved so that a variable can be defined as DO even though DO is the FORTRAN equivalent of `for`. These rules make FORTRAN's lexical analyzer extremely complex with little additional benefit to the programmer.)

Because the same ASCII character may be used in more than one token, ambiguities can arise. When this occurs, the analyzer selects the longest token that applies. For example, consider the following:

```
z=x---y;
```

Is this "z gets x-- minus y" or "z gets x minus --y"? Both possibilities make sense, but only one is correct. The longest token rule implies the answer must be the former. After finding the tokens `z`, `=`, and `x`, the lexical analyzer sees two possibilities: `-` and `--`. Since `--` is longer, the analyzer selects it.

Ambiguities such as these can be avoided by including white space. For example, the preceding statements could have been written more clearly as follows:

```
z = x-- - y;
//   or
z = x - --y;
```

The convention is not to include white space between a unary operator and its argument but to include white space in most other cases.

Notice that the lexical analyzer does not attempt to alter its decisions in the hope of making sense out of user input. The following is simply incorrect:

```
z=x----y
```

since it is parsed as

```
z = (x--)-- y;
```

even though it could have been interpreted as:

```
z = x-- - -y;
```

Once the tokens have been determined, the next step in the evaluation process is to interpret the expressions they represent.

Confusing Operators

C++ statements broadly fall into the three categories declarations: definitions, control structures, and expressions. Expressions are the basic statements that get the job done, such as `a = a + b`.

Since every operator produces a value, almost any operator can be used wherever an expression is required. This principle allows the programmer to produce compact, expressive constructs such as the following `for` loop, used to copy one string into another.

```
void copy (char *pS, char *pT) {
    for (; *pT = *pS; pT++, pS++);
}
```

The flexibility to mix and match expressions accounts for the popularity of C and C++ with programmers. However, this flexibility, combined with the lack of positional information, means that the C++ compiler has very little redundant information with which to determine whether the programmer has made an error.

The classic example of this is confusing the `=` (assignment) and `==` (equality) operators. For example, it is clear to the reader what is meant in the following function:

```
//higherLower - return a 1 if a>0, a -1 if a<0 and 0
                 //if a=0
int higherLower(int a) {
    if (a = 0)
        return 0;
    return (a > 0) ? 1 : -1;
}
```

However, the programmer might be surprised to find that this function always returns a -1, irrespective of the input value of the argument `a`. A moment's reflection reveals the reason. The first line of the function is incorrect.

```
if (a = 0)
    return 0;
```

says "store the value of 0 into a and return a zero if the result is nonzero," which of course it cannot be. Control then passes to the return statement which always decides that a is not greater than 0 (since it is now exactly 0), and the function returns a -1. What was intended, of course, was

```
if (a == 0)
    return 0;
```

which means "if a is equal to 0, return a 0." The corrected function works properly, as follows:

```
//higherLower - return a 1 if a>0, a -1 if a<0 and 0
                     //if a==0
int higherLower(int a) {
    if (a == 0)
        return 0;
    return (a > 0) ? 1 : -1;
}
```

This is such a common problem that most compilers generate a warning if an assignment is made within a conditional. In any case, the problem can be avoided by putting the constant first in the equality. A statement such as

```
if (0 == a)
```

is legal while the erroneous

```
if (0 = a)
```

is rejected with a compiler error.

Less likely but just as confusing are constructs like the following:

```
//inRange() - return a 1 if a is between min and max
int inRange(int a, int min, int max) {
    if (min < a < max)   //if a twixt min and max...
```

```
        return 1;         //...return a 1; otherwise, ...
    return 0;             //...return a 0
}
```

At first sight, the C++ programmer may be surprised that a statement such as this is accepted, since there is no "in the range of" operator. Executing the function reveals that the value returned from the function depends almost solely on the value of max — in any case, the function is not correct. C++ understands the following: "compare a to min; generate a 1 if a is larger and a 0 otherwise. Now compare max to the 0 or 1. If max is larger, return a 1, otherwise return a 0."

Coders have occasionally been fooled by inserting extra semicolons where they do not belong. For example, compiling the following function generates no error messages, but executing the function has no effect.

```
void printValue(int i) {
    printf;("The value is %d\n", i);
}
```

This is perhaps the most extreme example of freedom of syntax gone berserk. The function printValue() actually contains two expressions. The first expression, printf;, evaluates to the address of the printf() function, which is not used for anything and is discarded without comment. The second expression ("The value is %d\n", i); contains two subexpressions separated by the comma operator. Again, neither subexpression is used for anything and the results are discarded. The same problem occurs in for loops.

```
int i;

for (i = 0; i < 100; i++);
    printf ("i = %d\n", i);
```

Due to the misplaced semicolon at the end of the for, the printf() call is not part of the loop. The program loops 100 times — doing nothing — then prints once with i equal to 101.

Thus, the lack of redundancy and the syntactical flexibility that programmers so enjoy make it difficult for the compiler to distinguish exceedingly clever tricks from syntactical nonsense.

Syntactical Puns

Characters are necessarily shared between tokens. The ASCII set does not contain enough characters to avoid some overlap between tokens. Except for extreme cases, the overlap doesn't cause the programmer confusion anyway. Who cares, for example, that `for` and `do...while` share the letter o in the same position? Even the ambiguities introduced by + and ++ are easily avoided by proper use of white space.

It is quite another matter when an entire token may take on a different meaning, depending upon the context. The meaning of such tokens is context sensitive (compare this with the discussion of context sensitive grammars at the end of Chapter 4). Writing in the September 1991 edition of the *SIGCSE Bulletin*, R. P. Mody calls these **puns** and heaps substantial criticism on C and C++ for their existence. (To be fair, most other languages suffer from puns as well, but to a lesser degree.) Here are the worst offenders.

The Comma Operator The meaning of a comma in C++ is highly context sensitive. Consider the following:

```
int a, b, c[10];                    //declaration separator
void swap(int*, int*);


for (a = 0, b = 10; a < 5; a++, b--) //comma operator
    swap(&c[a], &c[b]);                 //argument separator
```

The comma is used in three different contexts with three different meanings: once to separate the members of a definition, twice to combine two subexpressions into a single expression, and once to separate the arguments to a function. One could argue that these meanings are similar; but a simple example can prove that they are not.

```
x = 0;                  //case #1
(x = 1, y = x);
```

```
x = 0;                          //case #2
f(x = 1, y = x);
```

In the first case, the comma refers to the comma operator and the results are defined (both x and y equal 1). In the second case, the comma is a function argument separator and the resulting value of y is specifically not defined — it could be 0 or 1, the standard does not say. (It was this pun in the comma operator that contributed to the previous fn; (a, b) error being overlooked by the compiler.) This pun can lead to further problems such as the following:

```
int i, j;
int matrix [10][20];
for (i=0; i<10; i++)
    for (j=0, j<20; j++)
        matrix [i, j] = 0;
```

The expression matrix[i, j] appears to the programmer to be the same as matrix [i][j]; in fact, it is synonymous with matrix[j]. The i is evaluated and discarded — the j is then evaluated and used to index into matrix. Further, the comma operator is overloadable for user-defined classes, whereas the comma separator is not.

The Four Faces of 0   The most glaring example of a context sensitive token in C++ is the 0. This symbol has four distinct meanings:

1. the integer zero
2. the address that cannot be the address of an object
3. logical FALSE
4. the terminator of a string

An experienced C/C++ programmer tends to think of these meanings as identical since they are all identified with the 0 token. However, consider the following example.

```
int c;
char *pC;
```

```
c   = 0;                //this is okay
c   = 1;                //as is this

pC = 0;                 //this is okay
pC = 1;                 //this is not
```

Both 0 and 1 are signed integers, so they may be assigned to the character `c` without generating a compiler error. Since 0 is also defined as an address, it may be assigned to a `char*`. As 1 is not defined as an address, however, it cannot.

The difference between these two meanings (`int` and `void*`) is highlighted by the fact that the ANSI Standard for C does not specify that the bit representation of the address 0 is the same as the integer 0 (although it is in all implementations with which I am familiar).

Some compilers define the constant `NULL` to be used in place of the illegal address, but different environments can't even agree on its definition — some define it as `0` and others as `(void*)0`. To further confuse the meanings, I have seen programmers refer to the first element of an array as `array[NULL]`. This ambiguity of meaning allows bugs like the following to go unnoticed by the compiler:

```
void toUpper(char* string) {
    char *pS;

    for (pS = string; pS; pS++)    //should be *pS in
                                   //conditional
        *pS = toupper(*pS);
}
```

The programmer clearly intended to check for the terminating character by asking whether the character pointed at by `pS` is `FALSE` (combining meanings 3 and 4). The incorrectly written program asks whether the address `pS` is `FALSE` (combining meanings 2 and 3). The correct code segment is:

```
void toUpper(char* string) {
    char *pS;
```

```
    for (pS = string; *pS; pS++)
        *pS = toupper(*pS);
}
```

This is also the source of the following common mistake:

```
char *pEnvLabel = "DBGCPP";

//look for string in the environment
char *pEnvString = getenv(pEnvLabel);
for (char* pS = pEnvString; *pS; pS++)
    *pS = toupper(*pS);
//...
```

Here the program looks up the string "DBGCPP" from the environment. The subsequent loop makes sure that all characters in the string are upper-case. The problem is that getenv() returns a 0 if the environment variable is not found. The programmer has reasoned that the loop will not execute if the string is NULL because of the *pS in the conditional portion of the for loop. However, this is confusing the condition pS == 0 with that of *pS == 0. NULL is not the same as the address of a NULL string; that is, NULL != "". The proper code segment should be:

```
char *pEnvLabel = "DBGCPP";

//look for string in the environment
char *pEnvString = getenv(pEnvLabel);
if (pEnvString)      //if a string is found convert it to
                     //all uppercase
    for (char* pS = pEnvString; *pS; pS++)
        *pS = toupper(*pS);
//...
```

Sometimes the location 0 does contain a 0, masking this common problem. Such a coincidence is simply bad luck and can certainly not be counted on. (I say bad luck since this circumstance makes a buggy program appear to work correctly during the debugging phase when the problem could be caught and corrected easily.)

Declaration Confusions   Some of the most difficult puns to catch are those that deal with variable declarations. Consider, for example, the following three declarations:

```
class MyClass {
  public:
    MyClass();
    MyClass(int f);
    MyClass(int f, int s);
};


MyClass a(1, 2);
MyClass b(1);
MyClass c();
```

One might assume that a, b, and c are all objects of class MyClass, each declared using a different constructor. In fact, this is not the case. While a and b are objects of class MyClass, c is a function that takes no arguments and returns an object of class MyClass.

To declare c to be an object using the default constructor, the declaration should have been written:

```
MyClass c;
```

Notice that an alternate form of the definition of b is allowed:

```
MyClass b = 1;        //equivalent to MyClass b(1);
```

This alternate form is only allowed for the single argument constructor. Although permitted, the following has a completely different interpretation.

```
MyClass a = b, c;    //not the same as MyClass a(b, c);
```

Instead of invoking the dual argument constructor, the preceding declares a with the single argument constructor and then declares a second object c using the default constructor.

Arrays of objects can be initialized from an initializer list. Each object is constructed with the next value from the list using the single argument constructor. The following definition constructs the object `array[0]` with the value 0, the object `array[1]` with the value 1, and so on.

```
struct MyClass {
    //...other stuff
    MyClass(int);
};
MyClass array[5] = {0, 1, 2, 3, 4}
```

To retain compatibility with C, C++ allows an aggregate class to be initialized directly without a constructor. (An aggregate class is a class that does not have a constructor, does not have any protected or private members, is not derived from a base class, and does not have any virtual functions; that is, a class that limits itself to C features.)

This generates the following:

```
struct One {
    int a;
    float b;
    char c;
};

struct Two {
    int a;
    float b;
    char c;
    Two(int, float, char);
};

One one = {1, 1.0, '1'};        //this is okay
Two two = {2, 2.0, '2'};        //this generates an error
```

The definition of `one` is allowed because class `One` is an aggregate class. The identical definition of `two` is not, because `Two` has a constructor. One might have thought that the second statement would invoke the `Two(int, float, char)` constructor in the same way that `c = 1` invoked the `MyClass(int)` constructor, but this is not the case.

Notice that if the initializer list is shorter than the array, the list is padded with zeroes. Thus, the following is not flagged as an error.

```
struct MyClass {
    //...other stuff
    MyClass(int);
};
MyClass array[5] = {0, 1};
```

The list is treated as if it were {0, 1, 0, 0, 0}. It is imperative when initializing arrays of aggregates to include braces wherever possible as shown in the following:

```
One faultyArray[3] = { 1, 1.0,
                       2, 2.0, '2',
                       3, 3.0, '3'};
```

The definition of `faultyArray` is probably not what the programmer intended. Since the first row omits a value for the character member, the character is assigned the first value on the next row. Initialization continues from this point with the initializer list out of synch. Zeros are padded onto the end of the list as needed. That is, the preceding definition is equivalent to the following:

```
One faultyArray[3] = {   1, 1.0, 2,
                       2.0, '2', 3,
                       3.0, '3', 0};
```

Adding braces at each level of nesting avoids the problem. The following definition:

```
One okayArray[3] = {{1, 1.0},
                    {2, 2.0, '2'},
                    {3, 3.0, '3'};
```

is equivalent to the much more benign

```
One okayArray[3] = {{1, 1.0, '\0'},
                    {2, 2.0, '2' },
                    {3, 3.0, '3'}};
```

Unfortunately, no parallel construct using the parenthetical format for initialization exists. The following is not legal. Even if it were, it would be confused with attempts to invoke the `MyClass(int, int, int, int, int)` constructor.

```
struct MyClass {
    //...other stuff
    MyClass(int);
};
MyClass array[5](0, 1, 2, 3, 4);
```

Another confusing aspect of initialization is that the use of = in definitions is actually a pun with respect to the assignment operator. The following two statements have completely different meanings.

```
int *pInt = 0;
    *pInt = 0;
```

The first statement defines a pointer `pInt` and sets the value of the pointer to 0. It says nothing about the value of the thing pointed at by `pInt`. The second statement is an assignment that sets the value of the thing pointed at by `pInt` to 0. It says nothing about the value of `pInt` itself.

Because of this pun, what constitutes assignment and what initialization is not always clear. For example, the code segment

```
int a = b = 1;
```

is assignment to `b` but initialization of `a`. The statement is equivalent to the following:

```
int a(b = 1);
```

One further pun exists in the definition of enumerated types. The following enumerated type is equivalent to defining three constants, `Color::red`, `Color::green`, and `Color::blue`.

```
struct Color {
    enum {red = 0, green = 1, blue = 2};
    //...other stuff
};
```

However, defining a `const` integer within a structure in the same way is not legal. Therefore, the following is not allowed.

```
struct Color {
    const int red = 0;
    const int green = 1;
    const int blue = 2;
    //...other stuff
};
```

Although using the = initializer with some members of an enumerated type and not with others is legal, it is a dangerous programming habit as the following example shows.

```
struct Color {
    enum {red, green, blue, cherry = 0, yellow};
    //...other stuff
};
```

Here, `red`, `green`, and `blue` are assigned the values 0, 1, and 2, respectively. Assigning `cherry` the value 0 resets the counter, however, so that `yellow` is then assigned the value 1. Although it may be clear to the programmer that `cherry` is equal to `red`, it will not be obvious at all that `yellow` is equal to `green`. Either let C++ assign values to all of the different members of the enumerated list or assign them all values explicitly.

The rules concerning white space and pointers in declarations also can be confusing. The following declares two pointers `pA` and `pB`.

```
int *pA, *pB;
```

One might assume that the following does the same, but, in fact, this statement declares `pA` to be a pointer to an integer and `pB` to be simply an integer.

```
int* pA, pB;
```

This makes defining types with `#define` macros subject to error as the following example shows. The results here are identical to the foregoing.

```
#define intPtr int*
//...much later...
intPtr pA, pB;
```

That is, pA is of type int* while pB is of type int. The desired effect can be achieved with a typedef, however. The following example defines both pA and pB to be pointers to integers.

```
typedef int *intPtr;
//...much later...
intPtr pA, pB;
```

A typedef acts as if each object were individually inserted into the declaration in place of the new type. Thus, the two lines are equivalent to

```
/*typedef*/ int *(pA);   //substitute pA in place of
                         //'intPtr'
/*typedef*/ int *(pB);   //substitute pB in place of
                         //'intPtr'
```

typedefs can be used to simplify complex declarations and to enhance maintainability. For example, without typedefs the following declaration of a is a bit difficult to read.

```
int (*a[])(int) = {f1, f2};
```

With the typedef it is much easier to see that a is an array of pointers to functions that accept an int argument and return an int.

```
typedef int (*ptrIntFn)(int); //ptr to an int fn(int)

ptrIntFn a[] = {f1, f2};
```

Further complexity is added to declarations by the volatile and const attributes. In the following example, it is clear that a is a constant integer (that is, a cannot appear on the left-hand side of an assignment). By analogy, it is also clear that pA is a pointer to a constant integer.

```
const int a;
a = 10;                  //not allowed since a is const
```

```
const int * pA;
*pA = 10;              //not allowed since *pA is const

int const * pB;
*pB = 10;              //this is also not allowed
```

Not so clear is that `pB` is also a pointer to a constant integer. To declare a constant pointer to an integer the following format must be employed.

```
int a, b
int * const pC = &a;
*pC = 10;              //this is allowed as *pC is a
                       //simple int
 pC = &b;              //this is not allowed as pC is const
```

Scope Considerations   Every object has a **scope**, that is, a range under which the object is accessible. The scope rules of C++ are a source of some confusion and, consequently, programming errors. It is important to know when an object goes into and out of scope since it is at that point that C++ invokes the constructor and destructor, respectively.

The following code segment defines four different objects, each with a different scope.

```
MyClass global;
static MyClass stat;

void fn1() {
    MyClass local;
    static MyClass localStatic;
}
void fn2() {
    int local;
};
```

Any function within the program that contains this code segment may access `global` (other modules must contain an `extern MyClass global` declaration), thus it is said to have **global** or **program scope**. A global object goes into scope and is constructed when the program begins execution.

By contrast, the object `stat` is only accessible to other objects within the same `.CPP` or `.CXX` source file. It is said to have **file scope** — that is, scope local to the file. Objects with file scope are also constructed when the program that contains them begins executing.

Members of a class have **class scope**. These objects have the same scope as the object of which they are a member.

The scope of an auto variable is limited to the block in which it is declared. Such an object is said to have **local scope**. Thus, `fn1::local` and `fn2::local` refer to two different objects that are in no way related — other than having the same name. A local object goes into scope when control passes through the object's definition. A local object goes out of scope when control passes out of the block in which the object was defined.

Similarly, the scope of a static local is limited to the block that contains its definition. Unlike a local object, the constructor for a static object is only invoked the first time the definition is encountered. This can lead to some interesting behavior. For example, in the following code segment the casual reader might assume that the local static object `localName` contains the name passed to the function in the variable `pN`. For example, if the function `fn()` were called with the argument "Brooktrout," the reader might assume that `localName` contains the name "Brooktrout." This does not follow, because we do not know if this is the first time the function has been called. The function `fn()` may have been invoked from an earlier point in the program (one of which we are perhaps not aware) with a different argument.

```
//Name - retain an individual's name
struct Name {
    char *pNameData;

    Name(char *pName) {
        pNameData = (char*)0;
        newName(pName);
    }
    ~Name() {
        newName(0);
```

```
    }
    void newName(char *pName);
};

//newName - store a new name into the object
void Name::newName(char *pName) {
    if (pNameData) {
        delete pNameData;
        pNameData = (char*)0;
    }
    if (pName) {
        int l = strlen(pName) + 1;
        if (pNameData = new char[l])
            strcpy(pNameData, pName);
    }
}

void fn(char* pN) {
    static Name localName(pN);

    //...what name is in localName?
}
```

Even when the arguments to the constructor are hard-coded, the reader cannot be sure of the contents of the object. For example, now what name is contained in `localName`?

```
void fn() {
    static localName("Schmekowitz");

    //...now what name is in localName?
    if (someCondition)
        localName("Simkovitch");
}
```

The object was initially constructed with the name Schmekowitz, but it is entirely possible that the function `fn()` has already been invoked with the value of `someCondition` set to TRUE, which changed the name to Simkovitch. There is no way to know from a static analysis of the program.

Programmers must be careful as to what constitutes a block. Although a function is a block, a block does not have to be a function. The following defines two different variables with the name `object`. The scope of the inner `object` is limited to the block that contains it.

```
void main() {
    MyClass object;


    {
        MyClass object;
    }
};
```

The scope of the outer `object` includes the inner block. Thus, C++ statements contained within the inner block may refer to any variable defined at a higher scope, including the outer `object`. Once the inner `object` has been declared, however, the new object definition overlays the older definition. All subsequent references to `object` access it.

Consider the following example:

```
#include <iostream.h>

struct MyClass {
    char *pN;
    MyClass(char* pName) {pN = pName;};
    void name() {
        cout << "I am the "<< pN << " object" << endl;
    };
};


void main() {
    MyClass object("outer");
    {
        object.name();                    //prints out 'outer'
        MyClass object("inner");
        object.name();                    //prints out 'inner'
    }
}
```

The first call to `name()` refers to the outer `object`, even though it appears within the inner block.

What is inside and what is outside of a block is not always clear. Consider, for example, a `for` loop. Given the classic definition of a `for` loop

```
for (expr1; expr2; expr3) {
    expr4;
}
```

expressions 1, 2, and 3 are considered outside of the block while expression 4 is within. Thus, the following program

```
void main() {
    MyClass o("outer");        //LINE 1
    int c;

    for (c = 0, o.name();
         o.name(), c < 2; o.name(), c++){
        MyClass i("inner");    //LINE 2
        i.name();              //LINE 3
    }                          //LINE 4
}                              //LINE 5
```

generates the following output. (The comments were added manually to identify the lines that generated the output.)

```
constructing outer              //line 1
I am the outer object           //expr1 of for loop
I am the outer object           //expr2 of for loop
constructing inner              //line 2
I am the inner object           //line 3
destructing inner               //line 4
I am the outer object           //expr3 of for loop
I am the outer object           //expr2 of for loop
constructing inner              //line 2
I am the inner object           //line 3
destructing inner               //line 4
I am the outer object           //expr3 of for loop
I am the outer object           //expr2 of for loop
destructing outer               //line 5
```

One by-product of this is that the scope of an object defined in the initialization expression of a `for` loop is not limited to the `for` loop. For example, the following is in error:

```
for (int i = 0; i < 10; i++ {
}
//i still in scope


//can't define two objects with the same name in
//the same scope
for (int i = 0; i < 10; i++) {
}
```

Polymorphic Declarations   Polymorphic (that is, virtual) method declarations are another source of software error. In the following class declarations the functions `f()` are both virtual, even though `D::f()` is not declared so (it inherits its "virtualness" from the base class `B`).

```
struct B {
    virtual void f(B*);
};


struct D : public B {
    void f(B*);
};
```

Thus, in the following program the calls within `fn2()` are polymorphic calls just as are those in `fn1()`.

```
#include <iostream.h>

struct B {
    virtual void f() {
        cout << "this is class B" << endl;
    }
};


struct D : public B {
```

```
            void f() {
                cout << "this is class D" << endl;
            }
        };

        struct F : public D {
            void f() {
                cout << "this is class F" << endl;
            }
        };

        void fn1(B& b) {
            b.f();              //late bound function call
        }

        void fn2(D& d) {
            d.f();              //this is bound late too
        }

        void main() {
            D d;
            F f;

            fn2(d);
            fn2(f);
        }
```

If class D were edited so that it no longer inherited from class B or so that it inherited from class B privately, the function f() would cease to be virtual in either class D or class F. Thus, changing the inheritance of a class can affect more than just the members of the class.

For the function f() to be virtual, all of the explicit arguments must match exactly. In the following declaration the two functions f() are not virtual with respect to each other.

```
struct B {
    virtual void f(B*);
};
```

```
struct D : public B {
    virtual void f(D*);
};


void fn(B& b) {
    b.f(&b);
}
```

Of course, the compiler does not generate an error in this case, as no rules have been broken. The programmer has merely declared two different methods that can be differentiated by their first explicit argument. The function `fn()` invokes `B::f()` whether passed an object of class B or class D. (A common mistake since the type of the `this` pointer is different between `B::f()` and `D::f()`. However, `this` is an implicit argument and cannot be used to distinguish between overloaded functions.)

When Declarations Are Ignored   Normally when a programmer adds a descriptor to a declaration, the compiler is expected to honor the request but this is not always the case. C++ has the flexibility to ignore the storage class of a declaration in two instances.

The `register` storage class can be used on variables that occur often within a function to ask the compiler to cache the variable in a register. The intent of adding the feature to the original Classic C language was to generate faster executing code by avoiding the loads and stores to memory. In C++, however, `register` is only a request — the compiler is free to ignore it.

Historically, compilers do a better job of optimizing variable accesses than programmers. A good optimizing compiler will cache a variable without being specifically instructed when doing so will generate optimum performance. Thus, many compilers choose to ignore the `register` attribute. Even in those that do not, the following is legal and must be accommodated.

```
register int obj;
void f(int&);


f(a);                    //call f() passing a reference to obj
```

In this case, C++ must assign `obj` a memory location, because the function `f()` expects to be passed `obj`'s address, not its value.

The second case where this arises is the `inline` attribute. Functions that are declared `inline` are normally expanded at the place where the function is called, like a `#define` macro and unlike a normal function. However, several conditions may force a function outline:

- declaring a method virtual (at least for those calls that are bound late)
- taking the function's address, as follows:

```
inline int max(int a, int b) {
    return (a > b) ? a: b;
}


int (*pFN)(int) = max;          //forces outline version
```

- recursion within the function, as in the following:

```
inline int factorial(int N) { //outline version created
    if (N > 1)
        return N * factorial(N - 1);
    else
        return 1;
}
```

- including a loop of any sort, as follows:

```
inline int factorial(int N) { //loop forces outline
    for (int total = 1;N > 1; N--)
        total *= N;
    return total
}
```

- multiple returns
- local array declarations
- being called from a previously defined inline function

Usually the compiler generates a warning when an inline function is forced outline, but there is no requirement to do so.

Forcing a function outline should not affect the way the function performs, other than making the resulting program slightly slower and smaller. In a few cases an inline function may not perform identically to its outline version, however. The most obvious cases occur when the function is invoked with arguments that have mutual side effects, as in the following:

```
a = max(b = c, b);
```

Even if the order of evaluation of the arguments to the function were such that the intended results were achieved when the function was inline, forcing it outline might change the order of evaluation, causing the expression to generate unintended results. During debugging it is a good idea to force all inline functions outline to make sure that they perform correctly in both modes. A compilation switch is included with most compilers for this purpose. In this way, the programmer is reasonably assured that no unpleasant surprises will arise later on if an inline function is inadvertently forced outline.

Evaluating Expressions

Most statements in C++ are expressions of one sort or another. Therefore, the rules for evaluating expressions must be clearly understood by all C++ programmers.

Constants   One might expect that the simplest expressions to write in C++ are those involving a single constant. Even here, however, programmers can become confused, introducing needless software bugs.

Even the original Kernighan and Ritchie C recognized the need for both decimal and octal constants. Quite early on hexadecimal constants were added. Unfortunately, C chose an unusual method of indicating the radix of a numerical constant: octal numbers begin with 0, hexadecimal numbers with 0x, and decimal numbers with any other digit. No problem exists with hexadecimal: the presence of the x is unequivocal. The problem arises with the octal. For the most part, programmers no longer use octal, so they tend to forget that octal constants are even supported. This leads many programmers to fall into the following trap:

```
unsigned long powersOfTen[] = {00000001, //10 ** 0
                                00000010, //10 ** 1
                                00000100, //10 ** 2
                                00001000, //10 ** 3
                                00010000, //10 ** 4
                                00100000, //10 ** 5
                                01000000, //10 ** 6
                                10000000};//10 ** 7
```

The programmer has attempted to adorn the constants by aligning their digits to highlight their relationship. The preceding listing is incorrect. Except for 10**7, all of the constants are powers of eight (8**1, 8**2, and so on) and not powers of ten because of the leading zeros.

The programmer may specify a character by its numerical value by preceding the number with a back-slash ('\'). This character is assumed to be a three-digit octal constant. (The leading zero is assumed.) Thus, the character '\10' is not a newline, even though a decimal 10 is the newline character. (The correct value is '\12'.) Even adding the zero can generate an incorrect result since a character constant cannot exceed three digits.

```
0101;        // constant 65
'\0101';                //the character 010 followed by '1'
```

For hexadecimal constants the situation is even worse.

```
0x41;        //constant 65
'\x41';      //equivalent to 'A'
'\0x41';     //equivalent to '\0' followed by 'x41'
```

Seeing the 0 following the back-slash, C++ assumes an octal constant is to follow. Since *x* is not a valid octal digit, C++ assumes the octal constant is complete and continues with the characters *x*, *4*, and *1*. Even though C++ only defines single-character constants, it does not specifically disallow multiple-character constants, so no error is generated. (Since they are implementation specific, multicharacter constants are not useful if portability is a concern.)

Octal and hexadecimal constants are assumed to be unsigned, while decimal constants are taken to be signed. This can lead to invalid comparisons between the two due to sign conversions. Character constants are generally always signed, whether ASCII, octal, or hexadecimal. (Characters can usually be made to default to unsigned with a compiler switch).

Precedence and Binding   Every programming language must address the ambiguity presented by compound expressions. How are the subexpressions to be combined? In cases such as the following, it makes little difference.

```
int a, b, c, d;

a = b * c / d;
```

In other cases, however, it makes quite a bit of difference.

```
a = b + c / d;
```

Is this "add b to c and divide the result by d" or "add b to the result of c divided by d"? Like most other languages, C++ solves this problem by assigning each operator a **precedence**. Operators with higher precedence are evaluated before operators with lower precedence. The precedence of the C++ operators is specified in Table 5–1. From this table we can see that the latter interpretation is the correct one because / has higher precedence than +. The order of evaluation can be influenced by adding parentheses. To divide b plus c by d, the programmer must write:

```
a = (b + c) / d;
```

Table 5–1. Precedence and binding of C++ operators

Precedence	*Operator*	*Binding*
1.	() [] -> :: . sizeof	L to R
2.	! ~ -(unary)	R to L
	++(preincrement) --(predecrement)	
	&(address of) *(dereference)	
	new delete (typecast)	
3.	++(postincrement)--(postdecrement)	R to L
4.	.* ->*	L to R
5.	*(multiply) / %	L to R
6.	+ -(binary)	L to R
7.	<< >>	L to R
8.	< <= > >=	L to R
9.	== !=	L to R
10.	&(arithmetic AND)	L to R
11.	^	L to R
12.			L to R
13.	&&	L to R
14.	||	L to R
15.	?:	R to L
16.	= *= /= %= += &= ^= |= <<= >>=	L to R
17.	,	L to R

The precedence of the operators was chosen to be as intuitive as possible, but surprises do occur. For example, the following expression does not generate an error but does not have the intended results.

```
//does not work
if (x = f() < 0)     //store results of f() in x
    x = -x;          //if result negative, make positive
```

The programmer probably intended to call function `f()`, store the results into a variable `x`, and then check to see if that variable is less than 0. However, since < has a higher precedence than =, the preceding is interpreted as if it were written as follows:

```
//equivalent to above
if (x = (f() < 0))
    x = -x;
```

The segment calls the function `f()` and compares the results to 0. The program then stores the resulting 1 or 0 into x. If the result is 1, it is converted to -1.

Since assignment is of low precedence, the rule of thumb is always to encase it in parentheses.

```
//this works
if ((x = f()) < 0)
    x = -x;
```

The bit-wise operators can also cause confusion, as the following example shows:

```
if (x.flags & OUTPUTBIT != 0) //if output flag set...
    x.output();                //...perform output
```

The precedence rules force the preceding to be evaluated as

```
if (x.flags & (OUTPUTBIT != 0))
    x.output();
```

This results in the least significant bit being checked, irrespective of what bit OUTPUTBIT actually is, since the result of the logical operator != is 1 for any nonzero value of OUTPUTBIT. Parentheses to the rescue — the proper code segment is

```
if ((x.flags & OUTPUTBIT) != 0)
    x.output();
```

One final example is provided by the shift operators as in the following segment:

```
unsigned int r;
unsigned char highByte, lowByte;
r = highByte << 8 + lowByte;
```

Rather than the expected addition, `lowByte` to `highByte` shifted left 8 bits, the preceding shifts `highByte` left by 8 plus `lowByte` bits. The corrected code segment is

```
r = (highByte << 8) + lowByte;
```

The problem exists in the opposite direction when the shift operators are overloaded to perform stream output. When used to perform output, the operators' precedence should be very low to avoid problems such as the following:

```
#include <iostream.h>

cout << "a + b = " << a + b;
```

Since addition has higher precedence than shift, this works as expected. Unfortunately, however, the following does not.

```
#include <iostream.h>

cout << "max(a,b) = " << (a>b) ? a : b;
```

Depending on the value of a and b, the code segment prints either a 1 or a 0, but nothing else. The proper interpretation of the preceding code is as follows:

```
(cout << "max(a,b) = " << (a>b)) ? a : b;
```

The result of the comparison a>b is output to the output stream `cout`. The result of this expression, which is the address of the `ostream` object `cout`, is nonzero, so the `?:` evaluates to a, but the results of this expression are discarded.

For expressions with operators of similar precedence, such as a / b / c, C++ uses the operator **binding** shown in Table 5–1. The table shows that most binary operators bind from left to right while most unary operators bind from right to left. Thus, a / b / c is interpreted as (a / b) / c.

The principle exceptions to the binary/unary rule are the assignment operators. Were the binding from left to right, the following would have the unexpected effect of first storing the value 0 into a and then the value 1 into b.

```
b = 0;
a = b = 1;
```

By binding from right to left, this expression has the desired effect of storing the value 1 into both a and b.

Order of Evaluation   Binding should not be confused with the order of evaluation. Although binding is always specified, most binary operators do not specify in what order their arguments are evaluated. The compiler is free to evaluate the two (or more) arguments in any order. Thus, the expression a/b gives no indication of the order in which a and b are evaluated.

This is not important unless a, and b represent expressions that have **mutual side effects**, that is, an impact on the other expression. Consider the following.

```
int i = 1;
cout << "1 = " << i++ << ", 2 = " << i++ << endl;
```

The two subexpressions i++ both change the value of i and, therefore, affect one another. The results of the expression depend upon the order of their evaluation.

The precedence rules indicate that the two expressions i++ are evaluated before any of the << operators. Which one is evaluated first, however, is unclear. You might assume that the subexpressions are evaluated from left to right, especially since the << operator binds in that direction. In fact, under the Borland C++ family of compilers, executing the preceding code generates the following curious results:

```
1 = 2, 2 = 1
```

indicating that the right i++ subexpression is evaluated before the left. However, C++ makes no promises. The order of evaluation is not affected by operator binding or precedence rules. Adding parentheses does not change the order of evaluation either.

The programmer can force the evaluation of the subexpressions by distributing them over more than one statement. Thus, the code segment

```
int i = 1;
cout <<    "1 = " << i++;
cout << ", 2 = " << i++ << endl;
```

generates the expected

```
1 = 1,  2 = 2
```

A coding mistake sometimes made by beginners is the following:

```
x = x++;
```

Obviously, the intent is to increment x, but the results of the preceding expression are not defined. The compiler might choose the following algorithms:

```
1. fetch the value of x into a register
2. store the value in the register back into x in memory
3. increment x in memory
```

This would result in the value of x being incremented as expected. However, an equally legal algorithm would be the following:

```
1. fetch the value of x into a register
2. increment x in memory
3. store the value in the register back into x in memory
```

This would result in the value of x being left unchanged. Either solution is valid — the standard simply doesn't say. Thus, the rule: **Don't include multiple subexpressions with mutual side effects in a single statement**.

The order of evaluation **is** specified for four operators. These are `&&`, `||`, `?:`, and `,`.

The logical operations `&&` and `||` promise that the left-hand expression is evaluated first and that the right-hand operator will not be evaluated at all unless necessary. This is called **short circuit evaluation**. In the case of `&&`, the right-hand argument is not evaluated if the left argument is false, since its value will not affect the outcome. In the case of `||`, the right argument is not evaluated if the left argument evaluates to true.

The `?:` operator evaluates either the second argument if the first argument is true or the third if it is false. It never evaluates both, however. In the following code segment either the function `f()` is invoked or the function `g()` but not both.

```
(a>b) ? f() : g();
```

Finally, the comma operator assures the programmer that the expression on the left side of the operator will be evaluated before the expression on the right. Of course, both expressions are always evaluated. Thus, in the following the variable y is assigned the value 6 and not 5.

```
int  x,  y;
x = 5;
x++,y = x;              //is  y  =  5  or  6  now?
```

These special operators can be used to avoid possibly fatal conditions within an expression. This is especially important in macro definitions. The following is a typical example:

```
#define ROUNDOFF(v, r)  if  (r)  v %= r;
```

Here the argument v is moduloed with the radix r. Since moduloing a number with 0 would result in a divide overflow, the macro checks to see if the radix is true (that is, nonzero). As we will see, macros containing control structures can cause problems. The && operator can be used to create an expression with the same effect as an if statement, as follows:

```
#define ROUNDOFF(v,  r)  (r && (v %= r), v)
```

If r is zero, the v %= r step is avoided by short circuit evaluation of the && operator. The 0 or 1 resulting from the && operator is discarded — the value of the macro is the resulting value of v, since the comma operator guarantees that the right-hand v is evaluated after the left-hand operation.

Although such tricks are common in C macro definitions, the inline function of C++ make them generally unnecessary. The following inline function is more maintainable, it is an expression with the same effect as the preceding macro with no added overhead.

```
inline int roundOff(int v, int r) {
    if (r)               //if radix is nonzero...
        v %= r;          //...modulo v with r
    return v;            //return result
}
```

The bitwise operations `&` and `||` are often confused with the logical operations `&&` and `||`. For many applications, such as the following example segment, the two generate identical results.

```
if ((a != 0) & (b != 0)) //if both a and b are nonzero...
    f(a, b);             //...call function f()
```

generates the same results as

```
if ((a != 0) && (b != 0))//if both a and b are nonzero...
    f(a, b);             //...call function f()
```

This works because the result of the `!=` operation is either 0 or 1. The bitwise ANDing of 0 and 0, 0 and 1, or 1 and 1 has the same effect as the logical ANDing of these same values. However, confusing the two operations is a common source of error. For example, the following expressions are no longer equivalent.

```
if (a & b)              //this comparison does something else
    f(a, b);

if (a && b)             //if both a and b are nonzero...
    f(a, b);            //...call function f()
```

Presumably a and b may have values other than 0 and 1. The truth table for `&` is not the same as for `&&` if the arguments are not limited to values of 0 and 1. (The first test is true if a and b have any bits set in common. The second test is true if both a and b have any bits set at all — quite a different thing.)

Further, `&` and `|` do not perform short-circuit evaluation. Thus, the following version of the `roundOff` macro is buggy, because it offers no protection against a zero denominator.

```
//no protection round off macro
#define ROUNDOFF(int v, int r) (r & (v %= r), v)
```

One could argue that if r is zero, the result of `r & x` must be zero, irrespective of the value of x, and x need not be evaluated. However, x is evaluated for the bitwise operators anyway.

Short circuit evaluation can introduce errors when the second sub-expression has side effects.

```
if (a && v[b++]) {
    //...continue
}
```

Once the `if` has been executed, it is not clear that `b` will be incremented. If `a` is false, the `v[b++]` is not executed.

Shifty Operators   The left and right shift operators also present some difficulties. In principle, their meaning is clear: shift the left-hand argument by some number of bits. Bits that are shifted out are lost. What should be shifted in to replace the lost bits?

The left shift operator always shifts zero bits in from the right. But for the right shift operator, there is some disagreement. In some applications, one would prefer that zeros be shifted in from the left, but in others one would prefer copies of the sign bit.

The C standard says that if the left-hand argument is unsigned, then the right shift operator must shift in zero bits. If the argument is signed, the right shift may insert either zeros or copies of the sign, whichever the implementation prefers.

```
unsigned int a = 0x8008;
         int b = 0x8008;
a >> 1;                 //result is 0x4004
b >> 1;                 //result may be 0x4004 or 0xC004
```

In addition, the right-hand argument to the shift operator must be less than the number of bits in the left-hand argument. For example, if an integer is 16 bits, then the following generates undefined results.

```
unsigned int a, b, n;
n = 16;
b = a >> n;
```

Here `b` need not be zero. In fact, the value of `b` is completely undefined.

Both of these rules allow the compiler to implement the shift operations with a minimum of assembly instructions. The shift operators are in the language to allow the programmer to write the most efficient code possible.

While all CPUs provide some type of shift operation, each CPU handles these questions slightly differently. If the compiler must add multiple tests to check for arguments or conditions that the base hardware cannot handle, the efficiency advantage of the operators is lost. (Of course, the programmer can overload the >> and << operators to add these checks during module debugging and remove them later.)

Programmers often use the shift operators as a faster alternative to integer multiplication or division by a power of 2. Programmers must be careful that the integer is nonnegative, however. Shifting a negative number does not have the desired effect; for example, (-1) >> 1 has the value -1 if the sign bit is inserted and the value 32767 if it is not (assuming a 16-bit word). (-1) / 2 produces a 0 on most machines.

C++ adds another context sensitivity to the shift operators by overloading them with the stream output operators. Consider the following example:

```
#include <fstream.h>

ofstream a("myfile.txt");
int b = 10;


a << 2;
b << 2;
```

The two applications of << have profoundly different effects. The first results in the integer 2 being converted to ASCII and written to the file myfile.txt, while the second shifts the value of b left two bits producing the value 40.

Division   Given the following definitions:

```
int Q, R, N, D;
Q = N / D;
R = N % D;
```

we would like the following three rules to hold true:

1. N = Q * D + R
2. Changing the sign of N changes the sign of Q, but not its magnitude.
3. the value of R is greater than or equal to 0, but less than the absolute value of D.

Unfortunately, all three conditions cannot be met simultaneously if N and D are of different signs. This is easy to prove. Take the case of N = -9 and D = 4. Rule 2 implies that Q should be -2, which combined with Rule 1 results in an R of -1 (`-9 = 4 * (-2) + (-1)`). However, this is in clear violation of Rule 3. Complying with Rule 3 with a Q of -3 and an R of 3 (`-9 = 4 * (-3) + 3`) would require that Rule 2 be broken.

Clearly division means nothing without Rule 1. However, a programming language may adhere to Rules 1 and 2 (**Rule 2 division**) or Rules 1 and 3 (**Rule 3 division**). Most languages specify Rule 2 division. C++ allows the compiler designer to choose whichever division the underlying hardware most naturally supports.

Rule 3 division can generate bugs when the modulo operator is used as a hashing operation as in the following:

```
//Decimal to ASCII digit - convert the decimal number to
//                         an ASCII digit
char dec2ADigit(int decimal) {
    char digits[] = {'0', '1', '2', '3', '4',
                     '5', '6', '7', '8', '9'};
    return digits[decimal%10];
}
```

Here the function accepts a number — nominally between 0 and 9 inclusive — and returns its character equivalent. The `%10` is to ensure that the index into `digits[]` is within the range; however, this test is insufficient. If `decimal` is negative, then `decimal%10` will be negative, and the index will access memory in front of the array. Either the function will return an undefined character, or the function will trap.

This type of problem is more easy to catch than the opposite. The following function is designed to collect readings from a meter and categorize each into its proper bin with the goal of building a histogram. Meter readings may take on values between -50 and +50. The histogram will be given 10 different values. Values between -49 and -40 will be assigned to bin 0, -39 and -30 to the bin 1, and so on.

```
int bins[10];
void histogram(int value) {
    //make sure value is in range
    if (value <= -50)
        value = -49;
    if (value >= 50)
        value = 49;
    //now, normalize to bin number
    value = value / 10 + 4;   //map [-49,-40] to bin 0,
                              //[-39,-30] to bin 1, etc
    //count it
    bins[value]++;
}
```

If the compiler uses Rule 2 division, then the range -9 to 0 and 0 to 9 both map to the same bin (bin 4). Thus, bin 4 receives too many counts and bin 9 never receives any. If the readings are uniform, someone should notice that one bin has too many readings. If the readings are not close to uniform, the problem may not be noticed for quite some time.

If, however, the compiler uses Rule 3 division, then a different problem appears. Now the range of -10 to 0 and 0 to 10 map to different bins, but the offset of 4 is incorrect. Under Rule 3 division -49/10 equals -5, which generates an offset into `bins[]` of -1.

Both problems can be solved, but the solutions are not compatible. If the program is to be portable from one compiler to another, the only safe solution is to force `value` to be nonnegative before the division is performed.

```
int bins[10];
void histogram(int value) {
    //make sure value is in range and positive
    unsigned uval = (unsigned)(value + 50);
    if (uval >= 100)
        uval = 99;

    //now, normalize to bin number
    uval = uval / 10;

    //count it

    bins[uval]++;
}
```

By forcing the numerator to be positive, Rule 2 and Rule 3 compilers generate the same results.

Mixed Expressions   Every language has difficulties with mixed expressions — for example, mixing signed and unsigned integers in the same expression — due to the differences in precision or range between different types. Is the result of the following expression an `unsigned int` or a `signed long`?

```
unsigned int a = 0x8000;
signed    int b = 0x0010;


a + b;                    //what is the type?
```

One could argue that an `unsigned int` could contain the resulting value but loses its "signedness." A `signed long` can both contain the value and retain its "sign," but requires that both values be promoted. C++ retains "signedness."

A programmer can get into trouble when mixing sizes as in the following code segment:

```
long a = 0xffff;
int  b = 0xffff;


if (a == b) {
//...continue on
```

One might assume that a and b are equal, but they are not. To make the comparison, b is promoted to a `signed long`, giving it the value `0xffffffff`, which is not equal to `0x0000ffff`. (This assumes 16-bit `int`s and 32-bit `long`s, the standard for PCs.)

Since `char`s default to signed, the same problem arises with some of the standard library functions, such as `getchar()`. The following test appears to scan the input stream until the character π is encountered; however, it does not work.

```
//Sample 1
#include <stdio.h>
void main() {

    while (getchar() != 'π'); //condition never satisfied
    //...program continues
```

Since `getchar()` is defined as an `int`, the character π is promoted from a `signed char` to a `signed int` before the comparison is made. The sign extension converts the π (`0xE3`) into the negative value `0xFFE3`. This is not equal to the nonsign extended `0x00E3` returned from `getchar()` when a π is entered, so the condition fails for all characters entered.

Surprisingly, however, the following code segment does work properly.

```
//Sample 2
#include <stdio.h>
void main() {
    char c;

    while ((c = getchar()) != 'π'); //condition okay
    //...program continues
```

The assignment `c = getchar()` converts the `int` returned from `getchar()` into a `char` before the comparison is made so that no sign extension of the `0xE3` π is necessary.

Macros

As has already been pointed out, software bugs can slip into a program in the form of incorrectly written macros. These errors are difficult to decipher because the preprocessor upon which macros rely is not part of the main body of the C++ language.

The preprocessor runs as the first step of the compilation process. The preprocessor looks only for lines beginning with a `#`. Lines beginning with `#define` contain macros that are expanded by the preprocessor whenever they are used. The resulting expanded text is processed by the C++ compilation step.

The following `for` loop repeats ten times.

```
#define LOOPCOUNT 10
void fn() {
    for (int i = 0; i < LOOPCOUNT; i++)
        //...
```

Macros allow argument substitution as well in the following `min()` macro.

```
#define min(x, y) (x > y) ? y : x

int fn(int a, int b) {
  return min(a, b); //expands to 'return (a>b)?b:a;'
```

Although this seems straightforward, the source of confusion is two-fold. First, the preprocessor is a language with a syntax that differs in some fundamental ways from C++. For example, preprocessor commands continue until a new line — they are not terminated by a semicolon. Thus, the following macro definition is incorrect.

```
#define min(x, y) (x > y) ? y : x;

int fn(int a, int b) {
    return min(a, b); //expands to 'return (a>b)?b:a;;'
```

Notice the appearance of two semicolons in the expansion of the macro. One came from the statement and the other from the macro expansion itself. In this particular case, it causes no problem, but in the following two cases it generates errors.

```
fn(min(a, b));    //expands to 'fn((a>b)?b:a;);'

if (flag)
    a = min(b, c);    //expands to 'a = (b>c)?c:b;;'
else
    a = 0
```

The `if` statement is in error since the extra semicolon appears as a separate, null statement that precludes the appearance of an `else` clause.

The following macro definition is also in error for the opposite reason.

```
#define min(a, b) (a > b) ?            //line 1
                          b :          //line 2
                          a            //line 3
int x, y, z;

x = min(y, z)        //expands to 'x = (y > b)?'
```

The preprocessor terminates the definition of the macro with the end of line 1. Lines 2 and 3 are not considered part of the macro and are left for the compiler to interpret. To extend a macro over more than one line, the last character on the line must be a \. Thus, the correct macro definition is as follows:

```
#define min(a, b) (a > b) ? \
                          b :\
                          a
```

When compilation errors occur, it is often difficult for the programmer to decipher the error message, especially if it was written by someone else. For example, the following line generated the error message "Operands are of incompatible type" under Turbo C++.

```
int *pI;
char *pJ;

pJ = min(pJ, pI);
```

Without knowing that the `min()` macro involves an implicit subtraction, the programmer would not realize to what operands the error message is referring.

The programmer can see the C++ program as the compiler sees it with all macros expanded. With most packages, a compile time switch suffices to generate a preprocessor output file. Some compilers, such as Borland's, provide a separate `cpp` utility. This can help locate macro-related problems; however, preprocessor output can be very difficult to interpret since all include files are also expanded.

Avoiding Control Structures in Macros   Errors can be especially confusing when macros contain control structures. Control structures are not expressions. Since a macro is designed to look and act like a function, which is an expression, it is important that a macro restrict itself to expressions. The control structures within a macro can interact with the structures in which the macro is used.

Consider the following error-checking macro that generates an error message if a field named `signature` is not equal to a predefined value.

```
//sigCheck - check to make sure an object
//            is of class MyClass
#define sigCheck(x)                                          \
if (x->signature != SIGVALUE) {                              \
    printf("Record %p signature failure\n", x); \
}
```

In general use, the macro appears as follows:

```
void fn(MyClass* pMC) {
    sigCheck(pMC);  //make sure its a valid pointer
    //...function continues
}
```

Now consider the following code segment.

```
void fn(MyClass* pMC) {
    if (pMC)               //if pMC is not NULL...
        sigCheck(pMC);     //...check to see if valid;...
    else {
        printf("Null pointer passed to fn\n");
        return;
    }
    //...function continues
}
```

This function does not perform as expected, generating the null pointer message for all values of pMC, except 0. Expanding the macro and realigning the if and else clauses for readability demonstrates why.

```
void fn(MyClass* pMC) {
    if (pMC)                        //if pMC is not NULL...
        if (x->signature != SIGVALUE) {
            printf("Record %p signature failure\n", pMC);
        }
        else {
            printf("Null pointer passed to fn\n");
            return;
        }
    //...function continues
}
```

This type of problem can be avoided by restricting macro definitions to expressions as in the following version of sigCheck().

```
//sigCheck - check to make sure an object
//            is of class MyClass
#define sigCheck(x)                                  \
(x->signature != SIGVALUE) &&                        \
    printf("Record %p signature failure\n", x), \
```

Here, short-circuit evaluation of the && operator precludes the printf() from being evaluated if the expression x->signature != SIGVALUE is not true. Since operator&& is an expression, the resulting macro is an expression and does not conflict with its usage within control structures.

Precedence, Side Effects, and Macros Unexpected macro expansions can also generate precedence and side-effect errors. Consider the following two test statements.

```
#define min(x, y) (x > y) ? y : x;

void main() {
    int i;
    int j = 0x20;

    i = 0x10;                       //test #1
```

```
    i = min(i & 0xfff0, j);

    i = 0x11;                          //test #2
    i = min(i & 0xfff0, j);
}
```

In the first test, i is assigned the value 0x10, as expected. In the second test, i is assigned the value 0x20. This is surprising since the & 0xfff0 should make the test insensitive to changes in the least significant nibble. The expanded tests show what is happening.

```
void main() {
    int i;
    int j = 0x20;

    i = 0x10;                          //test #1
    i = (i & 0xfff0 > j) ? j : i & 0xfff0;

    i = 0x11;                          //test #2
    i = (i & 0xfff0 > j) ? j : i & 0xfff0;
}
```

Since the precedence of the > operator is greater than that of &, the selector of the ? operator is evaluated as if it had been written (i & (0xfff0 > j)). The value of 0xfff0 > j is 1 (0xfff0 is unsigned). The resulting 1 is ANDed with i. Thus, any odd value of i results in the value of j and an even value of i results in the value of i & 0xfff0.

This problem can be solved by adding parentheses around the arguments to the macro, forcing evaluation in the expected order, as follows:

```
#define min(x, y) ((x) > (y)) ? (y) : (x)

i = min(i & 0xfff0, j);
```

now expands into

```
i = ((i & 0xfff0) > (j)) ? (j) : (i & 0xfff0);
```

This solves the precedence problem with respect to arguments to the macro. However, precedence problems still remain with respect to the outer expressions in which macros find themselves. Consider the following example:

```
#include <iostream.h>
#define min(x, y) ((x) > (y)) ? (y) : (x);
void main() {
    int i = 0x10;
    int j = 0x20;

    cout << "min(i, j) = " << min(i, j) << endl;

}
```

Executing this program generates the curious output:

```
min(i, j) = 0
```

The reason for this is only apparent after we view the expanded macro.

```
cout << ((i) > (j)) ? (j) : (i);
```

Since the precedence of << is higher than that of >, the expression is evaluated as if it had been written (dropping unnecessary parentheses for clarity):

```
(cout << (i > j)) ? j : i;
```

The comparison i > j generated the 0 output. The value of cout << 0 is nonzero, causing the overall expression to evaluate to the value of j, but this value is discarded.

This precedence problem can be solved by adding an outer set of parentheses rendering our simple min() macro a rather less readable:

```
#define min(x, y) (((x) > (y)) ? (y) : (x))
```

Readable or not, this is the way that macros must be defined to avoid generating unexpected results: each argument encapsulated within parentheses and an outer set of parentheses encasing the entire macro.

The side-effect problem is another issue. Consider the following function:

```
//copy - copy a string from one buffer into another.
//       Be careful not to exceed the length of the
//       target buffer.
void copy(char* pTString, int length, char* pSString) {
    int sOffset, tOffset;
    sOffset = tOffset = 0;
    while (pSString[sOffset]) {
        //copy the character over
        pTString[tOffset] = pSString[sOffset];

        //increment to the next character (be careful
        //not to exceed length of target buffer)
        ++sOffset;
        tOffset = min(++tOffset, length - 1);
    }
    pTString[tOffset] = '\0';
}
```

This function attempts to copy a string pointed at by `pSString` into a target buffer pointed at by `pTString`. The size of the target buffer is given by the argument `length` and is not to be exceeded. There are many ways to solve this problem, but the preceding approach seems reasonable. The offsets `sOffset` and `tOffset` are incremented after each character. In addition, the `min()` macro is used to make sure that `tOffset` does not exceed the value of `length`.

The function looks fine, but when it is tested with the following program

```
#include <iostream.h>
void main() {
    char buffer[40];

    copy(buffer, 40, "This is a string");
    cout << buffer << endl;
}
```

the results are unexpected.

```
T,h*i!s~ &i&s* )a% Cs@t*rai\nBg*
```

The buffer contains the expected string, but every other character of the string is garbage. The `copy()` function appears correct. Only by expanding the `min()` macro can the source of the problem be seen.

```
tOffset = min(++tOffset, length - 1);
```

expands into (again dropping unnecessary parentheses for clarity)

```
tOffset = (++tOffset > (length - 1)) ?
                    (length - 1) : ++tOffset;
```

`tOffset` is incremented twice because `++tOffset` appears twice in the expansion of the `min()` macro. The corrected call to `min()` is as follows:

```
//break statement into two lines
++tOffset;
tOffset = min(tOffset, length - 1);
```

The basic problem was that the `++tOffset` expression being passed to the macro had a side effect: the incrementing of the variable. Since arguments may appear many times within a macro, the programmer has no idea how often this expression will be evaluated. This problem cannot be solved by adding parentheses in the proper places. The rule must be do not invoke macros with arguments that have side effects.

Replacing Macros with Inline Functions   Programmers must be able to differentiate macros from functions. This is the reason macro names are all uppercase. Making the `min()` macro a `MIN()` macro does not solve the problems inherent in macros, but it does alert the programmer to the danger.

Unfortunately, not all programmers follow this convention. In particular, macros defined within the Standard C include files (such as `getchar()`) are not named with all capitals, so the programmer must remain constantly alert.

In C++, macros have been largely replaced with inline functions. Inline functions offer the same execution efficiency advantage of being expanded in place. However, an inline function is processed by the compiler, not by a separate preprocessor. Therefore, inline functions share the syntax of regular functions, including type-safe arguments. Inline functions generate far fewer surprises than macros. An inline version of min() appears as follows:

```
//min - return the lesser of two signed integers
inline int min(int a, int b) {
    int retVal;
    if (a > b)
        retVal = b;
    else
        retVal = a;
    return retVal;
}
```

The following expressions do not cause the problems previously demonstrated with macros.

```
i = min(i, j);                  //normal usage

i = min(i & 0xfff0, j);         //no precedence problems
cout << min(i, j);

i = min(++i, maxI);             //no side-effect problems
```

However, two common macro problems do remain with inline functions. First, inline functions and macros both execute as a single statement under the debugger. This makes debugging a faulty inline function or macro very difficult. Here the inline function still has the advantage, as most C++ compilers offer a compilation switch that forces inline functions outline during debugging.

Second, unwise use of either macros or inline functions can generate large amounts of object code. Consider the following harmless looking code fragment used to assign to the variable f the smallest of the five variables a, b, c, d, or e.

```
#define MIN(a, b) (a > b) ? b : a
int a, b, c, d, e, f;

f = MIN(a, MIN(b, MIN(c, MIN(d, e))));
```

Expanding the innermost macro call yields the following:

```
f = MIN(a, MIN(b, MIN(c, (d > e) ? e : d)));
```

Repeating the process, the problem becomes clear.

```
f = MIN(a, MIN(b,
    (c > ((d > e) ? e : d)) ? ((d > e) ? e : d)) : c);
```

As Andrew Koenig points out in *C Traps and Pitfalls*, repeating the process twice more results in the following extraordinary expression.

```
f = (a > ((b > ((c > ((d > e) ? e : d)) ?
    ((d > e) ? e : d) : c)) ?
    ((c > ((d > e) ? e : d)) ?
    ((d > e) ? e : d) : c)) : b))) ?
    ((b > ((c > ((d > e) ? e : d)) ?
    ((d > e) ? e : d) : c)) ?
    ((c > ((d > e) ? e : d)) ?
    ((d > e) ? e : d) : c)) : b)) : a;
```

To compare the effect, the following program was compiled using Borland's Turbo C++ compiler for DOS, and the size of the generated object code measured.

```
inline int min(int a, int b) {
    return (a > b) ? b : a;
}

#define MIN(a, b) (((a) > (b)) ? (b) : (a))

int minf(int a, int b) {
    return (a > b) ? b : a;
}
```

```
void main() {
    int a, b, c, d, e, f;

    a = 1; b = 2; c = 3; d = 4; e = 5;

    f = MIN(MIN(MIN(MIN(a, b), c), d), e);      // 1
    f = min(min(min(min(a, b), c), d), e);      // 2
    f = minf(minf(minf(minf(a, b), c), d), e);  // 3
}
```

Apparently, at least with this compiler, inline functions have the upper hand here as well. The macro expression on line 1 generated some 0xA5 bytes of object code. The inline version on line 2 generated some 0x44 bytes of code, less than half of its macro cousin. By comparison, the function version on line 3 generated some 0x25 bytes of code including both the function and the call.

Differences Between C++ and C

Another source of coding errors lies in the differences between C++ and C syntax. For the most part, C++ is a superset of and, therefore, compatible with C. This makes the differences that do exist that much more surprising. Fortunately, where differences exist, they are usually in C++'s favor.

Function Prototypes and Name Mangling   One of the most obvious differences lies with function prototypes. For historical reasons C treats the declaration `int  fn()` as if it were written `int  fn(...)`. C++ treats `int  fn()` identically with `int  fn(void)`.

C++ extends its strong typing into the link phase by adding type information to the name of the function in a process known as **name mangling**. For example, the C++ function `fn(int)` is turned into the symbol `fn__Fi` during the translation phase by the AT&T cfront translator. The `__Fi` at the end of the name indicates that the function takes an integer argument. Other argument types are added at the end of the name. For example, the function `int  fn(int, char, char*)` would become `fn__FicPc`. A list of other symbols used by cfront in name mangling appears in Table 5–2.

Table 5–2. Name mangling symbols used by cfront

Type	*Symbol*	
simple types		
void	v	
char	c	
short	s	
int	i	
long	l	
float	f	
double	d	
long double	r	
...	e	
amplifiers		
unsigned	U	
const	C	
volatile	V	
signed	S	
pointer to	P	
reference to	R	
array of	An_ where n is the size of the array	
function	F	

As a hybrid language, C++ must work with C functions. For example, C++ uses the functions of the Standard C library. To allow C++ to access these C functions, it must be possible to turn name mangling off. C++ introduces a new meaning for the `extern` statement for this purpose.

```
extern "C" {
   int fn1(int);
}
int fn2(int);

void main() {
   fn1(1);
```

```
   fn2(2);
}
```

During the link step, this program segment will attempt to link to the C compatible function _fn1 and the C++ function _fn2__Fi. It is possible, if unlikely, that confusion can arise between a mangled C++ function and an unmangled C function name, as in the following example:

```
in ModuleA.c:
   int fn__Fi(float f) {
      //...some C function
   }
```

```
in ModuleB.cpp:
int fn(int i);        //prototype of a C++ function
void main() {
   fn(1);
}
```

The C function name fn__Fi matches the mangled name for fn(int), but the argument type does not match.

Name mangling also presents a problem when attempting to link to libraries generated by different compilers. Not all manufacturers use the same mangling rules as cfront. For example, the function fn(int) when compiled under Borland's C++ compilers becomes fnqi. Thus, an object file from a Borland compiler cannot be type-safe linked together with one generated from a cfront-compatible compiler, as the function names do not match. It is possible to link objects from different C++ compilers if all shared functions are marked as extern "C" (assuming that there are no other incompatibilities).

Heap Allocation   The original C language provided a set of functions for allocating memory from the heap. The prototypical allocate function is malloc() and the return function is free(). Since these are functions in the Standard C library, they have no access to type information. Thus, their prototypes are void* malloc(long noOfBytes) and void free(void*). In use, they appear as follows:

```
MyClass *pMC;

pMC = (MyClass*)malloc(sizeof(MyClass));
//...other code
free(pMC);
```

This mechanism has several problems as far as C++ is concerned. First, it is not type-safe. Worse, the constructor cannot be invoked in this mechanism. C++ introduced a new heap allocation mechanism to address these limitations.

```
MyClass *pMC;
pMC = new MyClass(10, "ten object");
//...other code
delete pMC;
```

Since `new` and `delete` are keywords, they have access to the type of the object being allocated and can invoke the proper constructor.

In order to remain compatible with C, C++ retains the `malloc()`/`free()` mechanism; however, the programmer cannot mix the two. Thus, the following is not legal.

```
struct MyClass {
    int data;
    char string[10];

    MyClass(int d, char *pS);
    ~MyClass();
};

pMC = new MyClass(10, "ten object");
//...other code
free((void*)pMC);
```

This is much easier to do than it appears, especially when objects are allocated and deallocated in separate functions. The program cannot look at the pointer and tell whether it was allocated one way or the other.

Since `new` and `delete` access the same heap as `malloc()` and `free()`, the preceding segment might work; however, it is not guaranteed to work, so it is not portable. Moreover, the foregoing does not invoke the destructor on `*pMC` as it should when freeing the object.

The rule of thumb is either use `new` and `delete` or `malloc()` and `free()` but not both.

Miscellaneous Incompatibilities   In Standard C a variable can be defined more than once as long as the definitions are identical. This concession allows an include file with a definition to be inserted more than once without generating an error. This cannot be allowed in C++ as it would result in the constructor for the object being invoked twice.

This does not mean that an object cannot be declared `extern` more than once, as the `extern` declaration does not invoke a constructor. This is another reason why include files may include `extern` declarations along with class and function declarations, but should not define any objects themselves.

Another incompatibility between C and C++ relates to their treatment of `const` objects. Both languages understand `const`; however, C treats `const` objects as standard objects that the compiler can optimize since they cannot change. C++ considers `const` objects almost as typed `#defines`. Thus, the following is legal and desirable C++.

```
const int maxBufferSize = 10;
char buffer[maxBufferSize];
```

Such a `const` object is said to have internal linkage. Like a `#define`, the name `maxBufferSize` is simply replaced by the value 10 wherever used during the compilation process. To support C functions, a `const` object may be declared `extern`, giving it external linkage like a C object as in the following code fragment.

```
extern const int maxBufferSize = 10;
```

However, `const` objects with external linkage may no longer be used in place of `#defines`. Thus, the following is not legal.

```
extern const int maxBufferSize = 10;
char buffer[maxBufferSize];
```

Undoubtedly, other incompatibilities exist between C and C++ that I have not mentioned. As the ANSI C++ standard develops, it is likely to further diverge from C, and new incompatibilities will arise. The best advice I can offer the reader is to become immersed in C++ and learn its peculiarities.

Functions

The C++ syntax is a rich source of traps and pitfalls, but it is not the only trap into which the unsuspecting programmer can fall. C++ functions also can be abused, resulting in bugs that are difficult to isolate. Some of these problems will be examined next.

Invoking Functions

Function prototypes have solved many of the problems associated with improper or the incorrect number of arguments. An error such as the following is caught during compilation when it can be easily fixed.

```
void fn(int, int, char*);

void main() {
    int i, j;

    fn(i, "a string", j);//arguments in incorrect order
    //...more code
```

By requiring a function to be declared before use, C++ avoids the pitfalls introduced in Standard C by the inferred prototype (also known as the Miranda prototype — "if you cannot afford a prototype, a prototype will be provided for you"). In Standard C, when a function is used without a declaration, the compiler guesses its type from its first usage. This can lead to subtle problems such as the following:

```
void fn() {
    int  channel;
    float data[10];   //data from each of 10 channels
```

```
        readData(-1);    //-1 indicates initialize device
        for (channel = 0; channel < 10; channel++)
            data[channel] = readData(channel);
    }
```

Here the function `readData()` reads data from some type of external multichannel device. The first call with a channel number of -1 allows the function to initialize the device prior to taking data. The problem with this code segment is that without a declaration for `readData()`, the compiler must inferr its type from the first call. From this call, the type appears to be `int readData(int)`. When the compiler encounters subsequent calls to `readData()`, it attempts to interpret the returned floating point values as integers. This results in garbled data with no warnings of any kind.

C++ allows the programmer to use unspecified arguments when the number and type of arguments are not known. The only portable way that such arguments can be accessed is via the `stdarg.h` mechanism, as follows:

```
#include <iostream.h>
#include <stdarg.h>

//printData - this function accepts pairs of data as
//            arguments; the first argument indicates
//            the type of the second
enum {NOMORE,
      INT,
      CHAR,
      DOUBLE,
      CHARP};
void printData(int type, ...) {
    va_list pArgs;
    va_start(pArgs, type);

    int    intArg;
    char   charArg;
    double floatArg;
    char*  pCharArg;
    while(type) {
```

```
            switch (type) {
              case INT:    intArg = va_arg(pArgs, int);
                           cout << intArg;
                           break;
              case CHAR:   charArg = va_arg(pArgs, char);
                           cout << charArg;
                           break;
              case DOUBLE:floatArg = va_arg(pArgs, double);
                           cout << floatArg;
                           break;
              case CHARP:  pCharArg = va_arg(pArgs, char*);
                           cout << pCharArg;
                           break;
              }
            type = va_arg(pArgs, int);
        }
    va_end(pArgs);
}
//example of printData in use
void main() {
    printData(INT,     1,
              CHAR,    'C',
              DOUBLE, 1.5,
              CHARP,   "a string",
              NOMORE);            //terminates the list
}
```

On some machines, variable arguments could be passed to another function by simply passing the first argument in the list as follows:

```
void fn2(int firstArg, ...);

void fn1(int firstArg,...) {
    fn2(firstArg);
}
void fn2(int firstArg,...) {
    va_list pArgs;

    va_start(pArgs, firstArg); //get access to list
```

```
//...and so on
}
```

Here the function `fn1()` passes its first argument to `fn2()`. This function proceeds as if it now had access to all of the arguments passed to function `fn1()`. This may work on some architectures, but it is not portable — it will not work under any of the PC or Macintosh compilers.

The more portable way to pass a variable argument list to a function is as follows:

```
void fn2(va_list pArg);

void fn1(int firstArg,...) {
    va_list pArgs;
    va_start(pArgs, firstArg);
    fn2(pArgs);
    va_end(pArgs);
}
```

The pointer to the arguments on the stack, `pArg`, is first calculated in the function `fn1()`. This pointer is then passed to the function `fn2()` for processing. Even this is not guaranteed to work if the compiler passes arguments in the registers as well as on the stack.

Classic C resolved `float` into `double` for computational purposes. This included passing by value to a function. C++ no longer does this, treating `float` just like any other resolution type. Thus, if a function is declared `fn(float)`, then a `float` actually gets passed to it when called in C++. However, this is not the case for functions whose arguments are not specifically declared `float` as in the following code segment.

```
void fn(...);
float f = 1.5;

fn(f);
```

Here, the `floatf` is promoted to a `double` before being passed to the function in order to be compatible with Classic C. This problem is very difficult to detect and quite obscure. Programmers should never expect a `float` to be passed as a variable argument. (Note the absence of `FLOAT` as a type in the preceding `printData()` function.)

C++ allows functions to be assigned defaults for arguments that are not present in the call. These defaults are always supplied from the right to left, as in the following:

```
void fn1(int i, int j = 0);    //ok
void fn2(int i = 0, int j);    //not ok; j must have a
                               //default if i does
void fn3(int i = 0, int j = 1); //ok

fn3(10);                              //equivalent to fn3(10, 1);
```

It is possible to default an argument other than the last argument by overloading the function name as follows:

```
//declare function without defaults
void fn2(int i, int j);

//effectively provide a default for 'i'
inline fn2(int j) { return fn2(0, j);}
```

The arguments to functions are not resolved in any particular order. Thus, the results of the following call are not predictable.

```
void fn(char* pArg1, char* pArg2);

int main(int argc, char *argv[]) {
    //pass the first and second argument to function fn
    int i = 1;
    return fn(argv[i++], argv[i++]);
}
```

The function may be called as `fn(argv[1], argv[2])` or `fn(argv[2], argv[1])`, the standard does not say.

Pascal Functions   C++ compilers for the PC allow functions to be declared as `pascal` functions as in the following sample.

```
pascal int pascalFunc(int a, int b);

int normalFunc() {
    pascalFunc(10, 20);
}
```

Declaring a function `pascal` tells the compiler two things: arguments are pushed onto the stack from left to right instead of the C standard right to left order, and the called function is responsible for removing these arguments from the stack instead of the calling function. The `pascal` attribute serves two purposes. First, it allows C++ programs to call functions written in other languages, such as FORTRAN or Pascal. Second, it allows C++ programs to call Microsoft Window functions. Windows functions use the Pascal calling rules.

The default can be changed to `pascal` using a compiler switch: /Gc for the Microsoft compiler, and select Options/Compiler/Entry-Exit Code/Pascal under the Borland C++ compiler. Declaring a function `cdecl` forces the function to use C/C++ calling rules irrespective of the default.

There are several pitfalls unique to `pascal` functions. If `pascal` and `cdecl` functions are to be mixed in the same program then prototypes are critical. In addition, the prototypes should declare each function to be specifically `pascal` or `cdecl` type — the programmer should not rely on the default. Otherwise the following error can easily arise.

```
MODULE1.CPP:            //compiled with cdecl as default
int pascalFn(int arg);

void cppFn() {
    pascalFn(10);
}


MODULE2.CPP:            //compiled with pascal as default
int pascalFn(int arg) {
    //...normal processing
}
```

Since `MODULE1` contains only a C++ function, the programmer compiles it using Pascal as the default. If `MODULE2` is compiled using `pascal` default, then `cppFn()` does not call `pascalFn()` properly and a difficult to detect and fatal error occurs. The problem is avoided by including `pascal` and `cdecl` in the prototypes as follows:

```
MODULE1.CPP:
pascal int pascalFn(int arg);
```

C++ uses a different calling sequence from Pascal because C++ functions can be called with varying numbers of arguments — Pascal functions cannot. Thus, a `pascal` function cannot use `varargs` to extract a variable number of arguments. It is possible to declare a function as follows:

```
pascal void pascalFn(...);
```

However, doing so is very dangerous. The elliptical arguments deprive the compiler of the information it needs to check that the number and type of arguments are correct. Calling a `pascal` function with the wrong number of arguments leads to a difficult-to-find program crash when the function returns.

Standard Library Functions

C++ uses the same standard library of functions as that used by ANSI C with the addition of some C++ specific functions such as iostream support. These functions were accumulated from the most consistently useful functions written over the years. Individual groups of functions, most of which probably originated from a single source, are quite consistent. For example, most string functions use the same arguments. Other groups, however, are not so consistent, having been written by a different programmer in a different place.

While Standard C rationalized some of these functions, the ANSI standards committee did not feel that they could do too much to these functions without breaking most existing code.

Without going into every function, this section presents the major traps waiting for the unsuspecting programmer in the standard library.

strlen   The `strlen()` function simply returns the length of a string. However, this length does not include the terminating NULL at the end of the string. That is, `strlen("")` returns a 0. The result of this is that the following seemingly straightforward function does not work.

```
//makeCopy - make a copy of the supplied string using
//            memory taken from the heap
char* makeCopy(const char* pS) {
    int length = strlen(pS);     //find its length
    char* pT = new char[length]; //allocate a block of
                                 //same size

    if (pT)                      //if we got a buffer...
        strcpy(pT, pS);          //...copy source to
                                 //target

    return pT;
}
```

Since `strlen()` does not include the terminating NULL in its calculation, `pT` is actually one byte shorter than `pS`. Thus, the terminator is written one byte beyond the end of the buffer.

This problem is particularly difficult to find for two unrelated reasons. First, much of the time overwriting a character buffer by one character is harmless. For speed reasons, memory is generally allocated in 16-bit or 32-bit chunks, depending upon the word size of the machine. Unless the last character in `pT` happens to fall on the end of a word boundary, the next byte is unused anyway.

Second, if any data is overwritten, it is likely to belong to the next heap block. The program will operate correctly until the next call to `malloc()` or `free()` (whether directly or via `new` and `delete`). This may be in a function far removed from the source of the problem.

The corrected allocation line appears as follows:

```
char* pT = new char[length + 1]; //allocate a block of
```

This includes room for the terminating NULL.

Memory Copy Functions   Blocks of memory can be copied using the `memcpy()` function. Thus, the following example should add a directory name onto the beginning of a filename, assuming that sufficient room exists in the buffer for both.

```
void prePendDirectory(char *pFileName) {
    char directory[MAXDIRSIZE];

    //get name of current directory on current drive
    getcurdir(getdisk(), directory);

    //now move the filename down to make room
    int l = strlen(directory);
    memcpy(pFileName + l, pFileName,
            strlen(pFileName) + 1);

    //and then insert the directory name
    memcpy(pFileName, directory, l);
}
```

The problem with this algorithm lies in the way memcpy() works. If the source and destination areas overlap, the results of memcpy() are unpredictable. The first byte copied may overwrite another byte in the string that has yet to be copied, the second byte may overwrite the next, and so on.

When the source and destination ranges overlap, as in the preceding case, the programmer should use the memmove() function. This function works whether or not the ranges overlap. The memmove() function can be used when the ranges don't overlap, but it has a certain amount of extra overhead when compared to memcpy().

Character Functions Oddly enough, the character functions of the standard library, such as getchar(), do not return a char at all, but return an int instead. This is to allow these functions to return the noncharacter end-of-file (EOF) indication. This can lead to some peculiar results when the returned character is one of those above 0x7F in the ASCII sequence as was shown in the previous section on mixed expressions. The solution at that time was to assign the results of getchar() to a character before performing the comparison, as follows:

```
char c;

if ((c = getchar()) == 'π')
    //...code continues
```

This solution still allows the following to work, but the programmer should be very careful to understand why.

```
char c;

if ((c = getchar()) == EOF)
    break;
```

The assignment to `c` converts the `signed int` into a `signed char` (the default for `char` is `signed`). The comparison with EOF, which is the value -1, converts the `signed char` back into a `signed int` via sign extension. This is dangerous for two reasons. First, EOF and the character `'\xff'` are now mapped on top of each other. An `'\xff'` in the input stream will be treated like an end-of-file. Second, if the default for `char` is set to `unsigned`, the solution instantly stops working since an unsigned `'\xff'` converts into `0x00ff`.

Functions with Side Effects   Some of the most difficult functions to debug are functions that have side effects. A function that has the same effect every time it is called with the same arguments is easier to handle than one that does not — this principle was discussed under function encapsulation in Chapter 4.

Most of the functions in the standard library have no side effects, but a few do. The most notorious are those that store information away in static internal buffers. The function `strtok()` is one of these. The description of this function is as follows:

```
char *strtok(char *pString1, const char *pString2);

1st call:
    pString1 points to a string to be parsed
    pString2 points to an array of delimiters
    returns a pointer to the first token string up to
```

```
                       but not including the delimiter (NULL
                       terminated
```

```
subsequent calls:
    pString1 is NULL
    pString2 points to an array of delimiters
    returns a pointer to the next token
```

This function operates by copying the string pointed at by `pString1` into its internal buffer where subsequent calls can operate on it. This means that two strings cannot be parsed at the same time using `strtok`. For example, the following code segment will not work.

```c++
#include <string.h>

//compareTokens - compare the tokens contained in two
//                strings;
//                return a 1 if they are equal
//                a 0 if not
int compareTokens(char* pS1, char* pS2) {
    static char* pDelimiters = ", ";

    char *pT1, *pT2;

    pT1 = strtok(pS1, pDelimiters);
    pT2 = strtok(pS2, pDelimiters);
    while (pT1 && pT2) {
        if (strcmp(pT1, pT2))
            return 0;
        pT1 = strtok(0, pDelimiters);
        pT2 = strtok(0, pDelimiters);
    }
    return 1;
}
```

The two calls to `strtok()` interfere with each other.

The Global `errno`   One side effect that many standard library functions share is that they set the value of a global variable `errno` in the event the function returns an error. This variable is set to be an index into an array of `char*` called `sys_errlist`. After an error occurs, `sys_errlist[errno]` points to a string explaining the nature of the error. The library function `perror()` can be used to print this string out to `stderr`, or the programmer may access `sys_errlist` directly.

```
if ((pInputFile = fopen(pFileName, "rt")) == 0) {
    printf("Can't open file: %s\n", sys_errlist[errno]);
```

This is a clever scheme and very useful. The one danger is that the value of `errno` is reliable only in the event that the function returns an error. For example, the following does not work:

```
//this does not work
c = getchar();
if (errno) {
    printf("Error on getchar(): %s\n",
            sys_errlist[errno]);
```

Even resetting `errno` before making the call is not reliable.

```
//this is still not reliable
errno = 0;
c = getchar();
if (errno) {
    printf("Error on getchar(): %s\n",
            sys_errlist[errno]);
```

The programmer can test for an I/O error with the `ferror()` library function.

```
//this is reliable
c = getchar();
if (ferror(stdin)) {                 //on error, print out msg
    printf("Error on getchar(): %s\n",
            sys_errlist[errno]);
```

The functions in the standard library are time-tested, optimized functions. This discussion should not dissuade you from their use. At least the problems and shortcomings of these functions are well-known and documented.

Constructors and Destructors

Constructors and destructors are unique member functions invoked when an object goes into and out of scope, respectively. Constructors and destructors have a unique syntax that is not always consistent. For example, the following code segment creates an object `x` using the constructor `MyClass(int)`, but does not create an object `y` using the `MyClass()` constructor as one might expect — it declares a function `y` and not an object.

```
MyClass x(10), y();
```

Since constructors are invoked automatically when the object definition is encountered, these definitions must not be included in conditional statements if these objects are to be used outside of the conditional. One can see the problem with the following:

```
void fn(int i) {
    if (i < 10) {
        MyClass c(i);
        //...other code
    }
    c.access();
}
```

If the value of `i` is less than 10, the object `c` is not constructed but is accessed later on in the program anyway. This particular problem is caught by the compiler because the scope of the object `c` is restricted to the block in which it is defined. The reference to `c` outside of that block generates a compiler error. The following variation will not be caught as easily.

```
void fn(int i) {
    MyClass *pMC;

    if (i < 10) {
        pMC = new MyClass(i);
        //...other code
    }
    pMC->access();
}
```

Here, the scope of the pointer is not limited to the block even though its definition is. Problems such as these may be quite difficult to catch since the function works well for certain values of input (i less than 10).

A constructor is not restricted in the types of statements it contains. However, constructors are only intended to initialize the object to some legal initial state. Performing too many or the wrong types of operations in a constructor can lead to problems that are difficult to fix.

For example, consider the following simple program.

```
void sortArray(int length, int array[]);

class ProblemClass {
  private:
    int length;
    int *pData;

  public:
    ProblemClass(int l, int pArray[], int pSorted[]);
};

ProblemClass::ProblemClass(int l, int pArray[],
                           int pSorted[]) {
    //initialize the object
    length = l;
    pData = new int[l];
    int i;
    for (i = 0; i < l; i++ )
        pData[i] = pArray[i];

    //now make a copy of the sorted data
    sortArray(l, pData);
    for (i = 0; i < l; i++)
        pSorted[i] = pData[i];
}

void sortArray(int length, int array[]) {
    int swap = 0;
    int i;
```

```
do {
    for (i = 0; i < length - 1; i++)
        if (array[i] > array[i + 1]) {
            int temp = array[i];
            array[i] = array[i + 1];
            array[i + 1] = temp;
            swap = 1;
        }
} while(swap);
}
```

This class has two problems. First, the constructor performs functions unrelated to the job of initializing an object. Assuming that the data array does not need to be sorted, the call to `sortArray()` is not necessary. The constructor even copies data back into a return argument.

The second problem is that the `sortArray()` function has a bug. Using a simple bubble sort algorithm, `sortArray()` loops until it can go through the entire array without swapping two entries. However, the function fails to initialize the `swap` flag through each loop. As written, `sortArray()` never terminates.

This second problem demonstrates why doing too much in the constructor is a bad idea. The following program hangs even before the call to `printf()` that appears to be the first executable statement.

```
void main() {
    int sorted[5];
    int unsorted[5] = { 2, 3, 1, 0, 4};

    ProblemClass pc(5, unsorted, sorted);
    printf("Program starting\n");
    //...other code
}
```

Worse yet, the following program hangs before `main()` is executed.

```
int sorted[5];
int unsorted[5] = {2, 3, 1, 0, 4};
ProblemClass globalPC(5, unsorted, sorted);
```

```
void main() {
    printf("Program starting\n");
    //...other code
}
```

Since the declaration of globalPC may be in a different module from main(), what is causing the problem may not be at all clear. Since most conventional source code debuggers begin execution with main(), debugging such a problem with a debugger is often not possible. (Such programs can be cleaned up with an assembly language debugger. This process will be discussed in Chapter 8.)

Of course destructors are susceptible to the same problems when the program exits. The program may appear to execute properly only to crash after the program calls the exit() function.

Constructors and destructors that crash or hang are very difficult to debug. Keeping these functions as simple as possible reduces the likelihood that problems will arise. Constructors and destructors are susceptible to other problems that are outlined in the following sections.

The Copy-Initializer Constructor   The copy-initializer or c-i constructor is used to make copies of objects. The following code segment invokes the c-i constructor to create the object newMCObj.

```
void fn(MyClass& oldMCObj) {
    MyClass newMCObj = oldMCObj;
    //...more code
}
```

Notice that the preceding does not invoke the assignment operator as rewriting the example using the alternate syntax clearly shows.

```
void fn(MyClass& oldMCObj) {
    MyClass newMCObj(oldMCObj);
    //...more code
}
```

The c-i constructor is also used by the compiler to create copies of objects, as when passing an object by value to a function.

```
void fn(MyClass mcObj) {
    //...whatever code
}

void outerFn() {
    MyClass mc;

    fn(mc);              //invokes c-i constructor to make
                              copy
                         //of 'mc' to pass to fn()
}
```

A c-i constructor must be present. Like Miranda prototypes, if a class does not provide its own c-i constructor, C++ assigns a default. The default performs a member-by-member assignment from the source to the destination object. A copy of an object formed by simple member-by-member copying is known as a **shallow copy**.

Consider the following class:

```
#include <string.h>

class MyClass {
  private:
    int    data;
    char *pName;

  public:
    MyClass() {
        data = 0;
        pName = (char*)0;
    }
    MyClass(int d, char *pN) {
        data = d;
        pName = new char[strlen(pN) + 1];
        if (pName)
            strcpy(pName, pN);
    }
    ~MyClass() {
        if (pName)
```

```
            delete pName;
        pName = (char*)0;
    }
};
```

Since this class does not have a c-i constructor, it is provided one equivalent to the function below.

```
//equivalent to the default c-i constructor;
//performs member by member copy
MyClass::MyClass(MyClass& source) {
    data = source.data;
    pName = source.pName;
}
```

The default c-i constructor is fine for many classes, but in this case, a problem arises. The constructor allocates the memory for *pName off of the heap. Accordingly, the destructor for MyClass returns this memory to the heap. If a copy of a MyClass object is made using the default c-i constructor, however, then two different pNames will be pointing to the same piece of memory. Destructing the first object (either the original or the shallow copy) returns the memory to the heap — destructing the second object returns it again, corrupting the heap. (The general problem of corruption of the heap will be discussed in Chapter 6.)

A proper MyClass definition is as follows:

```
#include <string.h>

class MyClass {
  private:
    int    data;
    char *pName;

    void initObject(int d, char *pN) {
        data = d;
        pName = new char[strlen(pN) + 1];
        if (pName)
            strcpy(pName, pN);
    }
```

```
public:
  MyClass() {
      data = 0;
      pName = (char*)0;
  }
  MyClass(int d, char *pN) {
      initObject(d, pN);
  }
  MyClass(MyClass &source) {
      initObject(source.data, source.pName);
  }
  ~MyClass() {
      if (pName)
          delete pName;
      pName = (char*)0;
  }
};
```

Here the `MyClass` c-i constructor allocates a separate block of memory off of the heap into which the contents of `*source.pName` are copied. This type of copy is known as a **deep copy**. When the copy is destructed, it returns this block rather than returning the original block.

Even when not allocated off of the heap, shallow copies can lead to unexpected results if any of the data members are referential. Consider the following `MyClass`.

```
#include <string.h>
#include <iostream.h>

class MyClass {
    friend ostream& operator<<(ostream&, MyClass&);
  private:
    int*  pData;

  public:
    MyClass(int& d) {
        pData = &d;
    }
    int data(int d) {
```

```
            *pData = d;
            return d;
        }
};

ostream& operator<<(ostream& os, MyClass& obj) {
    return os << *obj.pData;
}

void main() {
    int i = 1;
    MyClass o1(i);
    cout << "o1 = " << o1 << endl;   //outputs a 1

    //create a clone of o1
    MyClass o2(o1);
    cout << "o2 = " << o2 << endl;   //outputs a 1

    //change the value of o1
    o1.data(2);
    cout << "o1 = " << o1 << endl;   //outputs a 2

    //value of o2 changed as well
    cout << "o2 = " << o2 << endl;   //also outputs a 2
}
```

Here, the class `MyClass` contains a pointer to another object stored somewhere else that it can modify through the method `data()`. The program constructs two objects, `o1` and `o2`. However, with a shallow copy c-i constructor, `o1` and `o2` point to the same integer. Thus, changing the `o1` object automatically changes the `o2` object as well. If unexpected, this side effect can lead to problems that are very difficult to understand. An argument of type `int&` has the same problem.

This discussion of the c-i constructor applies equally to the assignment operator. The default assignment operator performs a member-by-member shallow copy from source to target. The programmer must provide a c-i constructor and an assignment operator that perform a deep copy if:

1. the destructor returns resources such as heap memory
2. the data members are pointers or references to objects that the class can modify

Calls to Virtual Methods from Constructors   A call to a virtual method is normally polymorphic. That is, it is resolved at execution time so that a subclass object may invoke a different function than a base class object from the same call, as in the following:

```
#include <stdio.h>

class BaseClass {
  public:
    virtual void func();
};
void BaseClass::func() {
    printf("In BaseClass func\n");
}


class SubClass : public BaseClass {
  public:
    virtual void func();
};
void SubClass::func() {
    printf("In SubClass func\n");
}


void fn(BaseClass &obj) {
    obj.func();
}


void main() {
    BaseClass b;
    SubClass  s;

    fn(b);
    fn(s);
}
```

The first call to `fn()` generates the message "In BaseClass func," the second call to `fn()` generates the "In SubClass func" message.

However, calls made from a constructor do not reference a method of a subclass. This can be demonstrated by adding a `BaseClass` constructor that calls `func()` just as the previous sample function did.

```
BaseClass::BaseClass() {
    func();
}
```

Now a simple program such as

```
void main() {
    BaseClass b;
    SubClass  s;
}
```

generates the message "In BaseClass func" twice because the call in `BaseClass::BaseClass` refers to `BaseClass::func()` whether constructing a `BaseClass` object or a `SubClass` object.

It would sometimes be useful if the call to `func()` could invoke `SubClass::func()` when constructing a `SubClass` object, but it is clear why it cannot. At the point that the `BaseClass` constructor is executing, the constructor for `SubClass` has yet to be called. The object is still only of class `BaseClass` and is not yet a `SubClass`.

When Objects Are Destructed Twice   Several errors can lead to objects being destructed twice. You have already seen how shallow copies can lead to member objects being destructed multiple times. In addition, programmer error can lead to the destructor being invoked twice.

This problem can be detected or made harmless by following two simple guidelines. Objects should be assigned a signature field that is first checked and then zeroed in the destructor, as in the following:

```
class MyClass {
  private:
    unsigned int signature;
    void         *pBlock;
```

```
        //...other data members

    public:
      MyClass() {
          signature = 0x1234;
          //...further initialization
      }
      ~MyClass();
};
MyClass::~MyClass() {
    if (signature != 0x1234) {
        printf("Faulty signature on MyClass object\n");
        return;
    }
    signature = 0;
    //...further destruction code
}
```

In addition, all pointers should be zeroed after they are deleted as the
following addition to the preceding destructor shows.

```
MyClass::~MyClass() {
    if (signature != 0x1234) {
        printf("Faulty signature on MyClass object\n");
        return;
    }
    signature = 0;
    if (pBlock) {
        delete pBlock;              //free the memory
        pBlock = 0;                 //and zero the pointer
    }
}
```

These precautions can help catch or avoid some types of double-release
problems that are difficult to debug.

Overloaded Operators

When carefully chosen and written, overloaded operators can aid the programmer by simplifying and clarifying the application code. Improperly implemented, however, operators can be quite difficult to debug. Due to their obvious meaning, the programmer often overlooks the fact that the operator is itself a function call.

For example, in a function such as the following, if the function did not work, how many programmers would think to question the `[]` operator as the source of the problem?

```
void copy(Array& target, Array& source) {
    int i;
    int length = min(target.length(),
                     source.length());
    for (i = 0; i < length; i++)
        target[i] = source[i];
}
```

For this reason, overloaded functions should be carefully written and debugged. These functions should be exceptionally careful about checking input variables to make sure their value is in range. Consider the following assignment operator for the class `Array`.

```
#include <assert.h>

class Array {
  private:
    int length;
    int *pData;

  public:
    Array() {
        length = 0;
        pData = (int*)0;
    }
    Array(int l) {
        if (pData = new int[l])
            length = l;
```

```
        }
        Array(Array& s) {
            pData = 0;
            *this = s;
        }


        Array& operator=(Array& source);
        int&   operator[](int index);
};
Array& Array::operator=(Array& source) {
    if (pData)
        delete[length] pData;
    pData = (int*)0;
    length = 0;
    if (source.length) {
        pData = new int[source.length];
        if (pData) {
            length = source.length;

            int i;
            for (i = 0; i < length; i++)
                pData[i] = source.pData[i];
        }
    }
    return *this;
}


int& Array::operator[](int index) {
    assert(index < length);
    return pData[index];
}
```

This operator first deletes its own heap memory, if it has any. It then allocates a block of memory large enough to contain the source array and copies the length and data from the source array into the *this array.

This operator seems okay, but what if the user of class Array codes a rather innocuous looking statement such as the following:

```
void fn(Array& s) {
    Array *pS = &s;
    *pS = s;              //unnecessary but supposedly harmless
     //...other code
};
```

Here, `*pS` and `s` refer to the same `Array`. This proves catastrophic. The assignment operator first deletes any data it had, then attempts to copy from itself the data, which is now gone. The result is a zero length `Array`. The correct assignment operator first checks for assignment to itself.

```
Array& Array::operator=(Array& source) {
    //assignment to yourself is a no-op
    if (this == &source) {
        return *this;
    }
    //...continue as before
}
```

Notice the `Array::operator[]()` operator. Overloaded operators such as `operator[]` provide excellent opportunities to add range checks. These opportunities should not be missed.

Programmers sometimes forget that operators are overloaded independently even when related. For example, `operator+=()` is overloaded separately from `operator=()` and `operator+()`.

Of course, these operators may invoke each other or some common function. For example, it is common to implement `operator+()` as follows.

```
Array operator+(Array& a, Array& b) {
    Array temp(a);            //create a temporary with a
    temp += b;                //add b to a
    return temp;              //return the temporary
}
```

Clearly the addition operator should return an object of class `Array`. (The previous function does not return `Array&` because the temporary `temp` is an auto variable declared locally on the stack. Returning its address would be illegal, since the object is out of scope as soon as the return is executed. Returning the object by value copies the contents of `temp` back into the caller's space.) It is not so obvious that the different assignment operators should also return such an object.

Consider the difference between `operators+=()` and `operator*=()` defined as follows:

```
Array& operator+=(Array& target, Array& source);
   void operator*=(Array& target, Array& source);

void fn() {
    Array a, b, c;
    b += c;             //Line #1 works fine
    b *= c;             //Line #2 also works

    a = b += c;         //Line #3 works as well
    a = b *= c;         //Line #4 does not work
}
```

Lines 1 and 2 work as expected. Since the assignment operators bind from right to left, line 3 is parsed as if it had been written `a = (b += c)`. The result of `b += c` is of type `Array`, so the assignment is allowed. Line 4 is also parsed as `a = (b *= c)`; however, the return type of `b *= c` is `void`, which cannot be assigned to `a`.

Reentrancy

Reentrancy is an important consideration when writing a function, especially in a preemptive multitasking environment. In such an environment, a process may lose control of the CPU at any time. There is no guarantee that the function in which the process was executing will not be called from some other process during the time the process is waiting for the CPU. This is particularly true of access methods.

Thus the following `Array` class is prone to failure in an environment that supports multiprocessing, such as UNIX or OS/2, if the same `Array` object is accessible from several different processes.

```
class Array {
  private:
```

```
        int data[100];
        int offset;

    public:
        Array() {
            int i;
            for (i = 0; i < 100; i++)
                data[i] = i;
            offset = 0;
        }
        Array& operator[](int index) {
            offset = index;
            return *this;
        }
        operator int() {
            return data[offset];
        }
};
```

In a segment such as the following:

```
Array globalObj;
void fn(int i) {
    int value = globalObj[i];
    //...other code
}
```

operator[]() is invoked first. This version simply stores the value of
the index for later use by the int operator.

If two processes A and B attempt to execute a statement such as value
= globalObj[i], the following problem can arise. Process A executes
the [] operator, storing the index i into globalObj.offset. Before it
can perform the int operation, however, its time slice expires and Process
B begins execution. Process B performs both the [] and int operations
storing its own index into globalObj.offset, overwriting the index
stored by A. When Process A resumes, it fetches the value pointed at by
offset — the value last referenced by Process B.

This type of error is known as a **data collision**. Data collisions are
exceedingly difficult to debug due to their random, unpredictable nature. A

particular program might work for days, weeks, or months before generating unexplainable results due to a data collision of some sort.

Data collisions can arise in nonpreemptive environments, such as Windows and MS-DOS, when objects are accessible both to interrupt and non-interrupt routines. The non-interrupt routine may be in the middle of executing a method when an interrupt occurs.

Data collisions invariably involve two or more operations that depend upon one another and that can be disturbed by other processes. In the preceding example, the `int` operator was dependent upon the results of the `[]` operation. Thus, the window of vulnerability begins with the `[]` operation and ends once the `int` operation is complete. This is called the **critical section** of the algorithm.

If Process A could assure itself of retaining control throughout its critical section, the foregoing problem could not occur. Thus, one approach to avoiding data collisions is to disable rescheduling at the beginning of the critical section and reenable it at the end. If the critical section is very long, the user will notice some jerkiness caused by one process "hogging the system" over an extended critical section. If the critical section is accessible to interrupt routines, then interrupts must be disabled as well, which could lead to loss of data. Finally, many operating systems do not allow a user application to disable rescheduling or interrupts.

A less disruptive approach is to use a flag to control access to the critical section. Notice that losing control of the CPU in the critical section did not cause the data confusion in the previous example. The problem was the entry of Process B into the critical section while Process A was suspended within it. Thus, controlling access so that only one process is within the critical section at a time is sufficient. Such a control flag is called a semaphore.

An initial attempt might resemble the following:

```
int semaphore = 0;     //0 -> okay to pass

void enterCriticalRegion() {
    //wait as long as flag set
    while (semaphore);//Line #1

    //now mark the region as occupied
    semaphore = 1;     //Line #2
}
```

```
void exitCriticalRegion() {
    semaphore = 0;      //signal others it's okay to pass
}
```

This algorithm has at least two problems. First, waiting in a tight loop — called **spin waiting** — wastes CPU time. The current process cannot continue until the process in the critical section has executed long enough to call exitCriticalRegion(), thereby surrendering the semaphore. No other process will gain control of the CPU until the current process's time slice is up as long as it spin waits. Further, the process that has the semaphore may be of lower priority. It is far more efficient to give up control of the balance of the current process's time slice than to burn up CPU cycles in a tight loop. The improved functions are as follows:

```
int semaphore = 0;      //0 -> okay to pass

void enterCriticalRegion() {
    //wait as long as flag set
    while (semaphore) //Line #1
        reschedule(); //surrender remainder of
                      //time slice

    //now mark the region as occupied
    semaphore = 1;              //Line #2
}

void exitCriticalRegion() {
    semaphore = 0;      //signal others it's okay to pass
}
```

This algorithm has a critical section of its own. Suppose that Process A calls enterCriticalRegion() to determine whether it is safe to enter a particular critical region. The program checks semaphore on Line 1 and finds that it is 0; however, before it can continue on to Line 2 to set it, Process A is suspended. Then Process B comes along and, finding the semaphore to be 0, sets it to 1 and continues on. Once Process A is restarted, it continues with Line 2, sets the semaphore flag (which is still 1) and proceeds into the critical region where it collides with B.

The preceding critical region is very small: not more than three or four CPU instructions. However, there is an algorithm that has no critical region. The functions shown that follow are based upon **Peterson's algorithm** as set out by Tannenbaum.

```
//Peterson's semaphore - the following algorithm
//                        is designed for two processes
unsigned turn;
unsigned interested[2];

void enterCriticalRegion(unsigned process) {
    assert(process < 2);

    unsigned other = !process;
    interested[other] = 1;
    turn = process;
    while (turn == process && interested[other])
        reschedule();
}

void exitCriticalRegion(unsigned process) {
    assert(process < 2);

    interested[process] = 0;
}
```

In addition, all preemptive multitasking operating systems provide some type of semaphore system calls. In UNIX these are called mutexes and may take on values greater than 1, essentially recording the number of critical region requests.

When designing with semaphores, programmers must be careful to avoid lockouts. A lockout occurs as follows: Process A requests semaphore 1 to enter some critical region. While in that region, Process A is suspended and Process B gains control. Process B requests semaphore 2 to enter a separate critical region. Within that critical region, Process B requests semaphore 1 and is suspended, since Process A still has it. Process A regains control and requests semaphore 2, which it cannot get as long as Process B has it. Process A is now suspended waiting for Process

B to give up one semaphore while Process B is suspended waiting for A to give up another.

This situation is known as a **deadlock**. Detecting and avoiding deadlocks is of great concern to operating systems writers, but is somewhat beyond the scope of this book. Those interested are advised to refer to a good operating systems text such as Tannenbaum's *Operating System Design and Implementation.*

A good guideline for applications programmers to follow is to code all functions, especially methods, reentrantly. If this is not possible, the programmer must protect the critical region with a semaphore. Critical regions should be kept as small as possible and be clearly marked with comments. The `enterCriticalRegion()` and `exitCriticalRegion()` calls should be within the same function to avoid any possibility that the latter function call is somehow missed.

In addition, semaphores should be designed to impact the fewest processes possible. For example, a static semaphore would protect critical regions within a class as follows:

```
class MyClass {
  protected:
    static unsigned semaphore;//all instances of MyClass
                                 //share a common semaphore
    //...other data
    void enterCriticalRegion();
    void exitCriticalRegion();

  public:
    void someFn() {
        //...beginning of critical region
        enterCriticalRegion();
        //...critical code
        exitCriticalRegion();
        //...other code
    }
};
```

Declaring the semaphore static will affect all processes that attempt to access `MyClass::someFn()`. If the critical region centers around global or static data, this is correct. If, however, the critical data is local to a single object, then the semaphore may be local to the object as well, as follows:

```
class MyClass {
  protected:
    unsigned semaphore;    //separate semaphore for each
                           //each instance of MyClass
    //...continue as before
};
```

The result is that only calls to the same object are affected. Remember that DOS is not reentrant. Great pains must be taken if DOS functions are to be accessed from within an interrupt service routine. These tricks are documented in the DOS literature. (See "TurboC: The Advanced Art of Programming, Optimization and Debugging" by Stephen R. Davis, for a complete discussion of the challenges of writing and debugging interrupt functions, including Terminate-and-Stay Resident programs, that access MS-DOS).

Static Buffer Problems

Even when reentry is not a problem, programmers must be careful about storing information in static buffers. Rewriting the previous `Array` example slightly would create an even worse problem.

```
class Array {
  private:
    int data[100];
    static int offset;

    //...continues the same as before
```

Here the program has reasoned that the `offset` member is needed only for short-term storage. To avoid the overhead of keeping a copy of this element with every `Array` object, the programmer declared it static. Besides not being reentrant, single-threaded but compound expressions, such as the following, no longer work either.

```
int fn(Array& a, Array& b, int i) {
    return a[i] + b[99 - i];
}
```

The two `operator[]`s are evaluated before the two objects are cast to `int`, the second call overwriting the `static offset` left by the first. Thus, members should only be declared static when they truly describe every member of the class simultaneously.

Other Forms of Control Transfer

The common function call is not the only way in which control can be transferred outside of a function. Two other ways are the long jump and the exception. Both of these transfer mechanisms offer opportunities and dangers to the C++ programmer, as you will see.

The Long Jump
Three constructs are necessary to perform a long jump: the `setjmp()`, the `jmp_buf` aggregate class, and the `longjmp()`. These are defined in the include file `setjmp.h`. In use, they look like the following:

```
//structure into which to store computer's state
jmp_buf CPUState;

void main() {
    if (setjmp(CPUState))
        printf
                ("A serious error has occurred;
    //"starting over\n");
    //...continues on
}

void someOtherFn() {
    //...other code
    if (error == serious)
        longjmp(CPUState, 1);//this does not return
    //...continue on
}
```

The call to `setjmp()` stores into the `jmp_buf` object the CPU registers, instruction pointer, and whatever other information may be required to restore the state of the machine at some later time. This state may be restored at any time by passing this object to the `longjmp()` function.

Since restoring the state includes restoring the instruction pointer to the `setjmp()` function where it was when saved, the `longjmp()` function does not return to the caller but reappears from the `setjmp()` call. When the program first calls `setjmp()`, the function returns a zero. Long jumps pass a nonzero value that appears as the return value from `setjmp()`. This allows the program to differentiate between the initial return and subsequent returns.

Long jumps are typically used to return control to some earlier point in the program without bothering to return and check error codes back up through multiple levels of function calls. As such, they are quick and straightforward. Long jumps harbor several potential problems for the programmer, however.

The first problem relates to the amount of information the `setjmp()` can store. This function cannot save all of memory, nor can the system determine which variables may have been modified between the `setjmp()` and `longjmp()` calls. Thus, the programmer must be wary about constructs such as the following:

```
#include <setjmp.h>
jmp_buf CPUState;

void fn1() {
    //...some initial code
    MyClass aLargeObject(5);
    int aSmallObject = 0;

    setjmp(CPUState);

    //What are the values of aLargeObject and
    //aSmallObject at this point?
    //after a longjump the value of aLargeObject
    //will be 10 and of aSmallObject 1

    fn2(aSmallObject);   //however, even after the
```

```
                              //longjmp a value of 0 is
                              //passed to fn2()
    //...more code
    aSmallObject = 1;
    aLargeObject.setValue(10);
    //...even more code
}
```

Here the program defines two objects and initializes them. One of these objects is a simple integer, and the other is a complex object. Let's consider the complex object first. The `setjmp()` call memorizes the state of the registers, but not the state of `aLargeObject` in memory. At some later point in the program, the value of `aLargeObject` is changed. If the program long jumps back to the `setjmp()` call, the object will retain its modified values.

The integer object `aSmallObject`, is small enough to fit into a CPU register. Since `aSmallObject` has been referenced immediately prior to the `setjmp()` call, the value of `aSmallObject` may have been cached in a register. When passed by value to the function `fn2()`, the compiler may assume that the value of `aSmallObject` can be taken directly from the register. Since the register value was saved in the `setjmp` buffer, the value passed to `fn2()` would be 0 after the long jump even though its value in memory is 1.

Of course, without knowing whether the value was cached, the programmer cannot be sure what the value passed to the `fn2()` is. It depends upon the compiler. The programmer can force the matter by declaring `aSmallObject` volatile. This requires the compiler to reload it from memory on every access, thereby avoiding the problem.

Even so, the programmer should make no assumptions about the values of any variables after a `setjmp()` call unless specifically in the zero (initial call) return path. Upon a nonzero return from a `setjmp()`, the programmer should reinitialize the entire context, including all data objects.

Another potential problem is losing information that the `longjmp()` requires. Clearly, the following will not work.

```
jmp_buf *pJmpBuf;
void setJumpBuf() {
    jmp_buf localJB;
    pJmpBuf = &localJB;
```

```
    setjmp(localJB);
}

void main() {
    setJumpBuf();

    //...other code
}
```

In this case, `jmp_buf` is allocated off the local stack of the function `setJumpBuf()`. As soon as this function exits, `localJB` goes out of scope and its contents become corrupted. If another function attempts to long jump back, it will find the CPU registers corrupted.

Not so obvious, the following does not work either.

```
jmp_buf globalJB;
void setJumpBuf() {
    setjmp(globalJB);
}

void main() {
    setJumpBuf();

    //...other code
}
```

The `jmp_buf` structure remains in scope throughout the program, but the return address — which is necessary to return control from `setJumpBuf()` to `main()` once a long jump has been performed — does not. These traits make long jumps dangerous but manageable if handled carefully. For C++ programmers, long jumps have another problem that cannot be handled. Consider the following:

```
#include <setjmp.h>

jmp_buf CPUState;
void fn1(int) {
    setjmp(CPUState);
```

```
    MyClass mcObject(10);

    //...other code
}
```

The object `mcObject` is created after the call to `setjmp()`. Once the program long jumps back, `mcObject` is constructed again without the old `mcObject` ever having been destructed. If the constructor for `MyClass` allocates memory off of the heap, that memory is lost. If the constructor allocates some other resource, that resource is lost as well. There appears to be no solution to this problem.

The exception   Faced with a long-jump mechanism that was broken as far as C++ was concerned, the authors of C++ decided to seek a better solution. The long jump is used to handle exceptions that arise during processing. Under ANSI C, exceptions are trapped via the `raise()` and `signal()` functions defined in the `signal.h` include file. The prototype for these functions is as follows:

```
extern "C" {
    int raise(int __sig);
    void (*signal(int __sig,
                       void (* func)(int))) (int);
}
```

That is, `raise()` accepts an integer, and `signal()` accepts an integer and the address of a function that also accepts an integer. Every calamity that might befall a program is assigned an integer value. Values exist for divide overflow, illegal instruction, illegal memory access, and so on. When one of these errors occurs, the system raises an alarm by calling `raise()`, passing the value associated with that signal.

A signal function is associated with each signal value. The raise function invokes the proper handler for that signal. The function `signal()` allows the application program to assign a new handler for these signals. This is demonstrated in the following:

```
#include <stdio.h>
#include <signal.h>
#include <setjmp.h>
```

```
void trmFn(int signl);
jmp_buf CPUState;

void main() {
    void (*pOldHandler)(int);

    //intercept requests to terminate
    if (setjmp(CPUState) == 0) {
        pOldHandler = signal(SIGTERM, trmFn);
    }

    //...other code
}

void trmFn(int signl) {
    printf("Program attempted to terminate"
            " - start over\n");
    longjmp(CPUState, 1);
}
```

The function `trmFn()` is established as a handler of the `SIGTERM` signal, which is raised when the program attempts to terminate. Rather than terminate, this function displays a message and then starts the program over from the beginning.

Since signals could arise from almost anywhere, application programs cannot add error returns in the proper places to allow for a more controlled return to `main()`. Long jumps are required in this case. However, long jumps appear to have almost no other valid use. Thus, if a better technique could be devised to handle exceptions, C++ programmers could forget about `longjmp()` and its associated problems.

Draft 3.0 of C++ introduced the `throw/catch` exception handler to serve this purpose. Rewritten to use `throw` and `catch`, the previous example resembles the following:

```
#include <stdio.h>

class TerminateInfo;            //defined somewhere else
void trmFn(class TerminateInfo);
```

```
void main() {
    for(;;) {
        try {
            //...other code
            fn();
            //...more code
        }
        catch(TerminateInfo ti) {
            printf("Program attempted to terminate\n"
                    "error was %d - start over\n",
                    ti.error());
        }
        catch(...) {
            printf("Unknown error occur - exiting\n");
            exit(3);
        }
    }
}
void fn() {
    MyClass mcObject;

    if (error == SERIOUS) {
        throw TerminateInfo(error);
    }
    //...function continues
}
```

The `try` keyword introduces a **try block**. Immediately following the try block are one or more **catch blocks** designed to handle exceptions that arise within the program. When an error is detected, the exception handler uses the `throw` keyword to throw an object containing error information back to the first catch block it can find with compatible argument types. *First* here is defined in terms of an upward search through the called functions, not in terms of the order of the appearance within the module or program.

In the preceding example, the error is detected and thrown with an object of class `TerminateInfo`. This is caught back in main with the `catch(TerminateInfo)` handler that prints a message. If a different object were thrown, it would have been caught by the `catch(...)` handler, which will catch any thrown object.

The difference between this mechanism and the `signal/longjmp()` mechanism is that `throw`/`catch` unwinds the stack in a controlled fashion, invoking the destructors for objects that go out of scope along the way. Thus, the object `mcObject` is destructed properly before the catch handler is invoked.

Conclusion

This chapter has presented a compendium of potential problems and pitfalls with the C++ language. Topics discussed were

- tokenizing confusions
- puns
- precedence and binding
- macro expansions
- function side effects
- constructor/destructor confusions
- overloaded operators
- data collisions, and
- exceptions

Most of these pitfalls were inherited from C, but some were of C++'s own making. Missing from this list are programming pitfalls associated with pointer variables.

Pointer variables form a class of errors that are so common and pervasive, especially to beginning programmers, that they have been given a separate chapter of their own, Chapter 6.

Chapter 6

Pointer Traps and Pitfalls

One of the most attractive features of C++ is its elegant handling of pointer variables — variables that point at other objects. The programmer can calculate and manipulate addresses with efficiency of both expression and implementation. With power comes danger, however. Pointer pitfalls are some of the easiest to fall into and most difficult to climb out of.

Simple Pointers

Errors involving pointer variables fall into the same categories as errors involving other variable types. Some pointer errors are random, such as failure to initialize a pointer properly. Others are more systematic failures, such as those resulting from a misunderstanding on the part of the programmer. This sort of error includes illegal or improper casts from one pointer type to another.

Pointer problems differ from other types of errors in two important respects: they are more destructive and more difficult to find. Pointer problems can cause a program to terminate abnormally, often at a point far removed from the source of the problem, leaving the programmer with nothing to work with and little idea of what the problem might be.

As with other error types, knowledge and diligence avoid many pointer problems. This chapter will discuss the most common pointer problems and examine special checks that can be added to detect pointer problems as soon as they occur, thus simplifying the job of finding the problem.

Pointer Review

Readers not familiar with C/C++ pointer variables are referred to an introductory C book for a more complete discussion. In the interest of completeness, however, this section presents a quick review of pointer variables.

Pointer variables are declared like other variable types except that they are preceded by an * as in the following examples:

```
int anIntObject;
int *pIntObject;
```

The object `pIntObject` contains not an integer, but the address of an integer. In use, this object appears as follows:

```
pIntObject = &anIntObject;
*pIntObject = 1;
```

The & operator returns the address of the object to which it is applied. The first expression here says, "store the address of `anIntObject` into `pIntObject`."

When used in an expression, the * operator says "the `type` pointed at by" where `type` must be gleaned from the declaration. Thus the second expression in the foregoing says, "store the value 1 into the integer pointed at by `pIntObject`."

To make this more concrete, suppose the object `anIntObject` is stored at location `0x1200`. The first expression stores a `0x1200` into `pIntObject`. The second expression stores a 1 into address `0x1200`.

Pointers to all other types are possible.

```
float *pFloat;
MyClass *pCompoundObject;
int (*pFn)(int);
```

The last declaration is the most interesting, because it declares a pointer to a function. In use, `pFn` appears as follows:

```
int fn(int);

pFn = fn;                    //assign address of fn to pFn
int retVal = (*pFn)(10);    //call fn pointed at by pFn
```

Notice that the & operator is not required in the first assignment. A function name without trailing parentheses is assumed to refer to the address of the function. Similarly, the name of an array without trailing brackets refers to its address.

A pointer variable is not simply a pointer to an object but a pointer to a type object. The following assignment is not legal because the types of the left- and right-hand values don't match.

```
int *pInt;
float fObject;
float *pFloat = &fObject;

pInt = pFloat;                    //types don't match
```

Here pInt is of type pointer to integer, whereas pFloat is of type pointer to float. Similarly, in the preceding segment pFn is not simply a pointer to a function, but a pointer to a function that takes a single integer argument and returns an integer.

One pointer type can be converted to any other pointer type with a cast. A cast appears identical to the declaration of the target object with the object name removed. The cast is placed in parentheses in front of the object. Thus, the preceding assignment would be written as follows:

```
pInt = (int *)pFloat;        //cast changes type
```

More complex pointers are recast in the same way, as in the following:

```
void voidFn(int);
int (*pIntFn)(int);

pIntfn = (int (*)(int))voidFn;//cast is identical to
                              //declaration of pIntFn
                              //with name removed
```

The type of an object is often written as the cast that would produce that object type. For example, a pointer to an integer is generally abbreviated `int*`. A pointer to a function that takes an integer followed by a float and returns a character is written cryptically, but succinctly, as `char (*)(int, float)`.

Random Pointer Errors

The sources of random pointer errors are many. The most common is simply forgetting to initialize a pointer variable before using it. Fortunately, this is the easiest pointer problem to correct. Most compilers catch the obvious cases, generating a "Possible use before initialization" warning at compilation.

Another possibility is extending beyond the end of a neighboring field, causing the pointer variable to be overwritten. In the following code segment, the bounds of `array` are exceeded, resulting in the first byte of `pointer` being overwritten with a null character.

```
char array[10];
int *pointer;

//zero out the character array
int  index;
for (index = 0; index <= 10; index++)    //test should
be '<'
    array[index] = '\0';
```

This type of error is very unpredictable, because it depends upon the placement of variables within memory over which the programmer has very little control.

An illegal address that falls outside the bounds of the memory assigned to the program is said to be **out of range**. Improperly initialized pointers are usually out of range. On many CPUs, attempts to access an out of range location can be trapped and reported back to the operating system (O/S) which then terminates the program. An O/S that can trap out-of-range accesses is called a **protected mode operating system**.

Unfortunately, neither the 8086/88, upon which the PC family is based, nor the 68000, upon which the Macintosh line of computers is built, can trap illegal addresses. The 80286 and above and the 68010 and above, when equipped with an optional memory management unit (MMU), do support this feature but only when running a protected mode O/S, such as UNIX (including the AUX and Xenix variants) or OS/2. Neither MS-DOS nor the Mac O/S is a protected mode operating system. Even a protected mode O/S cannot trap accesses to illegal, but in-range, addresses.

When not trapped by the O/S, accessing an illegal address has different effects. Reading an illegal location does little harm other than returning garbage to the program. Writing to an illegal location will probably do no harm either, since at any given moment most memory is not being used. However, a wild write may overwrite a machine instruction or a critical data location. Such overwritten items act like land mines that lie dormant until the program happens to come upon them. By the time the overwritten instruction is executed or the overwritten data item is used, the programmer has no idea how the location came to be corrupted.

Several techniques can detect improperly initialized pointers. First, at program start global and static variables are initialized to 0, making this the most common illegal address. It is so common that 0 is never considered within range on a protected mode O/S. Even non-protected mode systems put special checks in for writes to location 0.

For example, the `exit()` function of both the Turbo/Borland C++ and Microsoft C++ compilers checks the first few bytes of the default data segment when the program exits. If this area is found to have been overwritten, the message "Null pointer assignment" is displayed. This is a flag that somewhere the program wrote to logical location 0.

Another effective technique to catch errant pointers to class objects is to assign each object a signature by which pointers to valid objects can be identified. This technique was used in Chapter 4 to detect an invalid index into an array of objects. The same technique is effective on other types of pointer problems as well.

The object is assigned a signature by defining a field within the class. The signature can be initialized in the constructor and cleared in the destructor. A `sigCheck()` method is then provided to allow the application program to check the signature.

```
#include <iostream.h>

#define MyClassSignature 0x1234
```

```
typedef unsigned int uint;

class MyClass {
  private:
    uint signature;
    //...other elements

  public:
    //set the signature in the constructor
    MyClass() {
        signature = MyClassSignature;
        //...initialize other elements
    }

    //clear the value in the destructor
    ~MyClass() {
        signature = 0;
    }

    void sigCheck() {
        if (signature != MyClassSignature) {
            cerr << "Bad pointer "
                 << (void*)this << endl;
            abort();
        }
    }

    //...other methods can (and should) check the
    //signature
    void anotherMethod() {
        sigCheck(); //make sure this is a valid ptr
        //...other code
    }
};

//global functions should check their arguments
//carefully
void globalFn(MyClass *pMC) {
    pMC->sigCheck();
```

```
        //...continue on now
}
```

Pointers should be checked at interfaces between different bodies of code, such as input to public methods of a class or global functions as in the example. Generally, pointers need not be checked within a function if they have been properly checked at the entrance to the function.

The `sigCheck()` method may be inlined for increased speed efficiency. However, it may not be static, since a static method is not bound to any object. In addition, the `sigCheck()` may not be declared virtual, as a virtual method cannot be invoked properly if the object is invalid. (This is explained in detail later in this chapter.)

File and line information can be added by using the ANSI C intrinsics `__FILE__` and `__LINE__` as arguments to the `sigCheck()` function as follows:

```cpp
void MyClass::sigCheck(char *pFile, unsigned lineNo) {
    if (signature != MyClassSignature) {
        cerr << "Bad pointer in file " << pFile
            << " #"                     << lineNo
            << " - "                    << (void*)this
            << endl;
        abort();
    }
}


//example usage
void fn(MyClass& mc) {
    mc.sigCheck(__FILE__, __LINE__);
    //...function continues
}
```

At compile time, the compiler replaces `__FILE__` with the name of the C++ source file and `__LINE__` with the line number of the call. The error message alerts the programmer to the exact spot where the error was detected.

Some programmers prefer to define a macro to invoke the signature check function, since it can be disabled after the program has been debugged, as in the following example:

```
#ifdef DEBUG
#define CHECKMCPTR(pMC)
        (pMC)->sigCheck(__FILE__, __LINE__)
#else
#define CHECKMCPTR(pMC) (void)0
#endif

void fn(MyClass& mc) {
    CHECKMCPTR(&mc);
    //...function continues
}
```

If DEBUG is defined at compilation, the CHECKMCPTR call at the beginning of fn() has the identical effect as the sigCheck() call in the previous example. If DEBUG is not defined, however, then the macro call has no effect. Using this technique, DEBUG is defined during the development and early test phases when errors are likely and performance is unimportant. Before final testing and product delivery, the source files are recompiled without DEBUG defined to remove the overhead of the signature checks.

Systematic Pointer Errors

The majority of pointer errors are not random. They result instead from a misunderstanding by the programmer. These systematic errors include improper arguments to functions, invalid casts, improper pointer arithmetic, and pointer aliasing. PC programmers must also learn to avoid an assortment of common segmentation errors.

The same signature fields so useful in finding random pointer problems also work against these more systematic pointer errors. However, familiarity with these problems can help the programmer avoid them.

Invalid Casts   C++ programmers are accustomed to casting a pointer from one type into another. In allowing a pointer cast to be made, the compiler assumes that the programmer has external knowledge. Suspending the strong typing rules limits the compiler's ability to protect the programmer from performing an illogical operation.

For example, there may not be enough room to accommodate the newly cast type as in the following:

```
void fn(int *pInt) {
    //...other code...
    *pInt = 0;
    //...function continues
}

void main() {
    char c;
    char anotherObject;

    fn(&c);                 //this is not allowed as the
                            //type is wrong
    fn((int*)&c);           //recasting the pointer
                            //removes the compiler
                            //error but the resulting
}                           //program is in error
```

The first call to `fn()` generates a compiler error since `char*` is not equal to `int*`, the expected argument type. The programmer's first instinct is to recast the pointer to the proper type. This is shown in the second call. Now, however, `fn()` writes an `int` into a space large enough to accommodate only a `char`. Depending upon the size of a `char` and the way auto variables are allocated, this may result in `anotherObject` being overwritten as well as `c`.

A variation of this bug occurs when passing pointer arguments to a non–type-safe function, such as `scanf()`. (A non–type-safe function is a function that has either no prototype or only an ellipsis prototype.) In the following code segment, it is obvious to the reader that the pointer `&arg` should be the address of a `float` and not an `int`, but there is no way for the compiler to detect this error.

```
//C I/O is not type-safe - this is a potentially fatal
//error
int arg;
scanf("%f", &arg);
```

Since it is type-safe, the iostream extractor avoids this problem.

```
//iostream I/O is type-safe
int arg;
cin >> arg;
```

The iostream inserters and extractors are so festidiously typesafe that the following problem can arise.

```
    void fn (unsigned char* pUString) {
        cout<< pUString<< endl
    }
```

C++ provides an inserter for chars; however, the default for chars is signed. Some environments, notably Borland C++, cannot use the signed char inserter or extractor on unsigned chars. (This is especially troublesome when selecting the Default chars to unsigned option.)

Problems of pointer alignment can also arise with improper pointer casts. The following moveBlock() function is intended to copy a block of data from one address to another. Rather than perform a byte-by-byte copy, however, the function copies an int at a time. Since an int is the "natural" word size of the base machine, this is almost certain to be more efficient.

```
//moveBlock - move a block of data from one location to
//            another. Transfer using long integers
//            to make the transfer faster.
void moveBlock(char* pTarget,
               char* pSource, int length) {

    //copy the majority of data in blocks of integers
    int lengthInInts = length / sizeof(int);
    int *pTI, *pSI;
```

```
        pTI = (int*)pTarget;
        pSI = (int*)pSource;
        for (int i = 0; i < lengthInInts; i++)
            *pTI++ = *pSI++;

        //copy whatever remains as characters
        int remainder = length % sizeof(int);
        pTarget = (char*)pTI;      //resume where left off
        pSource = (char*)pSI;
        for (i = 0; i < remainder; i++)
            *pTarget++ = *pSource++;
};
```

This function compiles without error, and on some machines, including the PC, it executes properly, but on many machines it does not work. The arguments pSource and pTarget are aligned to a char boundary that typically means byte alignment. Many CPUs (most notably some 680x0 processors) cannot perform word transfers if either the source or target address is not word-aligned.

Suppose that the function is passed a value of 0x4231 for pSource. This is a legal value for a char* but not for an int* on these architectures. Attempts to perform a word transfer using a non–word-aligned pointer generate a trap that the O/S uses to terminate the program. The 80x86 family of processors can perform nonaligned transfers, but at a slower rate.

Therefore, the moveBlock() function should first align the source and target pointers, if possible. The following version of the same function transfers data using char* until both addresses are int aligned. If they cannot both be int aligned simultaneously, the function attempts short int alignment. If that, too, is impossible, it continues with char alignment.

```
//moveBlock - transfer a block of data using the most
//            efficient pointer type possible
            void moveBlock(char* pTarget,
            char* pSource, int length) {
    int i;

    //check to see if source and target are both on int
    //alignment
    int target = (int)pTarget;
    int source = (int)pSource;
```

```
target %= sizeof(int);
source %= sizeof(int);
if (target == source) {
    //copy until pointers are int aligned
    for (i = 0; i < target; i++)
        *pTarget++ = *pSource++;
    length -= target;

    //copy the majority of data in blocks of ints
    int lengthInInts = length / sizeof(int);
    int *pTI, *pSI;

    pTI = (int*)pTarget;
    pSI = (int*)pSource;
    for (i = 0; i < lengthInInts; i++)
        *pTI++ = *pSI++;
    length -= sizeof(int) * lengthInInts;

    pTarget = (char*)pTI;
    pSource = (char*)pSI;
} else {

    //int alignment didn't work, try short int
    target %= sizeof(short);
    source %= sizeof(short);
    if (target == source) {
        //copy until pointers are short aligned
        for (i = 0; i < target; i++)
            *pTarget++ = *pSource++;
        length -= target;

        //copy the majority of data in blocks of ints
        int lengthInShorts =length/sizeof(short);
        int *pTS, *pSS;

        pTS = (int*)pTarget;
        pSS = (int*)pSource;
        for (i = 0; i < lengthInShorts; i++)
            *pTS++ = *pSS++;
        length -= sizeof(short) * lengthInShorts;
```

```
                   pTarget = (char*)pTS;
                   pSource = (char*)pSS;
          }
     }

     //copy whatever remains using character pointers
     for (i = 0; i < length; i++)
          *pTarget++ = *pSource++;
};
```

Some CPUs have other pointer restrictions as well. For example, on some older machines the format of a byte pointer is different from that of a word or double word. (This is true of old Hewlett-Packard, IBM 360 class, and Gould equipment, to name a few.) On these machines, alignment problems such as the one presented here are not caught by a CPU trap, but generate unpredictable results.

When assigning one pointer type to another, the `const`-ness or `volatile`-ness of the pointer must be considered as well. Tossing away a restriction upon a type without an explicit cast is prohibited. Thus, in the following segment the first assignment is legal but the second is not since it results in the `const`-ness being lost. The third assignment is legal since it contains the explicit cast.

```
int i;
int *pInt = &i;
int const *pConstInt;

pConstInt = pInt;            //#1
pInt      = pConstInt;       //#2
pInt      = (int*)pConstInt; //#3
```

Finally, casting pointer types can cause conversion problems. Casting an `int` into a `char` or a `float` allows the compiler to make the necessary conversions to generate a proper result. When a pointer type is recast, however, no conversion is performed on the target object. This can be useful, but it can also lead to unpredictable results. Consider the following example:

```
short int i = 0x1234;
char *pC = (char*)&i;
```

Assuming that a `short` is 16 bits wide and that a `char` is 8 bits wide, `*pC` might be equal to either `0x12` or `0x34`. Integers may be stored in either of the two methods shown in Figure 6–1.

Those CPUs in which `*pC` is equal to `0x12` have what is called **Big Endian** architecture since the front end of the integer is the more significant byte. (This is also known as **High Byte–Low Byte** architecture.) These machines include the 68000 and the IBM 360/370 processors. Those in which `*pC` is equal to `0x34` have a **Little Endian** or **Low Byte– High Byte** architecture. These include the 80x86 and the VAX family of processors.

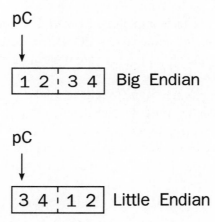

Figure 6–1. Possible internal organizations of a short integer

If we extend this problem to larger data types, the problem worsens.

```
long l = 0x12345678;
char *pC = (char*)&l;
```

Does `pC` now point at the character `0x12`, `0x34`, `0x56` or `0x78`? All four are possible, as shown in Figure 6–2. The programmer must be careful about any assumptions made concerning the layout of bytes in memory when casting from one pointer type to another. The practice should be avoided completely if portability is a concern.

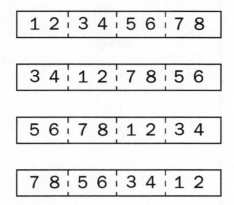

Figure 6–2. Possible internal organizations of a long integer

Pointer Arithmetic   Pointer arithmetic is another area of confusion with C++ programmers. All high-level languages provide some type of array construct, the individual members of which are accessed by indexing into the array with an integer index. The member is accessed by adding the index to the address of the array as follows:

```
char array[10], i;

array[i] <= is equivalent to => *(array + i)
```

Thus, both `array[2]` and `*(array + 2)` refer to the second element in `array`. (both refer to the `char` that is two bytes offset from the beginning `array`.) In Figure 6–3 you can see why this is the case.

In order for this equivalence to hold for types other than `char` arrays, addition to a pointer must be defined in terms of the size of the thing pointed at. If `array` were of type `int[]`, then `array + 2` should point to the `int` four bytes into the array. For a class `MyClass` defined below, `array[2]` might refer to the `MyClass` object some 20 bytes offset. In the general case, `array + i` refers to the object `i * sizeof(type of array)` bytes from the beginning of the array, as shown in Figure 6–4.

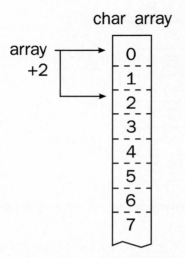

Figure 6–3. Indexing into a `char` array

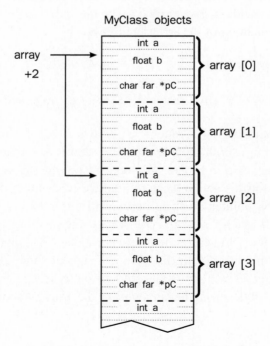

Figure 6–4. Indexing into a MyClass array

```
struct MyClass {
    int a;
    float b;
    char far* pC;
};
MyClass array[10];
```

Programmers occasionally forget this and create functions such as the following:

```
//setFlag - set the specified flag at the specified
            byte offset
//          in the data set
void setFlag(int* pData, unsigned byteOffset,
            int flag) {
    *(pData + byteOffset) |= flag;
}
```

The comment indicates that the programmer is attempting to set a flag at the byte offset specified by `byteOffset`. However, the flag is actually set at the byte offset `byteOffset * sizeof(int)` which is two or four times as far into the array as the programmer intended.

In addition, programmers are occasionally confused when a compiler error is returned on the following:

```
void setFlag(void* pData, unsigned byteOffset,
                int flag) {
    *(pData + byteOffset) |= flag; //now generates an
error
}
```

Since the function does not know what type of pointer it is to receive, the programmer has decided to declare `pData` to be of type `void*`. However, this also denies the compiler of the size information (`sizeof(void)` is not legal, so the addition is no longer allowed.

Operators related to addition, such as subtraction and equality, are also defined on pointer types. For example, the following `if` statement is true if the two pointers have identical numerical value.

```
void fn(int *pA, int *pB) {
    if (pA == pB) {
        //...true if pA is numerically equal to pB
    }
}
```

This can cause confusion in constructs such as the following.

```
void fn(char *pCommand) {
    //if command is RUN...
    if (pCommand == "RUN") {
        //...execute RUN code
    }
}
```

Here the programmer is attempting to compare the string pointed at by `pCommand` with the string `RUN`. However, the above `if` statement actually asks whether the value of `pCommand` is numerically equivalent to the address of the string "RUN". The answer to this question will always be no, irrespective of the contents of the string `*pCommand`. The correct function appears as follows.

```
#include <strings.h>
void fn(char *pCommand) {
    //if command is RUN...
    if (strcmp(pCommand, "RUN") == 0) {
        //...execute RUN code
    }
}
```

The function `strcmp()` compares the contents of the two strings passed to it. If they are found to be equal, it returns a zero.

Pointers may be subtracted from one another if they are of exactly the same type. The result is an integer that has been scaled down by the size of the thing pointed at by the pointer.

```
void fn() {
    int buffer[10];
    int delta;
    delta = &buffer[9] - &buffer[0];      //answer is 9
}
```

This makes pointer subtraction the inverse of pointer addition in the following sense:

```
given:
    Type *pA, *pB;
    int c;
```

```
if:
    pB = pA + c;
```

```
then:
    pB - pA is equivalent to c for all types Type
```

Since subtraction is defined in terms of the thing pointed at, addresses of type `void*` cannot be subtracted from one another.

Confusing a Pointer with an Array　　In many respects an array is like a pointer. The preceding address calculations demonstrate one way in which they are similar. In many C and some C++ books, the following equivalence is drawn:

```
Type arrayT[10];      //where 'Type' can be any type
Type *pT;
```

```
arrayT  <= is equivalent to => pT
```

This illusion of equivalence is heightened by the fact that C++ allows both of the following constructs, although they have different effects.

```
void fn() {
    char arrayC[20] = "this is a string";
    char *pC        = "this is a string";
}
```

The first line creates a 20-character array on the stack and initializes the first 17 characters with the array when the function is called. The second line creates a string in static memory at compile time. It allocates a pointer when the function is called and stores the address of this string into the pointer.

A pointer to an object and an array of objects differ in two fundamental ways, both of which can cause errors that are difficult to debug. First, `pT` is an lvalue, whereas `arrayT` is not. Thus, in the following example line 1 is correct, but line 2 is not.

```
Type t;
pT      = &t;          //#1
arrayT = &t;           //#2
```

This incompatibility creates a bug when the same global entity is declared differently in each of two modules, as in the following:

```
//in MODULEA.C
Type arrayT[20];

//in MODULEB.C
extern Type *arrayT;

for (int i = 0; i < 20; i++)
    arrayT[i] = new T;
```

Although the usage in MODULEB appears compatible with the declaration in MODULEA.C, the `extern` declaration is not identical. The function generates no compiler warnings, but it does not execute properly.

Second, `arrayT` allocates space for data objects, while `pT` does not. Until `pT` is assigned the address of an object, `*pT` is not a valid object. Memory for the two cases is represented in Figure 6–5.

The effect of this is shown in constructs such as the following:

```
char  arrayC[20];
char *pC;
strcpy(arrayC, "fileName");   //this line works ok
strcpy(pC, "fileName");       //this does not
```

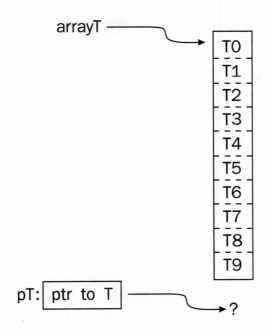

Figure 6–5. Memory comparison of `arrayT` **and** `pT`

Although the compiler does not complain, `pC` has not been assigned the address of a valid character string. The call to `strcpy()` generates unpredictable results, as the string is copied into a random location.

One final difference lies with inherited base classes. A pointer to a subclass can be used in place of a pointer to a superclass. However, an array of subclass objects cannot be passed to a function that expects an array of base class objects.

```
struct Base {
    int a;
    int b;
};
struct Derived : public Base {
    int c;
};

void clear(Base *pB, int index) {
    //vector into the array of objects
    pB[index].a = 0;
```

```
        pB[index].b = 0;
}

void main() {
    Derived d[10];

    for (int i = 0; i < 10; i++)
        clear(d, i);
}
```

In the function `clear()`, indexing is performed based on the size of an object of class `Base`. Since `Derived` is larger, `pB[index]` does not point to the beginning of a `Derived` object for any index except 0. No compiler warning is generated because the `Derived*` is compatible with `Base*`.

Pointers and Multidimensional Arrays   In general, the confusion between pointers and arrays increases as the number of dimensions increases. When passing a multidimensional array to a function, the beginning programmer is likely to produce the following:

```
void clear(int **ppMatrix, int, int);

void main() {
    int matrix[2][4];
    matrix[1][2] = 0;    //this calculates an offset
                         //from both inidices as
                         //in the following:
                         //*(matrix + 1 * 4 + 2)
    clear(matrix, 1, 2);
}

void clear(int **ppMatrix, int i, int j) {
    ppMatrix[i][j] = 0;  //line #4
                         //this is equivalent to:
                         //   *(*(ppMatrix + i) + j)
}
```

Although no compiler error is generated, `clear()` lacks the necessary size information to calculate correctly the position of `matrix[i][j]`. In fact, the foregoing comment shows the actual interpretation of line 4. The function `clear()` does not work as expected. Attempts to correct the problem by declaring `clear()` as follows do not help.

```
void clear(int *pMatrix[2], int i, int j) {
    pMatrix[i][j] = 0;    //line #1
}
```

Now `pMatrix` is an array of pointers to `ints`. Line 1 in this example has the identical effect as line 4 in the previous example. The proper solution is as follows:

```
void clear(int (*pMatrix)[2][4], int i, int j) {
    (*pMatrix)[i][j] = 0; // == *(pMatrix + i * 4 + j)
}
```

This declares a pointer to a 2x4 matrix of integers. (Notice the presence of the complete size information.) Indexing into the matrix now performs the desired multiplication rather than pointer indirection.

Aliasing Pointer and reference variables introduce another source of error to both the C++ programmer and the compiler, that of aliases. An **alias** arises when a pointer refers to an object that is already known by another name. Aliases appear often in C++ programs such as the following:

```
void fn() {
    char buffer[80];

    //first clear the buffer
    char *pC = buffer;
    for (int i = 0; i < 79; i++) {
        *pC++ = '\0';
    }
    //...and so on...
}
```

Here `*pC` is an alias for `buffer`. This type of alias causes the programmer few problems as the correspondence is clear.

Aliases also arise when programmers define references or pointers to objects to avoid calculating the object's address repeatedly.

```
struct Name {
    char first[40];
    char middle[10];
    char last[40];
    char title[8];
};
struct Person {
    int   age;
    Name name;
};
void fn(Person people[], int index) {
    //it is more efficient to define an alias for the
    //specific object rather than recalculate the
    //address each time
    Name& person = people[index].name;
    getName(person.first, person.middle, person.last);

    //...much later on
    //will programmer remember that person and
    //people[index] refer to the same object?
}
```

This type of alias causes problems if the programmer continues to use both the alias and the original name throughout the program. A good rule of thumb is to use only the alias, once it has been defined. If the alias is only needed in a small area, then its scope should be limited so that it cannot be used outside of that area, as in the following example:

```
for (int index = 0; index < 10; index++) {
    Name *pPerson = &people[index].name;
    getName(pPerson->first, pPerson->middle,
            pPerson->last);
}
```

is preferable to

```
Name *pPerson = &people[index].name;
for (int index = 0; index < 10; index++) {
    getName(pPerson->first, pPerson->middle,
            pPerson->last);
}
```

because the scope of the alias variable pPerson is limited to the for loop in which it is used.

Aliases can be much more subtle, as in the following:

```
include <string.h>
char globalBuffer[80];

//prePendDirectory - prepend the directory name to the
//                   given filename. Copy the result
//                   back into the filename buffer.
void prePendDirectory(char *pFileName,
                      char *pDirectory) {
    strcpy(globalBuffer, pDirectory);   //line #1
    strcat(globalBuffer, pFileName);    //line #2
    strcpy(pFileName, globalBuffer);    //line #3
}
```

This function prepends a directory name onto a file name. This code segment seems simple enough that it should work without problems and, in fact, most of the time it does. However, examine its use in the following:

```
#include <fstream.h>
extern char globalBuffer[];

//openInputFile - get filename, prepend directory and
//                open it. Return file handle
ifstream& openInputFile(char *pDirectory) {
    //open the file - use globalBuffer to store the
    //name since we only need it for a few lines
    cout << "Enter filename:";
    cin  >> globalBuffer;
```

```
    prePendDirectory(globalBuffer, pDirectory);
    ifstream& inputFile = *new ifstream(globalBuffer);
    return inputFile;
}
```

Here the function `openInputFile()` is already using the variable `globalBuffer` to hold the input file name. When passed to `prePendDirectory()`, the pointer `pFileName` becomes an alias to `globalBuffer`. Within `prePendDirectory()`, the source and destination refer to the same buffer and the program crashes.

Such alias-induced problems are difficult to detect. They can best be avoided by

1. limiting the scope of alias pointers and references to where they are actually used
2. using only the alias name once it has been defined, and
3. documenting any side effects a function might have.

Aliases can cause compilers confusion as well. Consider the following simplistic example.

```
void fn(int double) {
    int i, j;
    int *pI = &i;

    i = 10;              //assignment #1
    if (double) {
        *pI = 20;        //assignment #2
    }
    j = 2 * i;           //assignment #3
    //...function continues
}
```

Here `*pI` is established as an alias for the integer `i`. The programmer first stores the value 10 into `i`; if the argument `double` is set, this value is replaced with a 20. By referring to the object via the alias the second time, the compiler does not make the connection between assignment 1 and assignment 2.

The problem arises if the compiler retains the 10 used in assignment 1 to be used in assignment 3. Compilers do this to reduce the number of machine instructions. In this case, the value of `i` is no longer 10, but the compiler does not recognize this. This optimization is part of a technique known as register optimization.

Compilers use many different algorithms to avoid this type of problem. One algorithm assumes that pointer aliasing is always a possibility and always reloads values after referencing through a pointer. This avoids the problem but reduces performance when it generally is not necessary.

A less drastic solution is to assume that aliasing is a potential problem only with those subexpressions involving a variable whose address has been taken. Other techniques can avoid the problem most of the time, but one can still imagine scenarios in which aliasing is possible.

Aliasing problems resemble those involving register optimizations around `setjmp()` calls: when examined with the debugger, a variable has the proper value. In use, however, the variable seems to have an earlier value. A suspected aliasing problem can be confirmed if disabling optimization appears to solve the problem.

The programmer can avoid compiler aliasing problems by being careful not to refer to the same object via different aliases within the same function. When this cannot be avoided, declare `volatile` any variables that are referred to from different aliases.

Class Pointers

Pointers to class objects have the same problems as simple pointer types. This section examines pointer errors unique to class objects. Many of these problems involve casting pointers from one class to another.

Recasting Class Pointers

No language that allows pointer variables to be recast from one type to another can be said to support encapsulation in the strictest sense. Consider the following:

```
//contained in an include file
class MyClass {
  private:
    int a;
    int b;
```

```
  public:
    MyClass();
    int accessData();
};

//equivalent class defined locally with all
//members declared public
class NoClass {
  public:

    int a;
    int b;

    NoClass();
    int accessData();
};
void aFunc(MyClass *pObj) {
    NoClass pNCObj = (NoClass*)pObj;
    pNCObj->a = 1;  //accessing "private" members...
    pNCObj->b = 2;  //...generates no compiler errors
};
```

By recasting the address of the `MyClass` object into a pointer to an object of type `NoClass`, the programmer has obtained access to the `MyClass` object's private members. As C++ does not preclude this, code reviewers should be on the lookout for such antisocial behavior. Such shenanigans must not be allowed to remain in the final product.

There are, of course, legitimate reasons to recast a pointer from one class to another. Every time a virtual base function is invoked, for example, `this` is recast into the base class. Consider the following code segment:

```
class Base {
  public:
    virtual void method();
};
void Base::method() {
    //this is of type Base*
}
```

```
class Derived : public Base {
};

void fn();
    Derived derived;

    derived.method();      //derived is recast into Base*
                           //when passed to
                           //Base::method()
}
```

Although not particularly good style, the following code sample demonstrates one way to cast from one subclass to the other.

```
class Base {
  public:
    int type;          //indicates the actual type
    void *pOtherInformation;
};

class Type0 : public Base {
  public:
    void *pType0Info;

    Type0() {type = 0;}
};

class Type1 : public Base {
  public:
    void *pType1Info;

    Type1() {type = 1;}
};

class Type2 : public Base {
  public:
    void *pType2Info;

    Type2() {type = 2;}
```

```
};

void fn(Base *pObject) {

    //process pObject according to its actual type
    switch (pObject->type) {
      case 0:processType0((Type0*)pObject);
            break;
      case 1:processType1((Type1*)pObject);
            break;
      case 2:processType2((Type2*)pObject);
            break;
    }
}
```

Although declared `Base*`, it is clear that `pObject` actually points to one of the subclasses of `Base`. Which one is indicated by the value of `type`. Here `fn()` uses this information to recast the declared (or static) type to match the dynamic type. The programmer cannot recast a pointer to an actual base class object into a pointer to a subclass, as the following example demonstrates.

```
class Base {
  public:
    int a;
    virtual int f1();
};
class Derived : public Base {
  public:
    int b;
    virtual int f2();
};
void main() {
    Base base, *pB;
    Derived derived, *pD;

    pB = &derived;          //#1 - no problem
    pD = &base;             //#2 - illegal without a cast
```

```
    pD = (Derived*)&base;//#3 - legal but dangerous...
    pD->b = 10;             //...and here's why
    pD->f2();
}
```

Assignment 1 is allowed without a cast because `derived` is a member of a publicly derived subclass of `Base` — thus a `derived` is a `Base`. Assignment 2 is not allowed, however, since a `base` is not a `Derived`.

C++ allows the assignment to be made with an explicit cast in assignment 3, but at considerable peril since the next two statements access members of `Derived` that `base` does not have.

A privately derived class is not a subclass either.

```
class Base {
    int a;
    virtual int f1();
};
class Derived : private Base {
};

void main() {
    Base *pB;
    Derived derived;

    pB = &derived;          //illegal without cast

    pB = (Base*)&derived;//legal with cast; however,
    pB->f1();               //'derived' should not provide
                            //access to the members of
                            //Base
}
```

The first assignment is rejected with a compiler error. The second assignment with a cast is allowed; however, the user now has access to members through an object in which those objects are `private`. (In fact, it is not clear the `vtble` for `derived` does include `f1()`.)

Casting from a Class to a Subclass So far the discussion has covered cases in which recasting the pointer changed only its type. Recasting a pointer from a class to a subclass or back can change its value as well. Consider the following:

```
class BaseA {
  public:
    int i;
    int j;

    void aFn();
};


class BaseB {
  public:
    int k;
    int l;

    void bFn();
};


class SubClass : public BaseA, public BaseB {
  public:
    int m;

    void scFn();
};
```

The memory layout of an object of class `SubClass` is shown in Figure 6–6. The base class `BaseA` occupies the first two words of memory, followed by the base class `BaseB`, and then the data member unique to `Sub-Class`, member `m`.

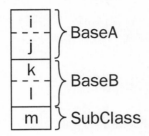

Figure 6–6. Memory layout of an object of class `SubClass`

The pointer `pSC` in the following code segment points to both the object `obj` of class `SubClass` as well as its `BaseA` portion of that object. It does not point to the `BaseB` portion of `obj`.

```
SubClass obj;
SubClass *pSC = &obj;;
```

You can see why this is of concern by considering what calls to the member functions `BaseA::aFn()` and `BaseB::bFn()` look like.

```
SubClass obj;

obj.aFn();            //no problem here
obj.bFn();            //here we may have a problem
```

Both of these functions receive a pointer to the current object, in this case `&obj`. `BaseB::bFn()` expects to receive the address of an object of class `BaseB`, which `&obj` is not.

To make both of the preceding calls work properly, C++ changes the value of the pointer when casting from a subclass to a base class by adding the offset of the base class within the subclass. Thus, in the following cast the pointer is moved down by the size of `BaseA` so that it points to the `BaseB` section of `obj` as shown in Figure 6–7.

```
SubClass *pSC = &obj;
BaseB *pBB;

pBB = (BaseB*)pSC;    //offset applied by cast
```

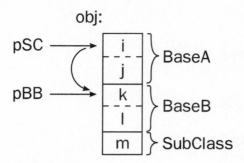

Figure 6–7. Casting from `SubClass*` **to** `BaseB*` **requires the addition of an offset**

The same adjustment is applied to the cast implicit in the previous call to `BaseB::bFn()`.

This addition of offsets to the address can cause confusion in two instances. First, by definition the `NULL` pointer does not point to an object, so the offset cannot be applied to it. Thus, the value of `pBB` in the following code segment remains zero despite is outward similarity to the preceding example.

```
SubClass *pSC = (SubClass*)0;
BaseB *pBB;
pBB = (BaseB*)pSC;   //no offset applied in this case
```

Second, a problem can also arise if the compiler cannot discern which subclass to select, as in the following:

```
class Base {
  public:
    int a;

    void baseFn();
};

class Path1 : public Base {
  public:
    int b;
};
```

```
class Path2 : public Base {
  public:
    int c;
};

class SubClass : public Path1, public Path2 {
  public:
    int d;
};
void fn() {
    SubClass obj;
    SubClass *pSC = &obj;
    Base  *pB;

    pB = (Base*)pSC;        //which Base class object?
    pSC->baseFn();          //these two calls illegal...
    obj.baseFn();           //...as well
}
```

Here the class `SubClass` inherits the base class `Base` twice, once in the base class `Path1` and again in the base class `Path2`. Thus, the cast from `pSC` to `pB` is ambiguous and the statement generates a compiler error. The two calls to the method `Base::baseFn()` are illegal for the same reason.

The ambiguity can be avoided by instructing the compiler as to which `Base` object to use. This is done by first casting the `SubClass` pointer into either a `Path1` or a `Path2` pointer or by explicitly specifying the subclass as follows:

```
void fn() {
    SubClass obj;
    SubClass *pSC = &obj;
    Base  *pB;

    //the following refer to Path1::Base
    pB = (Base*)(Path1*)pSC;  //no longer ambiguous
    ((Path1*)pSC)->baseFn();  //ditto
    obj.Path1::baseFn();      //here we use a
                              //different way
```

```
//these refer to Path2::Base
pB = (Base*)(Path2*)pSC;
((Path2*)pSC)->baseFn();
obj.Path2::baseFn();
}
```

Notice that if the base class is virtually inherited, then there is only a single `Base` class object in `SubClass` and the ambiguity does not arise.

The programmer must be very careful because the compiler does not generate any indication that the adjustment is (or is not) being performed when the pointer is recast.

Invalid Pointers to Class Objects

Using a class pointer that contains invalid data has the same general effect as using any other invalid pointer. In a few cases this is not true, however.

Since static members do not belong to any single object, they can be accessed successfully even with an invalid pointer. Consider the following:

```
class MyClass {
  public:
    static int classMember;
           int objMember;
};

void fn() {
    MyClass *pMC;
    pMC->classMember = 0;       //this access is valid
    pMC->objMember = 1;         //this access is invalid
}
```

The pointer `pMC` is not assigned a value. The member `pMC->objMember` is not set to 1, as one would expect. Surprisingly `classMember` is successfully assigned a 0 value since only the type of `pMC` is used in this case.

The situation regarding function members is similar.

```
class MyClass {
  public:
    int   data;

    static  void fn1();
            void fn2();
    virtual void fn3();
};
void MyClass::fn1() {
}
void MyClass::fn2() {
    data = 2;        //assignment #1
}
void MyClass::fn3() {
    data = 3;        //assignment #2
}

void fn() {
    MyClass *pMC;

    pMC->fn1();      //fn called successfully
    pMC->fn2();      //fn called by with invalid 'this'
    pMC->fn3();      //fn not called successfully
}
```

Here again the pointer pMC has an invalid value. Nevertheless, the call
of fn1() is successful. Static functions have no this pointer and so are
unaware that the address of the object is invalid. The call to fn2() is successful, but the this pointer passed to the function is invalid. Using the
invalid pointer, fn2() calculates an equally invalid address this->data
at assignment 1 generating the same unpredictable results one would
expect from addressing through any other invalid pointer.

The call to fn3() is not successful, however. Calls to virtual functions
are performed indirectly through a table called the vtble (pronounced
"vee-table"). Each object contains a pointer to the vtble for that object's
class. To see how this works, consider the two classes that follow:

```
class MC1 {
    int someData;

  public:
```

```
        virtual void fn1();
                void fn2();
        virtual void fn3();
        virtual void fn4();
};
class MC2 : public MC1 {
    int more Data;

  public:
    virtual void fn3();
    virtual void fn5();
};
```

The appearance of two objects of class MC1 and MC2 in memory is shown in Figure 6–8. Each has a pointer to a different vtble. These tables contain pointers to each of the virtual methods of the class — the function MC1::fn2() is not virtual and hence does not appear in the table. MC2::vtble points to the same functions as MC1::vtble except for fn3(), which is overloaded in the subclass and fn5(), which is unique to MC2.

A call to function fn3(), for example, is made by retrieving the vtble address from the object and then jumping indirectly through the address at offset 1 in that table. If the object address is faulty, the program will pick up a nonsensical vtble address and jump indirectly to some random location.

This problem can be particularly perplexing to debug. Even single-stepping the call does not help. The program crashes immediately without any indication as to the cause. This problem can be confirmed in two ways during debugging. First, determine whether the program even reaches the function either by single-stepping the call or setting a breakpoint at the beginning of the function. If it does not and the function is declared virtual, remove the virtual declaration and repeat the experiment. (Remember, a function is still virtual if it is declared virtual in a base class whether explicitly declared virtual or not. Without the virtual declaration the program may not call the same function.) If the program now reaches the function but with a bad this pointer, then the problem is confirmed. If it gets to the function with a correct this pointer, then suspect that something is overwriting the vtble.

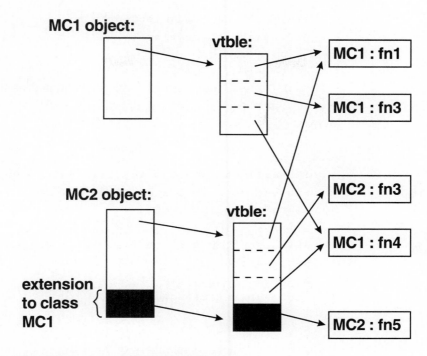

Figure 6–8. `vtble` **and virtual methods**

Signature checks are the most effective means of uncovering hard-to-find invalid pointer problems of all types. These checks can be added in a transparent fashion by overloading `operator->()` as well.

Member Pointers

Member pointers point to members of a class. Here I am not referring to a pointer such as the following:

```
class MyClass {
  public:
    int singleObject;
    int data[80];
};


void fn() {
    MyClass mcObj;
    int *pSObject= &mcObj.singleObject;
```

```
        int *pMOData = mcObject.data;
        //...function continues
}
```

Here `pSObject` and `pMOData` are conventional pointers that happen to point to members of a specific object. A member pointer is declared as follows:

```
void fn() {
    int MyClass::* pSO = &MyClass::singleObject;
    int (MyClass::* pData)[80];
    pData = &MyClass::data;

    //in use they must be tied to an object
    MyClass mcO;
    mcO.*pSO = 1;
    (mcO.*pData)[2] = 2;
}
```

These are pointers to members of an unspecified object. The actual object must be specified when the pointer is used. Pointers to nonstatic members are not compatible with conventional pointer types and cannot be made so until the member pointer is bound to an object.

```
void fn() {
    int MyClass::* pSO = &MyClass::singleObject;
    int *pInt;

    pInt = pSO;           //won't work
    pInt = (int*)pData;//won't work either
    MyClass mcO;
    pInt = &(mcO.*pSO);//this works as the address is now
                       //tied to the specific object mcO
}
```

A member pointer does not actually represent the address of an object, but rather the offset of that member within the class. The address of the member is not known until the offset is applied to the address in an object in that class.

Most errors involving member pointers relate to their sometimes confusing syntax. Such compile time errors are easily found, if not so easily fixed. Since a member pointer is similar to an index into an array, member pointer run-time errors resemble indexing problems, such as accessing offsets beyond the end of the object.

Pointers to Heap Memory

Heap memory is a powerful resource to the C++ programmer. The heap neatly solves the problem demonstrated by the following:

```
//parseDirectory - given a filename, parse out
//                 the first directory name
char* parseDirectory(char* pPathName) {
    int i;
    char dirName[80];
    int length = strlen(pPathName) + 1;

    //first copy the directory name into another buffer
    for (i = 0;
            pPathName[i] != '\\' && i < 80;
              length--, i++)
        dirName[i] = pPathName[i];
    dirName[79] = '\0';

    //now remove the directory name
    memmove(&pPathName[0], &pPathName[i], length);
    return dirName;
}
```

The problem with this function is that the object `dirName` goes out of scope with the return of the function and its memory is lost. Thus, the pointer returned by the function points to unallocated memory. One can solve this problem by using a buffer allocated globally. This introduces the reentrancy problem demonstrated by the following:

```
void fn(char *pSource, char *pTarget) {
    char* pSourceDir = parseDirectory(pSource);
    char* pTargetDir = parseDirectory(pTarget);
    //...function continues
}
```

The second call to `parseDirectory()` overwrites the global buffer before the contents stored there by the first call can be used. The solution is to allocate memory off the heap as follows:

```
//parseDirectory - given a filename, parse out
//                      the first directory name
char* parseDirectory(char* pPathName) {
    int i;
    char dirName[80];
    int length = strlen(pPathName) + 1;

    //allocate a buffer that is certainly long enough
    char *pDirName = new char[length];

    //first copy the directory name into another buffer
    for (i = 0; pPathName[i] != '\\'; length--, i++)
        pDirName[i] = pPathName[i];
    pDirName[i] = '\0';

    //now remove the directory name
    memmove(&pPathName[0], &pPathName[i], length);
    return pDirName;
}
```

Besides solving the scope/reentrancy problem, the heap solution does not suffer from any arbitrary buffer length limitations since the size of the buffer is determined at runtime. In the PC environment, the heap has one further advantage: `farmalloc()` can allocate blocks of memory larger than 64K. In fact, this is the only way to allocate such a block under DOS.

Of course, heap memory has its share of traps and pitfalls that the careful programmer should avoid. Heap errors fall into four classes as follows:

1. overrunning the end of a heap block
2. forgetting to return heap memory

3. returning heap memory more than once

4. using the heap block after it has been returned

Overrunning the end of heap memory is much like exceeding the bounds of a globally or auto allocated array. The programmer generally learns of the error when the next request for heap memory fails.

The next two problems stem from the programmer's responsibility to make sure that heap memory is returned properly. The language provides no help in this regard. Memory that is not returned properly is lost until the program terminates. Returning the same memory block twice corrupts the heap causing subsequent requests for heap memory to fail or, more likely, crash.

Detecting the fourth problem is easier if you always zero out a pointer to heap memory once the memory has been returned. Macros can help in this regard.

```
void fn() {
    MyClass *pMC = new MyClass;
    //...other stuff

    //release heap block and zero pointer
    delete pMC;
    pMC = 0;
}
```

The final three problems can be detected and avoided using a debugging tool known as a **heap wrapper**. The heap wrapper is a set of allocate and release functions that places information around the user-requested heap block. A well-written heap wrapper can

- detect most overrun problems
- detect and avoid multiple returns
- find lost blocks

A heap wrapper is strictly a debugging tool. Once the application is working satisfactorily, the heap wrapper should be removed. This can be handled easily by properly defining the appropriate macros. Many different heap wrappers can be used. My personal version is presented in the next section. (Some of the ideas on the wrapper were inspired by Robert Ward's article, "Debugging Instrumentation Wrapper for Heap Functions," in the *C Users Journal*.)

My Heap Wrapper

The principle behind a heap wrapper is simple: wrap the user data in an envelope of debugging information that the program can use to detect errors. This wrapper uses the data structure shown in Figure 6–9.

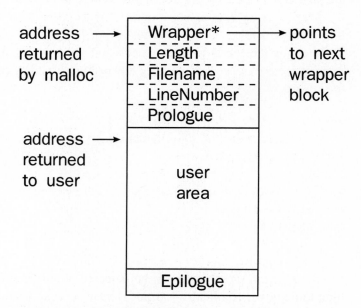

Figure 6–9. Memory layout of the heap wrapper

The first data item in the list is a pointer to the next allocated block. All blocks allocated by the heap wrapper are kept in a linked list. Blocks are removed from this list when freed. If during the freeing process the block is not found to be in the list, the block has probably already been released. Blocks remaining in the list when the program exits have never been released.

The second field contains the length of the user area. Next come the file name and line number of the call that allocated this block. Blocks not returned from the heap originate from a particular logic path. Knowing where these blocks are allocated will help determine the faulty path.

Finally, the last character before the user data and the first character after the user data are signature fields that can be used to detect buffer overruns. These fields are set to a unique value. When the wrapper is freed, these fields are checked to determine if they are still set at their original values. If not, then the application program has written outside of the prescribed buffer. It is possible for the application program to write outside of the buffer without overwriting either of the signature fields. The greater the number of signature characters, the more likely that an overrun will be detected; however, a larger string consumes more memory.

The following C++ module implements this wrapper.

```
#include <stdio.h>
#include <stdlib.h>
#include <alloc.h>
#include <string.h>

//Wrapper - the heap wrapper structure which we will
//          use to hold the prologue and epilogue
information
struct Wrapper {
    //prologue information
    Wrapper* pNext;
    int length;
    char fileName[8];
    unsigned lineNumber;
    char     prologue;
    int  :0;           //make sure user data falls
                       //on a word boundary
    //user data
    char data[1];

    //epilogue follows
};
Wrapper *pFirst = 0; //pointer to linked list of
                     //allocated blocks

//prototype declarations
```

```cpp
        static void werror(Wrapper*, char*, int = 0);
        //both new operators
        void* operator new(size_t);
        void* operator new(size_t, char* , int);
        void* allocateFn(size_t sizeBlock,
                         char *pFile, int lineNo);


        //and both delete operators
        void operator delete(void*);
        void operator delete(void*, size_t);
        void deleteFn(void*);
        void displayAllocated();


        //werror - display heap wrapper error message and quit
        static void werror(Wrapper *pBlock,
                           char *pErrorString, int fatal) {
            printf("Heap error: %s, Allocated: %s, %d\n",
                   pErrorString,
                   pBlock->fileName,
                   pBlock->lineNumber);
            if (fatal)
                exit(1);
        }


        //new - allocate a block from the heap and then tag on
        //      the debugging type, data information; return
        //      to the user the address of his data
        void* operator new(size_t sizeBlock,
                           char *pFile, int lineNo) {
            return allocateFn(sizeBlock, pFile, lineNo);
        }
        void* operator new(size_t sizeBlock) {
            return allocateFn(sizeBlock, "Unknown", 0);
        }
        void* allocateFn(size_t sizeBlock,
                         char *pFile, int lineNo) {
            Wrapper *pBlock;
            char    *pUserData;
```

```
        if (sizeBlock == 0)
            return (void*)0;
        else {
            //get a block from the heap
            pBlock = (Wrapper*)malloc(sizeBlock +
                                        sizeof(Wrapper));
            if (!pBlock) {
                return (void*)0;
            }

            //now fill in the data
            strncpy(pBlock->fileName, pFile, 7);
            pBlock->fileName[7] = '\0';
            pBlock->lineNumber = lineNo;
            pBlock->length = sizeBlock;

            //fill in the prologue and epilogue sections
            pBlock->prologue = 0x12;
            pUserData = pBlock->data;
            char *pEpilogue = pUserData + sizeBlock;
            *pEpilogue = 0x21;

            //and add it to the list
            pBlock->pNext = pFirst;
            pFirst = pBlock;
            //now return the user a pointer to his data
            return (void*)pUserData;
        }
    }

//delete - accept either form of delete function;
//         size information unnecessary
void operator delete(void *pUserData) {
    deleteFn(pUserData);
}
void operator delete(void *pUserData, size_t size) {
    deleteFn(pUserData);
}
```

```
//deleteFn - check out the heap block to make sure all
//           is kosher then remove it from the list
void deleteFn(void *pUserData) {
    //calculate the address of the original Wrapper
    //block
    int offset =  (int)&((Wrapper*)0)->data;
    //(offset is now the number of bytes the field
    //data is from the beginning of a Wrapper block)
    Wrapper *pBlock = (Wrapper*)((char*)pUserData -
                                offset);

    //check the prologue and epilogue
    if (pBlock->prologue != 0x12)
        werror(pBlock, "Prologue overwritten", 1);
    char *pEpilogue = (char*)pUserData +
                        pBlock->length;
    if (*pEpilogue != 0x21)
        werror(pBlock, "Epilogue overwritten", 1);

    //now unlink it from the list
    Wrapper *pWrapper = pFirst;
    int foundIt = 0;
    if (pWrapper == pBlock) {
        pFirst = pBlock->pNext;
        foundIt = 1;
    }
    else {
        while (pWrapper) {
            if (pWrapper->pNext == pBlock) {
                pWrapper->pNext = pBlock->pNext;
                foundIt = 1;
                break;
            }
            pWrapper = pWrapper->pNext;
        }
    }
    if (!foundIt) {
        werror(pBlock, "Block not in list;
                        //"released twice?");
```

```
    }

    //now free the block
    if (foundIt)
        free((void*)pBlock);
}


//displayAllocated - this function simply displays all
//                     of the heap blocks that
//                     are still "check out"
void displayAllocated() {
    Wrapper *pBlock;
    pBlock = pFirst;
    while (pBlock) {
        printf("%d bytes allocated at %s;%d\n",
                pBlock->length, pBlock->fileName,
                pBlock->lineNumber);
        pBlock = pBlock->pNext;
    }
}
```

The function `operator new()` overloads the global new operator. The first `operator new()` accepts the file name and line number from which the call was made. The second is provided in case the programmer forgets to supply this information.

The `allocateFn()` function uses `malloc()` to fetch a block off the heap and then fills in the prologue and epilogue information. Finally, the block is added to the linked list of allocated blocks. A pointer to the data buffer portion of the block is returned to the application. The zero length bit field declared in the `Wrapper` prologue ensures that this pointer will be on a word boundary.

The `deleteFn()` function first moves the pointer provided by the user back to the prologue information. If either the prologue or epilogue character is found to be overwritten, the program terminates with an error message. If these check out, the function attempts to find the block in the allocated linked list. If the block cannot be found, the function assumes that it has already been deleted. The function generates an error message and continues to the caller without freeing the block again.

Notice that a previously released block can fail the prologue and epilogue checks and, thus, generate a slightly misleading error message. Once a block has been returned to the heap, it can be picked up and used by other functions, thus destroying this information.

The `displayAllocated()` function loops through the blocks contained in the linked list and displays their saved information. In use, the functions resemble the following:

```
void fn() {
    MyClass *pMC = new (__FILE__, __LINE__)
                            MyClass(args);
    //...other stuff
    delete pMC; pMC = 0;
}
```

The intrinsics __FILE__ and __LINE__ are expanded by the preprocessor into the current source file and line number. Defining the following two macros can help with adding the file and line number information to all of the new calls.

```
#define NEW new(__FILE__, __LINE__)
#define DELETE(x) ((delete (x)),(x) = 0)
```

The NEW macro automatically provides the current line and file information. The DELETE macro deletes and then zeros the pointer as previously suggested. The example function now appears as follows:

```
void fn() {
    MyClass *pMC = NEW MyClass(args);
    //...other stuff
    DELETE(pMC);
}
```

Place the macro definitions in a universally included .H file during debugging. Replace the definitions with the following null definition after debugging.

```
#define NEW new
#define DELETE(x) ((delete (x)), (x) = 0)
```

Scheduling the `displayAllocated()` function to execute on program exit to display any remaining undeleted blocks may be helpful. Not deleting a block before exit is not an error in itself, as the exit function returns all heap memory to the system anyway. However, any unexplained blocks in the allocated list may indicate a memory loss problem. Functions can be called upon exit via the standard `atexit()` library function, as follows:

```
void main() {
    atexit(displayAllocated);

    //...other stuff
}   //displayAllocated executes here
```

Heap wrappers are valuable tools to find and remove heap-related errors easily.

Heap Pointers Within Classes

A class commonly contains pointers to heap memory. Besides the general heap problems already discussed, such classes suffer from two other common errors that the preceding heap wrapper is effective at uncovering. Both errors can be avoided by following the programming guidelines described here.

Consider the example class that follows:

```
class Name {
  private:
    char *pFirst;
    char  mI;
    char *pLast;

  public:
    Name(char *pL, char *pF = 0, char initial = '\0');
};
```

The constructor for `Name` allocates memory for the first and last names off of the heap as follows:

```
Name::Name(char *pL, char *pF, char initial) {
    pLast = pFirst = (char*)0;
    mI = initial;
    pLast = new char[strlen(pL) + 1];
    if (!pLast)
        return;
    strcpy(pLast, pL);
    if (pF) {
        pFirst = new char[strlen(pF) + 1];
        if (!pFirst)
            return;
        strcpy(pFirst, pF);
    }
}
```

If this class relied upon the default destructor, the memory allocated by the constructor would not be returned to the heap when the object was destructed. Therefore, any class that contains pointers to heap memory must have a destructor that returns memory to the heap.

A destructor for Name appears as follows:

```
Name::~Name() {
    if (pLast) {              //if there is a heap block...
        delete pLast;        //...return it
        pLast = (char*)0;
    }
    if (pFirst) {            //same applies here
        delete pFirst;
        pFirst = (char*)0;
    }
}
```

The reverse problem occurs if the class is not provided with a copy-initializer constructor and assignment operator. Remember, these methods are invoked when it is necessary to copy the object, as in the following:

```
void anotherFn(Name);

void fn() {
```

```
    Name srd("Davis", "Stephen", 'R');
    Name alterEgo = srd;        //invokes c-i constructor

    anotherFn(srd);             //uses c-i constructor to
                                //build copy on stack for
                                //anotherFn()
    Name suspect("???");
    if (iAmGuilty)
        suspect = srd;          //uses op=() to overwrite
                                //suspect with srd
}
```

The default c-i constructor and `operator=()` provided by C++ provide a shallow copy, member-by-member copy, from the source to the destination. When the class contains pointers to heap memory, these defaults are not correct.

Consider the declaration of `alterEgo`. Using the default c-i constructor both `alterEgo.pLast` and `srd.pLast` point to the same memory block. When `srd` is subsequently destructed this memory block will be returned, but when `alterEgo` is destructed this same block will be returned again.

A similar problem arises with the assignment operator. Not only is `srd.pLast` deleted twice, the original `suspect.pLast` pointer is overwritten and that block is lost. Thus, any class containing pointers to heap memory must have a copy-initializer constructor and assignment operator that perform a deep copy. The definition for the entire class, including the c-i constructor and assignment operator, appears as follows:

```
class Name {
  private:
    char *pFirst;
    char  mI;
    char *pLast;

    //functions to create and delete an object
    void  copyTo(char*, char*, char);
    void  deleteFrom();

  public:
    Name(char *pL, char *pF = 0, char initial = '\0') {
```

```
            copyTo(pL, pF, initial);
    }
  ~Name() {
        deleteFrom();
    }

    Name(Name& n) {
        copyTo(n.pLast, n.pFirst, n.mI);
    }
    Name& operator=(Name& n) {
        deleteFrom();              //delete the original...
        copyTo(n.pLast, n.pFirst, n.mI);
                                   //...before copying
        return *this;
    }
};

void Name::copyTo(char *pL, char *pF, char initial) {
    pLast = pFirst = (char*)0;
    mI = initial;
    pLast = NEW char[strlen(pL) + 1];
    if (!pLast)
        return;
    strcpy(pLast, pL);
    if (pF) {
        pFirst = NEW char[strlen(pF) + 1];
        if (!pFirst)
            return;
        strcpy(pFirst, pF);
    }
}
void Name::deleteFrom() {
    if (pLast) {
        DELETE(pLast);
    }
    if (pFirst) {
        DELETE(pFirst);
    }
}
```

Defining the two private methods `copyTo()` and `deleteFrom()` to perform the actual construction and destruction removes any duplication of code between methods.

Linked Lists

Linked lists are a powerful member of the C++ programmer's toolbox. Unlike simple arrays, linked lists can grow and shrink as required. In addition, linked lists can be combined into hierarchical structures to describe the relationships between classes.

Linked lists are subject to the same types of problems that affect other pointers. In addition, linked lists suffer from a few unique problems. For example, the following function is deceptively simple, but wrong.

```
//freeList - free linked list of heap blocks
void freeList(MyClass *pFirst) {
    MyClass *pMCObj;
    for (pMCObj = pFirst; pMCObj;
                        pMCObj = pMCObj->pNext)
        delete pMCObj;
}
```

Here the function attempts to use the object after it has been deleted. The corrected function appears as follows:

```
//freeList - free linked list of heap blocks
void freeList(MyClass *pFirst) {
    MyClass *pMCObj;
    MyClass *pMCNext;
    for (pMCObj = pFirst; pMCObj; pMCObj = pMCNext) {
        pMCNext = pMCObj->next();//get next pointer first
        delete pMCObj;                 //then delete object
    }
}
```

Other problems include lists that vector to nowhere or loops with unintended cycles in them that appear to go on forever. Linked list problems appear daunting to the beginner. The program generates either absolute gibberish or mysteriously goes silent as it sits in an infinite loop.

Fortunately linked list problems are relatively easy to identify. For example, the DELETE() macro presented in the previous section would have revealed the foregoing problem immediately by causing the pMCObj = pMCObj->pNext expression to fail.

The most powerful tool in finding problems in linked lists is the signature check presented earlier. An incorrect next pointer in a linked list usually points to a non-object. Non-objects do not have valid signatures. The preceding program with a signature check appears as follows:

```
//signatureError - display error message along with
//                 critical information to error log
int signatureError(MyClass *p,
                   char *pFileName, int lineNo){
    cerr << "Signature error on object "
         << (void*)p
         << ", Problem discovered on line "
         << lineNo
         << ", file "
         << pFileName
         << endl;
    exit(1);        //terminate on error
    return 1;       //this will never be executed
}


//following macro invokes the function errorHandler()
//if p->signature is not correct
#define CHECKSIGNATURE(p) \
    (p)->signature != MCSIGNATURE && \
    signatureError((p), __FILE__, __LINE__)

//freeList - free linked list of heap blocks
void freeList(MyClass *pFirst) {
    MyClass *pMCObj;
    MyClass *pMCNext;
```

```
    for (pMCObj = pFirst; pMCObj; pMCObj = pMCNext) {
        CHECKSIGNATURE(pMCObj);
        pMCNext = pMCObj->pNext;//get next pointer first
        delete pMCObj;              //then delete object
    }
}
```

The next most likely linked list problem is the infinite loop formed when one member incorrectly points to an earlier member of the list. This error can be detected by adding to the signature field a loop detection bit that works as follows.

Every time before traversing the list, the program links through each object clearing the loop detection bit. As soon as a member is found with the bit cleared or the end of the loop is reached, the function stops. During the actual loop traversal, the loop detection bit is checked. If it is found cleared, the bit is set indicating that this member was visited already. If, however, the bit is found set, then the loop curls back on itself and the program is terminated with an appropriate error message.

In practice, the loop detection bit appears as follows:

```
void clearLB(MyClass *pFirst);
void checkInfLoop(char *pFN = "?", int lineNo = 0);


//clearLB - clear the loop bit so that infinite loops
//          can be found without hanging
void clearLB(MyClass *pFirst) {
    MyClass *pMCObj = pFirst;
    while (pMCObj) {
        if ((pMCObj->signature & 0x8000) == 0)
            break;
        pMCObj->signature &= 0x7FFF;
        pMCObj = pMCObj->pNext;
    }
}


//checkInfLoop - use the loop bit to detect an infinite
//               loop in the linked list; be sure to call
```

```
//                     clearLB() before traversing the list
                       void checkInfLoop(MyClass *pMCObj,
                       char *pFileName, int lineNo) {
    if (pMCObj->signature & 0x8000) {
        cerr << "Infinite loop detected at object "
             << (void*)pMCObj
             << "discovered at " << pFileName << lineNo
             << endl;
        exit(1);   //terminate on error
    }
}
```

The `next()` method must set the loop bit (here chosen to be the most significant bit of the signature field) and check the loop bit of the next entry in the list. In addition, the `checkSignature()` method must mask off the loop bit before making the signature comparison. This might appear as follows.

```
//next - return the next member of the list
MyClass* MyClass::next(char *pFN, int lineNo) {
    signature |= 0x8000;
    if (pNext) {
        checkSignature(pNext, pFN, lineNo);
        checkInfLoop(pNext, pFN, lineNo);
    }
    return pNext;
}
```

The file name and line number arguments simply allow the file name and line number of the call to be passed to aid in debugging. They are not required.

Although these techniques are useful in identifying a problem, they do not locate the source of the problem. Once a problem has been identified, however, the programmer can zero in on the source of the problem by traversing the list after every major function. Consider the following simplified example.

```
void traverseList(MyClass *pMC) {
    while (pMC)
```

```
        pMC = pMC->next();
}

void majorFn(MyClass *pList) {
    transformA(pList);
    traverseList(pList);

    transformB(pList);
    traverseList(pList);

    transformC(pList);
    traverseList(pList);
}
```

If, for example, `traverseList()` was able to successfully traverse the list after `transformA()` but not after `transformB()`, then the programmer could conclude that `transformB()` contains the bug. This function could be further subdivided in the same way to narrow down the problem.

Hierarchical linked lists can be debugged in this fashion. Suppose, for example, that each object of class `MyClass` contained a pointer to a subordinate linked list of `UrClass` objects. By recursively traversing each `UrClass` list while traversing the `MyClass` list, the programmer can verify the entire structure. This type of test is especially useful before writing a database out to disk, as it reduces the risk of overwriting a good but older database with a newer but corrupted one.

Pointers on the PC

Every processor has its own architecture. This architecture includes the internal organization, the number and size of the internal registers, and the instructions. An essential part of any processor's architecture is its memory model.

This section will discuss the different memory models offered by modern processors — in particular, the 80x86 processors used to drive the IBM PC-compatible family of personal computers. Programmers already familiar with segmented pointers may choose to skip to the next section that examines some of the software errors associated with this architecture.

Memory Models

The processor's **memory model** is the way a processor handles memory. When an instruction reads a location in memory, the memory model describes the steps the processor takes to find and fetch the contents of that location. The memory model of a processor is so strongly tied to the internal organization of the CPU that few, if any, processors not built as clones of one another share an identical memory model.

Early processors had a simple memory model, usually known as the **flat**, or **linear**, **memory model**. In this model, each instruction generated a physical address directly without conversion. Thus, a logical address 0xC800 generated by an instruction referred to a physical address 0xC800 as well. This model is conceptually simple for the programmer and the compiler, but it has some severe limitations.

First, a program must know in advance the location in physical memory where it is to execute. A program designed to execute on an 8080 processor must know that it will execute at location 0x0100, for example; otherwise, addressing must be limited to Instruction Pointer (IP) relative modes. Second, this model provides no protection to catch out-of-range references. Finally, this memory model does not support virtual memory, so that all program code and data must be loaded into internal RAM memory simultaneously without extreme steps by the software.

Paged Memory Model   Most of these problems are addressed by a memory model known as the **paged memory model**. In this model, instructions generate a logical address that is translated through a page table into a physical address, as shown in Figure 6–10. The upper bits of the logical address are used as an index into the page table. Each entry in this table contains the physical address of a page of memory. Pages are typically 4K to 16K in length. The lower bits of the logical address are used as an offset into this page.

The paged memory model is just as simple for the programmer, since the logical address space is still linear. However, with this model an application can no longer know its physical address in memory. The page table determines where the program is to execute. The entries in this table are assigned by the O/S when the application is started. Thus, all programs may be linked to execute at the same logical address. Since each has its own set of page table addresses, each executes at a different physical address and no conflict arises.

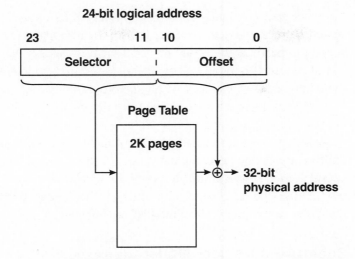

Figure 6–10. Logical-to-physical mapping in paged memory model

The paged model can support virtual memory as well. Most paged architectures provide a "Not present bit" in the page table entry, which is set when the physical memory page is not actually loaded in RAM. An attempt to access this page generates a trap that the O/S intercepts. The page is then loaded from disk and the physical address stored into the paged table. Finally, the "Not present bit" is cleared and the instruction is restarted.

The physical pages of memory need not be consecutive. The operating system may allocate physical pages in any order. To the application and its logical address space, the resulting memory appears consecutive.

Finally, some protection is provided: the operating system knows what logical addresses the application needs. Only the pages associated with these logical addresses are assigned to the application. Attempts to reference any other memory page generate an invalid memory reference trap. Some processors assign other protection bits as well, such as an execute-only flag. Pages containing code are marked "execute only," preventing the program from mistakenly overwriting an instruction with data. Most modern processors use some form of paged memory model.

Notice that nominally each memory access in a paged memory system would require two accesses: the first to load the page table entry and the second to perform the actual physical memory access. Various techniques have been used to avoid this overhead. One way is to load the entire paged table into very fast memory within the processor.

A second approach is to cache only the most recently used page table entries into fast internal memory. This is particularly advantageous since a program typically only executes out of three different pages at a time: the code occupies one page, the data another, and the stack a third. References outside of these pages, such as when the IP advances from one page to the next, cause the new page table entry to be loaded with the associated delay; however, such "cache misses" are infrequent.

Segmented Memory Model   In the late 1970s when Intel designed the 80286, the problems of paged memory must have seemed formidable. Including on the chip the logic to maintain a fast page cache stretched the technology of the day. To avoid this, Intel decided to force the programmer to maintain the internal page table entries via a set of special registers known as the segment registers. This gave the resulting model its name, the **segmented memory model**.

In the segmented memory model, the program loads the page table entries — now known as **segment descriptors** — into one of four segment registers labelled CS, DS, SS, and ES. The code segment is pointed at by the CS, the data segment by the DS, and the stack segment by the SS register; the ES, or extra segment, is used for special instructions or to avoid repetitive segment reloads when transferring data from one segment to another.

The segment register points to a segment descriptor that contains the address of the segment in physical memory. This 24-bit physical address is combined with the offset generated by the instruction to create a 24-bit physical address. A 24-bit address corresponds to a physical address space of 16 MB, as shown in Figure 6–11.

The 80286 segment descriptor also includes privilege flags and the length of the segment. Accesses beyond the end of the segment are trapped before they can cause damage. The privilege flags are used to implement further protection, such as "execute only" or "only accessible to the operating system."

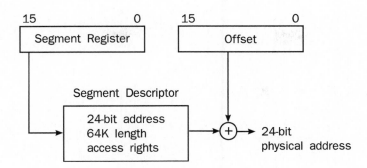

Figure 6–11. The 80286 segmented memory model

Unfortunately, Intel made two design decisions in implementing the 80286 segmentation scheme that seem very unwise today. First, it provided only a 16-bit offset. Although this makes instructions more compact, it effectively limits segments to 64K in length. Of course, a program can have as many segments as desired, so this does not limit the overall application. However, C++ counts on being able to calculate simple offsets to arrive at the address of elements within an array. Thus, the 80286 architecture limits individual arrays to 64K (without going through some complicated calculations that I will explain in a minute).

In some respects the second decision was even worse. Having decided upon the 80286 architecture, Intel realized that too many transistors were required. They could not achieve the segmented memory model they wanted on a single piece of silicon given the technology of the day. Unfortunately, time was of the essence. The Z80 processor from Zilog had already taken most of the market share away from Intel's flag ship 8080 and 8085 processors. Intel could not wait until the 80286 was achievable.

To bridge the gap between the 8080 and the 80286, Intel built a reduced processor, the 8086. This chip had the same basic instruction set and the same number and size of registers as the 80286. It even included segment registers to get programmers accustomed to the concept. However, instead of pointing into a segment descriptor table, the segment registers were simply used as offsets into physical memory. The 8086 arrives at a physical address by shifting the contents of the segment register left four bits and adding the offset, as shown in Figure 6–12.

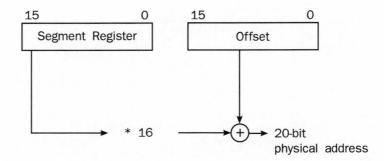

Figure 6–12. The 8086/8088 segmented memory model

Since both the segment register and offset are 16 bits, the resulting physical address of the 8086 is 20 bits for an address range of 1 MB. (Addresses from 0x100000 through 0x10FFFF wrap around.)

When IBM built its Personal Computer in 1982 (the third personal computer introduced by IBM), they considered using the Z80 processor. However, by that time it was clear that the Z80's 64K address range was too limiting. Therefore, they chose Intel's 8088 processor. Although this processor had an 8-bit external data bus like the Z80, it was internally identical to the 8086 processor. To drive this new machine, IBM arranged with Microsoft to produce a special version of the MS-DOS O/S known as PC-DOS. This O/S was provided free with each machine, virtually ensuring its success.

Of course, the IBM PC, with its open architecture, was a runaway success. Soon 8086- and 8088-based computers running the DOS operating system were appearing everywhere. Existing applications were ported over from the Z80-based CPM-80. When the 80286 was designed, no one knew of the coming IBM PC. By the time Intel got the 80286 processor into production, the PC boom was in full swing. No longer was the 80286 architecture considered the standard with the 8086 kludge the aberration, just the reverse. Intel had become a victim of its own success.

In a special mode that Intel called Real Mode, the 80286 supports the 8086's memory model. This was probably intended to allow the power-on software to set up the descriptor tables properly before turning on the 80286's base Protected Mode. By leaving the chip in Real Mode, however, the 80286 could support MS-DOS and its applications that were built around the 8086 memory model.

When IBM introduced the 80286-based PC/AT, everyone expected a Protected Mode operating system to be introduced quickly to make use of the extended features of the newer processor. This turned out to be more difficult than expected. By the time the new O/S could be released under the name OS/2, the 80286 was already considered an out-of-date chip. An even larger problem was that users did not perceive a need for it. At the time, programmers were finding ways to work around MS-DOS and its limitations. Since the 80286 could execute these programs handily, users were content to leave their 286 processors in Real Mode.

By the time work began on the 80386, the PC was already firmly established. Clearly the 80386 had to be able to support the 80286's protected memory model. To do otherwise would make obsolete the protected mode software that already existed. Just as clearly, the 80386 needed to offer a memory model that was significantly easier for operating system and application programmers to use.

To handle this, the 80386 offered two significant improvements, both of which are shown in Figure 6–13. First, the offset portion of the logical address was increased to a full 32 bits. This, plus a corresponding change to the segment size limit in the segment descriptor, meant that a single segment could be up to 4GB long. No longer could programmers complain that segmented memory was limiting the size of their arrays.

In addition, the Intel designers added a second stage to the address calculation logic. The intermediate address created by adding the offset to the segment's base address is passed through a conventional page table. This paged memory closely resembles most other modern processors, which allows general purpose operating systems such as UNIX to be easily ported to the 80386. Further, the paged portion of the memory system is invisible to the application program. This allows DOS and its applications to execute on the 80386 in a paged memory system (as is the case with DESQview and Windows 3.x).

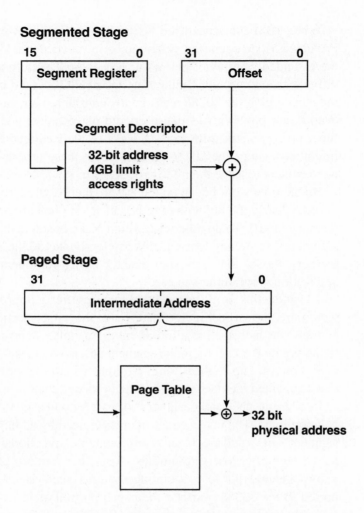

Figure 6–13. The 80386 segmented/paged memory model

Implications of Segmented Memory

The history of the 80x86 family of processors would be of little interest to the C++ programmer were it not for the implications it has for DOS programs.

Two different types of addresses are used on the PC: near addresses and far addresses. **Near addresses** consist of the 16-bit offset portion of the address, whereas **far addresses** consist of both offset and segment.

Each program is assigned a default data segment and a default code segment. A near address is an offset into the default segment. Near data objects are allocated space in the default data segment; near functions, in the default code segment.

The programmer controls the default pointer type with the Memory Model switch. Under the Small Model (/AS under Microsoft C++ and Small under the Options/Compiler window with Borland and Turbo C++), addresses default to near. Under the Large Model (/AL with Microsoft, Large with Borland), addresses default to far. Other memory models allow for mixtures of small and near defaults. Under either memory model, an object or a pointer can be explicitly declared near or far.

```
int near global1; //alloc space in default data segment
void near fn1();   //alloc space in default code segment

int near *pGlobal1 = &global1;//16-bit pointer
void (near *pFn1)()= fn1;

int far global2;
void far fn2();

int far  *pGlobal2 = &global2;//32-bit pointer
void (far  *pFn2)()= fn2;
```

Near pointers limit the programmer more than far pointers. A strictly Small Model program is limited to 64K of code with a separate 64K of data, including stack and heap — not enough room for most programs.

Even in Large Model, the programmer should be aware of problems associated with segmentation. Loading a far pointer involves two register loads, one for the segment and a second for the offset, while loading a near pointer involves only one. Thus, near pointer programs run slightly faster than their far pointer equivalents — sometimes as much as 10 to 20 percent faster. In addition, many pointer errors made by programmers writing for the PC involve confusing near and far pointers. These will be discussed in detail in the segmentation section.

Segmented Pointer Arithmetic

C++ pointer arithmetic is only performed on the 16-bit offset portion of
the address for all pointer types other than `huge`. This is what limits the
size of objects to 64K on the PC. Thus, the following function is suspect
since `byteOffset` may take on values larger than `0xFFFF`, the limit of a
16-bit pointer offset.

```
void setFlag(char* pData,
             unsigned long byteOffset,
             int flag) {
    pData[byteOffset] |= flag;
}
```

When a calculated offset exceeds `0xFFFF`, it wraps around to zero and
begins overwriting the beginning of the segment. No error is generated.

Even if `byteOffset` is an integer, the offset can still overflow since
the offset portion of `pData` is likely not to be 0. Consider the following
example:

```
pData          = 0x1234:0x2000      <- address of array
byteOffset     = +       0xF100     <- integer offset
                 ------------
                 0x1234:0x1100      <- offset overflow
```

To make sure that the offset portion of an array is zero, the programmer
may declare the array `far`, thereby forcing it into its own segment.

```
int far dataBlock[32000];    //occupies its own segment
```

This ensures that a full 64K is available to the array.

Offset calculations can also overflow as a result of multiplication prior
to the offset addition. Consider the following example:

```
void setFlag(int far* pData, int byteOffset,
             int flag) {
    pData[byteOffset] |= flag;
}
```

```
byteOffset   =  0xA000              <- integer index
             *       2              <- sizeof(int)
                ----------
                 0x4000             <- offset overflowed
pData        = +0x1234:0x0000       <- address of array
                --------------------
                 0x1234:0x4000      <- incorrect address
```

Thus, the number of elements one can have in an array is `64K / sizeof(a single element)`.

Pointer subtraction involves only the 16-bit offset portion of the pointer as well. Thus, the following subtraction gives somewhat surprising results.

```
void fn() {
    int far* pI1 = (int far*)0x12340000L;
    int far* pI2 = (int far*)0x12300040L;

    int i = pI2 - pI1;
}
```

One might expect the result to be 0 because the two addresses point to the same physical location; however, the answer is 32 (`(0x40 - 0x0) / 2 = 0x20`). As we will see, declaring the pointers `huge` solves the problem because it forces all 32 bits of the address to be included in the calculation.

Huge Pointers

If address calculations included the segment portion of a far address, segmentation would not restrict the size of an array. Most C++ compilers support a special pointer known as the **huge pointer**. Huge pointers have the same 32-bit `segment:offset` format of far addresses. They differ, however, in that arithmetic on a huge pointer includes the segment as well as the offset.

Since no 80x86 machine instructions support this, the compiler inserts a call to a special pointer addition function every time huge pointer arithmetic is required. This function constructs a 20-bit address from the `segment:offset` before performing the addition. The result is then converted back into a `segment:offset`. (The offset is always in the range of 0 through 0xF.)

Huge arrays have several limitations. First, the function call, along with the conversion to and from the 20-bit format, requires more time than a simple offset calculation. Thus, indexing a huge array is considerably slower than indexing a normal array. In addition, no single record may extend over a 64K segment boundary. The size of each record, then, must be a power of two bytes in length plus no single object can exceed 64K.

Finally, since individual segments are limited to 64K, huge arrays must be allocated off the far heap via the C library function `farmalloc()` as in the following:

```
void fn(long size) {
    int huge* pBigBlock;

    //size is not limited to 64k / sizeof(int)
    pBigBlock = (int huge*)farmalloc(size);
    //...
}
```

Often huge pointers can be avoided by dividing a large array into a number of smaller arrays, each less than 64K in length. Consider the following:

```
#include <stdio.h>
#include <stdlib.h>
#include <alloc.h>

int huge matrix1[256][256];    //128 kbyte array

void main() {
    int far*matrix2[256]; //array of pointers to arrays
    int i, j;

    //allocate data space for matrix2
    for (i = 0; i < 256; i++) {
        matrix2[i] = (int far*)farmalloc(256 *
                                    sizeof(int));
        if (matrix2[i] == 0) {
            printf("Heap exhausted @%d. Terminating\n",
                    i);
            exit(1);
```

```
        }
    }

    i = 10;
    j = 20;
    matrix1[i][j] = 0; //calls address function
    matrix2[i][j] = 0; //does not call address
                       //function, but performs
                       //extra level of indirection
}
```

Here `matrix2` is declared as an array of far pointers to arrays. The pointers must be far because in its entirety the data will consume more than 64K. (Remember, setting the memory model to Large enables the programmer to dispense with the `far` keyword since that becomes the default; however, it forces all pointers far.)

These smaller arrays must be allocated individually. In this example they are taken from the heap. In use, `matrix2` resembles its huge cousin, `matrix1`. The code generated by the access of `matrix2` is considerably simpler and quicker to execute than that generated by the `matrix1` access.

This works equally well for an array of large records when the total number is less than 16,000 (64K/`sizeof(void far*)`) as in the following example:

```
struct MyClass {
  private:

    //lots of data
    int data[1000];

  public:
    //methods allowed as well
    MyClass();
    void otherMethod();
}
```

```
void fn() {
    //if declared directly, array would have to be
    //declared huge since 100 * sizeof(MyClass) is
    //greater than 64K MyClass array[100];

    //an array of MyClass far* does not have to be
    //declared huge because 100 * sizeof(MyClass far*)
    //is only 400
    MyClass far* pArray[100];

    //to access a member
    pArray[i]->otherMethod();

    //...and so on as in the previous example
}
```

Segmentation Errors

Programmers who deal with the segmented memory model of the 80x86 family of processors are subject to further class of pointer errors. Segmentation errors are particularly difficult for the 80x86 novice to understand. By going over a few of the more common segmentation problems, the reader may be able to recognize them when they arise.

Programmers who feel uneasy about near and far pointers are encouraged to use the Large model exclusively so that all pointers default to far. This avoids many of the segmentation related problems presented here. Many segmentation problems involving mixed pointer sizes disappear when the program is recompiled using the Large model.

Mixing Different Size Pointers

Apart from attempts to address beyond the end of a segment, most segmentation errors involve mixing 16-bit near and 32-bit far pointers in the same expression. Many, but not all, combinations are allowed, as the following segment shows.

```
void far(int arg) {
    int far* pFar;
    int near* pNear;

    int (far* pFarFn)();
    int (near* pNearFn)();

    pFar = pNear;               //this is ok
    pNear = pFar;               //probably not ok; may
                                //generate compiler error
    pNear = (int near*)pFar;    //no compiler error, but
                                //not ok

    pFar = (int far*)pFarFn;    //this is okay
    pNear= (int near*)pNearFn;  //this is not okay unless
                                //CS==DS (tiny model)
}
```

Any pointer size can be assigned to a far pointer. The same holds true for huge pointers since they differ from far pointers only in the way they perform pointer arithmetic.

In general, a far pointer cannot be assigned to a near pointer, because the near pointer does not have room to hold the segment portion of the address. The compiler may generate a compiler error in the absence of a cast. With a cast, the compiler will likely perform the operation, but the resulting program will not work.

The only exception is if the programmer knows that the segment portion of the far address is equal to the default segment. For example, the following function works properly on most PC compilers.

```
//compiled under Large model
int buffer[100];    //allocated out of the default
                    //data segment
void main() {
    //initialize buffer with a near pointer because
    //it's faster - this is very dangerous
    int near* pBuf = (int near*)buffer;
```

```
for (int i = 0; i < 100; i++) {
    pBuf[i] = i;
}
}
```

Here the programmer is relying on the fact that a global array declared within a module and not specifically declared `far` is allocated from the default data segment for that module. By declaring `pBuf` to be near, the programmer hopes to achieve fractionally better performance. This is not a safe practice and should be avoided. The slight increase in performance is more than negated by the fragility of the resulting program.

Returning to our earlier example, notice that in general it is not correct to assign a near pointer to a function to a near pointer to data. Near data pointers use the default data segment, whereas near code pointers use the default code segment. These two segments are not equal (except in tiny model, which is seldom used anymore).

The same problem can arise when near pointers are assigned to global variables — that use the default data segment — to near pointers to auto variables that use the stack segment. To avoid this problem, the stack segment and data segment are assigned the same value in the small and medium models.

This is not true in the compact and large memory models, however, where the following problem can arise.

```
//compiled in Large model
int buffer1[80];
void fn() {
    int buffer2[80];
    int near* pBuf;

    pBuf = (int near*)buffer1;//okay, but dangerous
    pBuf = (int near*)buffer2;//not okay since buffer2
                              //comes out of the stack
                              //segment
}
```

This is also a problem when writing Terminate-and-Stay Resident and Interrupt Service routines. When the interrupt arrives, the function must first set the data segment register to what the function expects it to be. In compilers with this feature, this code is generated automatically by declaring the function `interrupt`. Once in the function, the stack segment and data segment registers remain unequal.

To solve this problem, many compilers include an ASSUME DS!=SS switch. Although the generated code is slightly slower, the problem is avoided. If this option is not available, the programmer can declare all variables global so that they will all be in the data segment.

Pointer Size and Function Prototypes

Although C++ makes function prototypes mandatory, C does not. However, mixed sized pointers require accurate prototypes while programming C modules.

In the absence of a prototype, pointers passed as functional arguments are compelled to the default size of data pointers in the current compilation memory model. Consider the following case, however:

```
extern "C" {
    void setFunctionAddress(...);
}
void fn() {
    void anotherFn();
    setFunctionAddress(anotherFn);
};

void setFunctionAddress(void (*pFunction)()) {
    static void (*pFuncToCall)();
    pFuncToCall = pFunction;
}
```

In compact or medium memory models, code and data pointers do not default to the same size. In medium models data pointers default to near, while code pointers are far. In a case such as this, the compiler can become confused and push a near address, assuming the pointer being passed to `setFunctionAddress()` is to data. The function itself is expecting a far address, since its argument is clearly declared as a pointer to a function. This problem also occurs when all pointer arguments are declared `void*` or `int*` and are recast immediately prior to use (this is common among pre-ANSI programmers).

A similar problem arises when attempting to access code in a small model program.

```
//hexDump - dump the given data to the screen in hex
//            format
void hexDump(void *pDataToDump, int length) {
    static char digit[] =
            {'0', '1', '2', '3', '4', '5', '6', '7',
             '8', '9', 'A', 'B', 'C', 'D', 'E', 'F'};
    char c1, c2;
    unsigned char *pData = (unsigned char*)pDataToDump;
    while (length) {
        for (int i = 0; i < 16 && length;
                                    i++, length--) {
            c1 = *pData >> 4;
            c2 = *pData & 0x0F;
            printf("%c%c ", digit[c1], digit[c2]);
            pData++;
        }
        printf("\n");
    }
}


void fn(char *pBuffer, void (*pFn)()) {
    hexDump((void*)pBuffer, 10);
    hexDump((void*)pFn, 10);
}
```

The function `hexDump()` is a general purpose function that dumps whatever it is given in hexidecimal format to standard output. The first call to `hexDump()` from function `fn()` works as expected. However, when `fn()` attempts to obtain a hex dump of the function `(*pFn)()`, the call does not work. The problem lies in the cast. When casting a pointer to a function into a pointer to data (or a `void*`), the default segment changes from the code segment to the data segment. Thus, the function `hexDump()` looks at the proper offset, but in the wrong segment to find the machine instructions to dump.

Properly declaring the size of a pointer returned from a function is important as well. Classic C functions generally assumed that a pointer could be stored in an integer, so functions such as the following were not uncommon. Here the return type of `oldStyleFunction()` defaults to `int`.

```
oldStyleFunction(size) {
    Block *pBlock;

    pBlock = malloc(size*sizeof(Block));
    return pBlock;
}
```

In the large and compact memory models, this is not true. An integer is 16 bits, while a far pointer requires 32 bits. Such functions must be provided with accurate prototypes when porting them over to the PC.

Declaring Function Types   Like data, functions may be declared near or far. All of the far functions declared within a single module are allocated space in a code segment unique to that module. All of the near functions declared within the program are allocated space in the default code segment. Unlike data, however, near functions and far functions are not compatible. None of the following mixed assignments is correct.

```
far   void farFn();
near  void nearFn();

void fn() {
    void (far*  pFarFn)();
    void (near* pNearFn)();

    pFarFn  = farFn;     //this is okay
    pNearFn = nearFn;    //so is this

    pNearFn = farFn;     //of course, this is illegal...
    pFarFn  = nearFn;    //...but this is too
```

```
     pFarFn  = (void(far*)())nearFn; //even with a cast
     (*pFarFn)();                //...the call does not work
}
```

While `pFarFn` is large enough to contain the full 32-bit address of `nearFn()`, the call to `(*pFarFn)()` is incorrect. The compiler assumes that any function pointed at by a far pointer is a far function and should be called as such. Although the call appears to work, the stack is not handled properly entering and exiting the function, and the program generates unpredictable results.

Memory Models and the Standard C Library   Because near functions and far functions are not internally identical, several copies of the Standard C library must be provided. When compiling in small model, the C++ compiler links with the small model version of the library (usually the name of the library carries some designator, such as CS.LIB for the small C library, CL.LIB for the large, and so on). These functions are designed to take the default size pointers for their memory model. This is indicated in the prototypes contained in the standard include files.

When include files are present, the compiler can recast pointers to the proper size before making the call. When this is not possible, an error is generated. For example:

```
#include <stdio.h>
void fn(char near* pNearBuffer) {
    printf("Enter your name:");
    scanf("%s", pNearBuffer);
}
```

When compiled under Small Model, the data pointers default to near and no conversion is necessary. When compiled under Large Model, however, the function `scanf()` expects a `char far*`. Since this is indicated in the prototype contained in `stdio.h`, the compiler recasts the `char near*` into a `char far*` before making the call.

One further problem concerns the use of the heap function `farmalloc()` available under most C++ implementations for the PC, including both Borland and Microsoft. In small and medium model programs, the heap must come from the default data segment. Since the program data and stack may not leave much room for heap variables, these compilers provide a separate heap, known as the far heap. Whatever memory is left over after the program has been loaded is allocated to the far heap.

The library function `farmalloc()` returns blocks of data from the far heap. Even though data pointers in these memory models default to near, `farmalloc()` returns a `void far*`. Thus, any pointer destined to receive the return from `farmalloc()` must be specifically declared far. Such a pointer cannot be passed to any other function whose argument is not also explicity declared far. This includes all of the C++ library functions when compiling in small and medium models. In large and compact memory model, the default `malloc()` call allocates memory off the far heap. The prototype for `farmalloc()` is in the include file `alloc.h`.

Protected Mode Programs   Protected mode programming is not particularly difficult. However, the details of how to write a protected mode program would fill a chapter on their own. When debugging a protected mode program, the programmer should watch out for several things.

- **Don't perform numerical computation on the segment portion of a far address.**

In real mode, a value can be stored directly into the segment portion of an address. For example, the text mode buffer of the graphics video adapter is located at physical address 0xB8000. It is not uncommon to see the following:

```
unsigned far* pVideo = (unsigned far*)0xB8000000L;
```

This stores a 0xB800 into the segment and a 0x0000 into the offset portion of the address. In protected mode, this will not work unless the operating system has previously set the selector 0xB800 to point to the video buffer. All segment selectors must come from the operating system.

- **Never store non-address information into a segment register.**

Segment registers should only be loaded with segment selectors set up by the operating system. This is more of a temptation to the assembly language programmer than the C++ programmer.

- **Don't access structures beyond their specified length.**

Returning to the video buffer example, the programmer knows how long the display buffer actually is. Rather than declare an array of that length, the programmer can declare a single-element array, knowing that the necessary space is pre-allocated anyway. Since protected mode segments contain lengths that are enforced by the hardware, this trick will lead to trouble in a protected mode environment.

- **Don't write into read-only areas.**

Programs should never write into code-bearing areas. The following should be avoided as well.

```
int diskNumber;                    //set externally
static char diskName[] = "ABCDEFGHIJ"; //names of disk
                                   //drives
char* addDiskToName(char *pPathName) {
    pPathName[0] = diskName[diskNumber];
    return pPathName;
}


char* createFileName() {
    return addDiskToName("?:\\MYDIR\\MYFILE");
}
```

Here the function `addDisktToName()` is attempting to overwrite the disk letter portion of the file name. The string passed to it is a constant string and might have been allocated from a read-only segment. The safer way to do this is as follows:

```
char *pString[80];
char* createFileName() {
    char *pConstString = "?:\\MYDIR\\MYFILE";
```

```
//copy the constant string to dynamic memory
strcpy(pString, pConstring);

//now pass this to the function
return addDiskToName(pDynString);
}
```

Other limitations and rules for protected mode programming will depend upon the operating system and the C++ environment you are using.

Conclusion

The past two chapters have examined many of the errors that befall the C++ programmer. After reviewing the syntactical errors that plague C++, trouble spots such as functions with unexpected side effects, incorrect constructors, overloaded operators, longjumps, semaphores, and reentry were discussed.

Pointer problems — including those associated with 80x86 addressing peculiarities — and the effects that bad pointers can have on programs have been examined so that the reader will be better able to recognize them when they arise. In addition, different ways of detecting bad pointers and tracking them back to their origin were reviewed.

As discouragingly long as this list might seem, many other errors have not been presented. No matter how careful you are as a programmer, you will make mistakes. These mistakes need to be discovered and removed before the product is delivered.

The next chapter will explore the next step in the program-writing process — testing. Only a careful, methodical test can ensure a quality product.

Part 2

Testing and Debugging

Chapter 7

Testing and Maintenance

The last five chapters have examined techniques for ensuring that a minimum number of errors make it through to the testing phase of development. This chapter will discuss how to deal with those that do.

Testing

Do not kid yourself into thinking that a good methodology applied during requirements, design, and coding will relieve you of the need to apply good techniques during the final phase, testing. Testing is the most important phase of a program and consumes the most time on a large project, but it is the phase least enjoyed by programmers.

Testing was not even identified as a separate phase of software development until the early 1970s, but the testing of software has undergone considerable study since then. Testing is too large a topic to be covered completely in a single chapter, but the main points of this important, though dreaded, subject will be reviewed in the following sections.

Why Programmers Don't Like to Test

Programmers do not like to test. Testing is considered "low tech," low excitement, and suitable for people with lots of time on their hands. Many programmers believe that once they have gone through the formality of running a few perfunctory tests against it, their code works. They designed and wrote it carefully. It works. They think spending a lot of time and labor in rigorous testing is not only wasteful, it's insulting.

This is a common attitude, and it is completely wrong. Humans can do many things amazingly well. We can identify shapes and find patterns buried in noise (both visual and audio) better than any computer. We can ponder our own existence. We can discover and invent things. We can even write C++ programs. However, humans make mistakes. Lots of them.

People admit this shortcoming in other areas of human endeavor: they purchase insurance, put on seat belts, prefer cars with air bags, place a napkin in their lap when eating, and become nervous when trapeze artists work without a net. In thousands of everyday events, we admit this frailty. Why then is it so hard to admit that programmers make errors in software?

When building an electronic circuit, a hardware designer goes over it carefully several times before ever applying power. In contrast, a software designer blithely takes a brand new, untested program and simply lets it run. If the program happens not to crash and even generates output that looks like it might be correct, the programmer is tempted to believe that the program works.

Case Study   I was once a part of a design presentation of a large system. During the presentation we described with pride how we intended to implement the receiver control, the data reduction, the reporting, and the database subsections of the system. As part of the database description, I went into some detail describing the error detection algorithms.

The algorithms were designed to uncover organizational errors in the database as soon as they occurred. These errors are otherwise notoriously difficult to debug, since they may lay dormant for hundreds of transactions before a function happens upon them and crashes.

Almost as soon as the error occurred, the system would write out a copy of the defective database for analysis before attempting to correct the problem. (The code was a good deal better at detecting problems than fixing them.) Armed with this information, the programmers would be better able to determine which transactions caused the problem. In addition, the hope was that errors that occurred in the field would be detected so the system could recover without crashing.

I was interrupted in the middle of my presentation by a worried customer who was concerned that we intended to ship a system that might have errors in the database code. Of course, we did not intend to ship a system with errors, but we knew we would ship a system with errors — it was unavoidable. I won the argument by countering that I did not intend to have a wreck on my drive home after the meeting, but I put on my seat belt anyway.

Total Quality I have stressed in this book that good programming techniques should be followed at every step of the software development process. This philosophy has not always been prevalent.

Assembly-line production methods have gone through a similar evolution over the last century. Around the middle of the 20th century, the prevailing theory was that production techniques were not as important as the testing methodology. A tremendous amount of effort was directed at writing ironclad requirements specifications and developing testing techniques to verify adherence to those requirements. The theory was that as long as the requirements were thorough and the product met those requirements, the product would be acceptable, irrespective of how the product was built. Meeting the letter of the requirements, often without regard to their meaning, became the order of the day.

In most respects, that outlook has been discarded. Modern production facilities use a technique known as Statistical Process Control or Total Quality Management that stresses a more holistic approach. SPC/TQM examines every stage of the production process, looking for ways in which the product can be improved or the cost reduced. Quality and accuracy must be built in at every step, in every human endeavor including writing C++ programs.

A good testing regimen is not sufficient by itself. However, a good testing regimen is required. Statistics reported by Boris Beizer in *Software Testing Techniques* show that a well-written program will still have one to three bugs per hundred lines. Programs that have not been purged of these errors are worthless, no matter how well written they were or how much effort went into their creation.

The Goals of Testing If I were to ask a dozen programmers what the goal of testing is, I would likely get at least ten responses to the effect that "the goal of testing is to demonstrate that a program is error free." Such a statement, however, is faulty on several accounts.

First, it establishes a goal that is impossible to achieve. A program will have errors. Attempts to prove that a program does not have errors will fail. Each subsequent error that is found only serves to demoralize the programmer by demonstrating how impossible the error-free goal is. No wonder, then, that testing is perceived as a painful exercise to be avoided as much as possible.

Second, the no-error goal tempts the programmer into a fraud. The only way to prove that a program has no errors is not to look very hard, especially at areas the programmer knows to be shaky. Maybe the programmer's understanding of the requirements was hazy in an area or perhaps several crashes occurred there that were never adequately explained. Doubtful sections of a program can be tested with just a few cases — enough to protect the programmer if challenged. To make up for inadequately testing some areas, a programmer may test the sections that are more certain doubly hard.

Of course, programmers don't consciously think this way. However, these are the types of games the human subconscious often plays.

Therefore, the goal of testing must be turned around. In *The Art of Software Testing*, Glenford Myers says "testing is the process of executing a program with the intent of finding errors." With this premise the situation for the tester is much rosier. The tester knows that errors are lurking in the code somewhere. Each error detected is perceived not as a failure but a success. The goal is to find them, and, like a challenging game, the job of finding errors in the program becomes more difficult with each error detected.

This change in approach encourages the programmer to spend less time testing the areas of the program that are clear and free of confusion. Those areas are well understood, and the bug density is not likely to be very high there. Software bugs live mostly in the murky areas near the edges where irregularities are common. Bug hunting is best in those places, and the tester will spend the most time there if the goal is to find errors.

Asking a programmer to shift from writing a program to testing it is like asking a bridge builder to spend weeks constructing a bridge and then stress it until it crumbles into the water. Nevertheless, that is exactly what is required to do a good job of testing. This is what is meant by **egoless programming**: attack the program without consideration for how its failure might reflect upon its creator, you.

In order for ruthless error detection to work, however, there must be no recriminations for the number of errors found. Some organizations keep statistics on how many errors are found per KLOC for different programmers. If statistics of this sort are to be kept, programmers must have a chance to test their own modules first and the errors found during this first round of testing MUST NOT be included in the statistics.

Egoless programming is difficult to achieve. Therefore, most software organizations have a separate department responsible for testing. This may be the Software QA Department or the Systems Department that was responsible for writing the specification in the first place.

Placing the responsibility for testing into a separate area allows a certain amount of healthy tension to develop between the two groups. Like a game of cat and mouse, the programmers try to anticipate all the ways the tester might choose to stress the program. Having anticipated them, the programmer then adds checks and tests out these conditions before releasing the software. The aim here is to deprive the tester of the satisfaction of finding a defect.

This is exactly what the software organization wants to occur. At first, the programmers react specifically to the testing organization. Eventually, however, programmers get into the habit of anticipating rigorous testing, irrespective of its source. This is called **sensitizing**. Making programmers aware of a particular error or test sensitizes them to that error, making it much less likely that the error will occur in the future.

The Developing Attitudes Toward Testing

According to Beizer, organizations go through five stages in their attitude toward testing:

Testing — An Extension of Debugging   In this phase the programmer considers testing merely a continuation of the unit testing/debugging cycle. Perhaps a little more formal, but essentially no different.

One could be charitable and conclude that such an organization pursues debugging with the same rigor and method as testing, but such is not the case. Organizations with this outlook perform almost no testing. What little testing they do perform is usually informal.

This was the standard industry attitude toward testing in the early days of programming. Convincing managers who were programmers during that era that this is not the best approach today can be difficult.

Testing Shows That a Program Works   This attitude recognizes a difference between debugging/unit testing and formal testing. Although debugging/unit testing is a type of testing and utilizes many of the same techniques, the formal testing phase is distinct and has different goals.

As noted, however, this attitude proposes an unachievable goal. Every non-trivial program has bugs — therefore, programmers and testers cannot hope to achieve the goal of showing that it does not. Holding to such a goal merely serves to demoralize the testers and the programmers who must support them.

Testing Shows That a Program Doesn't Work   This attitude divorces the goal of the developer from that of the tester, even when the programmer and tester are the same person. The tester now questions every assumption the designer made and every step the programmer took. Finding a problem whets the appetite of the tester to find more bugs. Testers envision ever more sophisticated test scenarios that might reveal a hidden problem.

Theoretically, this approach to testing leads to the most error-free software. The only problem is that there is no guideline established to tell the tester when to stop. You can never prove that no more bugs remain in a piece of software. If you have not found a problem, it may be because you are looking in the wrong place. That next test, no matter how contrived, might ferret out one more defect, and so the product continues to be improved but is never delivered.

Testing Reduces the Risk of Program Failure   This is the attitude that most progressive software corporations have towards program testing today. At this point, the tester realizes that producing error-free software is not possible. The best that can be hoped for is some level of software risk.

Risk is defined as the probability of an error weighted by the damage caused by that error summed over all of the errors remaining in the program.

This number is not calculable since it would require a knowledge of each remaining software error.

For a large system, this value can be estimated empirically, however. The longer the system is tested and the longer the system remains in the field under trial conditions without error, the lower the risk. However, even for a small system, the foregoing relation can be used to guide the testing plan.

The probability portion of the equation suggests that more tests should be planned for the parts of the program that are prone to error. Error-prone software results from poor design, the interfacing of code from different sources, and, the use of units written by inexperienced programmers. More testing also should be directed toward those areas of the program that are likely to be used the most.

The risk side of the equation suggests that programs whose failure would be catastrophic, such as aircraft control systems, must be tested more thoroughly than systems whose failure would be only inconvenient, such as an editor. It also suggests that more time be spent testing units within a program whose failure would have the highest negative effect.

Once the test team is satisfied that the system is sufficiently risk-free, the program can be delivered to the customer or offered on the market for sale. Since management knows that errors remain in the system, plans must be made for how errors that occur in the field will be reported and how bug correction versions will be created, retested, and distributed — in short, how the program will be maintained.

Testing is a State of Mind   The difference between this step and its predecessor lies primarily in the attitude of programmers and testers toward the developmental steps prior to testing. This is the attitude that quality, including testability, should be designed in from the beginning: Requirements should be reviewed for accuracy. Designs should be well thought out and rehearsed with the customer and programmers. Classes should be constructed defensively to detect errors early, and hooks should be included for checking control flow between classes. The test team or Software QA should be involved during each developmental phase to make sure that the goals of quality and testability are being pursued evenly. When software is constructed in this fashion, testing is a relatively painless process.

Organizing Testing

Like other aspects of software development, testing must be planned. The level of effort expended in planning should match the size of the program. For small, single-programmer projects, the plan can be informal. For large, multiprogrammer efforts, however, the test plan should be carefully designed.

The most important aspect of any test strategy is the test plan itself. While the plan may be informal or formal, it must be in written or recorded form. Testing should not be performed "on the fly" no matter how small the project.

The test plan should include a test schedule. The testing schedule need not specify firm dates, but should reflect the relative scheduling of testing phases on different parts of the program. Even the lone programmer should have an informal idea that certain classes will be tested first, followed by groups of classes, and so on.

Just as important as these aspects of testing organization is the Error Reporting Form with which software errors are reported and tracked.

The Written Test Plan

The **test plan** is a written document describing each test and how it will be conducted. In multiprogrammer organizations, the plan should also address organizational details such as who is responsible for approving the test, performing the test, and signing off on the test results.

The tests themselves should be laid out in a hierarchical fashion, much like the outline of a book. Higher levels describe the test environment and the goals of the tests contained in this section. Lower levels of the test plan contain the actual test steps to be performed. Tests that fail are reported on a standard error form that refers to the test step in question.

Why a Written Test Plan?   Beizer compares testing without a plan to small children playing pool. One steps up to the table and whacks the cue ball, perhaps aiming at a ball and perhaps not. In any case, the child takes credit for any ball that happens to fall into any pocket. Beizer calls this kiddie pool.

In **kiddie testing**, the programmer/tester thinks up some test at the terminal and then executes it. Neither the test nor the results are recorded. If the results look reasonable, the tester thinks up another test to try.

Kiddie testing is not acceptable for several reasons. First, subtle bugs often go undetected. Cases that produce reasonable but incorrect results are often overlooked. If the program does not crash, the programmer is predisposed to accept whatever output is produced. The tester might detect incorrect results, but if the output is anywhere close to the expected, it will be accepted as correct.

Second, results are not statusable. When a problem does arise, it is much easier to report that the program failed Step 1.2.1a of the test plan, for example. The programmer can then refer to the plan to see exactly what test step failed. The test plan should include sufficient instructions so that anyone well versed in the project can reproduce the test — it does not need to be written for the final user or for the "man in the street."

Once the problem has been fixed, the programmer can then report back that Step 1.2.1a is ready for retest. The tester marks in the plan that the test is ready to be rerun. When time allows, Step 1.2.1a is retested. The tester will probably want to revisit the related steps of section 1.2 to make sure that the new fix has not affected one of these ("Regression testing" is discussed later in this chapter).

Third, without a mapped out testing strategy, it is difficult to know when to stop. The tester has only a vague idea of what percentage of the program has been covered — management has absolutely no idea. What does it mean when the tester reports that testing is 50 percent complete? I presume this means that the tester's patience is 50 percent gone. What else could it mean? Without some written plan, no review or audit capability exists.

Finally, results are not repeatable without a written test plan. A good program will go through many revisions in its lifetime as features are added or existing features are modified to fit changing requirements. The previously used test plan forms the basis for the test plan for the new system.

When writing Version 1.1 of a program, what programmer would throw away the C++ source code for Version 1.0 and start over completely? Why then, would that same programmer throw away the test plan for Version 1.0 and develop a new test plan from scratch?

In starting with the test plan for the previous system, developers are reasonably certain that the new system can do at least what the old system could. Customers are much more tolerant of new features with problems than they are of features that worked in previous versions but no longer work in the new version.

The Format of a Test Plan   The test plan consists of two parts. The first section sets down the ground rules. This section should attempt to answer the following questions:

- What support software is required and what is the assumed hardware configuration?
- Who or what organization is to perform the test?
- How and when is the test plan to be reviewed by the designers and programmers?
- What type of regression testing is to be performed and how often?
- How are the tests to be run? How are the results to be verified? Who signs off on the tests?

The second section of the test plan lists the actual tests. This section is often kept as a separate document since it is subject to constant change and addition, while the first section is not. The tests should be laid out in hierarchical fashion, such as the following excerpt from a mythical test plan for the receiver control program developed in Chapter 3.

```
1.    User input section
```

```
The following section is designed to test that all
commands are interpreted properly and that illegal
input is rejected.
```

```
1.1   Frequency
```

```
The following tests check the commands that accept a
frequency. These tests verify that properly entered
frequencies are understood correctly and that
improperly entered frequencies are rejected.
```

```
1.1.1 Tests
```

```
For the following component tests, only the syntax
checking software need be running. A terminal is also
required. The system should be booted up as normal.

                a. Input: T 1234
     Response: Ok

     b. Input: T 9999
     Response: Frequency out of range
                       *
                       *
                       *
```

The test plan may assume the user has knowledge of the system. After all, it will be carried out by engineers who are intimately familiar with the program. For example, in the previous test plan it was sufficient to say "boot the system" without going into the details of how to do so. If this level of instruction is necessary, place the basic instructions in an appendix or some other easy to find place. Repeating this type of detail throughout the document adds needless bulk and makes the result more difficult to follow and maintain.

The Error Reporting Form

The **Error Reporting Form (ERF)** is a standardized form on which testers record test failures. Although this may seem trivial, large companies spend a lot of time determining what should be on the Error Reporting Form. In 1990 E-Systems, Inc. held meetings and reviews spread over six months on updating a one-page ERF.

For small organizations, the ERF need not be so formal, but even a one-programmer operation needs some type of ERF to keep track of test anomalies. At a minimum the ERF should contain the following information:

- a unique number that identifies the anomaly for future reference
- the number of the test step that failed
- the version of the software in which the problem was detected (more on this point in the next section)

- the name of the tester who found the problem. Any questions about the error report will be referred back to the original tester.
- the nature of the problem. What did the program do on that test step that was incorrect? The bug might be due to a misconception in which case the programmer may not see what the error is.
- the status of the ERF. A standard set of status indicators needs to be adopted. A good set is OPEN, IN WORK, FIXED, READY FOR RETEST, and CLOSED. An open ERF is one that has just been written. An in-work ER has been assigned to a programmer for debugging and fixing. A fixed ERF has been corrected but the fix has not been included in the software version currently being tested. A ready ERF is waiting to be retested. A closed ERF has been retested successfully and is closed.
- the priority of the ERF. Some bugs are more critical than others. In *Managing the Software Process*, Watts Humphries suggests the following severity levels:

  1 — an error that prevents the accomplishment of an operational or mission-essential function or jeopardizes personal safety.

  2 — an error that adversely affects the accomplishment of an operations or mission-essential function and for which no acceptable work-arounds are available

  3 — a severity 2 error for which a workaround does exist

  4 — an operator inconvenience that affects mission-essential functions

  5 — all other errors

- the name of the programmer fixing the bug
- the category of the bug. Test organizations keep statistics on software errors. This bug taxonomy is then used to develop future test plans that concentrate on those classes of bugs that occur most often.
- the modules affected. Knowing what modules were modified in fixing the bug tells the test team which regression tests to run in order to make sure the fix has not impeded another part of the program.

Once an error report is written it is turned over to the programmers or their supervisor for debugging. A copy may be retained by the test team to ensure that ERFs are not lost. Once the ERF is reported back ready, the test is reexecuted. If the problem has been fixed, the modified unit list is consulted to determine what regression tests are indicated. Once testing is completed, the ERF is closed and saved for post-project analysis.

The programmer may not agree that the software is in error — the test organization does not have a monopoly on truth. When a questionable error report arises, it is discussed among designers, programmers, and testers. The requirements are consulted, and a decision rendered. If the ERF is incorrect, it is immediately closed, but not destroyed.

Software Baselines

A **software baseline** is a version of the software that has been assigned a number for tracking purposes. Every version of the software has its own characteristics. Testing should proceed in an orderly and controlled fashion. Programmers cannot be allowed to insert changes willy-nilly during the middle of testing. The test team gets confused when steps that used to work suddenly begin failing and steps that used to fail start working without any obvious explanation.

To avoid this confusion, the team conducts tests against a baseline that is kept in a separate directory from the version on which the programmers are working. Error reports are reported against the baseline version and sent to the programmers for debugging as soon as they are discovered. After some time, a sufficient number of problems will have been discovered that it no longer makes sense to continue testing the current baseline. At that point, the corrections that have been unit-tested are accumulated into a new baseline of the source code. A new system is built by recompiling and relinking the source code, and it is assigned the next version number. This is called the **baseline candidate**. A high-level regression test is performed on the baseline candidate to make reasonably certain that the new version does not have such glaring flaws that its adoption would hinder testing. If the baseline candidate passes this test, it becomes the new baseline.

Baseline version numbers should be chosen so that the reader can tell whether the baseline is an internal version, a beta test version for limited distribution, or a version that was shipped to the customer. Some companies use three-digit numbers for internal releases and two-digit numbers for external releases. Thus, a company might offer for sale a Version 1.2, while retaining Version 1.2.3 for internal testing. Baselines generated prior to the initial release are assigned version numbers starting with 0; for example, 0.5.1. Some companies append a T onto test versions and a B onto beta versions. The details of the numbering scheme are not critical as long as the reader can, at a glance, determine whether the program is an internal version and which was the previously released version.

Source-code versions are usually maintained with the help of a **software configuration control system (SCCS)**. The SCCS allows previous versions of software to be archived. It also prohibits two or more programmers from editing a module at the same time.

Levels of sophistication vary depending on the SCCS being used, but at their simplest they all work something like the following. After the programmer has written a module and unit-checked it, the module is added to the SCCS library and assigned the version number 1.0. When a module requires modification the first time, a programmer attempts to check out the module. If it is already checked out, the request is rejected. If it is available, the module is checked out in the programmer's name. Once the corrections have been completed, the programmer checks the module back in. The programmer may enter a comment describing the nature of the change. The source module is assigned a new version number, probably 1.1. After major changes, the programmer may change the major version number, resulting in a Version 2.0.

The baseline version number has nothing to do with the versions of the source-code modules that make it up. Thus, a baseline 1.5.1 might be made up of Version 1.4 of Module A, Version 1.7 of ModuleB, and Version 2.0 of ModuleC. These module version numbers should be retained somewhere so that the programmers know which versions of each module comprise that baseline. There are different ways of doing this but my favorite is to bury this information directly into the executable. To do this, I define the following macro in an include file VERSION.H that all modules include.

```
#define UNIQUESTRING "MODULE/FILENAME"
#define VERSION(x) \
  static char _vrsn[]=UNIQUESTRING __FILE__ " " #x
```

This macro accepts as its single argument the version of the current module. It then creates a string _vrsn that contains a unique label followed by the name of the module and the supplied version number. The string is declared static so that its definition in one module will not interfere with its definition in other modules.

For example, within the module MODULEA.CPP the following statement:

```
VERSION(1.5);
```

expands into the following

```
static char _vrsn[] = "MODULE/VERSION MODULEA.CPP 1.5";
```

Placing this macro call at the beginning of the source code causes this string to become part of the object code. During the link step this string and others like it from other modules are linked into the executable.

I then use the following WHATSIT program to search for the string "MODULE/VERSION" and print out the module name and version number that follow it. (Of course, "MODULE/VERSION" can be replaced by anything you like as long as it is not likely to appear otherwise in the program.)

```
//Whatsit - look into an executable to determine what
//          versions of the source code were used to
//          build this executable.  The first argument
//          is assumed to be the name of the program to
//          search.  If no second argument is present,
//          then all version numbers found are printed.
//          If the second argument is present, it is
//          assumed to be the name of a module.  Only
//          that module's version number is printed.

#include <stdio.h>
#include <string.h>
#include <io.h>
#include <fcntl.h>
#include <sys\stat.h>
#include <iostream.h>
```

```cpp
#include "version.h"
VERSION(1.0);          //Version of current program

void printModuleMatch(FILE* pFile, char* pMName);

int main(int argc, char *argv[]) {
    FILE *pFile;
    //there must be at least one argument
    if (argc < 2) {
        cerr <<
            "Scan a file looking for module "
                "names and version numbers\n"
            "\n"
            "Incorrect number of arguments:\n"
            "You must specify at least the name "
                "of the file to scan.\n"
            "You may also specify a module name. "
                "If you do not\n"
            "you will receive the version numbers "
                "of all modules.\n"
            "If you do, you will receive only that "
                "module's version number"
            << endl;
        return 1;
    }

    //open the indicated file
    _fmode = O_BINARY;
    pFile = fopen(argv[1], "rb");
    if (pFile == NULL) {
        cerr << "Unable to open file "
                << argv[1] << endl;
        return 1;
    }
    //scan through the file for the signature
    char nextChar;
    int matchOffset = 0;
    while(!feof(pFile)) {
```

```
                //count each character which matches
                nextChar = getc(pFile);
                if (nextChar == UNIQUESTRING[matchOffset])
                    matchOffset++;
                else
                    matchOffset = 0;

                //when the entire UNIQUESTRING found,
                //we have a match
                if (matchOffset >= (sizeof(UNIQUESTRING) - 1))
            {

                    printModuleMatch(pFile, argv[2]);
                    matchOffset = 0;
                }
        }
}

//printModuleMatch - if no specific module name given,
//                   read the module name and version
//                   number and display them.
//                   if a module name is provided, only
//                   print the module and version name
//                   if the provided module name
//                   matches the module name read.
void printModuleMatch(FILE* pFile, char* pMNName) {
    char moduleName[80];
    char versionNumber[80];

    //read the next two fields: the module name and
    //the module version number
    fscanf(pFile, "%80s %80s",
                moduleName, versionNumber);

    //if a module name is provided, check it;
    //if there is no match then skip this module name
    if (pMNName)
        if (stricmp(moduleName, pMNName) != 0)
```

```
            return;

    cout << "Module "
         << moduleName
         << "; Version "
         << versionNumber
         << endl;
}
```

For example, executing WHATSIT on itself produces the following output:

```
whatsit whatsit.exe
Module WHATSIT.CPP; Version 1.0
Module ; Version
```

Notice that the marker string UNIQUESTRING actually appears twice inside WHATSIT.CPP, once with and once without a module name. Running WHATSIT on a program with multiple modules yields output like the following:

```
D>whatsit testmt.exe
Module TESTMT.CPP; Version 1.0
Module WORM.CPP; Version 1.5
Module DIRECT.CPP; Version 1.9
Module MTASK.CPP; Version 2.1
```

Since a single executable may contains dozens of modules, this list can become uncomfortably long. To avoid this, WHATSIT allows for a third argument, which is assumed to be the name of a module. If present, only the version number of the specified module is printed. Thus, asking WHATSIT for the version number of the module DIRECT.CPP produces output like the following (WHATSIT ignores case in module names):

```
D>whatsit testmt.exe direct.cpp
Module DIRECT.CPP; Version 1.9
```

Other information could be added besides the version number, such as the date of the last modification using the __DATE__ preprocessor directive or the name of the programmer who made the change. On my IBM PC programs, I even added an indication of which memory model was used to compile the module. The data that follow the marker strings are just ASCII strings separated by white space.

Phases of Testing

Just as the design phase could be divided into high-level and detailed design, testing can be divided into the following subcategories:

- unit testing/debugging
- component test
- integration
- system tests
- acceptance test
- field test
- regression test

Each of these testing phases will be considered in turn.

Unit Testing/Debugging   The first phase is known as **unit testing/debugging**. A **unit** is either a small group of related functions, as in a source file, or a class together with its methods.

Unit debugging and unit testing are two different aspects of this phase of development. Unit testing is the process of finding errors. Unit debugging, by contrast, is the process of finding and fixing the causes of the errors discovered by testing. During the unit phase, these processes are often lumped together since they are typically performed by the same person in a cyclic, reiterative process.

Unit testing can be formalized, using the same techniques as those employed for the other levels of testing. At least initially, however, not much is gained from using a formalized approach. At the beginning of unit testing/debugging so many errors exist that almost any technique can be used to find them. Simply working through functions using data chosen in "kiddie fashion" will suffice to surface bugs at this stage.

As testing progresses, however, the unit reaches a point where it essentially works. At this point, the unit can be turned over to the next phase of testing.

Component Testing   **Component testing**, sometimes known as **group testing**, is what beginning programmers think of when they think of the word *test*. A component is an aggregate of two or more units that logically go together. A component may be a group of source code modules, a set of related classes, or a program that operates within a system.

At this point, the units should be clean enough that many of the tests work the first time they are performed. A tester should not hesitate to send back any unit that does not work. To go through a formal test on such a unit is a waste of time.

Component testing should be formalized. In larger organizations, component testing is performed by the test organization. This group constructed the test plan while the software development groups were writing the software.

Integration   **Integration** is the act of combining into a completed system the components that have made it through component testing. As the components have already been through component testing, Integration testing is primarily directed at exposing problems between components. In many organizations, integration testing is used as a last sweep to pick up errors that were not caught during earlier phases.

Many programmers imagine that all system components are combined at one time and integration begins on the resulting system. This is not the case. Integration starts with two approved components being combined and the result tested. Once these appear to work, a third component can be added and further tests undertaken. The third component need not wait until all defects have been identified and corrected between the first two components — this would take too long. However, most bugs should have been identified and characterized before the next component is added.

This stepwise approach to integration is used for two reasons. First, all of the components are never ready for integration at the same time. Large projects require fewer programmers if the component completion dates are staggered. That is, programmer A can work on component 2 while component 1 is in component testing. The same programmer can then work on component 3 while components 1 and 2 are being integrated, and so on.

Not only does this make better use of personnel, but it is safer. Lessons learned during the component testing and integration phase can be applied in the development of later components, reducing the amount of rewriting that is required.

A second reason for the step approach is that the tester wants to maintain a controlled environment as much as possible. While reporting that a test has failed, is useful, knowing in what unit the test failed is more important. This level of control is not possible when too many variables are added at one time.

Notice that stepwise integration is not a violation of the Waterfall Scheduling Method. Each component cascades through the development stages from coding and unit testing through component testing into integration.

System Testing   System testing is a catchall phrase for a number of different tests, each designed to check some aspect of the system that requires the entire program, or at least most of it, to be available. For example, performance testing attempts to show that the program cannot meet throughput or response-time requirements.

Throughput and response-time requirements are often confused under the general heading "real-time requirements." A **throughput specification** states that the system must be able to process data at a given rate or higher. Generally, such a requirement names a peak rate and duration, and a lower, sustained rate. For example, a bank system to service automatic teller machines (ATMs) might contain a requirement like the following: "The system shall be able to handle a sustained rate of 50 transactions per second averaged over any 10-minute period with a burst rate not higher than 100 transactions per second for up to 10 seconds."

A throughput requirement says nothing about how long any given transaction might take to process. For this one needs a **response-time specification**. Our sample ATM system may have an additional requirement as follows: "Users must receive an acknowledgment of input within two seconds. Individual transactions must be completed within 10 seconds of final user input."

Without a throughput specification, the ATM system could process only a single transaction at a time. Without a response-time specification, the system could store all transactions to be processed between 10 P.M. and 8

A.M. when bank activity is very low. Neither solution would result in an acceptable ATM system, however.

Other forms of testing include security testing or stress testing. In both cases, the tester establishes a possible, if unlikely, scenario to determine how well the system responds to stress.

In the case of the security test, a tiger team of experts is set loose with the task of breaking into the system. The team has an ample but limited amount of time. Usually the goal of the tiger team is to extract private data from the system; however, sometimes the goal is simply to deprive other users of use of the system. (I have read of a multiuser operating system that was virtually impenetrable, but could be brought to its knees by repeatedly attempting to log in with the same invalid password at the 9600 baud allowed by a terminal.)

In stress testing, the system is deprived of assets to see how it responds. A system designed to work with a certain amount of RAM might be executed on a system with less and less memory. This type of testing is a little like the types of drug testing the FDA performs on mice: Rather than administer normal dosages to millions of mice, researchers give fewer mice large overdoses in the hope of generating a higher incidence of a side effect that would occur even at the lower dosage.

The results of stress tests must be interpreted carefully (one might almost say "compassionately"). Depriving a program of memory might cause the program to execute more slowly, but that is of little interest. The purpose of stress tests is to force the program to demonstrate errors that could surface anyway. Errors that arise under stress conditions but cannot occur under field conditions can be accepted without correction. For example, in the memory deprivation test eventually the point will be reached where the program cannot execute at all; however, as long as the program exits gracefully, generating meaningful error messages, the program can be said to have passed the test.

Other forms of system testing include compatibility tests designed to determine how compatible a system is with a previous system, availability tests designed to determine system reliability (mean time between failure), serviceability tests designed to determine time to repair (mean time to repair), and recoverability tests designed to determine if the system can recover properly after a crash, power outage, or other serious error.

Acceptance Testing   The **acceptance test** is a subset of the component and integration tests. Historically this is the test that a software developer performs to prove that the system is error-free and ready to be put into use by the customer.

Of course, such a test does nothing of the sort, but it is a useful milestone. A well-written acceptance test demonstrates that the functions of the system appear to work under normal conditions. An acceptance test should not attempt to be the end-all test. An error is an error and should be fixed even if it is not detected by the acceptance test.

On the other hand, passing does not mean that the system passed every single step of the acceptance test without error. Most large systems are shipped with errors outstanding with the understanding that these problems will be fixed as part of on-site testing. This is reasonable since both the software house and the customer know that new problems will be discovered once the system is installed.

Field Testing   Most testing should be performed at the development site. However, managers are sometimes tempted to ship a program that has yet to complete testing in order to meet a delivery deadline. A team of programmers is sent along to clean up the remaining problems on-site. This is always a mistake.

A software developer is always more efficient at home in familiar surroundings with all of the development and testing assets available. Forcing the developer to an unfamiliar site with only a skeleton crew and insufficient hardware only delays the program. Further, if a difficult problem should arise that requires a particular individual with specialized skills, it will be very expensive to ship that person to the site to handle the problem.

The only exception to this rule that I can imagine is shipping a product in which some, but not all, of the functionality is in place and tested with the intent that the system be completed at home and the complete system shipped later. This is especially true if the contractor is using the Recursive Scheduling Method.

Nevertheless, even a well-tested, completed program should go through a field test period before being turned over to the customer. This can take several forms.

The most limited form is **on-site support**. Here the product is shipped along with a few support programmers. Programmers with different areas of expertise are picked so that together all aspects of the program are covered with a minimal number of programmers. These programmers assist in the installation of the software. Problems that arise after the system is installed are isolated on the spot and reported back to the developer's home site where they are fixed and retested. Periodically an updated system is shipped and the fixed problems are retested on-site. When the on-site programmers are not isolating problems, they are training customer programmers in the maintenance of the program. After a prescribed period of time, the on-site programmers turn maintenance over to the customer programmers and return to their home base.

Another form of field testing is the **beta test**. Prereleased versions of the software are shipped to selected test sites. The earliest versions, called the alpha versions, are shipped to a very select group, perhaps only other departments of the developer's company. The later, beta versions have gone through component and integration testing, but perhaps not without errors. These versions are shipped to a wider audience, usually including highly regarded technical customers. The beta versions are supplied with an errata sheet describing the known problems. Users are encouraged to promptly report problems that they find. Beta testing is discussed further later in this chapter.

The most involved form of field testing is the **hot backup**, which is used when replacing a critical system. In this test, the existing system is allowed to continue operation while the new system is installed. The input to the old system is duplicated and fed to the new system. The installation and test programmers compare the output of the new system with that of the old system. This is shown in Figure 7–1. Since analysis may take much longer than the time required to produce the data, the new system is generally only turned on for limited time periods, perhaps once during peak loading, once during the evening, once during the day, and so on.

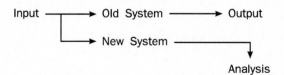

Figure 7–1. A hot backup on-site test

Only after the analysts are convinced that the new system is working does operation shift over. The old system is often retained for a short time as a backup in the event the new system fails.

Regression Testing   Systems undergo change, either during continued development or as a result of the addition of features in new versions. **Regression testing** is a rerunning of tests that were previously passed to make sure that newer modifications have not broken existing software.

When testing first begins, there is no regression test. As component testing proceeds, some subset of the tests that have been passed are thrown into what Watts Humphries calls the **regression bucket**. Periodically during the testing of the system, the tests found in the regression bucket are rerun.

Determining which tests should be in the regression bucket is a matter of judgment. Including all component and integration tests results in a comprehensive regression test that is so difficult to run that it cannot be performed often enough. Including only a few key tests results in a regression test that is easy to perform but doesn't demonstrate very much.

The best compromise is to build several regression tests:

- a large, comprehensive test
- a small, easily performed test
- a separate small test for each major component of the system

The smaller regression test can be rerun often, perhaps before the release of each software version to the testing team. The comprehensive test should be performed on a much less frequent basis, perhaps once every two months. The component regression tests should be run on a cyclical schedule so that each is performed once by the time the comprehensive test comes due.

After the program has been delivered into the field, the regression test plans and results are saved together with the source code and executable. As bugs are found in the field and the fixes applied, the new version is run through regression testing before being shipped back to the field.

Types of Tests

In addition to the phases of testing, many types of tests can be run. The different tests fall into the following broad categories:

- reviews
- static analysis
- proof of correctness
- structural tests
- functional tests

The following sections examine each of these types of tests, including its strengths and weaknesses. Finally, we will discuss which tests are most effective at locating what types of bugs.

Reviews

Many programmers do not consider peer reviews to be a testing technique at all. Yet to my mind peer review is the most effective test of all. Any bug that is found in a peer review will not need to be found and removed by some other means of testing. Reviews are an attractive testing technique for other reasons as well.

First, reviews tend to find bugs early when they are cheaper to fix. Most other test techniques require that the software be written before testing can begin. Requirements reviews can be performed even before the design is complete.

Second, reviews are more educational to the programmer than any other testing technique. Development programmers should not be divorced from the test phase of the project. A programmer who makes a particular type of error but is never shown the mistake will continue to make the same mistake over and over again. Testing should provide some type of feedback to the programmers to allow them to learn from their errors. Peer reviews provide the most beneficial and direct feedback of any of the testing techniques.

Third, peer reviews open up channels of information between programmers. Too often, a programmer is given the requirements or design for a single section of the problem and sent off to code it. That programmer may not understand how that piece fits into the remainder of the system until integration is well underway. Peer reviews allow each programmer to see how his or her piece fits with those of the other programmers to build the system.

Fourth, peer reviews are an educational process for both beginning and experienced programmers. The younger programmers learn proven techniques from the old hands, while the older programmers get to see some new ideas presented during these exchanges.

Finally, reviews motivate people to produce better work. When programmers know their work will be critically examined by their peers, they work more carefully and adhere more rigorously to standards either to avoid being embarrassed by sloppy work or to be able to display a superior product.

There are at least four different types of reviews:

- requirements reviews
- high-level design reviews
- detailed design reviews
- code reviews

Some researchers would add a test plan review to this list as well.

Reviewing the entire requirements, design, or code at one time is not necessary (or even desirable). Instead, sections of the requirements, design, and code are reviewed separately.

Requirements Reviews   Coming as early as they do in the development cycle, the requirements reviews are the most important of all of the reviews and probably the least likely to be performed. Their primary purpose is to discover inconsistent or misleading requirements. Just as important, however, are missing requirements — for example, a multiuser system with no throughput or response-time requirements. (The absence of these requirements does not benefit the developer — without a goal, programmers are apt to code faster and faster modules, eventually exceeding the required performance, at great cost.) Reviewers should also look for unquantifiable terms, like "the system shall show good response time." Such requirements only provide bones of contention when it is time for acceptance testing.

Requirements reviews also make sure that the requirements are testable. Including a requirement that is not sufficiently independent of other requirements nor sufficiently well-defined to be tested does little good.

Another aspect of the requirements review that is often overlooked is communication. The lead programmers are sometimes left to present the requirements back to the authors, the systems designers, and other programmers. This presentation forces the lead programmers to become intimately familiar with the requirements and allows the designers to test that knowledge. This is an effective communication technique.

Design Review   Once the requirements are understood, it is time to work on the design. Typically the problem is broken up into components that are designed separately and combined to form the complete program. Design reviews may be held on each component separately. Once high-level design on a component is completed, it may be subdivided for the detailed design step. If this is the case, the detailed design reviews should be held separately as well. The amount of material should be kept small enough to be easily reviewed in a one-hour period.

The goal of the design review is to ensure that the design meets the requirements, is well-structured, is feasible given the constraints of the system, and is testable and robust.

Code Review   Code reviews occur quite late in the development cycle. Before being submitted for review, the code module should be documented and have completed unit testing. In fact, code review is typically the last step the module undergoes before being checked in to source code management.

Surprisingly, code reviews are no more effective than the other reviews in finding software bugs — in fact, they are somewhat less so. Organizations just beginning to perform reviews spend more time in code reviews than in the others. However, after these same organizations have gained experience in the review process, the amount of time spent in code reviews drops while the amount of time spent in the other reviews increases dramatically.

Consider why this is so. A good detailed design has checked out the algorithm that the code is to use. Not much is left for the code review other than checking the programmer's logic and making sure that coding guidelines are being followed. Still the code reviews should not be skipped.

Often, more errors are found in preparing for code reviews than in the reviews themselves. Even if code reviews found no errors, knowing that they are there forces programmers to be more careful.

Conducting a Review   Reviews should be formal with a checklist of items to be accomplished. Studies have shown that informal reviews, called **walk-throughs**, are not as effective as formal reviews. Programmers should be provided with a handbook detailing the goals, requirements, attendees, and conduct of each review type. This handbook may consist of a few photocopied pages, but it should be complete. The review summaries that follow were adapted from just such a handbook developed for the programmers at E-Systems, Inc. of Greenville, Texas.

These guidelines appear quite formal and may seem like overkill for a small program. However, they have been applied with positive results on projects involving only two programmers and one designer after making some allowances for the small number of people involved. For projects involving five or more programmers, the benefits of this level of formality are undeniable.

Software Engineering Review Summary

Requirements Review:
Person responsible:	Lead Programmer
Presenter:	Lead Programmer
Audience:	Leads from other groups
	Programmers for this effort
	Software task leader
	Requirements developers
	Software QA
Time frame:	Prior to development of design
Purpose:	Demonstrate understanding of requirements

Top-Level Design Review:
Person responsible:	Lead Programmer
Presenter:	Programmer Coach
Audience:	Leads from other groups on same portion of the project
	Programmers for this effort
	Software task leader
	Software QA

Time frame: Prior to development of detailed design
Purpose: Demonstrate that requirements are being met
                     by a reasonable and workable design

Detailed-Level Design Review:
Person responsible: Programmer
Presenter: Programmer Coach
Audience: Software lead
                     Programmers for this effort
                     Software task leader
                     Software QA
Time frame: Prior to start of coding
Purpose: Demonstrate that requirements are being met
                     by a reasonable and workable design

Code and Test Review:
Person responsible: Programmer
Presenter: Programmer Coach
Audience: Software lead
                     Two programmers who attended design reviews
                     Software QA
Time frame: Prior to source code module being controlled
Purpose: Demonstrate that requirements are being met
                     by a reasonable and workable design

Requirements Review Guidelines

Purpose:
- Verify that the requirements are complete and correct. Detect problem area like definition deficiencies, performance, or storage restraints.

- Determine impact of requirements on design and coding effort.

- Demonstrate familiarity of the programming team with the requirements.

Preparation:
- The lead programmer reviews the requirements.

- The lead programmer reserves a room and invites attendees at least 24 hours in advance.

- The review script to be used during presentation and copies of the requirements to be reviewed must be provided to the review attendees with the letter of invitation. It is the responsibility of the review team to study this material before attending the review.

Review:
- Presenter hands out schedule.
- Presenter makes a high-level presentation of the requirements. Presenter may assume that the attendees are familiar with the requirements.
- Presenter leads discussion to any problems with the requirements or requirements that will be particularly difficult to meet.

Problem Resolution:
Requirements flaws are corrected together with requirements team.

High-Level Design Review Guidelines

Purpose:
- Verify that the design is complete and correct.

- Verify that the design is implementable and testable.

- Verify that the design meets requirements.

Preparation:
- Programmer completes high-level design. Programmer selects a "programmer coach." Together the programmer and coach go over the design until both feel it is ready to be reviewed. The coach may suggest changes in the design.

- The programmer reserves a room and invites participants at least 24 hours in advance.

- The programmer makes available at the time of invitation copies of all the PDL, flow charts, the names and rough description of any messages sent, data descriptions, and so on. It is the responsibility of the review team to study this material before attending the review.

Review:

- The coach hands out the schedule for the presentation. The coach presents a high-level description of the design.

- Reviewers challenge with any problems they found in the design. They should be particularly wary that:

    1. the design meets requirements
    2. error detection and recovery are covered
    3. interface to other units has been coordinated
    4. the design is testable
    5. the design is implementable
    6. the design is robust
    7. the design makes effective use of class abstraction
    8. the design is adaptable to changes and extensible
    9. the design is efficient

Problem Resolution:

Design problems are corrected and demonstrated to the lead programmer.

Detailed-Design Review Guidelines

Purpose:

- Verify that the detailed design matches the high-level design and that it is sufficiently complete to allow coding.

- Verify that some thought has been given as to what type of test bed will be required for unit and component testing.

Preparation:

- Programmer completes detailed design and finds and trains a coach. The coach may suggest changes to the detailed design.

- The programmer must reserve a room and invite participants at least 24 hours in advance.

- The programmer makes available to the reviewers at the time of invitation flow charts, PDL, detailed data definitions, message formats, and so on. It is the responsibility of the reviewers to study this material prior to attending the review.

Review:
- The coach hands out the schedule for the presentation. The coach presents a description of the detailed design. This design should be divided along the same lines that it will be implemented (that is, divided by major units and classes).

- Reviewers challenge with any problems they found in the design. They should be particularly wary that:

1. the detailed design matches the high-level design
2. error detection and recovery are covered
3. interface to other units has been coordinated (that is, message and data formats are provided in detail and match those demonstrated at other detailed designs)
4. the design puts inheritance, data hiding, and other object-oriented techniques to good use
5. sufficient detail is available to allow coding
6. sufficient test tools will be available at unit test

Problem Resolution:
Minor problems with the detailed design may be fixed and redemonstrated to the team leader.

Code and Test Review Guidelines

Purpose:
- Verify that the design has been correctly implemented.

- Verify that the proposed unit test is sufficient.

Preparation:
- Programmer completes detailed design and finds and trains a coach. The coach may suggest changes to the source code or the suggest the addition of further test cases.

- The programmer must reserve a room and invite participants at least 24 hours in advance. Reviewers should be chosen from attendees of the detailed design review.

- The programmer makes available to the reviewers at the time of invitation source code, include file listings, and unit test cases. It is the responsibility of the reviewers to study this material prior to attending the review. Both source code and test cases are reviewed against the requirements contained in the Coding Style Guide (see Chapter 4).

Review:
- The coach hands out the schedule for the presentation. The coach presents a description of the test cases chosen.

- Reviewers challenge with any problems they found in the source code or test cases. They should be particularly wary that:

  1. the code implements the detailed design
  2. the code matches the requirements of the style guide
  3. the test cases are reasonably complete
  4. the logic presented by conditionals is correct (if statements are formulated correctly, for loops terminate at the proper time, and so on.)
  5. the programmer has not fallen into one of the C/C++ traps (see Chapters 5 and 6)
  6. the programmer has made effective use of C++ features

Problem Resolution:
Minor problems with the detailed design may be fixed and redemonstrated to the team leader.

Reviews should be designed to last approximately one hour. In no case should a review extend beyond 90 minutes. The stress of such long meetings is too high and efficiency suffers. If a review extends beyond this time, it is usually because a disagreement has arisen. Such a review should be continued at a later date.

Attendees at reviews should be technical staff only, since the goal is to point out errors, not to punish programmers for mistakes. The presence of managers at reviews changes the perception of the programmers that it is they who are being reviewed. The results of the reviews, in the form of status reports, can be given to managers to assuage their curiosity. Attendees should receive the information to be presented at the review far enough ahead of time to allow them to study the material.

Notice that the preceding guidelines specify that the material should not be presented by the person who originated it. In the example, this presenter is called the **programmer coach**. The idea of a programmer coach may seem odd to those who have not tried it, but it has several benefits. First, the writer of the requirements, design, or code is naturally defensive of any criticism from the reviewers. The coach is in a better position to determine whether criticisms are justified or not. Second, the writer needs to be concentrating on the review discussions, not worrying about what to present next. Remaining in the audience gives the author more time to think about the discussions. Third, the coach must become familiar with the material before the presentation. It is an advantage to the group to have more than one programmer acquainted with the material.

The final reason has more to do with human nature. The coach does not want to be embarrassed by presenting flawed material any more than the author. Thus, the coach is obliged to study the material in detail. Anything suspicious will be discussed in the non-threatening environment of programmer coach to programmer. Experience has shown that more problems are discovered and corrected in the programmer/coach meetings prior to the presentations than in the reviews themselves.

A secretary is appointed at the beginning of each review. The job of the secretary is to fill out the checklist and note any problems that the review discovered. Checklists are generic for each review type, although they may be adapted to the needs of particular programs. They cover planning, preparation, conduct, and conclusion of the review. A sample of the first page of a checklist appears as follows:

Review Report

Project:_____   Date:_____

Unit Name:_____   Program:_____

Presenter:_____   Programmer:_____

Moderator:_____   Pass/Fail:_____

Review Type: Req_____ HLD_____ DD_____ C&T_____

Duration: ____ min.**Lines/pages reviewed:**_____

Reviewers:_____

_____

_____

No. of problems found:_____

No. of pages attached:_____

Subsequent pages of the review form are used to record problems. These appear below:

Page _____ of ___

Number of problems this page:____

Problem #:_____

Where found:_____ Problem taxonomy:_____

Description of problem:_____

_____

_____

_____

_____

Page _____ of ___

Number of problems this page:____

Problem #:_____

Where found:_____ Problem taxonomy:_____

Description of problem:_____

_____

_____

_____

_____

The problem taxonomy refers to the type of problem using the same taxonomic categories as used for the Error Reporting Form. Some of the data is for strictly historical reasons. For example, recording the amount of time spent in the review, number of errors, and whether those errors could have been discovered during testing allows for a post-project analysis of the effectiveness of reviews.

Each review must have a moderator responsible for making sure the meeting is conducted properly. The moderator also decides whether the material presented passes or fails the review. If the review is not passed, the presenter must make the necessary changes and present the material again later. If problems are found but they are not deemed to be serious, the fixes may be made and redemonstrated to the moderator. The moderator may be a senior programmer or a Software QA representative. It is best if a moderator has either training or previous experience in software reviews.

Review Effectiveness How effective are reviews at detecting errors? In one study reported by Watts Humphries in *Managing the Software Process*, AT&T Bell Laboratories reported that inspections were 20 times more cost effective in finding software errors than functional testing.

Statistics show that the efficiency of reviews varies considerably, depending upon the amount of experience and training of the participants. Humphries reports a study in which the initial efficiency for reviews was 15 percent, that is, for every 100 bugs, 15 were found during the review cycle. While even this rate of return might justify the cost of reviews, by the third release of the program, efficiency had risen to 61 percent. For every 100 defects in the software, a full 61 were isolated during the reviews (all review types included).

On one particular project, E. Yourdon reports in *Structured Walkthroughs* that when three experienced programmers reviewed a 200-line PL/1 program for 45 minutes, they found 25 bugs, 5 of which could not have been detected by functional testing.

Quoting a Freedman and Weinberg study, Humphries also reports that software quality on a large COBOL project went from an average of 450 errors per KLOC before inspections to 8 errors per KLOC after inspections were introduced — that a reduction by a factor of 50 in the number of errors making their way to test!

Static and Dynamic Analysis

Static analysis is the name given to a group of associated and interrelated software techniques for finding structural and semantic bugs. Static analysis tools analyze the code without actually executing it.

Static analysis is very good at detecting some types of errors, such as determining that a function is being called incorrectly or that a variable is declared but never used. Static analysis can also determine the likelihood — but cannot prove — that a variable is being used before it is assigned a value. Static analysis has a very difficult time with some errors. For example, static analysis cannot warn you that a function contains a division by zero (unless the zero is a constant). It cannot warn you that an index into an array is too large or that a pointer is invalid.

Some static analyzers are designed to work with C++ source code. In fact, all modern C++ compilers contain fairly sophisticated static analyzers that are responsible for generating warnings. Disabling the warnings robs you of the benefit of this testing tool.

Another class of static analyzer works not on the C++ source code but on the design written in some form of structured PDL. These tools can analyze designs for consistency and completeness. At one time in the late 1970s, the industry held great hope for PDL analysis tools, but the excitement seems to have dwindled since then.

Dynamic analysis executes the program with checks in place. This type of analysis is best performed during unit testing, since it involves executing the program with extra code added, often at much reduced speeds. Dynamic analysis tools are often designed to catch one particular type of problem, such as stack overflow or an invalid pointer reference. Such analysis may be very effective at catching the one type of error for which it is designed, but totally ineffective at detecting other serious errors.

Proof of Correctness

Some researchers have worked on the technique of proving programs correct. **Proof of correctness** starts by expressing relationships that must be true at the beginning of the unit. The next step is to express the relationships that are expected to hold when the unit completes. These are similar to Eiffel's entrance and exit assertions. The unit being tested is then converted into assertions of the relationships between the data variables within the unit. These assertions are evaluated using the lamda calculus. The proof consists of demonstrating that given the starting relationships and all of the assertions contained within the unit, the expected results must follow.

The difficulties of proof of correctness are daunting. First, the complexities of such proofs make it impossible to prove a unit correct as soon as the unit exceeds the size of a small function. Second, the proofs are extremely labor intensive and prone to error. Thus, if the proof contains an error, the unit itself may have errors.

If the derivation of the proof could be automated, both of these problems would diminish somewhat. The idea of allowing a super analyzer program to study and eventually prove that a program is correct is very attractive.

However, a third difficulty with proof of correctness is not so easily solved: the inability to prove the correctness of a program does not necessarily mean that the program actually has an error. The programmer can expend considerable effort modifying a unit that has no software defect to make it provably correct. In addition, if a program does have an error, the process does not indicate what that error might be.

Proof of correctness is not a reality today. It may become a reality someday for systems in which the cost of failure is very high, such as flight or rocket control systems. Software has a long way to go, however, before proof of correctness is an alternative for conventional software systems.

Provably Secure Operating Systems   Great impetus has been given to proof of correctness efforts by the National Security Agency (NSA). In carrying out its functions, this agency of the federal government must keep and maintain large amounts of classified material. In order to assure that material would not be leaked to personnel who do not have the proper clearance, the NSA established rules for handling classified data.

One of these rules stated that if classified material was stored in a computer system, only people with clearances were allowed access to the system. Enforcing this rule proved to be expensive. Purchasing a single VAX for a department was no longer sufficient. The NSA was forced to purchase a non-classified VAX as well as a classified VAX. The two were not allowed to communicate, so separate databases had to be maintained, and so on. Clearly the NSA could save a lot of money if they could loosen the access rule.

The only way to bend the access rule was to build an operating environment in which it would be impossible for an unclassified user to access classified material. Demonstrating a lack of access was not sufficient, the environment vendor had to prove that access was impossible.

Since the late 1970s operating system manufacturers have been working to develop such **provably secure operating systems**. This work has taught them something about the proof of correctness problem.

First, it is possible, but difficult to prove a design; it is not possible at this point to prove the source code. The current state of the art is to describe the design of the system and to prove that the design achieves its goals. Once the design has been proven, programmers manually encode the design into source statements.

Second, a system cannot be designed and then later proven to be secure. The design must be written to be provable from the beginning. In fact, the design will have to be changed many times before it can be proven, even though the original design may have, in fact, been secure.

Finally, provable designs are often less efficient than normal designs due to the measures one must take to allow the proof to be made.

In response to these problems, designers resorted to proving a secure nucleus upon which a conventionally designed and written, non-proven operating system relied. To reduce the costs, difficulties, and inefficiencies, this nucleus must be kept as small as possible. Unfortunately, while this technique allows provably secure operating systems to be built, it is not much help to the proof of correctness problem.

Structural Testing

To many programmers, structural testing is the only type of testing there is. **Structural testing** consists of providing input so as to achieve maximum coverage of the unit under test. This is often called **white box** or **glass box testing**, since structural testing requires an intimate knowledge of the internals of the unit. It is also called **path testing** because executing a carefully chosen set of paths results in a large percentage of the unit being tested.

The motivation behind path testing is clear. Executing every statement and every branch in a program should flush out the majority of bugs. Path testing is almost the only type of test programmers use when testing small units, such as individual functions.

Unfortunately the effectiveness of path testing decreases as the size of the unit increases. Path testing cannot be used on large components because the number of paths is too large to be covered.

Types of Path Coverage   Path testing is based upon the concept of a control flow graph. A **control flow graph** is a flowchart in which sequences of statements without branches either in or out are reduced to a single node (just like those used to calculate the McCabe Cyclomatic Complexity). These straight-line code segments are called **process blocks**. For example, the following main() function taken from the WHATSIT program earlier in this chapter can be broken into the flow graph shown in Figure 7–2.

```
//excerpt from WHATSIT
int main(int argc, char *argv[]) {
    FILE *pFile;

    //there must be at least one argument
    if (argc < 2) {
        cout <<
           "Scan a file looking for module "
                "names and version numbers\n"
            "\n"
            "Incorrect number of arguments:\n"
            "You must specify at least the name "
                "of the file to scan.\n"
            "You may also specify a module name. "
                "If you do not\n"
            "you will receive the version numbers "
                "of all modules.\n"
            "If you do, you will receive only that "
                "module's version number\n";
        return 1;
    }

    //open the indicated file
    _fmode = O_BINARY;
    pFile = fopen(argv[1], "rb");
    if (pFile == NULL) {
```

```
            cout << "Unable to open file "
                    << argv[1]
                    << endl;
            return 1;
        }

        //scan through the file for the signature
        char nextChar;
        int matchOffset = 0;
        while(!feof(pFile)) {
            //count each character which matches
            nextChar = getc(pFile);
            if (nextChar == UNIQUESTRING[matchOffset])
                matchOffset++;
            else
                matchOffset = 0;

            //when the entire UNIQUESTRING found,
            //we have a match
            if (matchOffset >= (sizeof(UNIQUESTRING) - 1))
{

                printModuleMatch(pFile, argv[2]);
                matchOffset = 0;
            }
        }
    }
```

A **path** is a sequence of instructions through a program. The length of the path is measured by the number of links in the chain, that is, the number of squares and triangles in the flow path, not by the number of executable statements. A **complete path** is a path that starts at the beginning of the unit and goes through until the end.

To perform a complete test one would like to exercise every complete path through the unit. Beizer calls this **100 percent path coverage**. This is clearly not practical for units of any size and is generally impossible for units with loops in them.

The next best test one could hope for would be to execute paths so that every link extending from every branch is executed at least once. This is known as **full** or **100 percent branch coverage**. Full branch coverage is achievable.

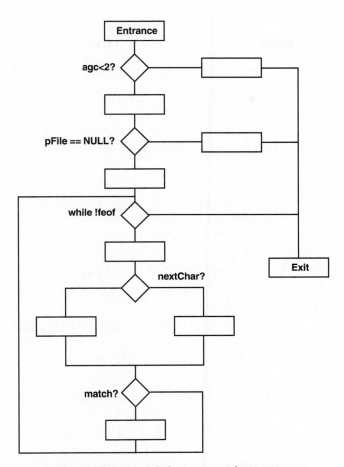

Figure 7–2. Control flow graph for `main()` **of** WHATSIT.CPP

Another alternative is to exercise paths so that every statement is executed at least once. This is known as **full** or **100 percent statement coverage**. Full statement coverage is a weaker test than full branch coverage. In the following function, for example, it is necessary to call abs() only once with a negative value to achieve full statement coverage. The function would have to be called twice, once with a negative value and once with a positive value, to achieve full branch coverage.

```
//abs() - return the absolute value of the argument
int abs(int x) {
    if (x < 0)
```

```
        x = -x;
    return x;
}
```

Full statement coverage is achievable and is the minimum acceptable level of testing. Any less than this implies that the programmer is willing to turn loose on the user code that has never been executed. The IEEE has established full statement coverage as the minimum for complete unit testing.

Programmers sometimes argue that statements belonging to paths that are executed only rarely, if at all, need not be tested. Two types of paths fall into this category: error paths and unusual command sequences. On the first account, untested code belonging to error paths may actually make the situation worse. For example, a programmer adds a check for illegal characters in the data stream but never tests it. That code contains a fatal error. Now what would have gone through as a garbage character crashes the system.

On the second account, programmers typically do not know which paths are common and which are unusual. The way the end user uses a system and the way a programmer who helped build it uses the same system is often radically different. On one large project, we kept a particular customer on call because of his uncanny ability to crash the system, usually within five minutes. Invariably the programmer's reaction upon learning of the crash was "Who would ever want to do that!?" The answer was, of course, "He did."

A slightly stronger testing requirement is **full predicate coverage** in which every predicate can achieve every possible value. In the absence of compound `if` statements this is the same as full branch coverage, but in their presence full predicate coverate implies multiple tests per branch. For example, calling the following function `factorial()` with the values -5 and 5 provides branch coverage. To provide predicate coverage, however, one must add a case that passes the first predicate but fails the second, such as 5.5. Notice that because the order of evaluation of && is defined, it is not necessary to provide a case to cover the opposite set of predicates, such as -5.5.

```
float factorial(float N) {
    float fact = 1.0;
    //if N is positive and has no fractional part
    //(within epsilon)
    if (N > 0 && abs(trunc(N)) < epsilon) {
        for (int n = (N + epsilon); n > 1; n--)
            fact = fact * n;
    }
    return fact;
}
```

Demonstrating Path Coverage To demonstrate that a particular level of coverage has been achieved, one starts by naming either the links or the nodes of a flow graph. For example, Figure 7–3 on the following page is the same as Figure 7–2 with labels added.

Begin tracing each path through the unit, marking down the names of either the nodes or the links. If statement coverage is your goal, you need only mark down the node names. If you are shooting for branch coverage, note the names of the links.

Consider how to achieve branch coverage for this function. Start by noting the straight-through path `abcde` along with the obvious error paths noted as `aor` and `abcpr`. Once the `while` loop is encountered beginning with node 6, a virtually unlimited number of paths exist, all with similar names:

abcdeq
abcdefghilnq
abcdefghilnfghilnq
...etc.

Shorthand names for these paths are as follows:

abcde(fghiln)^{0}q
abcde(fghiln)^{1}q
abcde(fghiln)^{2}q
...etc.

The different cases can be lumped together using the same nomenclature adopted earlier: * means 0 or more times and $^+$ means 1 or more times. Thus, the preceding set of paths can be given the name `abcde(fghiln)*q`. The general loop case is described using the `M/N` superscript where `M` is the maximum number of times through the loop and `N` is the minimum.

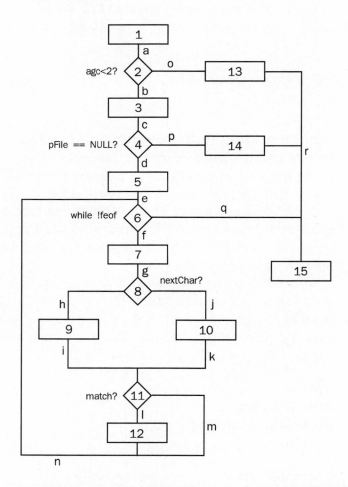

Figure 7–3. Control flow graph for `main()` of WHATSIT.CPP with labels

Alternative branches are noted using the + symbol, which is read as `or`. An expression such as `g(hi+jk)l` is read "the link `g` followed by either the links `hi` or the links `jk`, followed by `l`". Thus, the expression `abcde(fg(hi+jk)(l+m))n)*q` is a more complete flow description of the function. A variable can be assigned as shorthand for a particular sequence. For example, you might assign the sequence `abcde` the name `S`, the if statement (hi+jk) as I_1, and the if statement (l+m) as I_2. This would enable you to rewrite the foregoing expression as S(fgI$_1$I$_2$)*q.

Test cases are now constructed to handle each of the paths described by the control flow expressions. This usually involves establishing a test to handle one of the paths, either the shortest or the most obvious. A small variation on this test will usually be sufficient to force execution down one of the other paths. Occasionally, it is difficult to arrange a test to force execution down a particular path, especially error paths. Most debuggers allow the programmer to resume execution from a particular line. When there is no other way, this feature can be used to cause the program to branch down a particular link.

Some may consider devising multiple tests with only slight differences a waste of time. However, small changes from one test to the next imply gradual changes in the test setup leading to more rapid execution of the tests. In addition, by changing only one independent variable at a time, you have a good idea of where to look when a software error arises. Finally, there is really no other way to make sure that each of the different branches is executed.

Path Coverage and Loops   Loops that only execute a fixed number of times are essentially no different than any other path; however, loops that execute a variable number of iterations represent a particularly thorny problem for path coverage. In general, it is not possible to test all of the possible number of iterations such a loop can experience. The following guidelines will discover most bugs, however.

During unit testing, the first time a loop is tested, use a source code debugger. After each node, check the data that the node has referenced. Before each loop, check the values of all variables involved in the increment section and in the predicate. Single step through the loop a second time, rechecking the same data. Make sure that the termination condition appears reasonable and that any pointers are being updated properly (the easiest way to do this is to examine what the pointer points to). Glaring errors will be found rapidly this way, while the programmer will get a better feel for the algorithm.

Repeat this step for each path within the loop. The sample program actually presented two loop paths fghiln and fgjkmn. Both of these loops should be single-stepped twice.

Now try executing the loop one fewer than the maximum number of times and then the maximum number of times, if possible. Be sure to test the case where the loop is not executed at all and attempt to force the loop into infinite execution.

A **nested loop** is a loop that is contained within another loop. It has a description like (abc(defg)⁺h)*. Nested loops offer additional testing headaches. To test such loops, test the innermost loop as you would a single loop with all outer loops held to their minimum values. That done, move outward one level and test the next loop the same way. Continue until the outermost loop has been tested.

A further consideration are **concatenated** or **serial loops**. These loops occur along a single path, but are not contained within each other. If the two loops are independent, they can be tested separately. If, however, they are not independent, then they should be tested as much like nested loops as the code allows.

Data Flow Testing   In discussing the Figure 7–3 flow graph, we were only concerned with achieving some level of statement coverage. The same flow graph can be used to make sure that data coverage is achieved as well.

Start by noting the different states in which a data object can find itself.

Letter	C++ Meaning
c	created
a	assigned a value
d	destructed
u	used

Initializing a value at the time that the object is created, either via an initializer list or a constructor, we will note as ca. Similar states can be used for other types of data objects, such as files, but for this example we will use memory data objects.

Look again at the control flow graph noting the operations that occur to the data objects of interest. The result is known as a **data flow graph**. The data flow graph for WHATSIT.CPP appears in Figure 7–4 on the following page. Following the variable matchOffset down the path abcdefghimnfghimnfgjkmnq you can see the following transitions: cauauuauad. The description of loops in the data flow graph can be abbreviated the same way as in the control flow graphs, thus the path `abcde(fghimn)*q` results in the data transitions `ca(uau)*d`.

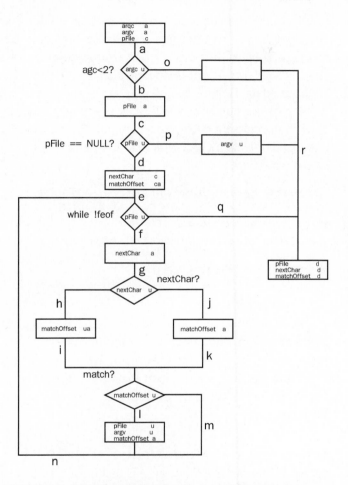

Figure 7–4. Data flow graph for `main()` of `WHATSIT.CPP`.

Full data coverage is achieved if each of the possible data transition graphs is tested. The goal of this testing is to isolate transitions that look suspicious such as the following examples:

`aa` - the second assignment overwrites the first without it being used; is this correct?
`cd` - this makes no sense unless the constructor for the object has side effects; either the object is not used or you have missed a reference

cu - this is a mistake; the object has been used without being assigned a value

Of course, full data coverage is as impossible to achieve for realistic functions as full path testing, so other lesser goals are attempted that are too numerous to detail here. For a more complete description see Boris Beizer, *Software Testing Techniques*, 2nd ed., 1990.

When data flowing pointers, you must decide whether to flow the pointer or the object at which it is pointing. Generally, you will want to flow both, but separately. For example, the following code segment allocates two objects: pObj, which is of type Object* and *pObj, which is of type Object.

```
ostream& operator<<(ostream&, Object&);

void fn(char *pName) {
    Object* pObj = new Object(pName);

    cout << *pObj;
}
```

The state diagram for the object pObj is caud. This poses no problems; however, when you look at the object *pObj, you find a state diagram of cau (new created the object, the constructor for Object assigned it a value, and the inserter uses the value). From this you can see that the object *pObj is never destructed and, thus, its memory never returned to the heap.

Other Types of Flow Graphs   Once the data transitions were added to the control flow graph, picking cases to test the possible data transitions was very similar to picking test cases to ensure control coverage, such as branch or statement coverage. In fact, the flow graph can be generalized to test for any desired property.

In path testing only the existence of the links was of interest. No value was assigned to the links themselves and all links were considered equal. In data testing, the links were annotated according to how they affected particular data objects. Testing strategies are based upon selecting test path segments that satisfy or examine some characteristic of the data.

The tester can invent other test paths by annotating the links with the effect they have on other aspects of the system. For instance, one might note what effect links have on heap memory. This is of interest since heap memory is often corrupted due to failure to release a heap object, releasing a heap object multiple times, or using a heap object after it has been released.

These attributes need not be strictly qualitative. Quantitative values may be assigned as well, such as the execution time or the amount of stack used by a particular link. When this is the case, the flow path nomenclature takes on further significance. Consider, for example, the flow graph in Figure 7–5, which is marked with the time to execute the different links.

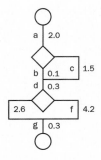

Figure 7–5. Hypothetical timing flow graph

The flow description for such a flow graph is `a(b+c)d(e+f)g`. By unfolding the paths through the `if` statements, the graph expands into the following `abdeg+abdfg+acdeg+acdfg`. You can then pose such questions as, "What is the maximum time through the system?" The possibilities are as follows:

abdeg	-> 2.0 + 0.1 + 0.3 + 2.6 + 0.3 =	5.3
abdfg	-> 2.0 + 0.1 + 0.3 + 4.2 + 0.3 =	7.0
acdeg	-> 2.0 + 1.5 + 0.3 + 2.6 + 0.3 =	6.7
acdfg	-> 2.0 + 1.5 + 0.3 + 4.2 + 0.3 =	8.3

Thus, the maximum time through the system is 8.3 time units. If probabilities were assigned to the paths, the average processing time of the routine could be calculated as well. For example, assigning the probabilities shown in the following list results in an average processing time of 6.1 time units. (These probabilities were derived based on a 60 percent chance of taking branch b as opposed to a 40 percent chance for branch c, and an 80 percent chance of taking branch e versus 20 percent for branch f). The probabilities are as follows:

```
abdeg      -> 0.48    * 5.3 = 2.5
abdfg      -> 0.12    * 7.0 = 0.8
acdeg      -> 0.32    * 6.7 = 2.1
acdfg      -> 0.08    * 8.3 = 0.7
                               ----
                               6.1
```

Loops are handled in a similar fashion. Given the following link execution times

Link	Time
a	1.1
b	0.5
c	2.1
d	4.2
e	1.2

a flow graph $a(b(c+d)e)^{10}$ would have the following maximum execution time:

```
a(bce)10  -> 1.1 + (0.5 + 2.1 + 1.2)*10 = 39.1
a(bde)10  -> 1.1 + (0.5 + 4.2 + 1.2)*10 = 60.1
```

If the number of iterations was indeterminate but bounded as in the graph $a(b(c+d)e)^{N/1}$, then the number N would be substituted for the 10 in the preceding calculation of maximum time.

Analyzing such simple flow graphs is reasonably straightforward. Analyzing more complex graphs can lead to a large number of different paths. Such problems can be solved piecemeal, the way function calls are normally handled. The lowest level function is analyzed, and the maximum execution time is calculated. The maximum time is then used in the analysis of any functions that call that function.

Figure 7–6 shows a flow graph that invokes a function fn(). To calculate the worst case execution time, the worst case time for fn() has been calculated separately and inserted into the flow graph. Path abcg has the worst case execution time of 9.3 time units. This does not include the time required for the call itself, which I assume is negligibly small in this case.

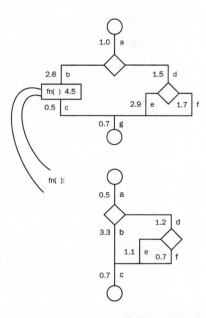

Figure 7–6. Flow control graph containing a function call

Fortunately, rules do exist for reducing the complexity of a large, compound graph to simplify this type of analysis. However, a discussion of such rules is beyond the scope of this book.

Functional Testing

The alternative to structural testing is **functional testing**, or **black box testing**. Functional testing treats the unit under test as a single unit without internal structure or, at least, with an internal structure that is not visible to the outside world (hence the name *black box*). Functional testing compares the output of the unit against the specification for the unit.

Functional testing starts by building a different type of flow graph, known as as the **transaction flow graph**. The transaction flow graph is a model of the system's behavior. A **transaction** is a unit of work as seen from the user's point of view. Transactions are started, typically from an external stimulus — such as a mouse click or a command — and lead to a set of outputs. The operator is usually powerless to stop the transaction until it, is complete, short of canceling it, or turning the computer off.

Consider the ATM example again. A withdrawal transaction flow graph for a hypothetical ATM system appears in Figure 7–7.

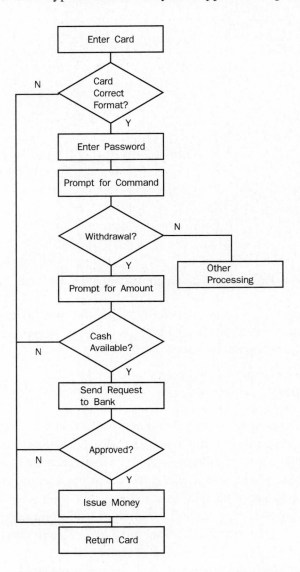

Figure 7–7. Withdrawal transaction flow graph for a hypothetical ATM

A transaction flow graph relates to the external events of the program, not its internal control flow. Thus, in the sample transaction flow there is a block called `Send request to bank`. In the actual program, this may be handled by a single functional node (at some level of abstraction) or it may not. In fact, it may not be possible to find any particular node or nodes in the control flow graph that correspond to a given node in the transaction flow graph.

A transaction flow graph is read the same as any flow graph is read: one starts a token at the beginning of the flow graph and allows that token to propagate through the nodes. In a control flow graph the token represents the CPU. Each of the steps and decisions that the token takes are the same steps and decisions the CPU will follow. This is not the case with the transaction flow graph — the token has no physical analog.

Functional testing attempts to cover the various paths of the transaction flow graph in the same way that structural path testing attempted to cover the paths through the control flow graph. Full path coverage, full branch coverage, and full statement coverage apply here as well.

Most of the transaction flows are easy to test. First, there are not nearly as many paths through the transaction flow as there were through the control flow. Second, loops in the transaction flow are relatively uncommon.

Testing the remaining 15 to 20 percent of transaction flows is often very difficult. These transactions correspond to errors, lockouts, race conditions, and so on, that require precise control of multiple, external events over which the tester may have no control. To generate these errors, the tester may be forced to

- set breakpoints and force execution down a particular error path
- mistune the system by reducing the number of available resources such as memory or disk space
- suspend key tasks in the middle of a transaction for several seconds and then unsuspend them to open up timing windows making collisions all but certain
- suspend input tasks to allow the input hopper to fill completely and then unsuspend the task to watch the system process transactions at full speed

In addition, testers should look for convoluted, obscure transaction paths. These paths usually execute large sections of code, involving the greatest number of data objects involved as well. The most common core paths are likely to have been examined and functionally tested by the programmers.

It's the uncommon threads that programmers like to sweep under the carpet and hope no one notices.

Analysis of transaction testing requires built-in tools to track the state of the transaction as it is processed. The tester will want to follow the path of the transaction token through each of the nodes in the flow graph. Since transaction testing must occur at full speed in order to be effective, this tool needs to be able to record this information for after-the-fact, leisurely analysis (see the section on built-in testing tools).

Domain testing

Every program receives data from the outside world. The set of all input can be viewed as a vector of values as shown in Figure 7–8 on the following page. This figure shows a block diagram for a simple program. The program accepts input from three different sources and generates four different outputs. Output may be to different devices or different windows on a single display. The same applies to the input.

An equivalent view of this program is shown below the block diagram. The input appears as a three-dimensional vector of the three inputs, the output appears as a four-dimensional vector, and the program itself is reduced to a transfer function between the two.

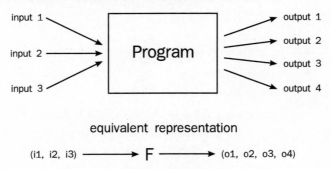

equivalent representation

$(i1, i2, i3) \longrightarrow F \longrightarrow (o1, o2, o3, o4)$

Figure 7–8. Input and output from a program unit

By generating all of the possible input values one should be able to generate all of the possible output values and, in so doing, test the transfer function. **Domain testing** takes this view of testing. Domain testing does not replace other testing techniques, it only augments them. Domain testing can be based on specifications or knowledge of the program. In practice it is generally based upon the specifications, making it a functional test technique.

An assumption implicit in domain testing is that all decisions are based upon input variables. This is not completely true, as some decisions are based upon the state of the system left over from previous input. To the extent that this internal state information is known, it can be accommodated as another input to the transfer function, as shown in Figure 7–9.

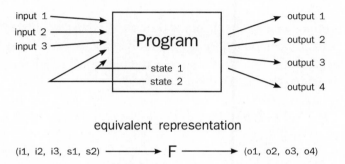

Figure 7–9. Input to a program unit with internal state data

Domain testing can be used during all stages of testing. During unit or component testing, the transfer function may be a single function. The input vector represents the input arguments plus any global variables the function accesses; the output vector represents the returned values plus the values passed to other functions.

Hyperdomains Let us call the set of all inputs I. This vector describes an N-dimensional space where N is the number of input variables. Each new input variable adds a dimension to that space.

Each input variable has a range of legal values. This range is known as the **domain** of that dimension. Domains may be infinite in both directions (minus infinity to plus infinity), infinite in one direction (for example, 0 to plus infinity), or finite (for example, 0 to 10). Domains may also be discontinuous, such as the range of all integers from 0 to 10.

The largest or smallest legal value for a dimension is known as a **domain boundary**. Boundaries may be closed or open. A closed boundary, noted with a bracket, includes the endpoint, whereas an open boundary, noted with a parenthesis, excludes the endpoint. Thus, the domain [0, 10) denotes the range from 0 to 10, including 0 but not including 10.

For every boundary there must be at least one predicate. For example, the following test

```
float x;
if (x < 0.0 || x >= 10.0) {
    cout << "x is not legal value" << endl;
    return -1;
}
//...function continues
```

defines a closed boundary at 0 (that is, x must be greater than or equal to 0 and an open boundary at 10). Individual processes may have domains as well. In the following example, the function f1() belongs to a subdomain bounded by x in the domain [0,5].

```
if (x >= 0 && x <= 5)
    f1();
```

The domain boundaries of a single input may be viewed as an (N-1)-dimensional surface in the N-dimensional input space. If the boundary does not depend on any other input variable, then the surface is a plane perpendicular to the axis describing the bounded variable. If the boundary does depend upon one or more input variables, then the surface slopes. Domains need not be linear. The formula $x^2 + y^2 < 10$ denotes a circular domain about the origin.

Applying Hyperdomains   Generally, it is impossible to test all the possible values an input vector can have. Fortunately, this is not necessary. Most bugs occur along domain boundaries. Domain testing attempts to describe these boundaries and explore them. The tester works hard to find the intersection of multiple domain boundaries and to select input points that lie barely on one side of the boundary or the other. (It is important to supply barely illegal as well as barely legal input.)

Domain testing is especially good at detecting certain classes of problems. The following list of errors that domain testing can detect is derived from Beizer.

- Poorly defined boundaries — for example, testing that a floating point number is within a closed range. Floating point representations are never exact, and the boundaries of a floating point range are necessarily fuzzy.

- Contradictory domains — when the design specifies two domains that are supposedly distinct but, in fact, overlap.

- Null domains — a domain specified in such a way that its volume is zero. For example, the following requirements cannot be simultaneously fulfilled: $x + 2y > 10$, $x < 5$, and $y < 2$.

- Closure reversal — a boundary that should be open when it is closed or vice versa.

- Faulty logic — a series of conditions specifies a domain that is not what was intended.

Another class of error that domain testing can isolate is mismatched boundaries. This condition is known as **closure incompatibility**.

Closure Compatibility　　The outputs of a processing unit are not limited to the values that unit returns to the caller. Output also includes variables that pass outside in calls to other units. Thus, in the following function `fn1()`, the variables a and b make up the input vector while the variable b makes up the output vector.

```
void fn(int a, int b) {
    //...some processing
    fn2(b);
}
```

The span of legal input values is known as the domain of the function. The span of possible output values is known as the **range** of the function.

The range of a variable in the calling function must match the domain of that variable in the called function. In the preceding example, the range of b in the call to `fn2()` must match the domain of the first argument of `fn2()`. If they match, the two processing units are said to have **closure compatibility**.

Closure incompatibility may take multiple forms. Possible relationships are shown in Figure 7–10. Ranges are shown immediately above the domains. In the first case the range and domain match exactly. For example, the variable b has a domain of [0, 10], while the function `fn2()` expects its first argument to take on values in the span [0,10].

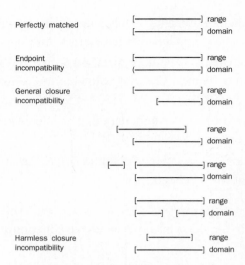

Figure 7–10. Several possible closure mismatches

The second case shown in Figure 7–10 is one of end-point incompatibility. The left end point is closed in the range but open in the domain. That is, `fn2()` does not expect `b` to take on the value 0. The remaining closure incompatibilities depict cases in which the range and domain do not match, either because they are offset from one another, not the same size, or irregular.

Not all closure incompatibilities indicate an error, however. The last entry in Figure 7–10 depicts a case in which the domain is greater than the range. The range of `b` is `[5,10]` while the domain of the first argument to `fn2()` is `[0, 20]`. Although suspicious, this is not necessarily an error: the caller is simply not using all of the capability of the function.

Test Applicability

No single type of testing succeeds at finding all types of software defects. Theoretically functional testing should be able to find all of the bugs in a program; after all, it is the program's function that the customer sees. If a software defect has no functional manifestation, one might argue that there is no bug.

However, even a medium-size program has too many functional paths to be tested properly. This is especially true of modern GUI-type applications in which commands may be entered in almost any order. Functional testing can be made to test all of the functional blocks, but this would leave untested the paths between the blocks. This, in turn, might leave paths through the functional blocks unexercised. Further, it would not prove that all of the data records were left in a valid state once the block was exited.

Almost any testing technique can be used to find any type of error. However, certain types of errors are more easily found with specific test strategies. The next section examines different error types and the tests to use against them.

Types of Errors   In *Software Defect Removal*, Robert H. Dunn divides the different types of non-compilation errors into the following seven categories:

- logic
- computational
- input/output
- data handling
- interface
- data definition
- database

Logic errors are the most common class of bugs. These errors include processing steps in the wrong order, improper conditionals, branches to the wrong statement, forgetting to check for a particular condition, incorrectly nested `if` statements, and infinite loops. These is the first type of error to come to mind when a programmer thinks *bug*.

Computational errors include incorrect equations, forgetting to place parentheses around an expression, mixing invalid data types, mixing improper units (for example, multiplying speed in miles per hour by the time in seconds).

The most common and hazardous **input/output error** in C++ is failure to provide sufficient buffer size on input or failing to limit input to the size of the buffer provided. Other I/O errors include opening files incorrectly (for example, open with truncation when you mean open for append), incorrect format, or not following protocol when communicating with another computer or external device.

Data handling errors include failing to initialize variables — especially pointers — before use, indexing arrays improperly, and manipulating pointers incorrectly.

Interface defects include mismatching the parameter list of a function, failure to return a legal value from a non-`void` function, failure to override inadequate defaults, and incorrect scheduling of other tasks. These errors are not as common in C++ as in some other languages (especially Classic C) due to its strong typing.

The two most common **data definition errors** in C++ are inadvertently declaring a signed value when an unsigned value was intended or vice versa and indexing arrays beyond their declared range. Other data definition errors include declaring a field improperly (for example, declaring a variable `int` when a `long` was needed) or improperly dimensioning arrays.

Database errors include misinterpreting the units of database entries, constructing incorrect queries, failure to balance trees properly, failure to follow locking protocols, and locking fields in the wrong order. One of the most common database errors when dealing with hierarchical databases is failure to update all database pointers properly when adding or removing an entry.

Tests to Use   Table 7-1 rates the efficiency of each type of test against the seven classes of error.

Table 7-1. Relative efficiency of different testing techniques

Defect	Reviews	Static Analysis	Proof of Correctness	Structural test	Functional test	Domain test
Logic	Med	Med	High	High	Med	Med
Comp	Med	Med	High	High	Med	Low
I/O	High	Med	Low	Med	High	High
Data hndl	High	High	Med	Low	High	Med
Interface	High	High	Low/High	High	Med	High
Data def	Med	Med	Med	Low	Med	High
Database	High	Low	Low	Med	Med	Med

* Low if proofs applied to single functions only; High otherwise

Reviews are the most efficient form of testing in terms of bugs found per hour spent for all error types. Unfortunately, reviews are weak in finding logic errors — the most common class of errors. However, structural testing is strongest in areas where reviews are weakest. This complementary aspect of reviews and structural testing is another argument for reviews in addition to normal structural unit testing.

Testing Classes

When most books discuss the testing of *units*, it is understood that they mean functions or groups of related functions. In C++ a unit can also be a class with its associated methods. Classes present some unique testing considerations as well.

First, a class is designed to work as independently as possible from its environment. This is a benefit to testing, as it allows the programmer to write a small test program to exercise the class alone. Testing a class as an independent body ensures that it is loosely coupled to its surrounding program.

If the class is new, the programmer must test the full range of advertised capabilities, not just those features of the class that the program uses. For example, in the following class Address, the programmer must test both the storeName() and the getName() methods even if the current program only uses getName().

```
class Address {
  private:
    char name[80];
    char street[80];
    //...other data

  public:
    Address(char* pName, char* pStreet);

    //retrieve the name or store a new name
    char *getName();
    char *storeName(char *pName);

    //...other methods
};
```

Object-oriented programmers like to pick up classes from existing, working programs and apply them to new programs being developed. They expect all of the methods of such classes to work, not just the ones required by the originating program. If the original programmer tested only some of the methods of the class, the borrowing programmer might inject unsuspected errors into the new program. If a class has a method that you do not intend to test, then remove it from the class.

As with a function, the programmer should single-step every instruction of each method of the class using a source code debugger at least once (full statement coverage). The programmer should continue to single-step these methods when they call methods of publicly inherited base classes, even if they have already been tested. A subclass is often tightly coupled with its publicly inherited base classes. The assumptions made in the base class must be carried over into the subclass if the inheritance is to be successful. If nothing else, single stepping through these methods reminds the programmer of how the base class works.

The structural testing of public inheritance hierarchies is handled much like composite testing. The programmer begins by testing the methods of the base class, including any virtual methods. Once the paths through the base class have been covered, the base class is declared unit tested and testing begins on the subclasses. Problems found during subclass testing may require changes in the methods of the base class. These changes must be tested against the base class as well as the subclass.

The coupling between a subclass and a privately inherited base class is no tighter than between a class and the surrounding program. Therefore, calls to the methods of privately inherited base classes can be treated like calls to any other external function.

Testing Class Intended for Reuse   C++ programmers are as much hybrids in their programming as the language they use. In Smalltalk, a pure object-oriented language, all classes become part of the environment and are considered reusable by future programs. In C++, however, programmers tend to think of some classes as general purpose, reusable class while others are held to be application-specific and not reusable. In fact, the programmer of a class does not know which classes will be reused in future designs and which will not, so all classes should be considered reusable.

However, when one speaks of reusable C++ classes one generally means classes that are set aside to become part of a class library. Reusable classes must be held to a higher standard of quality. The range of each method and the domain of all data members must be specified. The methods of the class must work properly over the entire domain of all input arguments. Values outside of the domain must be tested for and must generate a meaningful error message. Reusable classes must be tested using a special test program capable of generating all such illegal input values as well as recording the results. In addition, steps must be taken to generate all internal errors, such as insufficient heap space, NULL pointer arguments, and so on.

Any less than this negates the benefits of class reuse. Bugs found in a reusable class are especially expensive. The application programmer using the class may not understand how the class works internally. Thus, the originator of the class may have to be found. Second, reusable classes by definition are used in multiple applications. The more different applications, the more the savings in time and cost. An error in a reusable class may show up in many different applications. Worse, a problem found and fixed in one application may have been accepted as proper behavior in another. Fixing the bug in the class removes the problem in the first application, but creates a new bug that must be found and corrected in the second. Finally, there is the matter of programmer confidence. Reusing existing classes requires effort on the part of the programmer. Programmers will only expend this effort if they are reasonably assured of receiving a quality product.

Classes are normally designed and documented as part of the documentation of the program that contains them. Reusable classes must be documented independently. Assumptions and limitations must be specified. Cox suggests a format like that used in hardware circuits.

Beta Testing

Beta testing is an effective way of working out errors in applications intended for a wide audience. Versions of the program that have been through component and integration testing, but not necessarily without errors, are exposed to a hand-picked cross section of the user community. The idea behind beta testing is that only end users know all the ways in which a program will be used.

A well-managed beta test program is an effective test tool. End users have no visibility into the internals of the program, no preconceived idea of the right way to do things, and no knowledge about the program other than what it and the documentation tell them. Thus, end users are likely to execute commands in strange and illogical sequences (from the standpoint of the programmer). These sequences tend to flush out bugs that went unnoticed during testing.

In addition, beta testing exposes the program to a myriad of different hardware configurations, much more than any single programmer or company can afford to purchase or rent for testing. These are the same configurations a program is likely to see in actual use.

Managing a beta test program is critical to its success. First, the number of reviewers should be carefully controlled. The earliest versions, known as alpha releases, should be limited to the most trusted individuals, perhaps other departments within the same organization. These versions will have enough errors that even a small number of testers should be able to keep the programmers busy. Later, better tested beta versions can be opened up to an ever-expanding number of testers.

A point of contact must be named to handle responses from beta testers. The beta test point of contact should be supplied with a separate telephone number, different from those of the rest of the company. Programmers' time should not be wasted handling beta calls.

The beta point of contact has several responsibilities. Many reported errors will not be errors at all, but merely the misunderstandings of users unfamiliar with a new product. These must be filtered out. Valid error reports must be sorted according to type of error: error in the documentation (the program was never intended to do that), error in the user interface (the user is confused because the program is misleading), or errors in the software.

The beta test point of contact must maintain a database of known software errors. As errors are reported, this database is consulted to determine whether a new error has been reported or whether a known problem has bitten a new user. To do this, the beta test point of contact must know what version of the program a particular beta tester is using. This makes it imperative that some rational baseline numbering scheme be employed. Error reports from the field must include the baseline version. To facilitate this, the program should be capable of reporting its version number when asked, either via a `WHATSIT` type external utility or a `Get Info` command within the program.

The point of contact should keep statistics as well. These statistics are useful in planning beta releases. New beta releases are shipped when the rate of new errors being reported drops below a predefined level. Each new beta shipment results in an immediate increase in the number of errors reported as fixes of old bugs allow new bugs to be found.

In addition, the beta test point of contact must make sure that beta testers are actually using the program. Time is a limited resource and it is understandable if a beta tester cannot find the time to find and report errors in a beta version of a program. There should be no recriminations (unless, of course, the beta tester is being paid); however, a beta tester who fails to generate results should be removed from the list. There is no need to continue to ship beta versions of the program to a reviewer who generates no error reports.

On the other hand, productive beta reviewers represent a valuable resource. The reviewer database should not be discarded when beta testing is completed. These same reviewers can be used on future versions of the program or future applications from the same organization.

In addition, productive reviewers should be rewarded. Expensive, limited-edition programs are offered to beta reviewers at a substantial discount. Commercial applications such as editors and compilers are generally offered to beta reviewers without charge. Either way, it is important that all beta reviewers receive a copy of the final released product. Otherwise, the beta releases of the software, including bugs, will be left in service.

Finally, beta reviewers are a good source of ideas for improvements. Their opinions should be taken very seriously . . . perhaps more seriously than the programmers'. Beta reviewers are real, if perhaps advanced, users without the unique inside knowledge of the builders of the system. Of course, their requests must be weighed against the effort required and any long-term plans for the program. Improvements that can be easily accommodated should be adopted. Those that require substantial changes to the program must be delayed until future versions or not undertaken at all.

Testing Tools

Testing is still a manual process for most programmers. Automatic testing aids can be a great help, however. As the art of testing becomes the science of testing, the role of automatic testing tools will continue to grow.

Of course, testing tools carry a cost. Externally developed tools must be purchased; internally developed tools must be built. Does the benefit of these tools justify their cost? Beizer reports a survey of 200 Japanese software development organizations that rated test tools as having the highest productivity return of all products tested.

The following sections examine the different test tools available today.

Commercially Available Tools

Many different types of testing tools are available. Some tools generate large volumes of random input data on the theory that even if you can't see the target, if you shoot enough bullets you will hit it sometime. This type of tool has been found to be cost-ineffective because of the large amounts of output data that must be analyzed by humans.

The most developed commercial testing tools are the **static analyzers**. These compare the source code to the semantics of the language and to a list of common traps and pitfalls. Potentially incorrect constructs are flagged to the programmer. Only the programmer can determine whether the construct is truly incorrect, but the tool does draw the programmer's attention to the potential problem. A static analyzer is built into the C++ compiler. Another form of static analyzer is the **lint** analyzer. This type of tool will be discussed in detail in Chapter 8.

Dynamic analyzers execute along with the program under test, looking for some particular type of common error. The most common dynamic analysis tools look for illegal memory references. For example, the C-Debug tool from Softran Corporation examines every pointer reference within a program, including references into arrays and blocks allocated off of the heap. The tester links the program under test with the tool and then proceeds with normal testing. Any reference found to be beyond the bounds of the array is trapped and reported. Dynamic analyzers cannot find illegal accesses on paths that have not been executed.

The C++ compiler provides some dynamic analysis as well. For example, attempts to read a file that has not been opened are rejected as illegal.

Some dynamic checks are implemented by extra instructions inserted into the object code. Since they take time, these checks are usually optional. For example, most C++ environments allow the inclusion of checks for stack overflow. Limited dynamic analysis is performed by the hardware as well — for example, division by zero generates an interrupt. C++ compilers generate code to handle this interrupt, but the user may replace the compiler-generated code with a custom routine. Users can add sophisticated, but specific, dynamic analysis by overloading operators for user-defined classes.

Metric tools, such as those examined in Chapter 4, are also a form of test tool. The metric tools identify the modules with the highest complexity. This allows test designers to focus their efforts on those complex modules where the number of bugs is likely to be highest.

Coverage monitors are usually integrated into a test environment or provided as an interpreter. As the programmer performs structural testing, the coverage monitor notes which paths have and have not been taken through the unit under test. The programmer can then ask the tool what paths remain to be tested. The output of the coverage monitor is a form of proof that full coverage was achieved during unit testing. The fact that these tools are integrated environments makes them useful for unit or early component testing, but they may not be useful for testing larger components. In addition, the kind of coverage provided by these monitors is generally not specified. It may be statement coverage, branch coverage, or both.

A **flow path generator** is similar to a coverage monitor but simpler and cheaper. A flow path generator statically scans the source code looking for all possible flow paths, much like a McCabe complexity analyzer (in fact, a McCabe analyzer capable of generating graphic output of the flow paths works fine for this purpose). A sheet with all of the paths or branches is then output. As each of these branches is exercised during unit testing, the programmer can check it off the list. This form with all paths checked is required at the code review.

A completely different type of test aid is the **capture/replay** tool. The test is designed by whatever means desired, manual or automatic. The test is then performed with **capture mode** enabled. In this mode, the tool records input to the program and the resulting output. The input is recorded and organized into a database by test step. The output is recorded separately and associated with the input.

When rerunning the test, the tester uses the **replay mode** of the tool to play back the test from a menu of previously recorded tests. The programmer can specify a single test or a group of tests to be executed in order. The replay tool fetches the specified test, runs it, and compares the resulting output against the recorded output from the earlier run. Discrepancies are flagged for later manual analysis.

Capture/replay tools are great for rerunning tests that have previously failed. In this scenario, the tests are first performed with recording enabled. If a test fails, the recording of the test, including the incorrect output, is attached to the Error Report Form that is turned over to the programmer. The programmer can replay the test that failed as often as necessary for debugging purposes. Once the error is reported back corrected, the test is replayed and the new results recorded. If correct, the new results become a permanent part of the test database.

Capture/replay is also an aid in program maintenance. Tests captured from the previous version of the software can be replayed against the new version. Discrepancies are either due to differences in the new requirements or bugs in the new software. Once the new version has successfully executed all recorded tests, the tests are replayed and the results are recorded to be compared against the next version.

A tool similar to the capture/replay tool is the **record/replay** tool. This tool does not capture input to the program under test, but accepts input that is destined for the program without sending it.

The difference between this and the capture replay tool is similar to the difference between live and studio recordings. Recording a song sung in concert is similar to the capture/replay tool. The alternative is to record the song in a recording studio. Eventually the recording will be played for the benefit of an audience, but there is no audience at the time of the recording. The song may be recorded all at once or the instruments may be recorded separately from the voices and assembled into a complete piece later. This process is similar to the record/replay tool. The replay feature of the record/replay is identical to the replay portion of the capture/replay tool.

The record/replay tool has two advantages over the capture/replay tool. First, it is often easier to use. Complicated test cases with multiple simultaneous inputs are difficult to set up in real time. Using the record/replay tool, these test inputs can be assembled separately usually in non-real time, like the studio song. The different test tracks are played back synchronized together. Second, work can begin on constructing the test scenarios before the program is ready to be tested. Tests are recorded and stored in the test database while the program is being developed.

Custom Testing Tools

Although often not as sophisticated as commercially produced tools, testing tools built specifically for the program under test are almost invariably more effective. This is especially true of custom test tools built directly into the program. The reason for this is twofold.

First, the custom built test tool understands both the design and purpose of the program under test. Special consideration can be made for trapping data between program components or simulating input at critical junctures. Without this intimate knowledge, commercial tools cannot be as effective.

Second, relying on commercial test tools allows program designers to ignore testability issues during the critical design phase. Built-in test tools must be designed in from the beginning. Custom tools require the designers to face testability issues squarely even during high-level design. The result is a program that is more testable by whatever means.

Custom tools built to debug and test a program should be documented and maintained along with the source code for the program itself. It would be senseless to rebuild such tools for later versions of the system. The testing tools will need to be fixed and upgraded to match changes to the program as part of normal maintenance.

The best record/replay tools are those built specifically for the program under test. Such tools are knowledgeable of the input and output ports of the program. They can insert data at the proper points and record output. Since they have knowledge of the message formats, they can display the messages in readable form, rather than hexadecimal dumps.

For example, a good record/replay tool written for a hypothetical receiver controller program would be able to capture and replay input from the serial terminal. It could also capture and display in an easy-to-read format the messages being sent to and from the receiver.

Another class of custom-built test equipment is the **simulator**. A receiver simulator for the receiver controller program would consist of a small program to accept receiver commands and generate the appropriate receiver responses. A sophisticated simulator is a complicated and difficult tool to construct if it is attempting to simulate a complicated object. For testing purposes a simple simulator capable of echoing commands and generating simple output under human direction will usually suffice even when simulating complicated external devices.

Professional programmers consider simulators indispensable testing tools even when the external device or program is available. This is because it is easier to generate error or illegal purposes for testing purpose from a simulator than from the real thing. Often setting up a particular test is easier with a simulator. In addition, custom simulators can work together with custom record/replay tools to record commands and program responses.

Data acquisition tools are the most important class of built-in test tools. I remember clearly my first large program. It was supposed to play a game of baseball between two teams. Each team was assigned a series of nine batters. The batting average of each batter was read from a punch card. The program used random numbers to make all decisions. To determine if the batter got a hit, the program generated a random number between 0 and 1. If the number was less than the batting average, the hitter was credited with a hit. If it was a hit, the program had to determine what type of hit. Another random number was generated. If that number was less than 0.6, the hit was assumed to be a single; if it was between 0.6 and 0.8, it was a double, and so forth. The program continued in this fashion generating random numbers to direct the runners about the bases and decide their fate.

After working on this program quite some time I decided to let the program run and see what would happen. The program ran for several seconds only to produce the single line of output "Team A Wins." Somehow I had assumed that I would be able to watch the intricate decisions being made at each point of the game, perhaps reading them in the blinking lights of the front panel, but of course I could not.

Armed with a new realization, I returned to the program and added play- by-play WRITE statements at each decision point in the game as well as box scores at the end of each inning so that I could follow what was happening. Now the game generated a much more satisfying, "Batter 2 steps up to the plate. He gets a hit. It's a single. Runner on first tries to take third. He's picked off...," and so on. In the end, Team A still won, but I had much more confidence that they deserved the victory.

The moral of this story is that every program must provide some mechanism for allowing the tester to track the logic of the program. Without such information, the programmer is either left with almost no information to go on or forced to resort to the source code debugger for every problem.

Data acquisition can be built into the system in several ways. Simple `printf()` statements, inline functions that can be disabled with `#defines`, and line trackers are all possible. More sophisticated techniques involve rerouting intertask messages. Built-in data acquisition tools should allow for a verbose mode and a quiet mode in which messages are suppressed so as not to get in the way of normal execution. Functional testing is likely to be performed in verbose mode to allow the tester to track the path of the program. Structural testing is performed under quiet mode until a problem develops.

Since these tools are also sophisticated debugging, aids they are described in more detail in Chapter 8. The one type of data acquisition tool that is strictly for testing allows the tester access to internal calculations that are normally hidden deep within a program. For example, a stock market analysis program must perform a considerable number of complicated calculations. Most bugs cause the program to generate wildly incorrect results that are easily caught by the human observer. However, some bugs are considerably more subtle. The program may generate a buy or sell suggestion that, although suspicious, might be correct. It is difficult even for the programmer to determine whether the output is correct without considerable analysis.

These types of problems are easier to analyze if the program can output the intermediate results of its internal calculations. Then the programmer can see when a particular rate of return or tax rate has been calculated incorrectly resulting in slightly skewed results.

Software Maintenance

Software maintenance incorporates all of the tasks necessary to sustain an operational software system. The word *maintenance* is something of a misnomer. After all, software does not wear out like a car. Nevertheless, changes need to be made. As programs are exercised, previously undiscovered software errors surface. In addition, the program must keep up with evolving requirements as well as increasing user demands. Software maturation might be a better description of the process.

In *Software Maintenance Management*, B. Lientz and E. Swanson list three different types of maintenance changes along with their relative importance: corrective (21 percent), adaptive (25 percent) and perfective (50 percent) (the remaining 4 percent of maintenance modifications fall into an "other" category). Corrective changes fix a software defect detected in the field. These defects may have existed since the program was written but were not detected during testing. This is what most people first think of as software maintenance, yet it constitutes less than one-fourth of the maintenance pie.

Adaptive modifications add new features to the system in response to a new user requirement. Customers and designers analyze a problem and conceive of its solution in the form of a software program. Once the program is built, tested, and deployed, it usually becomes clear that not everything works the way it was envisioned. Using the program points out its weaknesses and things that could have been done better. Making these adjustments to the program is also part of software maintenance.

Perfective modifications adapt the program to unforeseen or poorly understood requirements. The world is constantly evolving: output formats change; new laws are passed; technology increases the capability of display devices, printers, and input devices, for instance. Scrapping a payroll program every time the tax code changes would be unacceptable. A color paint program must be updated to make use of the increasing resolution and numbers of colors offered by new video adapters. Programs are updated to account for changing conditions.

Managing Software Maintenance

Software maintenance must be managed in the same way that the development of the program was managed. Changes to the program must be coordinated between the developer and the customer. In addition, maintenance changes have the highest error rates per line of code modified of any programming endeavor. Thus, any maintenance modification must undergo proper testing.

Maintenance modification requests are tracked using the same mechanism used to track errors detected during testing. Rather than use the Error Report Form, however, some organizations adopt a similar Modification Request Form. The ERF has the negative connotation of a software error, while the MRF requests a modification without casting blame.

Modification requests need to be coordinated before being implemented. For custom programs that have only a single customer site, there are two primary concerns. Is the modification request within the scope of the long-term support agreement? If not, a separate agreement must be negotiated involving payment for the added features. If the customer has been provided with an on-site programmer as part of the purchase price of the program, then any change the on-site programmer can handle is automatically in scope.

All bug fixes should also be considered in scope although one might put some reasonable time limit on this warranty. After several years, the developer may no longer have on the payroll the same personnel who developed the program. Even if they are, they are not likely to remember much about the program. However, software defects encountered and reported within a reasonable period should be fixed without complaint.

The second problem concerns the long-term evolution of the program. Is the request in the long-term best interest of the customer? Does it fit with the customer's future needs and the program's design, or is it a quick fix designed to address an immediate problem? Working as they do without much knowledge of the program's internals, customers can be very short sighted in their requests. They may ask for several changes that are at cross purposes. All modification requests should be discussed at some length to give the customer time to consider what is really desired.

If the program has more than one customer, then a third factor must be included. Different users may have conflicting opinions about the direction in which the program should evolve. One company that uses relatively unskilled workers might want more mouse-accessible menus added. Simultaneously, another company that uses highly skilled workers might want more Quick Keys to allow operators to skip through the menus.

Most programs have more than one user even when custom written for a single organization. Companies are a collection of individuals. Each person who uses the program has a different opinion about what should be changed. A modification request from one of these individuals may not express the desires of the entire company.

The maintenance programmer starts by collecting all MRFs. No MRF should be rejected out of hand no matter how silly or unachievable it might appear. If it truly is silly, it will be easy enough to reject in the future. The MRFs are entered into a database. This may be as simple as a three-ring binder, but it should be accessible to the programmers, designers, and users. An electronic bulletin board can be used when the programmers and users are not in the same location.

Each MRF should be discussed first with the users. Is the modification truly needed or is it aimed at correcting a symptom of a deeper problem? Is there universal consensus among users for the modification or is the request coming from a single user? Does the modification fit the look, feel, and intent of the program or is it something the program was never designed to do?

At the same time the programmers can evaluate the MRF for its impact on the program. How much will the underlying design be affected? Approximately how many lines of code will need to be changed? How many added? Which regression tests will need to be rerun? Are any new tests required for this change?

From this, the program developers can draw up a long-term schedule for maintenance modifications. Approximate dates can be assigned to the modifications by comparing the level of effort required to the available manpower. Initial estimates of completion dates are likely to be inaccurate but collecting this metric information will allow calibration of subsequent estimates.

The ordering of modifications on the schedule is a value judgment. Low-difficulty, low-risk additions can generally be accommodated even if only a few users are requesting them. It may not be possible to accommodate high difficulty changes until a future major revision of the software no matter how many users request them. Some personnel should be held in reserve for fixing bugs especially during the periods immediately following installation of major modifications. Software defects are sure to be found with new revisions and those problems may require immediate attention. Provision should be made in the schedule for these adjustments.

When the program has a limited number of customers, the customers should be allowed to influence the modification schedule. The customer may feel that a modification is important enough to undertake even if other problems will not be fixed for some time. The developer should be ready to counsel the customer in making the right decision.

In addition to a short-term modification schedule, the developer (and customer) should have a long-term plan outlining what capabilities they would like to see in the program in several years' time. By acting as a guide in day-to-day modification decisions, this long-term plan ensures a coherent maturing of the program over its life span.

Software Maintenance Errors

The number of software errors per line of code is higher for maintenance than during any other phase of programming. Error rates for corrective maintenance are the highest of all. In *The Complete Guide to Software Testing*, Bill Hetzel reports that estimates range higher than 50 percent failure rates for corrective modifications. In his study more than half of all corrective modifications either did not work or disabled something else! There are several reasons for this high failure rate.

One is that typically not many lines are changed for each given fix. Modifications, especially bug fixes, often involve changing a line in one module, changing another line in another module or include file. Before the changes can be made, the maintenance programmer must read through the affected modules to understand all of the logic present, including any subtle nuances. Often overlooked nuances cause the errors. In *Maintaining Information Systems in Organizations*, E. Burton Swanson and Cynthia Mathis Beath note that the time spent studying existing functions before making a change is so great that typical productivity factors for maintenance code are 1,000 times lower than for new code.

The net effect is that the surface area of the changes to the remainder of the system is extremely large compared with the small volume of code changed, resulting in abundant opportunity for error.

Adaptive and perfective modifications usually involve larger, more centralized changes and additions to the software, resulting in software error rates that are more comparable to new code development rates.

A contributing factor to the high maintenance error rates is the fact that many changes add complexity to the program. This is especially true when the change cannot be easily accommodated by the existing software. Rather than rewrite one or more functions, kludgy patches are added to the existing code to handle the error cases. The increased complexity adds greatly to the possibility that an additional case will not be handled properly.

The high maintenance error rate makes testing of changes that much more important. Since thorough testing after every fix is an expensive proposition, many organizations accumulate several modifications before rerunning the full regression testing suite. Once the software has passed regression testing, it is released to the customer along with an errata sheet listing the modifications included.

Maintenance programmers should also keep statistics on corrective modifications by module. Modules with more than their share of software bugs were either not tested properly or inherently too complex. A complexity metric tool can be helpful in deciding which is the case. If the module was not tested properly, additional tests can be added to the regression test suite. Modules may be too complex either because they were written that way originally or because they have gotten that way due to changes accumulated over time. Complex modules should be rewritten.

A rule of thumb can be used to help decide when to rewrite complex functions. For example, the rule might be that a function should be rewritten if its complexity exceeds 150 percent of the development complexity limit. Thus, if a McCabe complexity of 10 was the limit during the development phase, then functions should be rewritten if their complexity exceeds 15 during the maintenance phase.

Object-oriented programmers fare somewhat better during maintenance than do structured programmers. A well-designed class is isolated from the remainder of the system except through the limited and well-documented interface formed by public methods. Even a one-line change within a class method can affect only the other lines within the class and cannot directly affect the other code outside the class.

Due to their wide exposure to the system, changes to interfaces are more error prone than changes within a function. Fortunately, studies reported by Denis Manel and William Havanas have shown that modifications in object-oriented C++ programs are less likely to result in an interface change than in non–object-oriented C or C++ programs (23 percent for OO C++ versus 38 percent for non-OO). The difference appeared to be primarily in the area of new features. New features required changes to one or more function interfaces 74 percent of the time in non–object-oriented programs, but only 41 percent of the time in object-oriented programs. The rates for corrective modifications were similar between the two types of programs.

Perhaps this results primarily from the ability of inheritance to allow additions to be made to classes without changing existing code. This view is consistent with the Cadre studies. Cadre had noted that the non–object-oriented version of their Teamworks product became very brittle over time. That is, it became difficult to modify the program without introducing an error. Experience showed that a modification to the object-oriented version of Teamworks was less likely to result in a new software error.

Conclusion

This chapter can be summarized as follows:

- "Testing is the process of executing a program with the intent of finding errors." (Myers, *Art of Software Testing*, 1979)
- Testing must be organized around a written test plan, a standardized Error Reporting Form including error categorization, and software baselines.
- The most effective types of testing are reviews and structural testing.
- The testing phase is divided into unit testing, component or group testing, integration testing, and acceptance testing. Other specialized testing is also possible.
- Maintaining a regression test suite is critical to the development of a program.
- Certain tools greatly increase testing efficiency — the most valuable of these are the capture/replay and simulator tools.
- Testing tools must often be built into the program. Hooks for such tools should be designed in from the beginning. The effort required to write such tools should be factored into estimates of the program cost from the beginning, as well.
- Maintenance should be handled in an organized fashion with proper planning and regression testing of all modifications to avoid allowing the program quality to degrade.

So far this book has covered the five phases of development: requirements, design, coding, testing, and maintenance. Techniques to avoid introducing bugs into software programs have been presented under the theory that an error that can be avoided is one less error to fix. Now it is time to turn to the actual job of finding and fixing software bugs. The next chapters will examine the proper use of debugging tools and some common approaches to debugging programs.

Chapter 8

Debugging Tools

Once a problem has been detected, it becomes the programmer's job to find the source of the problem and fix it. The next chapter will review some debugging techniques, including a sample debugging session. This chapter examines the debugging tools available to the C++ programmer.

The Programmer's Toolbag

This section presents some of the many debugging devices available to the C++ programmer. The order here is roughly chronological, starting with the older, simpler aids and continuing to the later, more powerful ones.

`printf()` Statements

The earliest debugging tool is the simple `printf()` statement, better known by its FORTRAN equivalent the **PRINT statement**. The principle is simple. The programmer begins by placing `printf()` statements in the program to display the value of variables that might be relevant to the problem.

Consider the following factorial function that contains a bug.

```
unsigned factorial(unsigned val) {
    unsigned accum = 1;
    while (val--) {
```

```
        accum *= val;
    }
    return accum;
}
```

For all values of `val`, the results of `factorial(val)` are 0. Knowing the initial value of `val` and the value of `accum` each time through the `while` loop might enable the programmer to determine what is wrong. Rewriting the function `factorial()` as follows:

```
#include <stdio.h>

unsigned factorial(unsigned val) {
    unsigned accum = 1;
    printf("initial value of val = %d\n", val);
    while (val--) {
        accum *= val;
        printf("accum = %d, val = %d\n", accum, val);
    }
    return accum;
}
void main() {
    factorial(5);
}
```

generates the following results when passed an argument of 5:

```
initial value of val = 5
accum = 4, val = 4
accum = 12, val = 3
accum = 24, val = 2
accum = 24, val = 1
accum = 0, val = 0
```

The decrement of `val` is in the wrong place. The factorial is calculated (albeit, incorrectly), then is multiplied by zero on the final pass through the loop. The corrected function appears as follows:

```
unsigned factorial(unsigned val) {
    unsigned accum = 1;
    for (; val; val--) {
        accum *= val;
    }
    return accum;
}
```

The `printf()` approach offers the C++ programmer a few advantages. First, it does not require the purchase of any other tools. The PRINT approach was the primary means of debugging in the early days of programming before other tools became available.

Unlike many other tools, such as a debugger, `printf()`s do not radically alter the timing of the program. This can be important when debugging a program that interacts with external hardware that cannot be kept waiting. For problems occurring in time-critical code, `printf()`s may be the only way to see what is happening. (Note that `printf()`s do change the timing somewhat. For very time-critical operations, `printf()`s don't work either.)

Weighed against this are numerous disadvantages. First, this approach is very slow. The programmer must decide what data to look at, add the necessary statements, recompile, relink, and reexecute the program. On the basis of these results, the programmer adds more `printf()` statements and repeats the process incrementally approaching the problem. The constant recompiling and relinking of the program slows the debugging process considerably.

In addition, `printf()`s can introduce bugs of their own. Adding an incorrect `printf()` statement can confuse the programmer, diverting attention away from the real problem. Once the problem has been corrected, the `printf()`s must be removed, which can introduce bugs through misediting as well.

Finally, `printf()` executes as part of the program that is being debugged. In rare instances, the added `printf()`s interact with the software bug being tracked changing its symptoms. Consider, for example, a program bug that corrupts the heap. Since `printf()` can allocate blocks off of the heap, adding a `printf()` may change the external appearance of the bug.

Some of the problems associated with `printf()s` can be handled by `including them in #ifdefs` as follows:

```
#ifdef DEBUG
printf("Error msg");
#endif
```

Defining DEBUG at compile time enables the messages. Removing the definition and recompiling, removes the messages.

Providing Command Line Control An extension of the `printf()` technique can be used to avoid repeated recompiling. This idea uses special arguments entered on the command line to enable and disable commands . Normally these commands are `printf()` statements, but they can be anything. (This idea is adapted from William McMahon's article, "A Generic Command-line Switch," *C User's Journal*, October 1991.)

The include file for this package is as follows.

```
//DBGRANGE.H - implement a printf() type debug facility
//             that can be controlled from the command
//             line instead of requiring recompilation

//parseArgs - this function parses the arguments to the
//             program.  These arguments are assumed to
//             be ranges within source .CPP files.
//             Arguments are in format:
//                 @FILENAME           or
//                 @FILENAME:L1        or
//                 @FILENAME:L1,L2     or
//             where FILENAME is the .CPP file in which
//             to look, L1 is the starting line # and
//             L2 is the finishing.  If FILENAME is
//             omitted, then all files pass.

void parseArgs(int argc, char** argv);

//min - return the minimum value of two integers
```

```
inline int min(int a, int b) {
    return (a > b) ? b : a;
}

//DBGRANGE - calls the function debugOn, passing the
//           file name and line number.  debugOn checks
//           this information to determine whether to
//           process the given command or not
#ifdef NDEBUG
#define DBGRANGE(c) (0)
      #else
      #define DBGRANGE(c)          \
      (DbgR::debugOn(__FILE__,__LINE__)?(c):0)
      #endif

//DebugRange - each debug range specified in the command
//             line is described by a DbgR block;
//             debugOn() then returns a 1 if called from
//             a line which is within one of these ranges
class DbgR {
  private:
    static DbgR* pFirst;
    DbgR*        pNext;
    char         fileName[20];
    unsigned     firstLine;
    unsigned     lastLine;

    int isIn(char* pName, unsigned line);

  public:
    DbgR(char*pFileName,unsigned fL=0,unsigned lL=0);
    ~DbgR();
    static int debugOn(char* pName, unsigned line);
};
```

The package consists of two parts: the function parseArgs() along with the class DbgR and the macro DBGRANGE.

A call to the function `parseArgs()` is added at the beginning of `main()`. This function examines the command line for arguments beginning with @. This character was used because it is unusual. Arguments that do not start with @ are assumed to be non-debugging arguments to the program itself and are ignored. The function updates `argv` to point to the first argument that does not start with an @.

Arguments beginning with @ are assumed to specify a range in the format:

```
@FILENAME:BEGINNINGLINE,ENDINGLINE
```

Since this line can be repeated, several ranges may be defined simultaneously.

The macro `DBGRANGE` accepts a single C++ expression as its only argument. If the `DBGRANGE` call falls within one of the ranges specified on the command line, the C++ expression is evaluated. If not, the C++ expression is skipped.

Consider the following example:

```
//MYPROG.CPP                                    //line 1
#include <stdio.h>                              //line 2
#include "dbgrange.hpp"                         //line 3

void main(int argc, char *argv[]) {             //line 5
    parseArgs(argc, argv);                      //line 6

    int i;                                      //line 8
    DBGRANGE(printf("At the start\n");          //line 9
    i = testFn()                                //line10
    DBGRANGE(printf("i = %d\n", i);             //line11
    for (int j = 0; j < 100; j++) {             //line12
        i = otherFn(j);                         //line13
        DBGRANGE(printf("i = %d, j = %d\n"));    //line14
    }
}
```

Executing the program as follows:

```
MYPROG @MYPROG.CPP:5,14
```

would generate output from the `printf()`s associated with all three DBGRANGE calls. Notice that MYPROG.CPP refers to the source file name, not the executable.

If the program is executed as follows:

```
MYPROG @MYPROG.CPP:11,11
```

only the DBGRANGE call on line 11 is executed. A range can be excluded by programming around it as follows.

```
MYPROG @MYPROG.CPP:1,10 @MYPROG.CPP:12,13
```

generates output from all DBGRANGE calls except the one on line 11.

All three values have defaults. If the source file name is missing, all source file names pass. If the ending line number is missing, then all line numbers after the starting line number pass. If the starting line number is missing, then all line numbers within the source module pass.

To use this technique the programmer spreads DBGRANGE() calls liberally throughout the program, specifying anything of interest. Without being enabled from the command line, these calls generate no output. When a problem arises, the programmer selectively enables the DBGRANGE() calls necessary to output the variables of interest.

The source code for the DBGRANGE package follows:

```
//DBGRANGE - implement the methods of DbgR

#include <stdio.h>
#include <string.h>
#include <ctype.h>
#include "dbgrange.hpp"

DbgR* DbgR::pFirst = (DbgR*)0;

DbgR::DbgR(char* pFileName, unsigned fL, unsigned lL) {
    strncpy(&fileName[0], pFileName, 20);
    fileName[19] = '\0';
    firstLine = fL;
    lastLine  = lL;
    //add to the front of the list
```

```
        pNext = pFirst;
        pFirst = this;
    }
    DbgR::~DbgR() {
        //remove current entry from the list
        if (pFirst == this)
            pFirst = pNext;
        else {
            DbgR *pEntry = pFirst;
            while (pEntry->pNext != this)
                pEntry = pEntry->pNext;
            pEntry->pNext = pNext;
        }
    }
    //isIn - check a filename and line number against
    //       the current entry; return a 1 if there is
    //       a match and a 0 if not
    int DbgR::isIn(char* pName, unsigned line) {
        //if filenames don't match, forget it
        //(if fileName is NULL match anything)
        if (*fileName)
            if (strncmp(pName, fileName, 20))
                return 0;

        //if no line numbers are provided then anything
        //within file matches
        if (firstLine == 0)
            return 1;

        //if first line given, line number must be after
        if (line < firstLine)
            return 0;
        if (lastLine == 0)
            return 1;
        return line <= lastLine;
    }

    //debugOn - check the given filename and line number
    //          against all of the debug areas; if none
```

```
//           match, return a 0
int DbgR::debugOn(char* pName, unsigned line) {
    DbgR* pEntry;
    for (pEntry = pFirst; pEntry; pEntry = pEntry->pNext)
        if (pEntry->isIn(pName, line))
            return 1;
    return 0;
}


//parseArgs - parse the command line arguments into
//            a series of DbgR records, one for each
//            debug range.
void parseArgs(int& argc, char** argv) {
    //check each argument, parse ones starting with '@'
    while (--argc > 0) {
        char* pCurrentArg;
        pCurrentArg = *++argv;
        if (*pCurrentArg++ != '@')
            return;

        //copy first 20 characters or until
        //colon or space encountered;
        char fileName[20];
        unsigned first, last;
        unsigned numsPresent = 0;
        first = last = 0;
        for (int i = 0;
                *pCurrentArg;
                    i = min(19, i + 1), pCurrentArg++) {
            if (*pCurrentArg == ':') {
                numsPresent = 1;
                break;
            }
            if (isspace(*pCurrentArg))
                break;
            fileName[i] = toupper(*pCurrentArg);
        }
        fileName[i] = '\0';
        //if numbers are present, parse them out as well
```

Chapter 8

```
        if (numsPresent) {
            //read beginning range
            sscanf(++pCurrentArg, "%d", &first);

            //now scan for the comma - if present
            //assume a last number exists
            numsPresent = 0;
            for (; *pCurrentArg; pCurrentArg++)
                if (*pCurrentArg == ',') {
                    numsPresent = 1;
                    break;
                }
            if (numsPresent)
                sscanf(++pCurrentArg, "%d", &last);
        }

        //use this to create a debug record
        new DbgR(&fileName[0], first, last);
    }
}
```

The function parseArgs() examines the arguments to the program
stopping at the first argument that does not start with @. Upon return,
argv points to the first argument that does not start with @.

For each argument range that parseArgs() finds, it constructs an
object of class DbgR. This object contains the file name as well as the first
and last line number of the range. These objects are maintained in a singly
linked list. Suitable defaults are provided for each in the event a value is
missing.

The macro DBGRANGE() generates a call to the method
DbgR::debugOn(), passing it the file name and line number from which
the call is made. In the event that the label NDEBUG is #defined during
compilation, the macro does nothing. This allows all DBGRANGE() calls
to be "removed" without editing the source file.

debugOn() searches the list of DbgR objects. If the current file name
and line number are contained within one of the ranges specified by a
DbgR object, then the function returns a 1; otherwise, it returns a 0. If
debugOn() returns a 1, DBGRANGE evaluates the expression passed as an
argument. If not, it evaluates the constant expression 0.

Since DBGRANGE is an expression, its value can be used as in the following:

```
void main(int argc, char *argv[]) {
    int array[10];
    parseArgs(argc, argv);

    //...
    if (DBGRANGE(1)) {
        //only executed if DBGRANGE is in a range
        for (int i = 0; i < 10; i++)
            checkValue(array[i]);
    }
    //...
}
```

Here, if DBGRANGE is called from within one of the ranges specified in the program arguments, DBGRANGE evaluates the provided expression 1, if not it evaluates a 0.

While DBGRANGE is flexible, it has several disadvantages. First, the code for each DBGRANGE is compiled into the executable whether it is executed or not. (Defining NDEBUG removes it.) In addition, it slows execution of the program somewhat, as every DBGRANGE invocation results in a function call and a search of the linked list of ranges. Nevertheless, for some real time applications this is a powerful and flexible tool.

Core Dumps

As soon as memory protection features were added to CPU architectures and protected mode operating systems were built, questions arose about what to do with a program that violates one of the protection features. The obvious answer was to terminate the program, but this gave the programmer little information about the nature of the problem.

Operating systems designers wanted to help the programmer find and fix the problem. Since the operating system had no idea what might have caused the problem, the best it could do was copy to disk the contents of all memory that belonged to the application at the time of the violation. Added to this usually were the contents of the registers and the instruction pointer at the time. This file was known as a **core dump**. (The most common form of internal RAM at the time was the magnetic doughnut, generally referred to as **core memory**, hence the name.)

The instruction pointer points to the instruction that caused the violation. The value of all data variables is contained within memory. The core dump should be an ideal debugging aid. In fact, this is generally not the case.

Core dumps are notoriously difficult to decipher. First, one must be intimately familiar with the machine code of the CPU. No interpretation of the binary codes is provided, so even knowledge of the assembly language is not sufficient. You have to know the binary codes for each instruction.

Second, you must know the architecture of the machine, the operating system, and the machine code generated by the language.

As other tools were invented, the core dump quickly faded away as a debugging tool for most programmers. Interestingly, however, some interest in the core dump returned when debuggers became clever enough to interpret them. Notably, xdb, the standard UNIX debugger, can analyze a core dump in the same way that it analyzes memory in an executing program. This makes analyzing a core dump more akin to normal debugging and, hence, much easier.

Debuggers

What a programmer really wants to do when debugging a program is to stop the program and examine what is going on inside of it. This capability was first provided by a tool that is so useful that it alone is given the name **debugger**. A debugger is itself a program. The debugger loads and executes the programmer's application as a child program. Before loading it, the programmer places stopping points within the child program. The stopping points are known as **breakpoints** since they break off execution of the application.

Each breakpoint is implemented by overwriting the application's instruction at the location with a jump back to the debugger (the PC uses a special, one-byte version of the INT 3 instruction designed specifically for this purpose). The application program executes until it encounters the jump, whereupon it jumps back to the debugger effectively halting its execution. Execution continues when the debugger replaces the original instruction and returns to the location, allowing the program to resume.

Using the debugger, the programmer loads the program, sets a few breakpoints, and starts program execution. When one of the breakpoints is encountered, the programmer can examine (and change) memory and registers. Depending upon what is found, the programmer may set further breakpoints and continue execution of the program until another breakpoint is encountered, repeating the process. Execution of the program can be restarted from the beginning at any time.

The Non-Symbolic Debugger   In the earliest debuggers, the locations specified by the programmer are logical addresses within memory. To relate these logical addresses back to function names, line numbers, and variable names, the programmer uses load map information generated by the linker. Consider the following small sections taken from the load map of DBGRANGE.CPP.

```
     Address           Publics by Name

    0000:19FB    operator delete(void near*,unsigned int)
    0000:19D5    operator new(unsigned int)
    0000:0239    DbgR::DbgR(char near*,unsigned int,
                 unsigned int)
    0000:0286    DbgR::~DbgR()
    0000:031F    DbgR::debugOn(char near*,unsigned int)
    0000:02C4    DbgR::isIn(char near*,unsigned int)
    01DE:00A8    DbgR::pFirst
    0000:0493    min(int,int)
    0000:034F    parseArgs(int near&,char near*near*)
//...

Line numbers for D:\DBGRANGE.OBJ(DBGRANGE.CPP) segment
_TEXT

    10 0000:0239   11 0000:024E   12 0000:0266   13 0000:026A
    14 0000:0270   17 0000:0276   18 0000:027B   19 0000:027F
    20 0000:0286   22 0000:028E   23 0000:0298   25 0000:029F
```

```
27 0000:02A5   26 0000:02A7   28 0000:02AB   30 0000:02C0
//...
```

Program entry point at 0000:0000

The upper section shows that the constructor DbgR::DbgR() is at off-set 0x0239 in the default code segment. The lower section shows that this is also line 10 in DBGRANGE.CPP. Thus, to stop execution whenever an object of class DbgR is constructed, a breakpoint should be set at CS:0x0239. Once the breakpoint is encountered, the programmer can continue to line 13 by setting a breakpoint at CS:0x026A and continuing execution.

This style of debugger is known as a **non-symbolic debugger** to differ-entiate it from the symbolic debuggers to follow. The DEBUG utility sup-plied with MS-DOS is a non-symbolic debugger.

The overall approach to debugging is similar to that used with printf() statements. The programmer allows the program to execute up to a point and then examines the values of critical variables. However, the debugger has two important advantages. First, it is an interactive tool. With printf() statements, the programmer must decide up front what data to collect. Once execution of the program begins, this decision cannot be changed. With the debugger, the programmer can make decisions in the middle of debugging the program based upon what was discovered at ear-lier steps.

Second, the debugger does not require the time-consuming recompiling and relinking to examine a new piece of data. The programmer determines the object's address from the load map and displays it. The debugger rep-resents a tremendous improvement in debugging technology.

Still, non-symbolic debuggers have a few disadvantages. Fortunately, even the earliest debuggers include disassemblers that translate the hexa-decimal machine instructions into assembly language mnemonics. How-ever, they still require a working knowledge of the assembly language of the machine and some knowledge of its architecture. In addition, some information is difficult to gather in such debuggers, most notably stack variables that do not have a fixed location can be tedious to locate. Finally, the need to reference the load map constantly is a time-consuming nuisance.

The Symbolic Debugger   The usefulness of a non-symbolic debugger is enhanced by automating the load map look-up process. That is, instead of requiring the programmer to enter `CS:0x0239`, allow him to enter `DbgR::DbgR()` or `DBGRANGE:Line10` and make the debugger look that value up in the load map. This new type of debugger is called the **symbolic debugger**. The `SYMDEB` debugger provided with earlier versions of Microsoft languages was of this type.

The original symbolic debuggers actually read the load map at start-up time and built an internal table of all of the symbols that it then used to look up references made by the programmer. Compiler and linker manufacturers quickly added this symbol table information to the `.EXE` file itself to allow the debugger to read the symbol information without referring to the load map. (Compile time switches are used to control whether symbol table information is included in the executable. Because it consumes a considerable amount of space, it is not included unless needed.)

The Source Code Debugger   The simple symbolic debugger still requires the programmer to have considerable knowledge of the assembly language. In addition, the programmer must keep print-outs of all source code from which to obtain line numbers and variable names.

With access to the .CPP source code and the line number information, the debugger does not need to display only assembly language information. When the debugger breaks execution at line 14, for example, it can display the source code with line 14 specially marked. This allows programmer to debug completely at the source code level, hence the name **source code debugger**. The current Microsoft debugger, CodeView, as well as the Borland Turbo Debugger are source code debuggers. All C++ compiler manufacturers include some form of source code debugger with their product.

The source code debugger is the most powerful weapon in the C++ programmer's arsenal. How to use a source code debugger will be discussed in detail later in this chapter.

Other Debugger Enhancements   Improvements on the source code debugger have centered around reducing the edit/compile/link/debug cycle time.

Combining these four phases into a single tool saves time and allows for a more consistent environment. The programmer can step through the problem using the built-in source code debugger. Having found a problem, the editor is instantly ready to correct it, and the compiler and linker are already loaded in memory ready to rebuild and start over.

The most successful of such environments has been the Borland/Turbo C++ and Microsoft C compilers, although C++ compilers from Topspeed, Zortech, and others offer this feature as well.

Another approach that has been used with the C language is not to compile at all, but to interpret the C source statements instead. An **interpreter** reads each source line as it comes to it rather than interpreting each line and storing the machine code equivalent into a stand-alone program as a compiler does. C interpreters are currently available from Gimpel Software (C-terp) and Rational Systems (Instant C). These companies have yet to market a C++ interpreter.

Interpreters have the advantage that changes to the source code take effect immediately. There is no need to recompile anything. In addition, interpreters maintain more information on the program in question and can often provide more help to the programmer than a debugger, even one built with a compiler.

Interpreters have a few disadvantages, however. First, syntactical errors are not discovered until the line containing the error is executed. Second, interpreters execute at least 100 times more slowly than compiler-generated code. For small programs this is not of much concern, but in a large program, it may take some time for the program to execute as far as the code containing the first breakpoint. The source code must be compiled at some point to generate a releasable product.

To address these limitations, at least one company provides a combined **compiler/interpreter**. Generally, the programmer is only interested in debugging a few modules at a time. In a large program, this may represent only a small percentage of the total.

A compiler/interpreter compiles most of the program like a combined environment; however, the programmer can flag certain modules to be executed interpretively. The overall program executes at near native program speeds with the execution slowing down only in the modules being debugged. Once debugging is complete, the programmer marks all modules for compilation to generate a standard executable file. Centerline offers the compiler/interpreter ObjectCenter (formerly Saber C++) for UNIX environments.

Cross-Debuggers   The machine on which the compiler, linker, and debugger reside is not always the same machine on which the eventual executable program will run. Certain embedded microprocessors, such as those found in microwave ovens, washing machines, and automobiles, do not have sufficient assets to support a C++ development environment. Such processors typically hold their source code in Read-Only Memory, have only a minimum of RAM, and do not have a disk at all.

To develop such applications, programmers use a separate computer — known as the **host** — on which they write, compile, and debug the application software before loading it into the embedded application — the **target** — for execution. In general, the host and target computers are not similar. They need not share the same CPU, memory architecture, or operating system. Debuggers that support this cross-development are known as **cross-debuggers**.

Cross-debuggers work in one of three ways. The first and easiest is the target **simulator**. Here compilation, linking, and debugging occur completely within the host processor. The simulator is built into the debugger to execute the target program by interpreting the target machine instructions. It simulates the target environment to the program so that the program believes it is executing on the target machine. Once debugging is complete, the program is burned into ROM and installed into the target machine.

Programmers often prefer simulators because they are an all software solution. The programmer does not need to worry about finding actual target hardware with which to work. On the other hand, simulators are often slow because they have to interpret each target instruction. In addition, they may not simulate the target environment perfectly, leading to problems when the code is installed in the actual target machine.

A second approach is the **remote debugger**, in which development occurs on the host processor as before. The host processor is connected to the target machine either via an RS232 serial connection or over a LAN. A small companion program to the debugger, a debugger stub, is installed on the target machine.

The user starts the debugger on the host machine. The host debugger transfers the executable to the debugger stub, which loads it into the target machine. The user performs all debugging operations on the host debugger including examining source code, setting breakpoints, and so on. The host transfers to the debugger stub on the target any instructions to be carried out.

This form of debugger avoids the problems of the simulator. The program executes in the actual target machine at target machine speeds. However, this debugger requires real target hardware. In addition, it makes certain demands of its own on the target. The target machine must have sufficient RAM to hold the program. The RAM can later be replaced with pin compatible ROM when the program is ready to be permanently installed.

In addition, the remote debugger may require that a communication port be added to the hardware design. The remote debugger can use an existing LAN connection in the target machine without affecting other LAN traffic, but it cannot use a serial port that is also being used by the application software.

Remote debuggers are the ideal solution for cross-development when these conditions can be met. They offer the convenience of a source code debugger while executing the target application at normal speeds in the real environment.

The host and target computers do not need to be colocated. As long as the communication path is reliable, the host processor can be many miles away. This makes remote debuggers ideal for distributed applications, such as telephone networks, point of sale equipment, and long distance communication.

The **In-Circuit Emulator** (or **ICE**) is a third form of cross-debugger. Here the CPU in the target processor is replaced by a probe that comes from the ICE in the host machine.

Undoubtedly, the ICE debugger is the most powerful of all. ICE boxes can execute programs stored in host memory or can download the program into target memory for execution. They can temporarily remap memory blocks or I/O ports. They can provide memory protection even if the target CPU has no memory protection features. ICE boxes provide a breakout switch to allow the programmer to stop execution in the target machine if that program has crashed. Some can even change the timing on the CPU pins to investigate the reaction of the hardware design to slightly out of spec parts.

ICE boxes are expensive. A good ICE costs in excess of $10,000, not including the host computer or cross-development software. Not too much for an industrial application, but out of reach of the individual programmer. In addition, ICE boxes tend to be less user-friendly than some of the other debugger types. Periscope offers some smaller, less expensive ICE solutions for the PC.

Other Debugging Tools

Besides those mentioned already, C++ programmers have available a series of different debugging aids, ranging from simple pretty printers through powerful lint programs and range checkers.

Pretty printers take the C++ source code and reformat it to make some semantic errors more obvious. For example, a pretty printer would take the following:

```
int factorial(int i) {
    int accum = 1;

    while (i)
        accum *= i;
        i--;
    return accum;
}
```

and reformat it into

```
int factorial(int i) {
    int accum = 1;
    while (i)
        accum *= i;
    i--;
    return accum;
}
```

making the misalignment of `i--` obvious. The types of errors that pretty printers can detect, however, are limited.

Pretty printers do become quite effective if formatting rules can be programmed in. In this mode, they act like source code watchdogs, making sure that the local coding standards are adequately enforced.

A **lint** syntax checker takes the concept of the pretty printer several steps further. The lint checker examines the source code meticulously, calling into question any structure that looks like it might be incorrect. Most of the C pitfalls outlined in Chapter 5 are detectable from a lint.

Tightened typing rules and improved technology allow compilers to build in some of the checks available in lints. For example, modern compilers generate warnings for declared but unused variables and errors for

functions called with improper prototypes. This has forced lint manufacturers to look for areas in which compilers cannot keep up. For example,
lint can examine the arguments passed to `printf()` to make sure that
they appear proper. Consider the output generated by PC Lint from
Gimpel Software for the following trivial program.

```
#include <stdio.h>

int main(int argc, char *argc[]) {
    int i;

    scanf("%d", i);
    printf("%f", i);
}
```

```
--- Module:   test.c
    scanf("%d", i);
test.c   6   Warning 560: argument no. 2 should be a
                pointer
test.c   6   Warning 534: Return mode of scanf
                inconsistent with line 149, file
                   c:\compiler\tc2\include\stdio.h
test.c   6   Warning 530: i (line 4) not initialized
                        —
    printf("%f", i);
test.c   7   Warning 559: Size of argument no. 2
                inconsistent with format
test.c   7   Warning 534: Return mode of printf
                inconsistent with line 145, file
       c:\compiler\tc2\include\stdio.h
   —
}
test.c   10  Warning 533: Return mode of main
                   inconsistent with line 3
test.c   10  Info 715: argc (line 3) not referenced
```

PC-Lint has detected several errors that the C++ compiler would not
have: line 6 should read `scanf("%d", &i)` and line 7 attempts to display an integer using a `%f` format.

Some software firms require a message-free output from lint before a source code module can be checked in. Since lints tend to generate a lot of false alarms, a lint should allow particular messages to be disabled for this to be practical.

Unfortunately, as of this writing there are no lints for C++, but several manufacturers are porting their lints.

Another debugging tool is the **range checker**. This device examines all memory references within the program during execution to make sure that none is outside the bounds of the object. These tools work in one of two ways.

One type of range checker uses the memory protection features of the CPU. For the PC this type of checker requires an 80386 or 80486 processor. These checkers are not necessary for protected mode operating systems, such as OS/2 or UNIX, since this capability is already built in.

A memory protection checker does not affect program performance, and need not be language specific. However, it cannot detect all incorrect memory accesses. Consider the following example using global arrays.

```
int array1[1000];
int array2[1000];

void fn() {
    array1[1500] = 0;
}
```

The access of `array1` is clearly out of bounds. Since it falls within `array2`, which also belongs to the program, a memory protection checker would not detect the error. In addition, the minimum granularity of the protection features of the 80386/486 is 4K. Thus, any overwrite within 4K might go undetected. Bounds Checker from Nu-Mega is a memory protection checker for the PC.

Another approach is to modify the source code, including source code statements around application lines of interest. These statements are calls to bounds-checking functions. For example, C-Debug from Softran takes the conservative approach placing checks around every access of the array or pointer. Other range checkers check only dynamically allocated memory and/or memory being passed as arguments to functions.

The source code modifier range checker is capable of finding more errors than the memory protection checker. For example, the error in the previous code fragment would be detected by a source code modifier checker. This type of checker is more difficult to use because it involves executing a prepass on the .CPP source file to properly instrument the source program before it can be compiled and linked. In addition, source code modifier checkers add to the size of the executable and can reduce performance.

Other Programmers

Perhaps the most powerful debugging aids the programmer has are fellow programmers. Despite their reputation as "nerds," a study of the best debuggers shows that they have excellent communication, negotiating, team building, and other social skills. (The study by T. R. Riedl et al. was reported by Victor Basili and John Musa in *IEEE* in September 1991.) In addition, programmers cultivate an extensive network of experts they can call on in a crisis.

Fellow programmers are useful in finding problems for several reasons. First, the originating programmers must organize their thoughts to present the problem to others. This time to step back from the problem and organize what is known into a format presentable to others helps the subconscious process. On several occasions a junior programmer has been in the middle of explaining a problem to me only to stop halfway through with the sudden realization of what the problem must be.

Second, other programmers have been there before. It is highly unlikely that you will have a problem that some old debugging veteran hasn't seen already. A few hours of other programmers' time, though valuable, can save you days. Even if experienced programmers can't see the problem immediately, they can probably point out dangerous or questionable practices that might be causing the problem.

Remember, it is for just these reasons that formal design and code reviews include both experienced and inexperienced programmers in the same group. Cross-fertilization between veteran programmers with their experience and rookies with their new ideas should be systematically encouraged.

Using a Source Code Debugger

Before source code debugging can start, the programmer must compile and link the program with symbolic information included in the executable file on disk. Since this symbolic information can be quite large — often two or three times as large as the program itself — the default for most compilers is not to include this information.

Once started, the source code debugger presents at least two windows to the user: the source window and the command window. In many debuggers the command window is replaced by a menu bar across the top of the display from which commands can be selected from the keyboard or with a mouse.

The following sections will discuss how to perform basic debugging functions with a source code debugger.

Controlling Execution

Under the debugger, the programmer has control of how the application program is executed. Normal operation is to set one or more breakpoints at places of interest before letting the program begin execution.

Breakpoints   Breakpoints are set by specifying the C++ line number where the program should stop. Window-oriented debuggers also allow the programmer to specify breakpoints with the cursor or mouse. After the breakpoints have been set, the programmer enters the run command to instruct the debugger to start executing the application.

When a breakpoint is encountered, execution is resumed with a continue command. Breakpoints normally remain until specifically removed. A breakpoint placed within a loop is encountered on every pass through the loop.

The programmer should be careful when executing from one breakpoint to another to keep straight what path was taken. Consider the following code segment:

```
char* faultyFn(char* pT, char* pS) {
    if (pS) {                                     //line 1
        if (pT != 0) {                            //line 2
            pT = new char[strlen(pS) + 1];        //line 3
```

```
        }
        strcpy(pT, pS);                           //line 4
    }
        pT = (char*)0;
    return pT;
}


void main() {
//...
    char *pCopy = faultyFn(0, "a string");        //call 1
//...
    faultyFn(pCopy, "a different string");        //call 2
}
```

Realizing that the function has a problem, the programmer sets a breakpoint at line 2 within `faultyFn()`. Seeing that `pT` is 0 and not noticing that the `if` statement is improper (it should be `if (pT == 0)`), the programmer deletes that breakpoint, sets a new breakpoint on line 3, and enters the continue command. The program stops on line 3 as expected, but the program is not where the programmer thinks it is. The first call stepped over line 3 due to the faulty `if` statement and returned. The second call to `faultyFn()` fell into the `if` statement and encountered the breakpoint. The programmer has unknowingly moved from the first call to `faultyFn()` to the second.

To guard against this, I always "guard the door" by setting a breakpoint on the entry to the function itself and leaving it there as long as I am debugging within the function. If the function returns without my knowledge and is subsequently called again, encountering the breakpoint at the beginning of the function alerts me to the problem.

Most debuggers also support conditional breakpoints. These are breakpoints that only stop execution if certain conditions are true. For example, the following breakpoint might mean "break on line 100 if `myObj` is negative."

```
(myObj < 0) b 100
```

These breakpoints are implemented like any other: execution of the application program is interrupted by the insertion of a jump back to the debugger. The debugger checks the specified condition. If it is not true, the debugger continues execution automatically. Setting a breakpoint within a tight loop that is executed often will affect the performance of the program even if the breakpoint condition is not fulfilled and the breakpoint does not appear to hit.

Normally breakpoints simply halt execution and return control back to the programmer for the manual entry of further debugger commands, but some debuggers support the inclusion of breakpoint commands. The following breakpoint might mean "break on line 200, print out the value of myObj and then continue execution."

```
b 200 p myObj c
```

This is particularly useful for time-critical applications. The programmer can stop execution, display a few values, and then continue execution before other tasks run out of time. This has the same effect as, but is more convenient than, printf() statements.

Single Stepping   A single step command allows the programmer to execute one C++ line. This operation acts as if the programmer set a breakpoint on the next instruction and depressed continue. This is very convenient when examining a particular portion of a program in detail. It also does not suffer from the problem mentioned above.

Confusion can arise as to what constitutes the next C++ statement. Consider the following example:

```
i = 0;          //line 1
fn2(i);         //line 2
j = 1;          //line 3
```

Single stepping from line 1, control passes to line 2. When line 2 is executed, control must pass through the function fn2(). Should the program stop on line 3 or on the first line of fn2()? Either is possible, so most debuggers provide a choice. Stepping over fn2() and stopping at line 3 is called a **step**. Stepping into fn2() to stop at the first line of fn2() is called a **trace**.

Notice that *over* and *into* are not accurate descriptions — either way, control passes into the function. The question is whether the programmer is viewing the function as a single C++ expression. If the source code to the function is not available, as would be the case for a call to one of the C++ standard library functions, many debuggers handle a trace identically to a step.

Debuggers can also generate confusing results when multiple sub-expressions are combined on a single line, as in the following:

```
for (int i = 0; i < 10; i++) array[i] = 0;
```

Most debuggers treat this as a single line so the individual loops cannot be single stepped. However, the following is considered two lines and can be single stepped.

```
for (int i = 0; i < 10; i++)
    array[i] = 0;
```

An in-line function is always treated as a single C++ expression. To trace the individual lines of such a function the function must be outlined. Most C++ compilers provide a compile-time option to outline all inline functions and thereby simplify debugging. If this option is not available, the programmer may insert the following at the beginning of the module to effectively remove all inline declarations.

```
#define inline
```

Viewing/Changing Data

Once stopped at a breakpoint, the programmer needs to be able to display variables. All source code debuggers provide some type of display command that allows the programmer to enter the name of a variable whose value is to be displayed. The debugger determines the format of output based upon the type of the variable. Consider the following variables.

```
int i = 1;
float f = 1;
int *pI = &i;
char *pS = "a string";
```

Assume that the address of `i` is `0x1234` and that "a string" is stored at address `0x5678`. Displaying these variables would generate the following results.

```
Display                  results:
    i                           1
    f                       1.000
   pI                      0x1234
  *pI                           1
   pS                    a string
  *pS                         'a'
   (void*)pS             0x5678
```

Notice the interpretation of `pS`. Since it is a `char*`, the debugger assumes the programmer is more interested in the entire string than the address. To see the address, the programmer must cast `pS` to some other pointer type.

Objects that have internal structure, such as class objects, are generally displayed in their entirety. The sophistication of this display is debugger dependent. A simpler debugger displays the values without interpretation as in the following:

```
Display              results:
struct {             {1, {1, 2, 3, 4, 5}, "a string"}
   int i;
   int array[5];
   char *pS;
} obj;
```

More sophisticated debuggers can display class relationships. This capability, known as a **browser**, gives the programmer a good overview of class hierarchy.

Certain variables are of particular interest, especially while single stepping/tracing through a function. To save the programmer the trouble of repeatedly displaying the value of objects, most debuggers offer a **watch window**. The programmer enters the names of objects whose values will be displayed every time the debugger stops the application.

Debuggers must also worry about scope rules. Consider the following functions:

```
void fn1() {
    for (int i = 0; i < 10; i++)
        fn2(i);
}

void fn2(int arg) {
    int i = 0;
    //...
}
```

If the program is halted within `fn2()` and the programmer asks to see the value of `i`, the debugger must assume that the programmer is referring to the `i` within `fn2()`. If the programmer actually means `fn1::i`, then the display command must refer specifically to that `i` by including the function name. The syntax details are debugger specific.

Data Breakpoints

In addition to normal breakpoints, most debuggers support some form of **data breakpoint**. Data breakpoints specify that program execution is to stop when a particular data object is accessed, modified, or set to a particular value. This type of breakpoint is used to find problems involving overwritten locations.

Without hardware help, to implement a data breakpoint the debugger must stop after every C++ instruction and check the data object. If the data condition is not fulfilled, the debugger automatically resumes execution. Executing a breakpoint after every statement slows execution of the program so much that data breakpoints are only effective if the range of the change to the data object can be restricted in some way.

Range limiting is usually handled with a watch variable. The programmer sets a watch variable on the data object that is being overwritten and single steps through functions until the object appears overwritten. The programmer then restarts the program and executes up to the offending function before setting the data breakpoint.

Fortunately, the 80386 and 80486 processors support up to four data breakpoints in hardware. Debuggers that support the 80386/486 use this feature to set data breakpoints without affecting the performance of the application. However, the programmer must be careful not to set more than four such breakpoints — otherwise, the debugger must revert to single stepping in order to implement them.

Assembly Language Debugging

Debugging C++ programs at the assembly language level is not often necessary, but when it is, few techniques are as effective. Assembly language debugging using a source code debugger is not nearly as difficult as debugging using an assembly language debugger.

A typical scenario involves a single C++ statement that does not work and the programmer cannot understand why. Simplifying a compound expression can often avoid the necessity of dropping down to the assembly level. Consider the following example:

```
//fn1 - input an integer and returns output;
//        return 0 if all ok, else error indication
int fn1(int input, int& output);

int fn2(int input);

void main() {
    int x, y;
    //...
    fn1(fn2(x % 5), y);
    //...
}
```

Before the call to `fn1()`, x is determined to have the correct value. Upon single stepping the call to `fn1()`, however, the resulting value of y is incorrect. What could be wrong? This expression can be made easier to debug if it is divided into its constituent subexpressions as follows.

```
    int temp1 = x % 5;
    int temp2 = fn2(temp1);
    int results = fn1(temp2, y);
```

Since they are now separated, the results of the individual sub-expressions can be examined. In addition, saving the error returned from a function gives the programmer an object that can be examined from the debugger to determine whether the function encountered a problem.

Occasionally expressions that do not work cannot be simplified any further. Consider the following:

```
#include <stdio.h>

struct MyClass {
  private:
    int p;                          //address of a function

  public:
    //save off the address of the function
    MyClass(int pF) {
        p = pF;
    }
    //call the function pointed at by p
    int call(int arg) {
        int (*pFn)(int) = (int(*)(int))p;
        int results = pFn(arg); //program crashes here
        return results;
    }
};


//aFunc - a trial function
int aFunc(int arg) {
    return arg * arg;
}

void main() {
    //declare an object and then try it out
    MyClass mco((int)aFunc);
    int results = mco.call(10);
    printf("results = %d\n", results);
}
```

All appears correct with MyClass except for the call to the function pointed at by pFn in the method call(). When compiled in large model, this function crashes the system. Setting a breakpoint on the trial function aFunc does not help, as control does not arrive there. Tracing this single expression crashes as well. This expression cannot be simplified any further. There is no choice but to look into the assembly language generated for that line.

First, I set a breakpoint on the call and execute in C++ mode up to that point. Before executing the call, however, I switch the debugger over to the assembly language mode and discover the following assembly language generated for the function. The C++ source appears as comments intermixed in the assembly language.

```
MyClass::call:  int call(int arg) {
    cs:00848040000         enter   0004,00
    cs:0088 56             push    si
#TEMP#12:  int (*pFn)(int) = (int(*)(int))p;
    cs:0089 C45E06         les     bx,[bp+06]
    cs:008C 268B07         mov     ax,es:[bx]
    cs:008F 99             cwd
    cs:0090 8946FC         mov     [bp-04],ax
    cs:0093 8956FE         mov     [bp-02],dx
#TEMP#13:   results = pFn(arg);
    cs:0096 FF760A         push    word ptr [bp+0A]
    cs:0099 FF5EFC         call    far [bp-04]
    cs:009C 59             pop     cx
    cs:009D 8BF0           mov     si,ax
#TEMP#14:   return results;
    cs:009F 8BC6           mov     ax,si
    cs:00A1 EB00           jmp     #TEMP#15 (00A3)
#TEMP#15:   }
    cs:00A3 5E             pop     si
    cs:00A4 C9             leave
    cs:00A5 CB             retf
```

Looking at line 13, the call itself, all appears correct. The argument is pushed on the stack. BP+0xA corresponds to the second argument to call(). The far call is performed to a location stored locally on the stack, which would be correct for pFn. Tracing into this call, however, control passes to the location 0x0000:0x0003, which is incorrect.

pFn is set up on line 12. Looking back to line 12, we can see the problem. The LES instruction loads the address of this, which is the hidden first argument to the function MyClass::call(). The MOV AX loads this->p, as expected. Why the CWD (Convert Word to Double)? The result of this is to sign extend a 0x0003 in AX into 0x00000003 in DX:AX. This should be the address of aFunc(). The actual address of aFunc() is CS:0x0003. The segment portion of the address of aFunc() has been lost because a 16-bit int cannot store a 32-bit address.

The problem can be solved by redeclaring p to be a long. However, the real solution is to declare p to be a pointer to a function. Once the class declaration has been corrected, I return to reexamine the assembly language to verify the fix.

```
#TEMP#12: int (*pFn)(int) = (int(*)(int))p;
    cs:009345E06            les      bx,[bp+06]
    cs:0096 268B4702        mov      ax,es:[bx+02]
    cs:009A 268B17          mov      dx,es:[bx]
    cs:009D 8956FC          mov      [bp-04],dx
    cs:00A0 8946FE          mov      [bp-02],ax
```

Now the full 32 bits are loaded from *this and stored into pFn.

You can see that single stepping a single C++ source code expression may involve executing several assembly language statements. Single stepping in assembly language mode executes only one machine instruction at a time. This gives extremely fine grain control. The programmer can execute each machine instruction of a C++ expression, examining the registers and variables at every point along the way.

The assembly language display will seem quite foreign to the C++ programmer at first. The programmer should attempt to execute up to the point of the problem in source code mode, flipping over to assembly language only at the last minute. This reduces the amount of detail. Single stepping individual assembly language instructions while watching the registers and data objects quickly teaches the programmer how the C++ instructions are being implemented.

Conclusion

Once a software error has been detected in testing, the programmer must find the source of the problem, fix it, and verify the fix. This chapter has reviewed the different debugging tools available. These tools range from simple `printf()`s through pretty printers, lint-type syntax checkers, and range checkers. However, the most powerful of all debugging tools is the source code debugger.

Every C++ programmer should become sufficiently familiar with a source code debugger that it comes to feel natural. When thinking about a problem, the programmer cannot be thinking about how to use the debugger as well.

The next chapter will go through the steps of using a source debugger to debug a sample C++ program.

Chapter 9

A Sample Debugging Session

Debugging a faulty program is much like fixing an extremely complicated car. The programmer starts by driving the program around the block a few times to hear the problem firsthand. Some problems generate symptoms that the experienced programmer can decipher quickly. Likewise, some symptoms usually are associated with particular types of errors.

Writing a fixed algorithm that can debug all problems all the time is impossible. Debugging must be guided by intuition that develops through experience. However, the beginner can follow some rules to help make the learning process as fruitful and short as possible.

First, understand the programming language. You should understand the syntax, the grammar, the standard library functions, everything. Whatever is not clear in your mind is a problem. You will find it very difficult to debug errors that occur in the murky areas of your understanding.

Second, be aware of the traps and pitfalls as well as their effects so you can recognize them when they occur. This is why I have spent so much time discussing the pitfalls of C++.

Third, understand your particular compiler. Read the manual carefully, even if on-line help is available. What you don't know will hurt you.

Fourth, understand your debugger. This is as much a development tool as your editor. Time spent learning how to use these tools is repaid many times with use.

Fifth, understand each module you intend to debug whether you wrote it or not. Step through it to get a feel for how it works. Not only will this give you some confidence that it works, but it will give your subconscious the raw material it will need to discover the cause of the problem.

Finally, try to understand how your computer works internally. This is a gradual process that takes time, often years. Times will come when you will want to drop down to the assembly level and examine the machine code put out by your C++ programs. I have encountered problems that I could not solve any other way. The ability to work comfortably at the machine level is a tremendous advantage.

Think

The sources of errors, in decreasing order of probability, are as follows:

- coding error (also the easiest to fix)
- logic error
- design error
- misunderstanding of a C++ feature
- compiler bug
- operating system bug
- software virus
- hardware error

The first three sources of error are by far the most likely. Given the complexity of the C++ syntax, misunderstanding of C++ features is also possible.

Compiler bugs are considerably less likely. Because they are unusual and somewhat beyond the programmer's control, when compiler bugs do occur, they can be quite difficult to find. This is why responsible compiler manufacturers do not hesitate to publicize known bugs in particular compiler versions. (These lists are usually maintained on electronic bulletin board systems — check with your compiler manufacturer.)

When you suspect a compiler bug, attempt to achieve the same goal with different C++ source code. It is possible that a specific construct, particularly if it is unusual or complicated, slipped through compiler testing. If you rewrite the function using different C++ source code and the problem does not go away, the problem probably is not with the compiler.

If the problem can be tracked down to a single, complicated expression, break the expression down into multiple, simple subexpressions. Not only does this help isolate the problem, but it simplifies the job of parsing for the compiler.

The only real way to verify a compiler problem is to examine the assembly language output from the statement. If the problem can be verified, document the problem using the smallest set of source code that exhibits the problem and send it to the manufacturer of the compiler. The manufacturer should fix the problem and add it to the list of known bugs for previous versions.

The last three sources of error are very unlikely and you should only consider them when all the evidence forces you to do so. There have been some notable exceptions, such as a particular version of the 80386 processor that could not perform 32-bit integer arithmetic properly.

Approaches to Problem Solving

One general approach programmers use to find a software bug is first to gather relevant data. Then execute the affected code, gathering facts and impressions. Next they might stop and ponder the problem for awhile. Simple problems can be found by stepping through the area with a debugger. More complicated problems will require either an inductive or deductive analysis.

Using the inductive process, the programmer begins by looking for some pattern in the data. The programmer devises one or more hypotheses, keeping the earlier probability list in mind. Always assume first that the problem is your own — you'll be right most of the time.

The programmer attempts to prove the most probable hypothesis. This very important step is often overlooked. Too often, the programmer will devise a fix based upon a hypothesis. This can be a waste of effort, as the fix will not fix anything if the hypothesis is incorrect. Worse yet, the fix might hide or change the symptom, making finding the real problem more difficult.

This does not mean that problems noticed during the course of investigating an error should not be fixed. For example, I might discover that a particular condition is not handled properly even though it is not the condition that is causing the current problem. I devise checks for these conditions but hold them in reserve to be installed only after the current problem has been tracked down, fixed, and tested.

Proving a hypothesis is generally just a matter of setting a breakpoint in the proper place and examining the proper data objects. If the hypothesis is rejected, attention must turn to remaining hypotheses. Once a hypothesis has been confirmed and it explains all of the facts, a fix can be devised, applied, and retested.

Another approach is to use deductive reasoning. In this case, the programmer starts by collecting relevant information as before. The programmer then writes down all possible hypotheses on a piece of paper and compares them with the facts. The hypotheses that do not agree with all of the facts are crossed off the list.

Once the list has been pared down to a few likely candidates, each remaining hypothesis is expanded and refined. The programmer repeats the process on each refined hypothesis until arriving at a set of hypotheses that can be tested using either new test cases or the source code debugger. This final step is identical to the inductive process.

Give your subconscious time to think about the problem. All debugging is performed in the subconscious, and I do not pretend to know how it works. It sometimes requires several hours or days to work out the problem. If you reach a dead end on a particular problem after a few hours, drop it and move on to something else for the day. Return a day or two later and the problem will seem more approachable.

Describe the problem to a friend. The act of describing the problem forces you to think about it in a more logical, cause-and-effect way. In addition, the friend may have seen the same or a similar problem before and may be able to suggest a new hypothesis that you can test.

If a solution cannot be found right away, avoid forcing it. Whatever you do, do not attempt to correct the problem with random fixes. This is the **shotgun approach**, and it is never effective. Even if the symptom goes away, you will not know what the problem was. Therefore, you will not know whether you really fixed the problem, and you will not know where else in the program you may have committed the same error.

A Sample Program

This section will combine the foregoing suggestions with the pointers set out in earlier chapters to debug a sample program. This program was written to solve the following problem:

```
Write a program that enters the names of the members
of families along with their ages and how much each
smokes. The program should then display the name of
each family followed by each of its members and a
health risk analysis factor. In addition, the average
health of each family should be displayed. The health
risk is calculated as follows:

Non-smokers:
    Risk factor = 1.0 + # of years above 40 / 10
For smokers:
    Risk factor = 1.0 + # of years above 30 / f
    where f =
                7.5 for 1 pack  per day
                7.0 for 2 packs per day
                6.5 for 3 packs per day
                        etc.
```

(This problem is for illustrative purposes only. The health risk factor has no medical basis.)

This problem is not particularly difficult to program. My solution to this problem follows. Be forewarned, however, that this program contains several errors. Examine the program and write down on a piece of paper or in the margins all of the problems that you can spot (use Chapter 5 and 6 for suggestions).

I will use Turbo C++ from Borland International as the compiler/environment. I will use the integrated debugger for all my debugging. Any good C++/debugger combination should generate nearly identical results, however.

```
//LAB - the following program inputs the names of family
//      members, their ages, and their smoking status and
```

```
//      then sorts them within the family by health risk
//      and outputs them to a file.
//      This program has several bugs
#include <stdio.h>
#include <stdlib.h>
#include <ctype.h>
#include <string.h>
#include <iostream.h>
#include <fstream.h>

class Family;
class Person;

//Family - families consist of groups of people
//          contained in a linked list
class Family {
    friend class Person;
  private:
    //class members
    static Family *pFirst;

    //instance members
    unsigned signature;
    Family *pNext;
    Person *pMembers;
    char    name[20];
    void    checkSignature();

  public:
            Family(char *pName);
    static Family *first()   {return pFirst;}
            Family *next()      {return pNext;}
            Person *members() {return pMembers;}
            char*    perName() {return name;}
            float    healthRisk();
            void    display(ostream& os);
};
void operator<<(ostream& os, Family& f) {
    f.display(os);
```

```
        }
        Family* Family::pFirst;//allocate space for static member

        //class Person - describe the people who are members of
        //              the family; this class may be inherited
        class Person {
          protected:
            unsigned signature;
            Family  *pFamily;          //base family
            Person  *pNext;            //next member of family

            char      lastName[20];
            char      firstName[20];
            int       age;

          public:
            Person(char *pN, int a, Family f, char *pLN = 0);
            Person* next() {return pNext;}
            void checkSignature();
            void display(ostream& os);
            float healthRisk();
        };
        void operator<<(ostream& os, Person& p) {
            p.display(os);
        }

        class Smoker : public Person {
          private:
            int  noPacksPerDay;

          public:
            Smoker(char *pN, int a, int packsPerDay, Family f,
                    char *pLN = 0) : Person(pN, a, f, pLN) {
                signature = 0x4322;
                noPacksPerDay = packsPerDay;
            }
            virtual float healthRisk();
        };
```

```
//-------------define Family methods----------------
Family::Family(char *pName) {
    //fill in signature
    signature = 0x1234;

    //fill in the data
    strcpy(name, pName);

    //add to beginning of name list
    pNext = pFirst;
    pFirst = this;
}


//checkSignature - check the signature
void Family::checkSignature() {
    if (signature != 0x1234) {
        cout << "Signature mismatch on family "
            << *this << endl;
        abort();
    }
}


//healthRisk - calculate the avg health risk of family
float Family::healthRisk() {
    checkSignature();

    float avgHR = 0.0;
    int count;
    float curHR;
    Person *pPerson = pMembers;
    while (pPerson) {
        pPerson->checkSignature();
        curHR = pPerson->healthRisk();
        avgHR += curHR;
        count++;
        pPerson = pPerson->next();
    }
    avgHR /= count;
    return avgHR;
```

```
        }

        //display - display a family to the specified stream
        void Family::display(ostream& os) {
            checkSignature();
            cout << "Family " << name;
        }


        //---------------now the methods of Person-----------
        Person::Person(char *pN, int a, Family f, char *pLN) {
            //check Family argument
            f.checkSignature();

            //fill in signature
            signature = 0x4321;

            //add the person to the family
            pFamily = &f;
            pNext = pFamily->pMembers;
            pFamily->pMembers = this;
            age = a;

            //now fill in data members
            strcpy(firstName, pN);
            strcpy(lastName, pLN);
        }
        //checkSignature - check the signature
        void Person::checkSignature() {
            if (signature != 0x4321) {
                cout << "Signature mismatch on person "
                     << *this << endl;
                abort();
            }
        }


        //healthRisk - calculate the overall health risk to
        //             the individual. This expression
        //             is purely fictional.
        float Person::healthRisk() {
```

```
    checkSignature();

    float risk = 1.0;              //assume normal risk
    if (age > 40.0) {              //above forty slightly...
        risk += (age - 40.0) / 10.0; //...upward trend
    }
    return risk;
}

void Person::display(ostream& os) {
    checkSignature();

    char *pLN;
    strcpy(pLN, lastName);
    if (*pLN == '\0') {
        strcpy(pLN, pFamily->perName());
    }
    cout << pLN << ", " << firstName;
}


//healthRisk - risks for smokers are higher than for
//             non-smokers.  These risk calcul-
//             ations are purely fictitious.
float Smoker::healthRisk() {
    checkSignature();

    float risk = 1.0;         //start with normal risk
    if (age > 30.0) {         //trend starts earlier
                              //and rises faster
        risk += (age - 30.0) / (8 - .5 * noPacksPerDay);
    }
    return risk;
}


//----------now define the general functions----------
//getFamily - return a family object, 0 if no more
Family* getFamily() {
    printf("Another?");
    char answer;
```

```
        scanf("%c", answer);
        if (answer == 'N' || answer == 'n') {
            return (Family*)0;
        }

        printf("Enter family name:");
        char buffer[132];
        gets(buffer);
        return &Family(buffer);
}

//getPerson - return a person object
Person* getPerson(Family family) {
    printf("Enter first name:");
    char first[132];
    gets(first);
    if (first[0] == '\0') {
        return (Person*)0;
    }

    printf("Enter last name if different from family:");
    char last[132];
    char *pLast = last;
    gets(last);
    if (!isalpha(*pLast)) {
        pLast = (char*)0;
    }

    int age;
    printf("Enter age:");
    scanf("%d", age);

    int pks;
    printf
       ("# of packs smoked per day (0 for non-smoker)");
    scanf("%d", pks);

    Person *pPerson;
    if (pks > 0) {
```

```
            pPerson = &Smoker(first,age,pks,family, pLast);
        }
        else {
            pPerson = &Person(first, age, family, pLast);
        }
        return pPerson;
    }


void main() {
    //load up the family data
    Family *pFam;
    while (pFam = getFamily()) {
        while (getPerson(*pFam));
    }

    //now output it to the file OUTPUT
    //ofstream oFile("OUTPUT");
    //during debug output to cout where we can see it
    ostream& oFile = cout;
    pFam = Family::first();
    Person *pPer;
    while (pFam) {
        oFile << *pFam << " - "
              << pFam->healthRisk() << endl;
        pPer = pFam->members();
        while (pPer) {
            oFile << "   "   << *pPer
                    << " - " << pPer->healthRisk()
                    << endl;
            pPer = pPer->next();
        }
        pFam = pFam->next();
    }
}
```

I start by generating a minimum set of test cases to run. The first three tests in the list that follows are designed to exercise all of the different functions. They are purposely kept minimal to allow single stepping through the functions. As debugging progresses, cases may arise that I will want to add to the list.

Notice that the risk results for some of the cases are "don't care." I am saying that I don't particularly care what the output is as long as the program does not die. Industrial applications may not be so forgiving, specifying for example that a particular output range not be exceeded or that an error message be generated.

Family	Person	age	packs	risk

Simplest case for initial testing:

Family	Person	age	packs	risk
Case 1 - Davis				1
	Randy	36	0	1

Simplest smoker case:

Family	Person	age	packs	risk
Case 2 - Davis				2.5
	Randy	40	3	2.5

Simplest case with different last name:

Family	Person	age	packs	risk
Case 3 - Davis				1
	Randy,Brown	40	0	1

Multiple families/members with different healthRisks; includes both smokers and non-smokers in same family:

Family	Person	age	packs	risk
Case 4 - Davis				1.3
	Randy	50	0	2
	Jenny	30	0	1
	Lee	8	0	1
Brown				4.7
	Tom	50	2	3.8
	Jackie	60	3	5.6
Kirkland				3.5
	Adalbert	60	1	5
	Jessica	50	0	2

Family members with illegal ages or very long names:

Family	Person	age	packs	risk
Case 5 - Abcdefghijklmnopqrstuvwxyz				don't care
	<100 a's>	0	0	don't care

B	0	1000	don't care
C	1000	0	don't care
D	30000	30000	don't care

No members in the family:
Case 6 -   Davis   don't care

No families:
Case 7 -   don't care

Start the debugging process by compiling the preceding program with all warnings and errors enabled. This will give the compiler a chance to scan the work for errors.

```
Error  99: Value of type void is not allowed in function Family::checkSignature()
Warning 128: Parameter 'os' is never used in function Family::display(ostream near&)
Error  152: Value of type void is not allowed in function Person::checkSignature()
Warning 174: Possible use of 'pIN' before definition in function Person::display(ostream near&)
Warning 179: Parameter 'os' is never used in function Person::display(ostream near&)
Warning 200: Possible use of 'answer' before definition in function getFamily()
Warning 231: Possible use of 'age' before definition in function getPerson(Family)
Warning 235: Possible use of 'noOfPacks' before definition in function getPerson(Family)
Warning 250: Possibly incorrect assignment in function main()
Error  262: Value of type void is not allowed in function main()
Error  266: Value of type void is not allowed in function main()
Warning 272: 'oFile' is declared but never used in function main()
```

Line 99 refers to the statement cout << "Signature mismatch on family" << *this << endl. From the error message you can deduce that something must be of type void. Since this is of type Family, the logical place to look is Family::operator<<(). In fact, this operator is declared type void.

As mentioned earlier, insertion operators should be declared type ostream& to allow them to be chained with other inserters. The identical problem generates the second error. To correct the problem, I rewrite the operators as follows.

```
ostream& operator<<(ostream& os, Family& f) {
    f.display(os);
    return os;
}
ostream& operator<<(ostream& os, Person& p) {
```

```
        p.display(os);
        return os;
}
```

The line 128 warning points to the end of the function `Family::display()`. The compiler wants to know why `os` is passed to the function if it is not used. Upon reflection, it is clear that output should be to the ostream `os` instead of `cout`. It is not uncommon to automatically send output to `cout` without thinking. The fix here consists of replacing `cout` with `os` within the function and in `Person::display()`.

The next warning complains that pLN is being used before it has been assigned a value in the call to `strcpy()` in function `Person::display()`. That's odd since it is the call to `strcpy()` that is supposed to initialize pLN. Here, I have confused an array with a pointer. Remember, an array defines a storage area and assigns it an address — a pointer defines a place to store the address of another storage area, but does not allocate that area. What was intended was the following:

```
void Person::display(ostream& os) {
    checkSignature();

    char lN[20];
    strcpy(lN, lastName);
    //...etc.
```

The next three messages warn that variables are being used before they have been initialized in the functions `getFamily()` and `getPerson()` at statements such as the following:

```
char answer;
scanf("%c", answer);
```

Of course `answer` has not been initialized, since I intended for it to be initialized by the call. You may be tempted to ignore the warning ("it's only a warning after all") and continue. This temptation must be resisted until you fully understand the warning and its cause.

In this case the compiler has pointed out a real error. The value of `answer` was passed instead of its address. Like any function that expects to change the value of an argument in the caller, scanf() expects a pointer or a reference to an object. The corrected call is as follows:

```
char answer;
scanf("%c", &answer);
```

Care must be taken to make sure that the format string matches the types of the actual arguments. Here scanf() is not type-safe, and if the types are wrong, the compiler will not generate a warning. Here %c matches the type of answer. (The extraction operator, which is type-safe, could have been used.)

The next warning was generated on the following line:

```
while (pFam = getFamily()) {
    //...etc.
```

No error has occurred, but the compiler is concerned that perhaps I may have confused = with ==. Examing the statement carefully, I can see that the statement is correct. Rather than disable the warning, since it might uncover a real bug in the future, I will get rid of the warning as follows:

```
while ((pFam = getFamily()) != 0) {
    //...etc.
```

The last two errors refer to the operator<< problem already fixed. The final warning occurs because oFile is used only on lines that had compiler errors. You can ignore this error until the previously mentioned compiler errors are fixed. If the error recurs, address it then.

Recompiling the program produces no errors or warnings.

It is now time to step through the program. Resist the urge simply to "let it run and see what happens." Since all new programs contain errors, I know that errors still exists in this program and I want as much information as possible to use to find them later. I place the cursor on the while in main() and select "Go to cursor." Tracing from there immediately takes me into the function getFamily().

From here I step over the printf() and scanf() statements. Debugging a program that performs input from the keyboard can be confusing. Remember that control will not return to the function being debugged until input has been completed. At the first prompt I enter *y*, then press Enter.

Checking `answer` using the evaluate window reveals that `answer` is set correctly. The `if` statement here only checks for *N* or *n*. Any other input is assumed to be yes. This may not be acceptable. I may want to ignore and requery if an unexpected character is entered, but for now I will assume that this is okay and push forward.

Stepping further brings me to the `gets()` statement. Attempting to single step this function returns immediately with no string input. Although not obvious, `gets()` is seeing the Enter left there from the previous input. When inputting individual characters the Newline at the end of an input line counts as a character as well. This is especially troublesome since `scanf()` tends to leave the Newline in the input buffer after input. Modifying the line as follows reads both the answer and the Newline.

```
char answer, nl;
scanf("%c%c", &answer, &nl);
```

I can rebuild the program and restart by placing the cursor on the next line after the `scanf()` and pressing "Go to cursor." For family name I use `Davis` as per test case 1. Tracing from here takes me into the constructor for `Family`, which executes uneventfully. Returning to `main()`, the first function called is `getPerson()`. I trace into this function and as I do when entering any function for the first time, I inspect the argument. Surprisingly `family` appears to contain garbage. How could the object have been overwritten between the return from `getFamily()` and the call to `getPerson()`?

When an object suddenly appears to be overwritten, suspect either an assignment to a bad pointer or a scope problem. In this case there were no assignments of any kind. Turning to the latter possibility, you can see that the function `getFamily()` returns to the caller an object allocated off of its own stack. This object is overwritten when `getPerson()` reuses the same memory.

Since `getFamily()` must create an indeterminate number of objects, a static buffer solution is not correct either. `getFamily()` should allocate `Family` objects from the heap. The corrected function is as follows:

```
//getFamily - return a family object, or 0 if no more
//            to be entered
Family* getFamily() {
```

```
    printf("Another?");
    char answer, nl;
    scanf("%c%c", &answer, &nl);
    if (answer == 'N' || answer == 'n') {
        return (Family*)0;
    }

    printf("Enter family name:");
    char buffer[132];
    gets(buffer);
    return new Family(buffer);
}
```

Every time you fix a problem, especially one as fundamental as this, step back and ask yourself what else might have the same problem and what might also be affected. Written in a similar style, `getPerson()` has the same problem, which is fixed in the same way. Normally I would return the heap memory explicitly, but in this case I can allow the `exit()` code to take care of this on program termination. Nothing else is affected.

Recompiling and starting over, I reenter my family name to create the `Family` object, followed by my given name, age, and smoking habits to create the `Person` object. Single stepping through the constructors for both reveals no problems.

After entering test case 1, I stop and reexamine `*pFam` from the function `main()`. The Inspect command displays the object members by name and type. `pFirst` points to the first (and only) object in the list, `*pFam`. The `signature` and `pNext` appear correct (0x1234 and 0, respectively). `pMembers`, the pointer to the `Person` list, contains a possible but suspicious `DS:0xFFFA`. This address is suspicious because the location is near the top of the stack and `Person` was not allocated off of the stack. Examining `*pMembers` reveals that the address is not correct. The signature is wrong and none of the data appear to be present.

Either `pMember` contains invalid data or the object pointed at by `pMember` was overwritten. When `*pFam` is constructed, the member list should be empty, so this is as good a place to start as any. Glancing through the constructor, you can see that `pMember` is not initialized to anything. Forgetting to initialize all of the members in the constructor is a common problem. The corrected constructor appears as follows:

```
Family::Family(char *pName) {
    //fill in signature
    signature = 0x1234;

    //fill in the data
    strcpy(name, pName);

    //add to beginning of name list
    pNext = pFirst;
    pFirst = this;

    //start with an empty member list
    pMember = (Person*)0;
}
```

Confident that I found the problem, I rerun test case. Inspecting *pFam from within main(), I am disappointed to find that *pFam is still not correct. Remember, when a problem has been found and fixed, always rerun the test case that detected the problem and reinspect the suspicious data — further bugs may be lurking behind the one that was just corrected.

Examining *pFam from within main(), I now find that pMembers no longer contains garbage. It now persistently remains null.

Since *pFam looks correct as returned from getFamily() and since the data within *pFam is not being overwritten (the signature field and other data appear correct), the problem must be within getPerson() after *pFam is constructed. To examine the object at each step, I set a watch on *pFam. Remember that a watch redisplays *pFam at each breakpoint. As written, the scope of pFam is local to main(), so that as control moves into other functions, the watch window indicates that pFam is unknown. Temporarily moving pFam outside of main() gives it global scope so that the watch remains valid through subordinate functions, such as getPerson() and the functions that it calls.

```
Family *pFam;    //***global scope for debug***
void main() {
    //...continues on the same
```

Sometimes reentrancy considerations do not allow the variables to be moved to global scope, even temporarily. However, in this case it causes no problems. I make a note in the comment to move it back inside `main()` when debugging is complete.

My preference when setting a watch on a pointer is to set a watch on both `pFam` and `*pFam`. The former gives the address of the object pointed at and the latter its contents.

I now repeat the same steps as before. I am most interested in the constructor for `Person`, since this is where the `Person` object is added to the member list. Single stepping the following instructions in the constructor is rather perplexing.

```
pF = &f;
pNext = pF->pMembers;
pF->pMembers = this;
```

This appears to change the `pMembers` member of our `Family` object, but `*pFam` does not change. Perhaps the program is storing into the wrong object. In fact, this is the case. Looking at the address of `f` and of `pFam`, I see that the object `f` is not the same `Family` object as `*pFam`. However, the signature field and other valid data reveals that `f` is a valid `Family` object, just not the same one as `*pFam`. Thus, it appears that `f` must be a copy of `*pFam`.

Whenever you suspect that an unintentional copy of an object is being created, add a c-i constructor to the class, put a print statement in the constructor, and watch for the message. Automatically created objects are also automatically deleted, so I include an appropriate destructor as well.

```
Family::Family(char *pName) {
    create(pName);
}
Family::Family(Family &f) {
    f.checkSignature();
    printf("Constructing a copy of family %s\n", f.name);
    create(f.name);
}
void Family::create(char *pName) {
    //fill in signature
    signature = 0x1234;
```

```
        //fill in the data
        strcpy(name, pName);

        //add to beginning of name list
        pNext = pFirst;
        pFirst = this;

        //start with an empty member list
        pMembers = (Person*)0;
    }

Family::~Family() {
    printf("Destructing family %s\n", name);

    //remove it from the family list
    Family *pF = pFirst;
    if (pF == this) {
        pFirst = pNext;
    } else {
        while (pF->pNext != this) {
            pF->checkSignature();
            pF = pF->pNext;
        }
        pF->pNext = pNext;
    }
    pNext = (Family*)0;
}
```

Moving the constructor code into a private method, create(), allows multiple constructors to share the same code. The c-i constructor contains the printf() statement. Single stepping the program I now find that the message originates from the call to getPerson(). The creation of the copy is verified by examining the chain of Family objects. The Turbo C++ display appears in Figure 9–1.

```
|----------------------------------LAB.CPP----------------------------------|
|       return (Family*)0;                                                  |
|                                                                           |
|                                                                           |
|   }                                                                       |
|                                                                           |
|   printf("Enter family name:");    |--------Inspecting Family::pFirst ---2----|
|   char buffer[132];                |8F38:0A4A » ds:FFDC                      |
|   gets(buffer);                    |pFirst                          ds:FFDC  |
|   return new Family(buffer);       |signature              4660 (0x1234)     |
|}                                   |pNext                           ds:1336  |
|                                    |pMembers                          NULL   |
|//getPerson - return a person objec |name "Davis\x0>YTû\b\x1\x0\x0\x0\x0\x0\x1 |
|▲Person* getPerson(Family family) { |------------------------------------------|
|   printf(Enter first name:");      |class Person *                            |
|   char first[132];                 |-----[■] ----Inspecting---pNext---3--[↑]--|
|   gets(first);                     |#8F38:FFDE » ds:1336                   ▲ |
|                                    |#pFirst                     ds:FFDC ■ |
|   if (first[0] == '\0') {          |#signature             4660 (0x1234)# |
|      return (Person*)0;            |#pNext                        NULL # |
|   }                                |#pMembers                     NULL # |
|                                    |#name "Davis\x0\x0\x0\x0\x0\x0\x0\     ♥ |
|   printf("Enter last name if differen#▲################################▲ –# |
|   char last[132];                  |#class Family *                      # |
|-----248:1----------------------------#------------------------------------------|
F1 Help  Alt-I Set index range  F10 Menu
```

Figure 9–1. Display of debugger with multiple Family objects

This display shows the program halted at the beginning of `getPerson()`. Two `Family` objects have already been added to the list, both with the same name. Since the constructor for `Family` adds objects to the beginning of the list, the first member is the copy. Notice its address — `0xFFDC`. Addresses so near `0xFFFF` are typical of stack objects. The second object at address `0x1336` has been allocated off of the heap.

Examination of the function prototype reveals that `getPerson()` function accepts a `Family` object by value. Whenever an object is passed by value, the c-i constructor is used to create a copy and it is the copy upon which the function operates. Changing the function to accept its argument by reference allows the function to operate on the original and not a copy. The corrected function appears as follows:

```
Person* getPerson(Family& family) {
    //...continue as before
```

Scanning the entire program, I find that the same problem occurs in the constructors for `Person()` and `Smoker()`.

After fixing the problem, I again single step through the same case of a single family with a single member, noticing that this time the c-i constructor is not invoked.

Entering the constructor for `Person()` everything appears to be in order with a `pLName` of 0, indicating the person's last name is the same as the family name. Single stepping through the constructor, all is well until the statement:

```
strcpy(lastName, pLName);
```

If `pLName` is NULL, this statement copies the string at location 0. This is a case of confusing `(char*)0` with `""`, both of which are sometimes referred to as the null string. The problem is avoided by replacing the preceding with the following:

```
//(replace 0 pointer with null string)
char* pLast = pLName ? pLName : "";
strcpy(lastName, pLast);
```

Upon exiting from the `while(pFam = getFamily())` loop, I reexamine `*pFam` and its members. This time everything appears to be in order. Continuing into the output loop, I single step into `Family::healthRisk()`. This function, in turn, invokes `Person::healthRisk()`, which correctly calculates a 1 for a non-smoker less than 40. Completing the loop, `Family::healthRisk()` computes a number that is much too small. After verifying that the averaging equations appear correct, suspicion turns toward improper initialization of either the numerator (`avgHR`) or the denominator (`count`). In fact, `count` has not been initialized. The function is updated to initialize `count` to 0 before entering the loop.

However, this brings up another problem. What if there were no members of the family? The variable `count` would remain zero in the denominator. To avoid this, I add a check for `count == 0`.

```
float Family::healthRisk() {
    checkSignature();

    float avgHR = 0.0;
    int count;
    float curHR;
```

```
        Person *pPerson = pMembers;
        count = 0;
        while (pPerson) {
            pPerson->checkSignature();
            curHR = pPerson->healthRisk();
            avgHR += curHR;
            count++;
            pPerson = pPerson->next();
        }
        if (count)
            avgHR /= count;
        return avgHR;
}
```

The corrected program now works with the first data set generating the following output:

```
D>lab
Another?y
Enter family name:Davis
Enter first name:Randy
Enter last name if different from family:
Enter age:36
# of packs smoked per day (0 for non-smoker)0
Enter first name:
Another?n
Family Davis - 1
  Davis, Randy - 1

D:\
```

The output from test case 1 looks correct, so I move on to test case 2. I can step over functions through which I have already single stepped as part of test 1. However, I am careful to single step any previously unvisited paths.

The constructor for Smoker seems to execute properly. Into the display loop, all appears okay until the program begins displaying the message "Signature mismatch on person" in an endless loop.

Why the signature mismatch? Either a pointer is incorrect, the object was destroyed, or the signature was set up incorrectly in the constructor. Examining the `Person` object more carefully reveals the last case.

Here, `Smoker` uses a different signature from `Person`, since it is a different class. The `checkSignature()` method must be updated to handle the different valid signatures. One approach is to make the `checkSignature()` method virtual. This would defeat the purpose since invoking a virtual method with an invalid object is fatal. Another approach is to assign signatures to the different subclasses so that they differ in only one or two bits and modify `checkSignature()` so that it does not check these bits except when it is important to distinguish between related classes. Choosing the latter approach, I update `checkSignature()`.

Before fixing `checkSignature()` function, however, I must analyze how the infinite loop came to be. I know that the `checkSignature()` error message is involved, so I set my first breakpoint there. With the test 2 input data reentered, the program immediately hits the breakpoint. Single stepping from there the problem quickly becomes obvious.

In the event of an error, `checkSignature()` outputs the offending `Person` object. However, the display function itself calls `checkSignature()` on the object. The programmer must be careful that none of the functions invoked from within the error handler check for errors that might result in invoking the error handler. When this cannot be avoided, special semaphores can be added to avoid the infinite loop. For example, an error handler might be written as follows:

```
void errorHandler() {
    static int semaphore = 0;   //0 -> okay to enter

    if (semaphore == 0) {      //if not already active...
        semaphore = 1;          //...allow through

        //...call whatever functions you like

        semaphore = 0;          //ok; we're leaving
    } else
        printf("Error handler loop\n");
}
```

The static flag `semaphore` is used to indicate that `errorHandler()` is active. When called the first time, the semaphore is checked. If 0, it is set to 1 and processing continues. If any of the functions within the error handler detect an error and try to report it by calling `errorHandler()`, the semaphore will not be 0 and the function will print a simple message and quit, thereby avoiding the infinite loop.

In the example, the loop can be avoided by not attempting to output the `Person` object when the signature is bad. The corrected `checkSignature()` appears as follows:

```
//checkSignature - check the signature.  Ignore the
                   last 2 bits
//                 since they differ between subclasses
void Person::checkSignature() {
    if ((signature & 0xfffc) != 0x4320) {
        cout << "Signature mismatch on a Person "
             << endl;
        abort();
    }
}
```

Rerunning the test case, all appears to work properly except that the calculated health factor appears as 1.0, which does not match the test plan prediction. Since 1.0 is a reasonable value, I might have missed the error had the test plan not included the predicted output values.

The objects appear to be correct. Tracing through the call to `pPer->healthRisk()`, however, does not call `Smoker::healthRisk()`, but `Person::healthRisk()`. This indicates that the call is being bound early. Apparently `healthRisk()` is not declared `virtual`. Examination of the class definition for `Person` substantiates this. (Even though the method is declared virtual within class `Smoker`, it is not virtual in class `Person`. Therefore, calls to `healthRisk()` from objects of class `Person` are bound early.) Declaring `healthRisk()` virtual in `Person` solves the problem.

The remaining test cases run smoothly until case 5. The extremely long family name causes the program to bomb. Examining the constructor for `Family`, one can easily see why. The name array is limited to twenty characters in length, but no such limitation is made on the `strcpy()` call. Replacing `strcpy()` with `strncpy()`, which does allow a limitation, does not completely solve the problem. The constructor must make sure that the name array is properly terminated even if the input string is longer than twenty characters. The corrected copy is as follows:

```
//fill in the data
strncpy(name, pName, 20);
name[19] = '\0';              //make sure it's terminated
```

Scanning the program reveals that the same problem exists in the constructors for `Person` and is solved the same way.

A related problem exists with the calls to `gets()` in `getFamily()` and `getPerson()`.

```
printf("Enter family name:");
char buffer[132];
gets(buffer);
```

Here the calling program cannot be sure that the buffer is large enough to hold the input string. If the user enters an absurdly large name, the buffer will overflow. The best one can do with `gets()` is to allocate a large buffer and hope for the best. The iostream extractor solves this problem by allowing the programmer to set the input width to ensure that the buffer length is not exceeded. The width can be set either via the method `width()` or the manipulator `setw()` (use of manipulators requires inclusion of `iomanip.h`).

The default for stream input is to skip leading white space. Since this is not the default for `gets()`, the `ios::skipws` flag must be cleared before `operator>>(char*)` can be used as a replacement for `gets()` in this program. In addition, stream input does not read out the final Newline character — this becomes critical if skip white space is reset. Explicitly extracting the Newline takes care of the problem.

Together they appear as follows:

```
//set inserter to not skip leading whitespace so it acts
//more like gets()
cin >> resetiosflags(ios::skipws);

//now set input width so that it does not overflow the
//input buffer  (explicitly extract the \n at the end)
```

```
char buffer[132], nl;
cin >> setw(132) >> buffer >> nl;
```

The width setting must be reset after every input (or output) operation, whereas the skip white space setting remains until explicitly reset.

Other illegal data also causes the generation of nonsensical health factors. This is acceptable since the test case specifies that the output is unimportant as long as the program does not bomb.

The remaining test cases reveal no additional problems.

Once debugging is complete, it is a good idea to return and rescan the program armed with a much better understanding of how the parts operate. The knowledge gleaned from the test cases may allow you to spot an error that was not tested for or a test that should be added. The test cases with wildly invalid age and smoking data draw my attention to the `health-Risk()` methods. I notice that if a `Person` smoked sixteen packs a day, the denominator would become zero. It therefore seems prudent to limit the number of packs to a reasonable value short of sixteen packs. I set the upper limit at ten. Since the `age` appears only in the numerator, it does not need to be limited.

Now that debugging is almost complete, some of the debugging tools must be removed, as follows:

- I remove the print statements from the `Family` c-i constructor and destructor
- I move the declaration of `pFam` back inside `main()`, and
- I allow output to go to the file `OUTPUT` instead of `cout`. The signature checks could be removed as well at this point. Finally, I rerun the tests to make sure that all components still work as intended.

The revised and debugged program is as follows:

```
//LAB - the following program inputs the names of family
//      members, their age, and their smoking status and
//      then sorts them within the family by health risk
//      and outputs them to a file.

#include <stdio.h>
```

```
#include <stdlib.h>
#include <ctype.h>
#include <string.h>
#include <iostream.h>
#include <fstream.h>
#include <iomanip.h>

class Family;
class Person;

//Family - families consist of groups of people contained
//          in a linked list
class Family {
    friend class Person;
  private:
    //class members
    static Family *pFirst;

    //instance members
    unsigned signature;
    Family *pNext;
    Person *pMembers;
    char    name[20];
    void    checkSignature();
    void    create(char* pName);

  public:
            Family(char *pName);
            Family(Family&);
           ~Family();

    static Family *first()   {return pFirst;}
            Family *next()    {return pNext;}
            Person *members() {return pMembers;}
            char*   perName() {return name;}
            float   healthRisk();
            void    display(ostream& os);
};
ostream& operator<<(ostream& os, Family& f) {
```

```
        f.display(os);
        return os;
}
Family* Family::pFirst;//allocate space for static
                         member

//class Person - describe the people who are members of
//               the family; this class may be inherited
//               by specialized classes
class Person {
  protected:
    unsigned signature;
    Family  *pFamily;          //base family
    Person  *pNext;            //next member of family

    char     lastName[20];
    char     firstName[20];
    int      age;

  public:
    Person(char *pName, int a, Family& f, char *pLN = 0);
    Person* next() {return pNext;}
    void checkSignature();
    void display(ostream& os);
    virtual float healthRisk();
};
ostream& operator<<(ostream& os, Person& p) {
    p.display(os);
    return os;
}

class Smoker : public Person {
  private:
    int  noPacksPerDay;

  public:
    Smoker(char *pName, int a, int packsPerDay,
                Family& f, char *pLName = 0);
    virtual float healthRisk();
};
```

```
//----------------define Family methods---------------
Family::Family(char *pName) {
    create(pName);
}
Family::Family(Family &f) {
    f.checkSignature();
    create(f.name);
}
void Family::create(char *pName) {
    //fill in signature
    signature = 0x1234;
    //fill in the data
    strncpy(name, pName, 20);
    name[19] = '\0';              //make sure its terminated

    //add to beginning of name list
    pNext = pFirst;
    pFirst = this;

    //start with an empty member list
    pMembers = (Person*)0;
}

Family::~Family() {
    //remove it from the family list
    Family *pF = pFirst;
    if (pF == this) {
        pFirst = pNext;
    } else {
        while (pF->pNext != this) {
            pF->checkSignature();
            pF = pF->pNext;
        }
        pF->pNext = pNext;
    }
    pNext = (Family*)0;
}
//checkSignature - check the signature
```

```
    void Family::checkSignature() {
        if (signature != 0x1234) {
            cout << "Signature mismatch on family "
                 << *this << endl;
            abort();
        }
    }


//healthRisk - calculate the avg health risk of members
float Family::healthRisk() {
    checkSignature();

    float avgHR = 0.0;
    int count;
    float curHR;

    Person *pPerson = pMembers;
    count = 0;
    while (pPerson) {
        pPerson->checkSignature();
        curHR = pPerson->healthRisk();
        avgHR += curHR;
        count++;
        pPerson = pPerson->next();
    }
    if (count)
        avgHR /= count;
    return avgHR;
}

//display - display a family to the specified stream
void Family::display(ostream& os) {
    checkSignature();
    os << "Family " << name;
}

//--------------now the methods of Person------------
Person::Person(char *pN, int a, Family& f, char *pLN){
    //check Family argument
    f.checkSignature();
```

```
    //fill in signature
    signature = 0x4321;

    //add the person to the family
    pFamily = &f;
    pNext = pFamily->pMembers;
    pFamily->pMembers = this;
    age = a;

    //now fill in data members
    strncpy(firstName, pN, 20);
    firstName[19] = '\0';
    //(replace 0 pointer with null string)
    char* pLast = pLN ? pLN : "";
    strncpy(lastName, pLast, 20);
    lastName[19] = '\0';
}


//checkSignature - check the signature.  Ignore the
//                 last 2 bits since they differ
//                 between subclasses
void Person::checkSignature() {
    if ((signature & 0xfffc) != 0x4320) {
        cout << "Signature mismatch on person " << endl;
        abort();
    }
}


//healthRisk - calculate the overall health risk to the
//             individual. This expression is
//             purely fictional.
float Person::healthRisk() {
  checkSignature();

  float risk = 1.0;          //assume normal risk
  if (age > 40.0) {          //above forty...
      risk += (age - 40.0) / 10.0; //...upward trend
  }
```

```
        return risk;
    }

    void Person::display(ostream& os) {
        checkSignature();

        char lN[20];
        strcpy(lN, lastName);
        if (lN[0] == '\0') {
            strcpy(lN, pFamily->perName());
        }
        os << lN << ", " << firstName;
    }

    //-----------define the methods of Smoker------------
    Smoker::Smoker(char *pN, int a, int packsPerDay,
        Family& f, char *pLN) : Person(pN, a, f, pLN) {
        signature = 0x4322;
        noPacksPerDay = packsPerDay;
    }

    //healthRisk - risks for smokers are higher than for
    //             non-smokers.  These risk calcu-
    //             lations are purely fictitious.
    float Smoker::healthRisk() {
        checkSignature();

        float risk = 1.0;        //start with normal risk
        if (age > 30.0) {        //trend starts earlier
                                 //and rises faster
            if (noPacksPerDay > 10) //don't let denom...
                noPacksPerDay = 10; //...to go negative
            risk += (age - 30.0) / (8 - .5 * noPacksPerDay);
        }
        return risk;
    }

    //-----------now define the general functions---------
    //getFamily - return a family object, 0 if no more
    Family* getFamily() {
```

```
        //input yes or no to continue
        cout << "Another?";
        char answer, nl;
        cin >> answer >> nl;
        if (answer == 'N' || answer == 'n') {
            return (Family*)0;
        }

        //input family name (do not overflow buffer)
        cout << "Enter family name:";
        char buffer[132];
        cin >> setw(132) >> buffer >> nl;
        return new Family(buffer);
    }

//getPerson - return a person object
Person* getPerson(Family& family) {
    //get first name if it's null return
    cout << "Enter first name:";
    char first[132];
    char nl;
    cin >> setw(132) >> first >> nl;
    if (first[0] == '\0') {
        return (Person*)0;
    }

    cout << "Enter last name if different from family:";
    char last[132];
    char *pLast = last;
    cin >> setw(132) >> last >> nl;
    if (!isalpha(*pLast)) {
        pLast = (char*)0;
    }

    int age;
    cout << "Enter age:";
    cin >> age >> nl;

    int noOfPacks;
    cout <<
```

```
                    "# of packs smoked per day (0 for non-smoker)";
        cin >> noOfPacks >> nl;

        Person *pPerson;
        if (noOfPacks > 0) {
            pPerson = new Smoker(first, age, noOfPacks,
                                    family, pLast);
        }
        else {
            pPerson = new Person(first, age, family, pLast);
        }
        return pPerson;
    }

void main() {
    cin >> resetiosflags(ios::skipws);

    //load up the family data
    Family *pFam;
    while ((pFam = getFamily()) != 0) {
        while (getPerson(*pFam));
    }
    //now output it to the file OUTPUT
    ofstream oFile("OUTPUT");
    pFam = Family::first();
    Person *pPer;
    while (pFam) {
        oFile << *pFam << " - "
                << pFam->healthRisk() << endl;
        pPer = pFam->members();
        while (pPer) {
            oFile << "   "   << *pPer
                    << " - " << pPer->healthRisk()
                    << endl;
            pPer = pPer->next();
        }
        pFam = pFam->next();
    }
}
```

Unusual Cases in Debugging

Now that you have seen how to approach the debugging of a moderately sized C++ module full of common errors, let's focus on a few unusual types of programs and some of the unique bugs that accompany them.

The types of programs presented here are not common. They tend to be DOS specific. However, when confronted with these categories of assignments, you will need any help you can get.

Interrupt Service Routines

An interrupt to a computer is similar to an interrupt to a human: it acts like a tap on the shoulder to stop what you are doing and perform some other, hopefully short, function before returning to the original task. In computers, interrupts are handled at the CPU level. An external piece of hardware, such as a printer or modem, asserts a voltage on a line going into the computer. This is converted by external support circuitry — including the **Programmable Interrupt Controller (PIC)** — into a signal to the CPU and an 8-bit interrupt number.

The CPU responds by completing the current instruction, then saving the instruction pointer (`IP`), `CS` register, and flag register onto the stack and jumping to the **Interrupt Service Routine (ISR)**. The ISR addresses are retained in the first `0x400` bytes of physical memory, one far address per interrupt. This area is called the **Interrupt Vector Table**. Thus, interrupt 0 is serviced by the routine contained in location `0x0000:0x0000`, interrupt 1 in location `0x0000:0x0004`, interrupt 2 in location `0x0000:0x0008`, and so on.

An ISR services whatever hardware is associated with the hardware interrupt. For example, the modem may be informing the computer that another byte of data is ready to be read. The ISR for this interrupt would read the byte out of the input buffer and store it into some FIFO queue to be read by the application.

Debugging an ISR is similar to debugging a normal function, except for a few special problems. Depending on the hardware, interrupts may occur many times a second. Most debuggers disable interrupts while the program is on a breakpoint. If the program encounters a breakpoint in the ISR, further interrupts will not be serviced and will remain pending until the programmer attempts to continue execution. This is likely to disrupt the further processing of the interrupt.

If the debugger does not disable interrupts while paused at a breakpoint, the situation is even worse. The processing of the first interrupt is halted by the debugger, but subsequent interrupts process right through into undebugged code.

DOS and Windows programmers must also deal with DOS's non-reentrancy. Since most debuggers perform DOS calls, encountering a breakpoint in an ISR is likely to crash DOS. This problem is not unique to debuggers either: you absolutely cannot debug ISRs with `printf()` statements.

Lately the situation has improved. Many modern debuggers, such as the Turbo Debugger and Codeview, have found ways around these and other problems associated with ISRs. Even so, ISRs can be debugged quite adequately even with older debuggers using the following guidelines.

First, keep the ISR as small as possible. For space and timing reasons, this is a good idea anyway. Input messages should not be processed within the interrupt. The ISR should read them in and queue them up for processing by a non-interrupt function.

Second, execute and debug the program as a non-ISR before attempting to run it as an ISR. This can be done easily by calling the function from within a specially constructed loop. Consider the following:

```
void myISR();               //declared as a regular fn()

void main() {
    for (;;) {
        myISR();            //"invoke the interrupt"

        //...if necessary, read any data from
        //   input queue...
}
```

In this mode, the ISR can be debugged normally since it is not operating as an interrupt function.

Once the function has been debugged and appears to be working in this mode, install the ISR in an unused interrupt that can be invoked from within main() as in the following:

```
void interrupt myISR();

void main() {
    //install into otherwise used interrupt
    installISR(0x67, myISR);

    //now invoke the interrupt
    for (;;) {
        geninterrupt(0x67);

        //...same as before
    }
}
```

This example installs `myISR()` as an ISR and then invokes the ISR via the software interrupt instruction. The DOS-specific `geninterrupt()` performs this function. (The same effect can be achieved by including `asm {INT 0x67}` if your compiler accepts inline assembly language or `__emit__(0xCD, 0x67)` if your compiler accepts inline machine code.)

This debugging step is similar to the previous step. Even though installed as an ISR, `myISR()` is not being invoked from a hardware interrupt and so is not subject to any of the debugging restrictions mentioned earlier.

With the debugger, make sure that all of the registers are stored properly upon entry into the ISR and restored properly upon exit. If any of the registers differ after return from the interrupt call, the function will not work as an ISR — even if it functions properly in this mode.

Only after the ISR works correctly during these three steps should you attempt to install it into the actual hardware interrupt. If you can control the rate of interrupts, during initial debugging try to generate a single interrupt and trace the results. If problems arise, try to step back to one of the previous debugging steps to analyze, fix, and retest the function.

Member Functions as ISRs   Classes are often built as abstractions of physical objects. This makes it attractive to wrap a class around an external hardware device. Access to the external hardware is then controlled by the class. Future changes to the hardware can be accommodated either by modifying the class or inheriting the old class into a new sub-class with modified methods. Including the ISR for that hardware within the class definition is not particularly difficult.

Consider the following IOPort class designed to be the program interface to the I/O hardware.

```
//DataBlock - used to transmit blocks of data to and
//              from the IOPort class
struct DataBlock {
    int length;
    unsigned char *pData;  //variable length data array
};


//Input/Output Port
class IOPort {
  private:
    //interrupt service routine
    static void interrupt isr();

  public:
    //constructors and destructor
    IOPort(unsigned hardwareAddr, unsigned intNo);
    ~IOPort();

    //process interrupt (called from isr())
    virtual void processInterrupt();

    //access methods
    virtual int send(DataBlock* pData);
    virtual DataBlock* receive();
    virtual int status();
    virtual int setRate();
};
```

In this class, several methods are provided to send data, receive data, and retrieve port status. The actual ISR, isr(), is a static method of the class. This method must be static because the interrupt is invoked without an object. When the interrupt occurs, isr() must determine which object is responsible for the interrupt. Once the object is identified, isr()

invokes the virtual method `processInterrupt()` against the object to process the interrupt.

Making the method `processInterrupt()` virtual allows the processing of the interrupt to be modified in subsequent subclasses as in the following:

```
class SerialPort : public IOPort {
  public:
    SerialPort(unsigned addr, unsigned intNo);
    ~SerialPort();

    //process interrupt (called from isr())
    virtual void processInterrupt();

    //access methods
    virtual int send(DataBlock* pData);
    virtual DataBlock* receive();
    virtual int status();
    virtual int setRate();
};
IOPort     port1(0xFF80, 0x67);
SerialPort port2(0xFF88, 0x61);
```

The program attaches a generic `IOPort` object to interrupt `0x67` and a `SerialPort` object to interrupt `0x61`. This technique provides an expressive description of the class relationships involved and accommodates new hardware types through the addition of new subclasses.

When using the class solution, it is convenient to allow the constructor to install the ISR and the destructor to remove it by replacing the previous value stored in the interrupt vector. This is shown in the following:

```
//PIR is a pointer to an interrupt routine
typedef void interrupt (far* PIR)();

//Input/Output Port
class IOPort {
  private:
    //interrupt service routine
```

```
        static void interrupt isr();

        //previous interrupt vector contents
        PIR pPrev;
        unsigned intNum;

        //hardware address
        unsigned portAddr;

    public:
        //constructors and destructor
        IOPort(unsigned hardwareAddr, unsigned intNo) {
            portAddr = hardwareAddr;
            intNum = intNo;

            //install isr but save previous value
            pPrev = (PIR)IOPort::isr;
            pPrev = installISR(intNo, pPrev);
        }

        ~IOPort() {
            //restore the previous value
            installISR(intNum, pPrev);
        }
};
```

The member pPrev is used to store the previous contents of the interrupt vector until needed by the destructor.

Removing the ISR is critical if the interrupt can occur after the program
has terminated. Otherwise the interrupt vector will point into memory that
is no longer allocated and is subject to being overwritten. Once the space
is overwritten, the next occurrence of the interrupt will be fatal.

Consider the following example:

```
IOPort com1(0x3F8, 0x0C);        //COM1:
```

The object com1 has been assigned to interrupt 0x0C, which is the
interrupt address through which COM1: is processed. COM1: is one of the
normal serial ports on the PC. Since COM1: interrupts are certain to occur

even after the program terminates, the ISR must be deactivated at program exit.

Unfortunately, destructors for global objects may not be invoked if the program terminates abnormally. Thus, if this technique is to be used, the programmer must make sure that any signals are handled in an orderly fashion.

Programs that Crash on Start-Up

As noted earlier, global objects are constructed before `main()` is called at program start-up. If any of the constructors invoked from these global objects contains a fatal error, the program appears to die even before it starts.

When using Borland's Turbo Debugger, which executes the program automatically up to `main()` as soon as the program is loaded, the program dies before the programmer has a chance to set the first breakpoint. To debug such programs, the programmer can start the debugger with the `TD -1` command line option. Ostensibly, this tells the debugger to begin in "assembly language mode." This has the added effect of beginning execution with the first assembly statement in the program and not proceeding automatically to `main()`.

The same problem arises if a `#pragma startup` function contains a fatal error. This problem does not arise with Microsoft's CodeView or other debuggers that do not go to `main()` until told to do so.

Normally constructors for classes should be completely tested on locally declared variables before being invoked from global objects. However, a subtle problem can arise when global objects refer to each other. Consider the following example:

```
class IOPort {
  private:
    //interrupt service routine
    static interrupt isr();

  public:
    IOPort(unsigned portAddress, unsigned interruptNo);
    unsigned setBaud(unsigned newRate);//rets old rate
    ~IOPort();
```

```
};

class Terminal {
  private:
    IOPort *pIO;

  public:
    Terminal(IOPort *pPort, unsigned rate) {
        pIO = pPort;
        pIO->setBaud(rate);
    }
};

IOPort port1(0xFF80, 0x67);
Terminal t1(&port1, 9600);

int main() {
    //...remainder of program
}
```

The programmer is attempting to create a `Terminal` object that is attached to the `IOPort` at I/O address `0x0800`. The objects `port1` and `t1` have been declared globally, perhaps because several functions access them.

Notice that the constructor for `Terminal` accesses the port, setting the baud rate. Thus, the object pointed at by `pPort` must exist before the `Terminal` object can be created. Since `port1` is declared before `t1`, the programmer might assume that the previous condition is fulfilled. However, the language definition of C++ does not explicitly say so.

The definition does say that all null valued globals are initialized first. However, it goes on to say, "no further order is imposed on the initialization of objects from different translation units." (See *The Annotated C++ Reference Manual* by Margaret Ellis and Bjarne Stroustrup, 1990.) If `port1` is defined in one module and `t1` in another, the programmer has no idea which object is constructed first and no way to reliably control the order of construction.

One approach is to avoid accessing member functions of one class from the constructor of other classes. Thus, if `Terminal` saved the `IOPort` address without accessing it until later, no problem would arise.

A safer and less restrictive approach is to manually construct all such objects. The preceding example becomes the following:

```
IOPort* pPort1;
Terminal* pT1;

int main() {
    //construct global objects
    pPort1 = new IOPort(0xFF80, 0x67);
    pT1 = new Terminal(pPort1, 9600);

    //...remainder of program
}
```

Pointers to the objects are declared globally where they can be accessed by other functions. The objects themselves are allocated under program control, however. By explicitly creating each object, the programmer can influence the order of construction, in this case insuring that the IOPort object has been constructed before it is accessed from the Terminal constructor.

As an aside, it is interesting to note that a signature field check would have detected this problem. That is a checkSignature() call within setBaud() would have noted that the base object had not been constructed.

Programs that Crash at Termination

Perhaps the most frustrating fatal error is one that occurs as the program is attempting to exit. A program might fail to terminate properly for several reasons. In a manner analogous to the start-up problems mentioned earlier, a destructor invoked from a global object may contain a fatal bug. In addition, the programmer cannot count on the order in which global objects are destructed (except that it is exactly the reverse of the order in which they were constructed).

Forgetting to restore an interrupt vector upon exit will cause an unprotected operating system like DOS to crash after the program terminates. This is often indistiguishable from a program that crashes during termination.

Finally, some compilers include extra checks in the program termination code to look for writes to offset 0 in the default data segment. If this code determines that this area has been overwritten, the somewhat cryptic message "Null pointer assignment" appears. As noted in Chapter 6, writing to location 0 is a common error and is never correct. Therefore, this is a helpful indication that something went wrong during the execution of the program.

This problem should be attacked like any other wild write: start by placing a watch on `DS:0` and executing the program until the location changes. If this is not practical, set a "Break on write" type breakpoint at location `DS:0`, and execute the program until the breakpoint occurs.

Conclusion

No debugging occurs without thinking. Allow yourself time to think about a problem. If the solution doesn't come to you within an hour or so, go on to something else even if that means going home and forgetting about it for the day. When tomorrow arrives, things will appear much clearer.

Try to understand every aspect of the problem. First, the program itself, what it does, how it does it. Look both at the logic flow and the programming details. Think about the problem at different levels of abstraction.

Understand C++. It's a big language and this is a tall order, but it is the language you have chosen to work with so you better make the best of it. Study the traps and pitfalls presented in Chapters 5 and 6. Every one of these problems has occurred in real-world programs (most of them have occurred in my programs at one time or another). Understand your environment, including the compiler and debugger.

Like any other endeavor, debugging takes practice. The pointers in this chapter should help you increase your proficiency more quickly.

Part 3

Error Message Desk Reference

Error Message Desk Reference

This section includes a list of the most common C++ compilation errors. Due to space constraints not all error messages are included. Omitted are those errors for which the compiler-generated message should provide sufficient help or errors that are so trivial the programmer should be able to see the problem immediately.

Each error includes an example of the problem, the error messages generated by both the Borland and Microsoft C++ compilers, and an explanation. Where possible, the explanation includes a sample program that has been corrected to avoid the error.

Also provided is a list of related errors that are sufficiently close to the listed error as to be covered by the explanation given. A separate error message index is provided to help the reader correlate compiler-generated error messages with the explanations provided. The Borland index is in alphabetical order according to the first word of the message itself. If the first word of the error message is variable, then the error is in order by its second word. The Microsoft index is in numerical order of the error number.

The error messages were generated by the Borland C++ Version 3.0 and Microsoft C/C++ Version 7.0 compilers. In both cases, all warnings were enabled including strict ANSI compatibility mode.

The include file `compat.h` is included by many examples to avoid incompatibilities between the Borland and Microsoft compilers. Other compilers can be handled in the same way, as they are likely to resemble one of these two standards. The include file is as follows:

```
#ifndef __BORLANDC__
#define near __near
#define far  __far
#define cdecl __cdecl
#define pascal __pascal
#define interrupt __interrupt
#elseif
#define __near near
#define __far far
#define __cded cded
#define __pascal pascal
#define __interrupt interrupt
#endif
```

Error Message Index

Borland Error Message

< expected, 678

Access can only be changed to public or protected, 677

Address of overloaded function *f* doesn't match type, 593

Ambiguity between *f1* and *f2*, 586, 659

Ambiguous operators need parenthesis, 563

Array allocated using new may not have an initializer, 572

Array must have at least one element, 570

Array of references is not allowed, 571

Array size for 'delete' ignored, 563

Array size too large, 573

Assignment to this not allowed, 628

Attempt to grant or reduce access to *id,* 667

Attempting to return a reference to a local object, 591

Attempting to return a reference to a local variable, 591

Bad syntax for pure function definition, 635

Base class *c1* is inaccessible because also in *c2,* 663

Base class *c* is included more than once, 667

Base class *c* is initialized more than once, 654

Base initialization without a class name is obsolete, 655

Call to function *f* with no prototype, 584

Cannot allocate a reference, 564

f1 cannot be distinguished from *f2*, 586

Cannot call near class member function with a pointer, 608

Cannot cast from *t1* to *t2*, 601

Cannot convert type *t1* to *t2,* 592, 593, 595, 603, 604, 607, 669, 670, 673, 674, 675, 681

Cannot create instance of an abstract class, 636

Cannot define a pointer or reference to a reference, 565

Cannot find class *c::c(c&)* to copy a vector, 612

Cannot find class *c::operator=(c&)* to copy a vector, 612

Cannot find default constructor to initialize array . . . , 611

Cannot find default constructor to initialize base class c, 611

Cannot find default constructor to intialize member id, 611

Cannot have a near class member in a far class, 668

Microsoft Error Numbers

Error Number	Page Number	Error Number	Page Number
C2022	561	C2143	559
C2027	565	C2152	593
C2036	597	C2166	650
C2039	671	C2171	671
C2040	592, 605	C2172	585
C2041	562	C2173	585
C2049	560	C2174	585
C2050	576	C2180	554
C2059	564	C2184	587
C2061	567, 581	C2186	554
C2062	557, 581, 609	C2187	603
C2065	567, 584, 652	C2197	585
C2073	611	C2198	585
C2079	565	C2202	587
C2083	574	C2203	563
C2086	613	C2205	568
C2087	570	C2229	570
C2088	574	C2234	571
C2089	573	C2238	609
C2100	594, 595	C2239	602
C2106	628	C2241	664
C2107	595	C2244	689
C2108	595	C2246	654
C2109	595	C2247	665
C2110	597	C2248	618, 621, 664, 665
C2111	597	C2249	665
C2112	597	C2250	660
C2113	597	C2252	625, 635
C2125	573	C2253	635
C2131	581	C2255	664

Error Number	Page Number	Error Number	Page Number
C2637	670	C2817	641
C2638	670	C2818	646
C2639	676	C2819	647
C2640	676	C2821	639
C2641	676	C2824	640
C2643	674	C2829	637
C2650	642	C2831	638
C2652	617	C2833	643
C2653	653	C2835	645
C2658	659	C4017	605
C2659	616	C4054	604
C2660	584, 585, 631	C4055	604
C2661	585	C4121	570
C2662	608, 649, 651	C4130	598
C2664	585, 589, 615, 617, 631	C4138	556
C2668	586	C4149	668
C2671	630	C4301	605
C2672	641	C4302	603
C2733	583	C4303	603
C2734	579	C4304	603
C2767	574	C4305	605
C2800	643	C4306	605
C2801	644	C4385	659
C2802	637, 639	C4510	620, 624
C2803	637, 644	C4512	623, 624
C2804	637	C4610	620
C2805	637	C4620	648
C2806	637	C4706	554
C2807	648	C4709	555
C2808	637	C4758	607
C2809	637	C4759	603
C2810	641	L2025	568
C2815	641	L2029	581
C2816	641	R6001	590

Assignment within conditional expression

Borland: • Possibly incorrect assignment

Microsoft: • C4706: assignment within conditional expression

Example:
```
void fn(int a) {
    int local = 10;
    if (local = a) {
        //...continue on
    }
}
```

Explanation: Since assignment is itself an operator with a return value, that value can be used within a conditional expression so the foregoing `if` statement is correct. However, there is a good possibility that the programmer really meant `if (local == a)` so the compiler generates a warning. To avoid the warning, split the expression into two statements.

```
local = a;
if (local) {
```

Non-expression provided where expression expected

Borland: • Expression syntax
related: • Expression expected
                  • Not an allowed type

Microsoft: • C2062: type 'int' expected
related: • C2180: controlling expression has type void
                  • C2186: id: illegal operand of type void

Example:
```
int oFn();
void fn() {
```

```
if (int i = oFn()) {
    //...other code
}
}
```

Explanation: A non-void complex expression can be provided wherever a simple expression (such as a constant) is expected; however, not all statements are expressions. In particular, control structures (such as if, do, while, case, and break) and declarations are not expressions. Statements other than non-void expressions cannot be used in control statements, as arguments to functions, as initial values to declared objects or with most operators.

The distinguishing characteristic of a non-void expression is that it has a value.

```
void fn() {
    int i;
    if (i = oFn()) {
        //...other code
    }
}
```

A void function does not have a value — therefore, a void function cannot be used in such situations.

Misusing the comma operator

Borland: • no error message

Microsoft: • C4709: comma operator within array index expression

Example:
```
void fn() {
    int m[10][10];
    m[1,2];              //what does this do?
}
```

Explanation: Although the comma operator allows some fiendishly clever code to be generated by those who are so inclined, its presence allows many programmer errors to go undetected. For example, the expression `m[1,2]` is legal, but almost certainly not what the programmer intended. It evaluates the first expression within subscript 1 and then throws that result away. It then evaluates the second expression within the subscript 2 and uses it as an index into the matrix `m`. The result is of type `int*`. Almost certainly what was meant was `m[1][2]`, which is of type `int`.

---

*/ found outside of a comment

Borland   • Expression syntax

Microsoft   • C4138: '*/' found outside of comment

Example:
```
void fn(int a) {
/* comment out this section
    if (a == 0)                 /*if a is invalid...*/
        return;                 /*...return now*/
*/
    return 1 / a;
}
```

Explanation: Although some compilers support nested comments, the standard is for comments not to nest. Without nested comments, the `*/` of the inner comment terminates the outer comment as well. (With nested comments, the comment is not terminated until the same number of `*/`'s as `/*`'s have been encountered.)

The proper way to handle a block of code that may include comments is by using the preprocessor.

```
#include "compat.h"
void fn(int a) {
#if 0
    comment out this section
```

```
        if (a == 0)              /*if a is invalid...*/
            return;              /*...return now*/
#endif
    return 1 / a;
}
```

`else` clause with no `if` statement

Borland: • Misplaced else

Microsoft: • C2143: syntax error: missing ';' before 'else'

Example:
```
#include <stdio.h>
int fn(int a) {
    if (a > 0)
        printf("a is greater than 0");
        return 1;
    else
        printf("a is not greater than 0");
        return 0;
}
```

Explanation: An `if` statement is followed by a clause, either several lines surrounded by { }, or a single C++ line. Immediately following this may appear an `else` clause to be executed if the first clause is not. In the preceding example, the second line (the `return 1`) precludes the appearance of the `else` clause. The corrected function is as follows:

```
#include <stdio.h>
int fn(int a) {
    if (a > 0) {
        printf("a is greater than 0");
        return 1;
    } else {
        printf("a is not greater than 0");
        return 0;
```

```
        }
    }
```

This condition can arise in a number of subtle ways. For example, a macro that erroneously contains a ; may also generate the error as follows:

```
#define max(x,y) (((x) > (y)) ? (x) : (y));
int fn(int a, int b) {
    if (a > 0)
        return max(a, b);
    else
        return 0;
}
```

When the macro `max()` is expanded inline, the results appear as follows:

```
return x > y ? x : y;;
```

The first ; is provided by the macro itself. The second ; appears to the compiler as a separate, null statement. The second statement precludes the appearance of an `else` clause.

Suspected macro problems can be confirmed by examining the output from the preprocessor. Some compilers use a special compile time switch — others provide a separate utility for this purpose.

In general, the C++ programmer should convert a macro into an inline function that uses C++ function syntax and is much less error prone.

Performing comparison within case clauses

Borland: • Duplicate case

Microsoft: • C2049: case value '0' already used

Example:
```
int fn() {
    const int c = 10;
```

```
switch (c) {
  case c < 10:
      return -1;
  case c == 10:
      return  0;
  case c > 10:
      return  1;
  };
};
```

Explanation: What is probably intended is something like the following:

```
if (c < 10) {
    return -1;
}
if (c == 10) {
    return 0;
}
return 1;
```

However, this is not the way the switch statement works. Instead, the cases list constants or expressions that can be evaluated at compile time. In this case, case c < 10 evaluates to case 0 since c is a constant 10. case c == 10 evaluates to case 1. case c > 10 evaluates to case 0, which is already used.

Hexadecimal with more than 3 digits

Borland: • Hexadecimal value contains more than 3 digits

Microsoft: • no message generated
related: • *n*: too big for character

Example:
```
void fn() {
      char *pC = "There are:\x0095 pages per section";
};
```

Explanation: The ANSI standard for C specifies a maximum of three hexadecimal digits per character constant. Thus the special character in the preceding string is `'\x009'` or Tab followed by the character '5'. However, the trailing 5 appears to be part of a constant `'\x95'`. Since this was legal in Standard C, the Borland compiler generates a warning.

Numbers can be lost in the same way. For example, in the following fragment the 5 is inadvertently combined with the `\x9` to form a very large character constant.

```
char *pC = "There are:\x95 pages per section";
```

Character constants on the PC cannot exceed `0xFF`.

Remember that special characters are defined for the common functions, such as tab. The preceding is clearer when written as follows:

```
void fn() {
    char *pC = "There are:\t5 pages per section";
};
```

Improper octal constant

Borland: • Illegal octal digit

Microsoft: • C2041: Illegal digit '8' for base '8'

Example:
```
int powersOfTwo[] = {001, 002, 004, 008,
                     016, 032, 064, 128};
```

Explanation: C was originally written for a machine (the PDP/8) whose tools preferred octal notation — therefore, C++ supports octal constants to this day. Since hexadecimal is much more common today, many programmers forget that any constant beginning with a zero is assumed to be octal. When dealing with bit constants, hexadecimal is safer.

```
int powersOfTwo[] = {0x01, 0x02, 0x04, 0x08,
                     0x10, 0x20, 0x40, 0x80};
```

Ambiguous operators need parentheses

Borland: • Ambiguous operators need parentheses

Microsoft: • no error generated

Example:
```
int bitsInCommon(int a, int b) {
    if (a & b == 0)
        return 0;                //no bits in common
    return 1;                    //at least one in common
}
```

Explanation: The precedence of operators is not always what the programmer expects. For example, this function does not have the desired effect. Since == has higher precedence than &, the preceding code first checks to see if b is equal to zero. The resulting 0 or 1 is then ANDed with a. If the result is nonzero, the function returns a 0, otherwise it returns a 1.

Since precedence problems are a common source of errors, many compilers generate warnings when operations with expected precedence are used in the absence of parentheses. The warning (and the danger of unintended results) can be avoided by including parentheses.

```
int fn(int a, int b) {
    if ((a & b) == 0)
        return 0;                //no bits in common
    return 1;
}
```

Array size for delete is obsolete

Borland: • Array size for 'delete' is ignored

Microsoft: • C2203: delete operator cannot specify bounds for an array

Example:
```
class MyClass {};
void fn() {
    MyClass *pMC = new MyClass[100];
    //...other stuff
    delete [100] pMC;
}
```

Explanation: Earlier versions of C++ required the programmer to specify how many objects to delete when removing an array of objects. Later versions of the C++ specification waived this requirement. The Borland compiler generates a warning and ignores the array size; the Microsoft product generates an error.

Remember, the destructor is invoked for each `MyClass` object separately.

Allocating reference incorrectly using `new`

Borland: • Cannot allocate a reference

Microsoft: • C2059: syntax error: ';'
related: • C2464: cannot use new to allocate a reference

Example:
```
void fn() {
    int &rI = *new int&;
}
```

Explanation: The reference portion of a declaration is not part of the type of an object. Thus, the type of `rI` is not `int&` but `int`. The preceding should be declared as follows:

```
void fn() {
    int &rI = *new int;
}
```

Defining a reference or pointer to a reference

Borland:
- Cannot define a reference or pointer to a reference

Microsoft:
- C2528: illegal pointer to a reference
- C2529: illegal reference to a reference

Example:
```
void fn() {
        int i;
        int &rI = i;

        int& *prI = &rI;
        int& &rrI = rI;
}
```

Explanation: Since reference is not part of the type, the preceding syntax is incorrect. Every use of a reference variable after its declaration is identical to the use of the object to which it refers. The foregoing should be written as follows:

```
void fn() {
        int i;
        int &rI = i;
        int *prI = &rI;
        int &rrI = rI;
}
```

Using a structure prior to declaring it

Borland:
- Undefined structure 'A'
- Type name expected

Microsoft:
- C2079: 'a' uses undefined class/struct/union 'A'
- C2501: 'c': missing decl-specifiers

related:
- C2027: use of undefined type *id*

Example:
```
struct B {  //both of the following are in error
    struct A a[10]; //with 'struct' keyword
    C c[10];        //without 'struct' keyword
};
struct A {
    int data;
};
struct C {
    int data;
};
```

Explanation: Here both A and B are defined, eventually; however, at the time that B is defined, A is not known. C++ will not look ahead to determine the type of some future defined class. Changing the order of the declarations is sufficient to remove the error.

```
struct A {
    int data;
};
struct C {
    int data;
};
struct B {
    struct A a[10];
    C c[10];
};
```

When including the keyword `struct`, which is not required for C++, the error message generated is somewhat more informative because the compiler knows that the object must be some type of structure. In fact, in applications that do not need to know the size of the structure or any of its members, no error is generated. Thus, the following is legal.

```
struct B {
    struct A *pA;
};
struct A {
```

```
    int data;
};
```

A more acceptable approach, however, is the following:

```
struct A;//declare it to be a structure
    struct B {
    A *pA;//legal to reference it but not its size
    A  a[10];//this is illegal since it needs size info
};
struct A {//now expand on the declaration
    int data;
};
```

Declaring an object in an `if` clause

Borland:
related:

- Declaration not allowed here
  - Goto bypasses initialization of a local variable

Microsoft:
related:

- C2065: 'mc': undeclared identifier
  - C2360: initialization of *id* is skipped by case label
  - C2361: initialization of *id* is skipped by default label
  - C2362: initialization of *id* is skipped by *goto label*

Example:
```
class MyClass {
    public:
        MyClass(int);
};
void otherFn(MyClass*);
void fn(int i) {
    if (i)
        MyClass mc(i);
    otherFn(&mc);
}
```

Explanation: Declaring an object in a logic path that may not be executed is not allowed. Although the space for an auto object is allocated as soon as the function that contains its declaration is entered, the object is not constructed until the declaration is encountered. If control passes around the declaration, the constructor will not be executed. The problem does not arise in the following:

```
if (i) {
    MyClass mc(i);
    //...other code
}
```

The object `mc` is constructed upon encountering the declaration and is destructed at the closed brace. The object is not known outside of the block following the `if` statement. The Microsoft compiler treats the earlier example as if a block had been defined.

extern **object cannot be initialized**

Borland: • _data defined in module ERR.CPP is duplicated in ERR2.CPP

Microsoft: • L2025: class MyClass __near data: defined more than once
related: • C2205: id: cannot initialize extern variables with block scope

Example:
```
ERR.H
class MyClass {
  private:
    int d;
  public:
    MyClass();
    MyClass(int);
};
ERR.CPP -
#include "err.h"
extern MyClass data = 10;
ERR2.CPP -
#include "err.h"
MyClass data;
```

Explanation: The keyword `extern` in ERR.CPP declares an object but does not allocate space for it. The compiler assumes that the space is allocated in a separate module, in this case ERR2.CPP. However, the compiler cannot initialize the object without allocating space. Thus, with the initialization present, the compiler ignores the `extern` keyword. During the link step, two `data` objects are found.

The solution to this problem is to provide initialization data only on the non-`extern` declarations.

Initialization only partially bracketed

Borland: • Initialization is only partially bracketed

Microsoft: • no message generated

Example:
```
struct MyClass {
      int i;
      char *pC;
      float f;
      int   array[5];
} mc[] = {1, "1", 1.0, 0, 1, 2, 3, 4,
          2, "2", 2.0, 5, 6, 7, 8, 9};
```

Explanation: Although not illegal, the preceding initialization is prone to error. Misalignment of any data element will force all subsequent elements to misalign as well. Including internal curly braces guards against misalignment and renders a more readable program.

```
struct MyClass {
    int i;
    char *pC;
    float f;
    int   array[5];
} mc[] = {{1, "1", 1.0, {0, 1, 2, 3, 4}},
          {2, "2", 2.0, {5, 6, 7, 8, 9}}};
```

Placement of members sensitive to alignment

Borland: • no warning generated

Microsoft: • C4121: 'MyClass': alignment of a member was sensitive to packing

Example:
```
struct MyClass {
    int i;
    char c;
    float f;
} mc[] = {{1, '1', 1.0},
          {2, '2', 2.0}};
```

Explanation: The placement of the f member of MyClass is dependent upon compiler switches. If word-alignment is chosen, then c will be allocated an entire word, even though it needs only a single byte. Even though both modules use the same definition of MyClass, if one source module is compiled with word-alignment and another with byte-alignment, linking the two modules together will generate errors that are difficult to track down. Forcing all members to use a full word or placing char members at the end of the structure is a safer approach.

```
struct MyClass {
    int i;
    float f;
    char c;
} mc[] = {{1, 1.0, '1'},
          {2, 2.0, '2'}};
```

An array must have at least one element

Borland: • Array must have at least one element

Microsoft: • C2466: cannot allocate an array of constant size 0
related: • C2087: *id*: missing subscript

- C2229: type *id* has an illegal zero-sized array
- C2503: *c*: base classes cannot contain zero-sized arrays

Example: `int array[0];`

Explanation: An array with zero elements cannot normally be declared, but in some cases that does happen. For example, when the size information is not necessary or the space is allocated somewhere else. This can occur in one of several ways:

```
extern int array[]; //space allocated in another module
void fn(int array[]) {//pointer to array passed to fn()
}
```

In addition, some compilers allow arrays declared as the last item in a structure to be of an unspecified size.

```
class MyClass {
    int i;
    float f;
    char c[]              //unspecified array size
}
```

The assumption is that objects of this type will be allocated off the heap only when the length of `c` is known. The unspecified array must be the last member of the object; therefore, any class that contains a zero length array cannot be a base class for another class. Declaring zero length arrays in classes is a dangerous practice that should be avoided.

Cannot declare an array of references

Borland:
- Array of references is not allowed

Microsoft:
- C2234: arrays of references are illegal

Example:
```
int i, j, k;
int& arrayOfRef[] = {i, j, k};
```

Explanation: The programmer is attempting to bind three separate `ints` to an array of references. This is not allowed, because the members of an array are assumed to appear sequentially in memory, but no such restrictions can be made on `i`, `j`, and `k`. The desired effect can be achieved by resorting to pointers as follows:

```
int i, j, k;
int* pArrayOfInts[] = {&i, &j, &k};
```

Now the programmer may index the three members as `*pArrayOfInts[index]`. Notice, however, that this introduces one extra level of indirection.

Array allocated with new may not have an initializer

Borland: • Array allocated using 'new' may not have an initializer

Microsoft: • C2538: new: cannot specify initializer for arrays

Example:
```
class MyClass {
  public:
    MyClass();
    MyClass(int);
};
void fn(int x, int y) {
    MyClass *pMC = new MyClass[3](x, y);
}
```

Explanation: Specifying a different constructor than the default constructor is not allowed when allocating an array of objects using `operator new`. The best alternative is to construct the objects with the default constructor and then initialize them by using a subsequent call to a standard method, as in the following:

```
void fn(int x, int y) {
    MyClass *pMC = new MyClass[3]; //alloc w/ default
    for (int i = 0; i < 3; i++)
```

```
            pMC[i].init(x, y);              //now init with arg.s
    }
```

Non-huge arrays larger than 64K are not allowed

Borland: • Array size is too large

Microsoft: • C2125: 'largeArray': allocation exceeds 64K

Example: `int largeArray[0xC000];`

Explanation: Pointer arithmetic normally involves only the offset portion of an address on the 80x86 CPU. This implies that an entire array must fit within a single 64K segment.

Arrays larger than 64K may be allocated off the far heap using Borland's `farmalloc()` as shown in the following. For Microsoft C++, use the similar `halloc()` library function.

```
#include <alloc.h>
int huge * pLargeArray;
void fn() {
    pLargeArray =
            (int huge*)farmalloc(0xC000L * sizeof(int));
}
```

The address returned by the `farmalloc()` or `halloc()` call is stored into a huge pointer, since address computations on huge pointers include both segment and offset portions, allowing access to more than 64K. Huge pointers are considerably slower to manipulate than other pointer types, however.

Classes larger than 64K are not allowed

Borland: • Structure size too large

Microsoft: • C2089: 'MyClass': 'struct' too large

Example:
```
struct    MyClass {
     int    iData[20000];
     float fData[10000];
};
```

Explanation: A single object must be wholly contained within a single segment; otherwise, accessing the members of the class would involve segment arithmetic. This implies that the memory used by all of the data members cannot exceed 64K.

There is no huge class that would waive the size restriction as there is with the far heap. However, individual members may be replaced with pointers to huge memory. In this example, no single array is larger than 64K, but the total of all arrays together surpasses the 64K limit. Removing the arrays from the structure as follows solves the problem.

```
class MyClass {
  public:
    int    *pIData;
    float *pFData;

    MyClass() {
        pFData = new float[10000];
        pIData = new int[20000];
    };
};
```

The arrays are now allocated individually off the heap. The `MyClass` structure consists of only the two pointers.

Scalar operations on user-defined types

Borland: • Illegal structure operation

Microsoft: • C2767: binary '==': 'class ::MyClass' does not define this operator or a conversion to a type acceptable to the built-in operator.

related:
- C2083: binary '==': struct/union comparison illegal
- C2088: binary '==': illegal for 'class ::MyClass'

Example:
```
class MyClass {
    private:
        int d;

    public:
        MyClass();
};
void fn() {
    MyClass a, b;

    if (a == b) {
        return;
    }
}
```

Explanation: The C++ intrinsic operations, other than assignment, are not normally defined for user-defined types. Such operations are defined if a coercion path exists between the class and a scalar type. Changing the class definition as follows removes the error.

```
class MyClass {
    int d;

  public:
    MyClass();
    operator int() {
        return d;
    }
};
```

Now the compiler coerces `MyClass` objects a and b into `int`s before performing the comparison using `operator=(int,int)`.

Of course, the operation is also legal if defined for the class as follows:

```
class MyClass {
    int d;

  public:
    MyClass();
    int operator==(MyClass& o) {
        return d == o.d;
    }
};
```

Now no coercion is necessary. A user-defined operation will be used even if coercion operators exist.

Non-scalar object used where scalar required

Borland: • Switch selection expression must be of integral type

Microsoft: • C2450: switch expression of type 'ComplexInt' is illegal
related: • C2050: nonintegral switch expression

Example:
```
class ComplexInt {
  public:
    int real, imag;
    ComplexInt();
};
int fn() {
    ComplexInt ci;

    switch (ci) {
      case 0:
          return 0;
      default:
          return 1;
    }
}
```

Explanation: Statements that require integer expressions cannot normally accept objects from user-defined classes. Interestingly, however, if a coercion path to `int` or `long` is provided, it will be used in the preceding situation.

```
#include <math.h>
#include "compat.h"
class ComplexInt {
  public:
    int real, imag;
    ComplexInt();
    operator int() {
        return (int)(sqrt(real * real + imag * imag));
    };
};
```

When used in a `switch` statement, objects of class `ComplexInt` are cast into an `int` that is then compared to the selection cases.

Type compatibility of arguments to ternary operator

Borland: • Two operands must evaluate to the same type

Microsoft: • C2446: ':' : no conversion between 'struct ::A' and 'struct ::B'

Example:
```
class A {
  public:
    A();
};
class B {
  public:
    B();
};
class C {
  public:
    C();
    C(B&);
    C(A&);
```

```
    };
    void fn(int n) {
        A a;
        B b;
        C c;
        c = a;                       //these two lines okay
        c = b;
        c = n ? a : b;               //this line generates error
    }
```

Explanation: The ternary operator is not simply a replacement for an `if` statement. It is a true expression, and like other expressions it attempts to coerce its operands into the same type. Since class A and class B have no coercion path to a common type, it cannot be done. This is true even though either a or b can be assigned to c (coercion paths are provided by the `C(A&)` and `C(B&)` constructors).

One solution is to provide a coercion path between A and B. A simpler solution might be to replace the ternary operator with a simple `if` statement.

```
    if (n)
        c = a;
    else
        c = b;
```

Cannot modify a constant object

Borland: • Cannot modify a const object

Microsoft: • C2166: lvalue specifies const object

Example:
```
    void fn() {
        const int i = 10;
        i = 20;
    }
```

Explanation: const objects, including pointers, cannot be modified. Therefore, the following is illegal as well.

```
void fn() {
    int i;
    int * const pI = &i;
    pI++;            //this generates error
    (*pI)++;         //this is ok
}
```

The pointer pI is declared constant so that pI++ is in error. However, the int pointed at by pI is not constant, so (*pI)++ is allowed — the parentheses are required because ++ has higher precedence than *. To declare pI to be a normal pointer to a constant integer, use const int *pI.

Must initialize constant or reference variable at declaration

Borland:
- Constant variable 'i' must be initialized
- Constant variable 'pI1' must be initialized
- Reference variable 'rI' must be initialized

Microsoft:
- C2734: 'i': non-extern const object must be initialized
- C2734: 'pI1': non-extern const object must be initialized
- C2530: 'rI': references must be initialized

Example:
```
const int i;              //these are all in error
int * const pI1;
int& rI;

extern const int j;       //this is okay
const int *pI2;           //this is okay too
```

Explanation: Since a constant object cannot be modified after it has been declared, it must be assigned a value at declaration. External constants, on the other hand, are initialized in the module that allocates space for them.

In addition, declaring a normal pointer to a constant integer without initializing the pointer is permitted. The pointer can be modified in a later statement, but the integer to which it points cannot.

Similarly, a reference object such as `rI` must be initialized when declared. All subsequent uses of `rI` refer to the integer referenced by `rI` and not to `rI` itself.

Temporary required for referential declaration

Borland:
- Temporary used to initialize 'ri'

Microsoft:
- C2440: 'initializing': cannot convert from 'const int' to 'int&'
- C2607: 'initializing': cannot implicitly convert a 'int' to a non-const 'int&'

Example:
```
int intFn();
void fn() {
    int& ri1 = 0;
    int& ri2 = intFn();
}
```

Explanation:
A referential object normally indicates another object. Since a referential is an lvalue, the object to which it refers must also be an lvalue — that is, it must have an address in memory. If it does not, the Microsoft compiler generates an error message. The Borland compiler generates a temporary object, initializes it with the rvalue, and allows the reference to refer to the temporary object. The temporary object is destroyed when the function exits. Thus, the preceding is identical to the following:

```
int intFn();
void fn() {
    int temp1 = 0;
    int& ri1 = temp1;
    int temp2 = intFn();
    int& ri2 = temp2;
}
```

This version generates no warnings under either compiler.

Cannot declare objects with conflicting type modifiers

Borland: • Conflicting type modifiers
• Conflicting type modifiers

Microsoft: • C2131: more than one memory attribute
• C2062: type 'int' expected

Example:
```
near far int i;
cdecl interrupt func();

const volatile int j = 10;      //this is okay
```

Explanation: Declaring an object both `near` and `far` makes no sense, as these descriptions are mutually exclusive. Similarly, `cdecl`, `pascal`, and `interrupt` are mutually exclusive function descriptions. However, `const` and `volatile` are not mutually exclusive — an object so declared is subject to change at any time but not by the program itself.

Neglecting `extern "C"` when linking C++ with C routines

Borland: • Undefined symbol cFunc(int) in module ERR.CPP

Microsoft: • L2029: 'void __near __cdecl cFunc(int)':unresolved external

Example:
```
File ERR.CPP:
#include "cincl.h"           //C include file

void main() {
  cFunc(10);
}
```

```
File CINCL.H:
void cFunc(int);

File CINCL.C:
#include "cincl.h"
void cFunc(int i) {
}
```

Explanation: C++ uses "name mangling" to encode the argument types into the name of the function to provide type-safe linking (see Chapter 1). C simply places an underscore before the names of its functions. To link C++ object files with C object files, the programmer must use the `extern` "C" construct to indicate function prototypes for C functions.

Include files intended to be used with either C or C++ programs, such as the include files that accompany the compiler package, already contain the extern "C" constructs where necessary. However, include files intended only for C compilers do not. This problem can be solved by encasing the include file in an `extern` "C" block as follows:

```
#include "compat.h"
extern "C" {
#include "cincl.h"
}
void main() {
  cFunc(10);
}
```

Remember, C functions cannot be overloaded.

Cannot extern with other than C or C++

Borland: • Unknown language, must be C or C++

Microsoft: • C2537: 'pascal': illegal linkage specification

Example:
```
extern "pascal" {
      int pascalFunc(int);
```

```
}
```

Explanation: Two different problems associated with function declarations were solved by two different groups in completely incompatible ways. One issue addressed by the `extern` "C" mechanism concerns whether names are to be mangled. Declaring a function within an `extern` "C" block allows C++ programs to call C functions. This mechanism was invented by the originators of C++ in the cfront translator.

The other issue is the difference in calling conventions between C/C++, Pascal, and FORTRAN. Declaring a function `pascal` assigns it Pascal calling convention. This mechanism was introduced by Microsoft for C for the PC. Thus, the preceding sample should be written as follows.

```
pascal int pascalFunc(int);
```

Only one overloaded function can be `extern` "C"

Borland: • Only one of a set of overloaded functions can be "C"

Microsoft: • C2733: second C linkage of overloaded function 'fn' not allowed

Example:
```
extern "C" {
    int fn(int);
    int fn(int, int);
}
```

Explanation: An `extern` "C" function cannot be overloaded by another `extern` "C" function. (This is because `extern` "C" functions are not mangled during compilation — see section in Chapter 1 on name mangling.)

However, "C" functions can be overloaded with C++ functions. Consider the following example in which the most generic C function `fn(char *pF, char *pM, char* pL, int age)` is overloaded by C++ functions.

```
extern "C" {
    void fn(char *pF, char *pM, char* pLast, int age);
}
void fn(char *pF, char *pL, int age = 0) {
    fn(pF, "<NMI>", pM, age)
}
void fn(char *pL, int age = 0) {
    fn("<NFN>", "<NMI>", pL, age);
}
```

Since the C++ function names are mangled, they cause no confusion with the single unmangled C function name.

Incomplete or missing function prototypes

Borland:
- Extra parameter in call to cFunc1()
- Function 'cFunc2' should have a prototype

related:
  - Call to function *function* with no prototype
  - No declaration for function *function*

Microsoft:
- C2660: 'cFunc1': function does not take 1 parameters
- C2065: 'cFunc2': undeclared identifier

Example:
```
void cFunc1();          //incomplete prototype
void main() {
  cFunc1(10);
  int i = cFunc2();     //cFunc2 not prototyped at all
}
```

Explanation: Pre-ANSI C compilers used "incomplete" prototypes. These function prototypes specified the return type of the functions but not the types of the arguments. Further, since the default for global functions is `int`, `int` functions often were not prototyped at all.

C++ insists on complete prototypes. The proper fix is to supply complete prototypes.

```
void cFunc1(int);
int  cFunc2(void);
```

This condition arises most commonly when incorporating an older C include file that accompanies a third-party C object file or library. Contact the vendor for the updated, fully prototyped include files, if possible; otherwise, edit the include file, specifying either the proper arguments, if known, or (. . .), if not known.

Calling a function with incorrect arguments

Borland:
- Too few parameters in call to 'oFn(int,int)'
- Extra parameter in call to 'oFn(int,int)'
- Type mismatch in parameter 1 in call to 'oFn(int,int)'

related:
- Extra parameter in call
- Too few parameters in call
- Type mismatch in parameter *n*
- Type mismatch in parameter *parameter*
- Type mismatch in parameter *parameter* in call to *function*

Microsoft:
- C2660: 'oFn': function does not take 1 parameters
- C2664: 'oFn': cannot convert parameter 2 from 'class ::MyClass' to 'int'

related:
- C2172: *f*: actual parameter is not a pointer
- C2173: *f*: actual parameter is not a pointer: parameter *n*, parameter list *n*
- C2174: *f*: actual parameter has type void: parameter *n*, parameter list *n*
- C2197: *id*: too many actual parameters
- C2198: *id*: too few actual parameters
- C2661: *f*: no overloaded function takes *n* arguments

Example:
```
class MyClass;
void oFn(int, int);

void fn() {
    oFn(10);
    oFn(10, 20, 30);
```

```
        oFn(10, mc);
}
```

Explanation: Obviously the function `oFn` is not invoked correctly. What is interesting about this error, however, is that it may generate completely different error messages such as "failure to prototype" during compilation, or "unresolved external" at link time. Since a function may be overloaded with several different versions, each with different arguments, it is not obvious that `oFn(10)` refers to the same `oFn` prototyped earlier. Perhaps the programmer is referring to some `oFn(int)` different from the `oFn(int,int)` appearing in the prototype.

Two functions are ambiguous

Borland: • Ambiguity between 'ambFn(int)' and 'ambFn(int,int)'
related: • `function1` cannot be distinguished from `function2`

Microsoft: • C2668: 'ambFn': ambiguous call to overloaded function

Example:
```
void ambFn(int a, int b = 0);
void ambFn(int a);

void fn() {
    ambFn(0);                    //which function?
}
```

Explanation: C++ considers the function arguments to be as much a part of the description as the name itself. (In fact, through name mangling the arguments become part of the name.) This allows the programmer to define multiple functions with the same name as long as the functions can be differentiated in use by the arguments.

Two overloaded functions must differ sufficiently in their arguments to be differentiated when called. For example, does `ambFn(0)` invoke `ambFn(int)` or `ambFn(int, int)` with the second argument defaulted to 0? Ambiguous functions arise under the following conditions:

• functions differ only in their return type (see below)

- two functions differ only in unspecified (elliptical) arguments
- two functions differ in defaulted arguments

Two functions are ambiguous (Part 2)

Borland: • Type mismatch in redeclaration of 'oFn(int)'

Microsoft: • C2556: 'oFn': overloaded functions only differ by return type

Example:
```
void oFn(int);
int  oFn(int);

void fn() {
    oFn(10);              //which oFn?
}
```

Explanation: C++ does not require a program to use the value returned by a function. In the preceding example the compiler cannot tell whether the programmer is attempting to call `void oFn()` knowing there is no returned value or is calling `int oFn()` and ignoring the returned value. Two overloaded functions cannot differ only in their return type.

Non-void functions must return a value

Borland: • Function should return a value

Microsoft: • C2202: 'inverse': not all control paths return a value
related: • C2184: illegal return of a void value
• C2561: id: function must return a value

Example:
```
float inverse(float x) {
    if (x != 0.0)
        return 1 / x;
}
```

Explanation: A function declared with return type other than `void` must return a value from every return statement including the implicit return at the `}`. The preceding can be rewritten as follows:

```
float inverse(float x) {
    if (x != 0.0)
        return 1 / x;
    return 0;
}
```

Most compilers can determine when all possible branches end in a value return. For example, the following alternative generates no error message.

```
float inverse(float x) {
    if (x != 0.0)
        return 1 / x;
    else
        return 0;
}
```

Compilers cannot be expected to compare logical operations in separate `if` statements, however. In the following example, the compiler does not notice that the two `if` statements are mutually exclusive and the same error is generated.

```
float inverse(float x) {
    if (x != 0.0)
        return 1 / x;
    if (x == 0.0)
        return 1;
}
```

Void functions cannot return a value

Borland: • fn(int) cannot return a value

Microsoft: • C2562: 'fn': 'void' function returning a value

Example:
```
float global;
void fn(int x) {
    if (x == 0) {
        return -1;
    }
    global = 1.0 / (float)x;
}
```

Explanation: A void function cannot return a value down any of its control paths.

Calling referential function with a constant

Borland:
- Temporary used to initialize 'rI'
- Temporary used for parameter 1 in call to 'oFn(int&)'

related:
- Reference initialized with *type1*, needs lvalue of *type2*

Microsoft:
- C2440: 'initializing': cannot convert from 'const int' to 'int&'
- C2607: 'initializing': cannot implicitly convert a 'int' to a non-const 'int&'
- C2664: 'oFn': cannot convert parameter 1 from 'const int' to 'int*'

Example:
```
int oFn1();
void oFn2(int&);
void fn() {
    int &rI = 10;
    int &rI2 = oFn1();
    oFn1(10);
}
```

Explanation: Constants, such as 10 in the example, have no address in memory. Thus, they cannot be assigned to a reference variable or passed by reference to a function. Attempts to do so under the Microsoft compiler generate an error. The Borland compiler circumvents the problem by creating a temporary object on the stack, initializing it with the constant, and assigning the reference to the temporary object. The message generated is a warning to alert the programmer in case it causes problems.

The problem can be avoided by giving the values addresses before making the call.

```
void fn() {
    int i;
    oFn2(i = 10);
}
```

The same problem arises with class objects and can be solved in the same way.

```
class MyClass {
  public:
    MyClass(int);
};
void oFn(MyClass&);
void fn() {
    oFn(MyClass(10));
}
```

Null pointer assignment

Borland: • Null pointer assignment

Microsoft: • R6001: null pointer assignment

Example:
```
int *pI;           //Small Model - same as 'int near* pI;'
void main() {
    *pI = 10 ;
};
```

Explanation: Since it is declared globally, the pointer `pI` is initialized with the value 0. The assignment `*pI = 10` stores a 10 at `DS:0000`, that is, offset 0 within the data segment. Since this is so common, both compilers reserve the first few bytes of the data segment. Upon program termination, the exit code checks to determine whether these locations have been overwritten. If they have, the `null pointer assignment` message is generated.

The same error is fatal when `pI` is a far pointer as would be the case if the example were compiled in Large Memory Model. In this case, `*pI = 10` would overwrite 0000:0000, the first two bytes of memory. This is part of the interrupt table.

Returning the address of a local object

Borland: • Attempting to return a reference to a local variable 'temp'
related: • Attempting to return a reference to a local object

Microsoft: • no error message

Example:
```
class Complex {
    public:
        int real, imag;
        Complex();
        Complex(Complex&);
};
Complex& operator+(Complex& a, Complex& b) {
    Complex temp;
    temp.real = a.real + b.real;
    temp.imag = a.imag + b.imag;
    return temp;
}
```

Explanation: A function cannot return a reference to an object declared `auto` in the function. The object is destructed and the space deallocated as part of the return process from the function, thus the reference is to invalid memory. To solve this problem, the programmer can return an object (as opposed to a reference to an object) as follows:

```
Complex operator+(Complex& a, Complex& b) {
    Complex temp;
    temp.real = a.real + b.real;
    temp.imag = a.imag + b.imag;
```

```
    return temp;
}
```

Now the local object `temp` is copied back into the caller's stack before it is destructed and deallocated.

Several proposals have been made for ways to avoid this seemingly unnecessary copying of temporary objects from one function's stack to another. One proposal is to flag local objects that are intended to be returned from referential functions. Another is to declare these objects as special parameters to the function, like arguments. As yet no standard method has been adopted, however.

Changing pointer type without a cast

Borland:
- Cannot convert 'char*' to 'int*'
- Cannot convert 'void*' to 'int*'

related:
- Nonportable pointer conversion
- Suspicious pointer conversion

Microsoft:
- C2446: '=': no conversion between 'int*' and 'char*'
- C2446: '=': no conversion between 'int*' and 'void*'

related:
- C2040: operator: different levels of indirection
- C2519: cannot convert type1* to type2*
- C2551: void* type needs explicit cast to nonvoid pointer type

Example:
```
int *pI;
char *pC;
void *pV;

void fn() {
    pI = pC;
    pI = pV;
    pV = pI;
}
```

Explanation: In Classic C, a pointer was considered assignment-compatible with any other pointer type. In C++ a pointer to one type is not assignment-compatible without a cast to another, except that any pointer type can be assigned to a void pointer (the `pV` = `pI` does not generate an error). Providing a cast solves the problem.

```
void fn() {
    pI = (int*)pC;
    pI = (int*)pV;
    pV = (void*)pI;      //not required but good practice
}
```

Assigning function address to incomplete pointer

Borland:
- Cannot convert 'void (*)(int,int)' to 'void (*)()'

related:
- Address of overloaded function *function* does not match type

Microsoft:
- C2446: '=': no conversion between 'void (*)(void)' and 'void (*)(int,int)'

related:
- C2152: id: pointers to functions with different attributes
- C2563: mismatch in formal parameter list
- C2564: formal/actual parameter mismatch in call through pointer to function

Example:
```
void oFn(int, int);

void fn() {
    void (*pF)();
    pF = oFn;
}
```

Explanation: This is the same case as the previous error. Function arguments are considered part of the function's description. They are also part of the description of a pointer to that function. The somewhat cryptic cast `void (*)(int,int)` is read "a pointer to a function taking an `int` and an `int` and returning nothing."

Defining the pointer completely is the preferred solution.

```
void fn() {
    void (*pFn)(int, int);
    pF = oFn;
```

```
}
```

Providing a cast also removes the error.

```
void fn() {
    void (*pF)();
    pF = (void (*)())oFn;
}
```

The pointer declaration must match its use. For example, the following is an error.

```
void fn(void (*pF)(int)) {
    (*pF)();
}
```

pF is declared as a pointer to a function that takes an int. The function must be called this way when using pF.

Changing function type with a cast is almost always an error. For example, all of the following casts are dangerous.

```
cdecl near void fn();
cdecl void (far*pF1)() = fn;
pascal near (*pF2)() = fn;
```

Near functions are invoked differently from far functions, and cdecl, pascal, and interrupt functions are all invoked differently. Thus, changing their types via a cast leads to a pointer that cannot be used without crashing the program.

Casting an extern "C" function to a conventional pointer is safe.

Non-lvalue pointers

Borland:
- Lvalue required
- Not an allowed type

Microsoft:
- C2100: illegal indirection

Example:
```
#include "compat.h"
void fn() {
    void (*pFn)() = fn;
    void *pV;
    *pFn = 0;              //ptr to fn is not an lvalue
    *pV = 0;               //can't store to void
}
```

Explanation: The result of applying the * operator to an address is usually, but not always, an lvalue. Neither a function pointer nor a void pointer resolves to an lvalue or points to a valid data object. (The Microsoft compiler did not generate an error for the first assignment — this appears to be a bug.)

Dereferencing non-pointer

Borland:
- Cannot convert 'int' to 'int*'
- Invalid indirection

Microsoft:
- C2446: '=': no conversion between 'int*' and 'const int'
- C2100: illegal indirection

related:
- C2107: illegal index; indirection not allowed
- C2108: nonintegral index
- C2109: subscript on nonarray

Example:
```
void fn() {
    int *pI;
    pI = 0;              //this is legal
    pI = 1;              //but this is not
    *0 = 0;              //neither is this
}
```

Explanation: To preserve compatibility with C, the token 0 can be understood to be `void*` and can be assigned to any other pointer type. No other integer constant can be used as a pointer without an explicit cast. In addition, 0 cannot be directly dereferenced since the type of object pointed at is not known. Providing a cast removes the error messages.

```
#include "compat.h"
void fn() {
    int *pI;
    pI = 0;
    pI = (int*)1;
    *((int*)0) = 0;                    //store a 0 into the int at
                                       //location 0
}
```

Be careful when casting constant integers into pointers, however, as the meaning of the cast may depend upon the memory model in force at the time of compilation. For example, (int*)0 points to the beginning of memory when compiled in Large Model but only to the beginning of the segment in Small Model. To avoid ambiguity, the programmer should specify near and far attributes explicitly.

```
*((int far*)0) = 0;        //store to beginning of memory
```

A long int can be used to generate pointers to known memory locations (such as video memory) as follows:

```
unsigned far* pVideo = (unsigned far*)0xB8000000L;
```

Pointers to functions can be generated from integer constants in the same way. Consider the following:

```
#include "compat.h"
void (far *pFn)(int) = (void (far *)(int))0x12345678L;
void interrupt (far * pGraphicsFn)() =
        *((void interrupt (far * far*)())0x00000040L);
void fn() {
    (*pFn)(10);      //call the function at 0x12345678
}
```

Here, pFn is defined as a pointer to a function that accepts an integer argument and returns nothing. Somehow the programmer knows this function starts at the address 0x12345678. The expression (*pFn)(10) invokes the function at that address.

The second declaration is considerably more involved. In the PC, the address of the graphics BIOS routines are stored in interrupt `0x10`, which is at address `0x00000040`. The cast changes the integer `0x40` into the address of the address of an interrupt function. The address contained in interrupt `0x10` is then stored in the local variable `pGraphicsFn`.

Indexing an array performs both pointer arithmetic and dereferencing.

```
int array[100];
array[i] = 0;             //equivalent to *(array + i) = 0;
```

Operations defined on pointers

Borland:
- Invalid pointer addition
- Size of the type is unknown or zero

related:
- Illegal use of member pointer
- Illegal pointer subtraction
- Illegal use of pointer
- Nonportable pointer comparison
- Size of *identifier* is unknown or zero
- *sizeof* may not be applied to a function

Microsoft:
- C2110: pointer + pointer
- C2036: 'void*': unknown size

related:
- C2111: pointer+nonintegral value
- C2112: illegal pointer subtraction
- C2113: pointer subtracted from nonpointer

Example:
```
void fn() {
    int i;
    int *pI1 = &i, *pI2 = &i;
    void *pV;

    pI1 = pI1 + 10;            //legal
    pI1 = pI1 + pI2;           //not legal
    pI1 = pI1 - 10;            //legal
    i   = pI1 - pI2;           //legal
```

```
        pV = pV + 10;                    //not legal
}
```

Explanation: Most scalar operations are not defined for pointer types. However, certain combinations of addition and subtraction are allowed.

An integer may be added to a pointer, but the result is defined in terms of the object pointed at. Therefore, the following is true.

```
T *pT;
pT + x <==> (T*)((char*)pT + x * sizeof(T))
```

$pT + x$ increases the numerical value of pT by $x * sizeof(T)$ bytes. In the preceding example $pI1 + 10$ moves the pointer over 10 $ints$, not just 10 bytes.

In addition, two pointers may be subtracted if they are of the same type, the result being the number of objects between them. The variants of addition and subtraction, such as += and ++ are also defined.

No arithmetic operations are defined for pointers for which $sizeof()$ is zero or undefined. This includes $void$ pointers, function pointers, and pointers to classes that have been declared but not defined.

Comparative operations are also defined on pointer types. Thus, it makes sense to ask if two pointers are equal or if one pointer is greater than another. (See 'Misinterpreting comparative operations on pointers' and 'Comparing two far pointers', however.)

Misinterpreting comparative operations on pointers

Borland: • no message generated

Microsoft: • C4130: '==': logical operation on string constant

Example:
```
int greetings(char *pC) {
    if (pC == "Hello") {       //what is this comparison?
        return 1;
    }
    return 0;
}
```

Explanation: The problem here is both obvious and subtle, depending upon your background. The `if` statement asks whether the value of the pointer object `pC` is numerically equivalent to the address of the string "`Hello`." (The answer is certain to be no, irrespective of what `pC` points to.)

If the intent was to determine whether the string pointed at by `pC` is "`Hello`", the corrected function is as follows:

```
#include "compat.h"
#include <string.h>
int greetings(char *pC) {
    if (strcmp(pC,"Hello") == 0) {
        return 1;
    }
    return 0;
}
```

If the global `operator==(char*, char*)` has been overloaded, then the `if` statement may, in fact, be correct, but the result is user-defined.

Ambiguous function pointers

Borland: • Overloaded 'oFn' ambiguous in this context

Microsoft: • C2244: 'oFn': unable to resolve function overload
related: • C2568: id1: unable to resolve function overload

Example:
```
void oFn(int);
void oFn(char);
void fn() {
    +oFn;
}
```

Explanation: Overloaded functions must be sufficiently different to be distinguishable when invoked. This generally means that they must differ in the type of at least one argument. Return type and storage class are not sufficient, but the type of any argument, including sign and nearness or farness of a pointer, is sufficient.

Even an unambiguous function becomes ambiguous in a context that does not include the function arguments. Without these arguments the compiler cannot differentiate between overloaded functions. C functions may not be overloaded.

Cannot cast from one overloaded function to another

Borland: • Overloaded 'oFn' ambiguous in this context

Microsoft: • no error; this is apparently incorrect. Should have generated:
C2547: 'oFn': illegal cast of overloaded function

Example:
```
void oFn(int);
void oFn(float);

void fn() {
    void (*pFn)(int);
    pFn = oFn;                         //this is okay
    pFn = (void (*)(int))oFn;          //this is not
}
```

Explanation: The first assignment is okay, because only one version of `oFn` is assignment-compatible with `pFn` without a cast. With the cast, however, either `oFn` function could be used; thus, the assignment is ambiguous.

Casting function pointers is not a good idea, because it defeats the typing mechanism that is so adept at catching coding errors. It is better to make the pointer type correct from the beginning and avoid the cast (as in the foregoing first assignment).

If the cast must be performed, clarify the assignment through the use of an intermediate as follows:

```
void fn() {
    void (*pF)();
    void (*pTemp)(int);
```

```
        pTemp = oFn;
        pF = (void (*)())pTemp;
    }
```

Since the pTemp declaration is identical to one of the overloaded functions, the initial assignment is not ambiguous. This unambiguous pointer subsequently can be recast in any way.

Cast is ambiguous

Borland: • Cannot cast from 'Derived*' to 'Base*'

Microsoft: • C2386: ambiguous conversion from 'Derived*' to 'Base*'

Example:
```
class Base {
    public:
        Base();
        aMethod();
} b;
class D1 : public Base {
};
class D2 : public Base {
};
class Derived : public D1, public D2 {
    public:
        Derived();
} d;

void oFn(Base* pObj);

void fn() {
    Derived *pD = &d;
    Base *pB;
    pB = (Base*)pD;              //both expressions incorrect
    oFn(pD);
}
```

Explanation: The compiler cannot recast a pointer from a derived class to a base class if the base class is inherited more than once since it does not know which base class is intended. This is true whether the cast is explicit as in the assignment or implicit as in the function call.

    This problem can be solved in one of two ways. First, why is the base class inherited twice? If it can be inherited virtually, then only one copy of the base class is generated and the cast is not ambiguous. Otherwise, the pointer must be recast to an intermediate base class from which the cast is no longer ambiguous.

```
void fn() {
    Derived *pD = &d;
    Base *pB;

    pB = (Base*)(D1*)pD;
    oFn((D2*)pD);
}
```

    This problem is closely related to the problem of name collisions discussed under **ambiguous inheritance**.

Confusing near/far with __near/__far

Borland: • Declaration syntax error

Microsoft: • C2239: unexpected token '*' following declaration of 'far'

Example:
```
int __far*  pFarMicrosoftStyle;
int __near* pNearMicrosoftStyle;

int far*  pFarBorlandStyle;
int near* pNearBorlandStyle;
```

Explanation: Microsoft began the practice of declaring 32-bit pointers `far` and 16-bit pointers `near`. Most other compilers, including the Borland C++ compiler, continue the practice today. Microsoft has since changed `near` to `__near` and `far` to `__far` to fall in line better with the ANSI C standard. When writing programs for one compiler, the programmer should use the style preferred by the compiler. When compatibility with multiple compilers is preferred, these discrepancies can be handled with a compatibility include file such as compat.h (described at the beginning of this section).

```
//both styles accepted by either compiler with the
//compat.h file included
#include "compat.h"
int __far*  pFarMicrosoftStyle;
int __near* pNearMicrosoftStyle;


int far*  pFarBorlandStyle;
int near* pNearBorlandStyle;
```

Casting far pointer to near pointer

Borland:
- w/o cast: Cannot convert 'int far*' to 'int *'
- w/ cast: no error generated

Microsoft:
- C4304: truncation during pointer conversion
- C4759: segment lost in conversion

related:
- C2187: cast of near function pointer to far function pointer
- C4302: truncation during conversion of pointer to function
- C4303: truncation during conversion of pointer to function to pointer to object
- C4304: truncation during pointer conversion

Example:
```
#include "compat.h"
void fn() {
    int a;
    int near* pNear;
    int far *  pFar;

    pFar = &a;              //this is okay
    pNear = (int near*)pFar;  //this is dangerous
}
```

Explanation: A far pointer contains a 32-bit address whereas a near pointer contains only a 16-bit offset into a default segment. Converting a near pointer into a far pointer is generally okay — the compiler provides the default segment as the segment portion of the far address. Convert a far pointer into a near pointer is generally not okay since the segment portion of the address will be lost. The only case in which this conversion is allowed is when the far address specifies the default segment.

Calling a function through a different-sized pointer is always incorrect even if the segments agree, since a far function is called differently than a near function. Thus, the following is incorrect even though it does not generate a warning message with either compiler.

```
#include "compat.h"
void near fn();
void (far*pFn)() = (void (far*)())fn;
```

Mixing near data pointer with near code pointer

Borland: • Cannot convert 'void (*)()' to 'int *'

Microsoft: • C2446: '=': no conversion between 'int*' and 'void (*)(void)'
related: • C2260: function pointer cast to a data pointer
                  • C2261: data pointer cast to function pointer
                  • C4054: function pointer cast to a data pointer
                  • C4055: data pointer cast to a function pointer

Example:
```
#include "compat.h"

void fn() {
    int near* pData;
    pData = fn;               // w/o cast
    pData = (int near*)fn;    // w/ cast no error message
}
```

Explanation: This conversion bears special mention since it is almost never correct. Both near pointers to code and near pointers to data are offsets into default segments but not the same segment: code pointers use the code segment and data pointers the data segment. In Tiny Memory model these are equal; however, in no other memory model are these the same.

If the intent is to access the bytes that make up a function like data, then the data pointer must be declared far.

```
#include "compat.h"

void fn() {
    int far* pData;
    pData = (int far*)fn;
}
```

Casting far pointers to integers

Borland: • no error generated

Microsoft: • C4301: truncation during conversion of pointer to integral type
related: • C2040: *operator*: different levels of indirection
• C4017: cast of int expression to far pointer
• C4305: truncation during conversion of integral type to pointer
• C4306: conversion of integral type to pointer of greater size

Example:
```
#include "compat.h"
int far *pI;
void fn() {
    int i = (int)pI;
}
```

Explanation: Older C programs assume that integers and pointers are essentially equivalent. Much of this older code continues today. Even when cast properly, as in the preceding example, an `int` is not large enough to hold a far pointer. The resulting value contains only the offset portion of the address.

Comparing two far pointers

Borland: • no message generated

Microsoft: • no message generated

Example:
```
#include "compat.h"
int compareFar(void far* pS1, void far* pS2) {
    return pS1 == pS2;
}
```

Explanation: This function compares two far pointers for equality. If they are equal, the function returns a 1, otherwise it returns a 0. The problem here is that two far pointers are equal if and only if they are arithmetically equal. However, two pointers can point to the same location and not be arithmetically equal.

```
void fn() {
    void far* pF1 = (void far*)0x00400010;
    void far* pF2 = (void far*)0x00000410;
    compareFar(pF1, pF2);
}
```

The first pointer specifies a segment value of $0x40$ and an offset of $0x10$ for a physical address of $0x410$. The second address specifies a segment address of $0x0$ and an offset of $0x410$, which also corresponds to physical address $0x410$. Thus, the two pointers point to the same location. Since they are not numerically identical, however, compareFar() returns a 0.

This problem can be neatly solved by declaring the arguments huge. Huge pointers are first normalized.

```
#include "compat.h"
int compareFar(void huge* pS1, void huge* pS2) {
    return pS1 == pS2;
}
```

The addresses `0x00400010` and `0x00000410` are now equal since they both normalize to `0x00410000`. In applications not involving a function, the pointers can be assigned to two huge pointers before comparison.

```
//...other code
void huge* pTemp1 = pS1;
void huge* pTemp2 = pS2;
if (pTemp1 == pTemp2) {
        //...program continues
```

Using near pointers when DS!=SS

Borland: • Cannot convert 'char _ss *' to 'char*'

Microsoft: • C4758: address of automatic (local) variable taken, DS!=SS

Example:
```
#include <string.h>
void fn() {
    char buffer[80];
    strcpy(buffer, "my name");
}
```

Explanation: Near pointers are offsets into a default segment; however, auto variables are allocated from the stack segment, and global variables are allocated from the data segment. This makes near pointers to global objects incompatible with near pointers to auto objects. To avoid this problem, all PC compilers make the default stack segment and default data segment the same for small model programs.

As part of their entry code, interrupt functions reload the expected data segment value so that they have access to global objects. These functions must use the stack segment they are provided, however. Thus, for these functions `DS != SS`. To allow for this, most C++ compilers for the PC provide a switch. When the switch is set, evaluating any expression that results in the address of an auto object generates a warning.

To correct this problem, either avoid taking the address of objects declared on the stack or compile the module in large memory model where no assumptions are made about the segment.

Calling a far class with a near object

Borland: • no message generated

Microsoft: • C2599: 'near': local functions are not supported

Example:
```
#include "compat.h"
class far MyClass {
  public:
    aMethod();
};
void fn() {
    MyClass near* pMC;
    pMC->aMethod();
}
```

Explanation: Declaring a class near implies that the address of the objects passed to a non-static method (the `this` pointer) will be a 16-bit, near pointer. Classes default to near in Small Model. Declaring a class far defines `this` pointers to be 32-bit, far pointers. This is the default in Large Model.

In this example, the pointer pMC is near, whereas the class is declared far. The Borland compiler performs the call by automatically promoting pMC to a far pointer before making the call — the Microsoft compiler generates an error. Including an explicit cast removes the problem for both compilers.

```
void fn() {
    MyClass near* pMC;
    ((MyClass far*)pMC)->aMethod();
}
```

Calling a near class with a far object

Borland: • Cannot call near class member function with a pointer of type 'MyClass far*'

Microsoft:
- C2662: 'aMethod': cannot convert 'this' pointer from 'struct ::MyClass *' to 'struct ::MyClass *const'

Example:
```
#include "compat.h"
class near MyClass {
  public:
    MyClass();
    void aMethod();
};
void fn() {
    MyClass far* pMC;
    pMC->aMethod();
}
```

Explanation: Here, the compiler cannot convert a far pMC into the near pointer that the class expects without losing information. (See the previous error description.)

To solve this problem the programmer can declare the class far as follows. Under the Microsoft compiler this will require that all accesses from near pointers be recast to far.

```
class far MyClass {
  public:
    MyClass();
    void aMethod();
};
```

Constructor/destructor not defined properly

Borland:
- Constructor cannot have a return type specification
- Constructor cannot be declared 'const' or 'volatile'
- 'MyClass::~MyClass(MyClass&)' must be declared with one parameter

related:
- Function *function* cannot be static
- Destructor cannot be declared 'const' or 'volatile
- Could not find a match for *constructor*

Microsoft:
- C2380: type[s] preceding 'MyClass'
- C2062: type 'int' expected
- C2238: unexpected token[s] preceding ';'
- C2524: 'MyClass': destructors must have a 'void' formal parameter list

related:
- C2461: *c*: constructor syntax missing formal parameters
- C2533: *id*: constructors not allowed return type
- C2534: *id*: constructor cannot return a value
- C2542: *id*: class object has no constructor for initialization
- C2577: *id*: constructor cannot return a value
- C2583: *id*: illegal const/volatile this pointer used for constructor/destructor
- C2610: identifier id can never be instantiated; user-defined constructor is required
- C2631: destructors not allowed a return type

Example:
```
class MyClass{
  public:
    void MyClass();
    const MyClass(int);
   ~MyClass(MyClass&);
};
```

Explanation:
The constructor carries the name of the class. No other member may be so named. A constructor has no return type, not even `void`. A constructor does not explicitly return the object it is constructing. In addition, a constructor cannot be declared `const`, `static`, `volatile`, `virtual`, or `interrupt`. The constructor may be overloaded with different arguments.

Each object declaration must have a matching constructor. For example, the following requires a constructor `MyClass(int, char*)`.

```
MyClass mc(0, "global object");
MyClass *pMC = new MyClass(1, "heap object");
```

In the absence of a constructor that matches exactly, the compiler will attempt to coerce any of the arguments to match an existing constructor.

The destructor carries the name of the class preceded by a tilde. Only a single destructor may be defined for a given class — therefore, the destructor may not carry any arguments (the Borland error message is a bit misleading — the "one parameter" probably refers to the hidden `this` pointer). The destructor also cannot be declared `const`, `static`, `volatile`, `virtual`, or `interrupt`.

A default constructor and destructor are provided by the compiler unless any other user-defined constructor is present.

No default constructor

Borland:
- Could not find a match for 'MyClass::MyClass()'
- Cannot find default constructor to initialize array element

related:
- Cannot find default constructor to initialize base class *class*
- Cannot find default constructor to initialize member *identifier*

Microsoft:
- C2512: 'MyClass': no appropriate default constructor available
- C2073: 'a': partially initialized array requires default constructor

related:
- C2539: id: no default constructor to initialize array of objects

Example:
```
class MyClass {
  public:
    MyClass(int i);
};
void fn() {
    MyClass s;
    MyClass a[3] = {1, 2}; //a[2] init'ed with
                           //MyClass()

}
```

Explanation: A non-aggregate class (a class that has member functions or nonpublic members or that inherits from another class) must have a default constructor if any objects are to be declared without an initial value.

If the user does not define any other constructors, C++ automatically provides a default constructor that calls the default constructors of all base classes and members. However, if the user defines any constructors, the compiler will not then automatically provide a default constructor. If any objects are constructed without initial values, a user-defined default constructor must be defined as well.

```
class MyClass {
  public:
    MyClass();
    MyClass(int i);
};
```

No copy-initializer constructor or assignment operator

Borland:
- Cannot find 'A::A(A&)' to copy a vector
- Cannot find 'A::operator=(A&)' to copy a vector

related:
  - Compiler could not generate copy constructor for class *class*
  - Compiler could not generate operator= for class *class*

Microsoft:
- no message generated

related:
  - C2558: *id*: no copy constructor available
  - C2582: *id*: operator= function is unavailable

Example:
```
class A {
  public:
    A();
    A(A&, int = 0);   //looks like c-i when int
                          //defaulted
    A& operator=(int);//an assignment operator
};
class B {
    A m[10];
  public:
};
void fn(B& b1) {
    B b2 = b1;          //needs A(A&) constructor to make
                        //copy of member m
    b2 = b1;            //needs op=(A&) to copy member m
}
```

Explanation: The copy-initializer constructor is used to create copies of class objects — the assignment operator is used to copy one class object over another. If they are not defined by the user, the compiler provides defaults that perform member-by-member copy.

User-defined copy-initializer constructors or assignment operators are used in preference to the defaults. However, if the arguments do not match identically, the Borland compiler will not use the user-defined device under certain circumstances, such as those in the preceding example. The Microsoft compiler generates no error messages in such a case — the difference probably stems from different interpretations of a C++ definition still in flux.

This problem can be solved by providing the appropriate copy-initializer constructor and assignment operator.

```
class A {
  public:
    A();

    //break c-i construct with default into two cases
    A(A&);
    A(A&, int);

    //add a new assignment operator
    A& operator=(A&);
    A& operator=(int);
};
```

The same problem can arise if the user defines a copy-initializer constructor or assignment operator and declares them private so that they are inaccessible to the application or derived class. Their presence precludes the compiler from generating a default while their restricted access prevents them from being used.

Defining an object more than once

Borland: • Variable 'mc' is initialized more than once

Microsoft: • C2086: 'mc': redefinition

Example:
```
class MyClass {
  public:
    MyClass();
};
MyClass mc;
MyClass mc;
```

Explanation: In C an object could be defined many times as long as the definitions were identical; this practice is not allowed in C++, as it would result in the constructor being invoked more than once. *The Annotated C++ Reference Manual* requires that "there must be exactly one definition of each object, function, class, and enumerator used in a program." As yet no consensus has been reached by the C++ ANSI standards committee as to what this means.

This problem arises most often when including C `.h` files. The solution is to add `extern` to declarations found in the `.h` files and define the objects in a separate C++ source file.

Cannot initialize non-aggregate class with list

Borland: • Objects of type 'Two' cannot be initialized with { }

Microsoft: • C2552: 'two': non-aggregates cannot be initialized with initializer list

Example:
```
struct One {
    int a; float b; char c;
};
struct Two {
    int a; float b; char c;
    Two();
};
One one = {1, 1.0, '1'};
Two two = {2, 2.0, '2'};
```

Explanation: To remain compatible with C, C++ allows a structure to be defined without any constructor. Such "C structures" are called aggregate classes. (An aggregate class cannot have a constructor, any private members, or any member functions. In addition, it may not inherit from another class.) Such a class can be initialized using C-like syntax.

Two is a non-aggregate class because of the presence of the default constructor. Therefore, two cannot be initialized with a C-like initializer list. A constructor should be generated and invoked as follows:

```
struct Two {                    //remember: 'class' is same as
    int a; float b; char c;// 'struct' with default of
    Two();                      // public
    Two(int, float, char);
};
Two two(2, 2.0, '2');
```

Invoking multiple argument constructor incorrectly

Borland: • Could not find a match for 'MyClass::MyClass(int)'

Microsoft: • C2664: '__pascal MyClass(const struct ::MyClass&)__near': cannot convert parameter 1 from 'const int' to 'const struct ::MyClass &'

Example:
```
class MyClass {
   public:
     MyClass(int,int);
};
MyClass a = 1, 2;
```

Explanation: While it is legal to invoke a single argument constructor using the assignment format as follows:

```
MyClass a = 1;  //equivalent to MyClass a(1)
```

this is not allowed for multiple argument constructors.

```
MyClass a = 1, 2; //not equivalent to MyClass a(1,2);
```

To invoke `MyClass(int, int)`, use the new initialization format.

Invoking default constructor improperly

Borland: • Lvalue required

Microsoft: • C2659: '=': overloaded function as left operand

Example:
```
class MyClass {
  public:
    MyClass();
    MyClass(int, int = 0, int = 0, int = 0);
    MyClass(MyClass&);
};
MyClass three(1, 2, 3);
MyClass two(1, 2);
MyClass one(1);
MyClass none();
void fn() {
    none = three;    //this is the illegal statement
}
```

Explanation: The three objects one, two, and three are all objects of class MyClass, and each is constructed with a different constructor. Despite its similar appearance, none is not declared an object of class MyClass but a function that returns an object of class MyClass. This unfortunate pun arises from the need of C++ to remain compatible with C.

To declare an object using the default constructor, omit the parentheses.

```
MyClass none;
```

Failure to provide the proper constructor

Borland:
   related:
- Could not find a match for 'MyClass::MyClass(int)'
  - Could not find a match for *constructor*

Microsoft:
- C2664: '__pascal MyClass(const ::MyClass&) __near': cannot convert parameter 1 from 'const' int to 'const class ::MyClass&'

Example:
```
class MyClass {
    public:
        MyClass();
};
void fn() {
    MyClass s(1);                //error on this line...
    MyClass a[2] = {1};          //...this line as well
}
```

Explanation: Here a constructor is provided, but not a constructor that matches the type of the initializer. (The somewhat confusing error message from the Microsoft compiler appears to stem from the fact that a constructor `MyClass::MyClass(MyClass&)` is provided by default, so the compiler attempted to convert the `int` into a `MyClass&` to use it but failed.)

The error message on the second line stems from the initialization of `a[0]` that is provided a value. `a[1]` initializes using the default constructor provided without comment.

Copy constructor cannot take a non-reference argument

Borland:
- The constructor 'MyClass::MyClass(MyClass)' is not allowed

Microsoft:
- C2652: 'MyClass': illegal copy constructor: first parameter may not be a 'MyClass'

Example:
```
class MyClass {
    public:
```

```
        MyClass(MyClass);
};
```

Explanation: Since the copy-initializer constructor is used to pass an object by value, it cannot accept its argument passed by value. Otherwise, the constructor contains a call to itself. Older compilers, which did not check for this case, generated an infinite loop when this constructor was invoked.

In most ways, the assignment operator is like the c-i constructor, however, `operator=(MyClass)` is allowed. Consider its effect in the following:

```
class MyClass {
  public:
    MyClass();
    MyClass(MyClass&);
    MyClass operator=(MyClass);
};
void fn() {
    MyClass b, c;

    b = c;
}
```

The assignment `b = c` uses the c-i constructor to make a copy of `c`, which is passed to the assignment operator. Thus, the copy of `c` is copied into `b`. This is almost certainly incorrect — the assignment operator should be declared `operator=(MyClass&)`.

Declaring constructor private

Borland: • 'MyClass::MyClass()' is not accessible

Microsoft: • C2248: 'MyClass::MyClass': cannot access 'private' member declared in class 'MyClass'

Example: `class MyClass {`

```
    MyClass();
};
void fn() {
    MyClass mc;
}
```

Explanation: The default access for class is private; however, declaring the constructor private means that no non-friends of the class will be able to construct an object of that class.

This is normally an error. Declaring the constructor public, as follows, solves the problem.

```
class MyClass {
  public:
    MyClass();
};
//or
struct MyClass2 {
    MyClass2();
};
```

This can be a useful technique, however, for restricting the number of functions that can create objects of that class. Consider the following example, which is also correct.

```
#include "compat.h"
class MyClass {
    friend void fn();
  private:
    MyClass();
};
void fn() {
    MyClass mc;
}
```

Here only the function fn() can create MyClass objects.

Declaring constructor private (Part 2)

Borland: • Compiler could not generate default constructor for class 'Derived'

Microsoft: • C4510: 'Derived': default constructor could not be generated
• C4610: struct 'Derived' can never be instantiated — user-defined constructor required
• C2512: 'Derived': no appropriate default constructor available

Example:
```
class Base {
   private:
      Base();

   public:
      Base(int);
};
class Derived : public Base {};
Derived d;
```

Explanation: A class with no non-private constructors can only be instantiated by a friend of the class. Declaring the default constructor private, however, means that the object can never be instantiated without some type of initial value. This may be useful.

One side-effect of this, however, is that any derived class must define a default constructor that invokes a different constructor of the base class. (The default constructor provided by the compiler invokes the default constructor of the base class as well.) For example:

```
class Derived : public Base {
   public:
      Derived() : Base(0) {
      }
};
```

Alternatively, the programmer can declare the default constructor in the base class `protected`, in which case outside functions cannot invoke the class without an initial value but the derived class can.

Declaring destructor private

Borland: • Destructor for 'MyClass' is not accessible

Microsoft: • C2248: 'MyClass::~MyClass': cannot access private member declared in class 'MyClass'

related: • C2262: id: cannot be destroyed

Example:
```
class MyClass {
  public:
    MyClass();

  private:
    ~MyClass();
};
```

Explanation: Declaring a destructor private or inheriting from a class in which the destructor is declared private has the effect of preventing the program from creating any instances of the class since these instances would be indestructible. Unlike constructors, destructors have no arguments. Thus, while it is possible to declare a single constructor, like the default constructor, private to prevent its use, declaring the destructor private makes the entire class uninstantiable.

Declaring the destructor protected makes it accessible to subclasses of MyClass. Thus, in the following example, MyClass cannot be invoked but SubClass can.

```
class MyClass {
  public:
    MyClass();

  protected:
    ~MyClass();
};
class SubClass : public MyClass {
  public:
    SubClass();
```

```
        ~SubClass();
    };
```

No place to store referential temporary

Borland: • Reference member 'ri' needs a temporary for initialization

Microsoft: • C2439: 'ri': member could not be initialized
                • C2440: 'initialization': cannot convert from 'const int' to 'int&'
                • C2607: 'initialization': cannot implicitly convert an 'int' to a non-const 'int&'

Example:
```
int fn(int);
class MyClass {
  public:
    int& ri1;
    int& ri2;
    MyClass(int x) : ri1(0), ri2(fn(x)) {};
};
```

Explanation: A referential object must refer to another object. Since a referential object is an lvalue (that is, it can appear on the left-hand side of an equal sign), this object must have an address. Consider a normal referential declaration.

```
void fn() {
    int i;
    int& ri = i;

    ri = 10;
}
```

The assignment to `ri` is allowed because the object to which `ri` refers has an address that receives the new value. In the preceding example, neither 0 nor the return value from a function have an address, thus there is no address to which the reference can refer. In addition, a temporary cannot be generated to house the objects since there is no obvious place to store the temporary.

Reference or constant not initialized in constructor

Borland:
- Constant member 'si' is not initialized
- Reference member 'ri' is not initialized

Microsoft:
- C2578: 'si': must be initialized in constructor base/member initializer list
- C4512: 'MyClass': assignment operator could not be generated

Example:
```
class MyClass {
   public:
      const int si;
      int& ri;

      MyClass(){};
};
MyClass mc;
```

Explanation: Members of a class may be declared either constant or referential. However, they must be initialized in the constructor initializer list, as follows:

```
class MyClass {
  public:
     const int si;
     int& ri;

     MyClass() : si(0), ri(si) {};
     MyClass(int i) : si(i), ri(si) {};
};
```

Reference or constant member with no constructor

Borland:
- Constant member 'MyClass::si' in class without constructors
- Reference member 'MyClass::ri' in class without constructors

Microsoft:
- C4510: 'MyClass': default constructor could not be generated
- C4512: 'MyClass': default constructor could not be generated

Example:
```
class MyClass {
  public:
    const int si;
    int& ri;
};
```

Explanation: Normally a constant or referential object is initialized where it is defined; however, a constant or referential member of a class must be initialized by the constructor. If the class has no constructor, the members cannot be defined. In addition, the compiler cannot generate a default constructor since it does not know to what to initialize the constant and referential members. Provide a constructor as follows:

```
#include "compat.h"
class MyClass {
  public:
    int i;
    const int si;
    int& ri;
    MyClass() : si(0), ri(i) {};
};
```

Here `si` is initialized to 0 and `ri` is established as an alternate name for the member `i`.

Static member cannot be initialized with an object

Borland: • 'sI' is not a non-static data member and can't be initialized here

Microsoft: • C2438: 'sI': cannot initialize static class data via constructor

Example:
```
class MyClass {
  public:
    static int sI;
    MyClass() : sI(0) {};
};
```

Explanation: A static member, such as sI, is invoked once per class. Static members are shared by all instances of the class. In other OOPLs, they are known as class members. Static members may not be initialized within a constructor, because the constructors are invoked against individual objects. The corrected example is as follows.

```
class MyClass {
  public:
    static int sI;
    MyClass();
};
static int MyClass::sI = 0;
```

Non-static member cannot be initialized without an object

Borland: • Cannot initialize a class member here
• Multiple declaration for 'MyClass::d2'

Microsoft: • C2252: 'd1': pure specifier can only be specified for functions
• C2258: illegal pure syntax, must be '=0'
• C2350: 'MyClass::d2' is not a static member

Example:
```
class MyClass {
```

```
      public:
        int d1 = 1;
        int d2;
        MyClass();
    };
    int MyClass::d2 = 0;
```

Explanation: Non-static members are invoked separately for each object. Thus, if they are to be initialized, they must be initialized in the constructor as follows:

```
class MyClass {
  public:
    int d1;
    int d2;
    MyClass : d1(1) {        //this is allowed
        d2 = 0;              //so is this
    };
};
```

The Microsoft errors stem from the similarity of the erroneous declaration of d1 to that of a pure virtual function.

```
class MyClass {
  public:
    virtual int fn() = 0;
};
```

A pure virtual function must be declared as shown with the `virtual` at the beginning and the `= 0` at the end — the constant value must be zero.

Object passed to/returned from function by value

Borland: • Structure passed by value

Microsoft: • no message generated

Example: `class MyClass {`

```
  public:
    MyClass();
};
void oFn(MyClass);
void fn() {
    MyClass mc;
    oFn(mc);
}
```

Explanation: In C++ passing a class object to a function by value is legal. In many pre-ANSI C compilers, class objects were passed by reference. Therefore, many C++ compilers issue a warning when an object is being passed to or returned from a function by value.

When passing or returning a class object by value, the copy constructor is used to create a copy on the stack. Thus, passing a function by value to add a class object to a linked list is always an error since the copy, not the original object, gets added to the list. Passing/returning by reference is more efficient and avoids these problems.

```
void oFn(MyClass&);
```

Returning by reference is not an option if the calling function is not prepared to destruct the returned object properly. Consider the following:

```
MyClass& operator+(MyClass& a, MyClass& b);
void fn() {
    MyClass a, b;
    c = a + b;
}
```

Being declared with a referential return type, `operator+()` must return the address of a `MyClass` object to the caller. This object is then copied into `c` using `operator=()`. The returned object cannot be declared off of `operator+()`'s stack, as it is deallocated upon return. If it is allocated off the heap, the calling function would have no way of returning it. Thus, such operators should always return by value.

```
MyClass operator+(MyClass& a, MyClass& b);
```

Assignment to `this` not allowed

Borland: • Assignment to 'this' not allowed

Microsoft: • C2106: '=': left operand must be lvalue

Example:
```
class MyClass {
   private:
      int size;
      int data[1];
   public:
      MyClass(int s) {
          void *pBlock = new int[s + 1];
          this = (MyClass*)pBlock;
          size = s;
      };
};
```

Explanation: Under cfront, the AT&T C++ to C translator, the programmer could define a dynamically sized class by allocating the necessary memory off of the heap in the constructor and assigning the resulting pointer to the `this` pointer. Assigning a new address to `this` had the effect of replacing the existing object with the new object in all future references.

This trick is not supported under modern C++ compilers. There are several ways around this problem. The easiest is to allocate the data portion off the heap as follows:

```
class MyClass {
  private:
     int size;
     int *pData;
  public:
     MyClass(int s) {
         pData = new int[s + 1];
         size = s;
     };
};
```

Non-static member cannot be used without an object

Borland:
- Member cannot be used without an object
- Use . or -> to call 'MyClass::method()'

Microsoft:
- C2352: 'MyClass::method': illegal call to a non-static member function
- C2597: 'MyClass::data': does not specify an object

Example:
```
class MyClass {
    public:
        int data;
        void method();
};
void fn() {
    MyClass::data = 0;
    MyClass::method();
}
```

Explanation: Non-static data members of a class are allocated as part of a class object. That is, given a `MyClass` object `mc1` and another `mc2`, `mc1.data` and `mc2.data` are independent. Similarly, non-static member functions must be referenced by an object. The preceding references should appear as follows:

```
void fn() {
    MyClass mc;
    mc.data = 0;
    mc.method();

    //same thing with a pointer
    MyClass *pMC = &mc;
    pMC->data = 0;
    pMC->method();
}
```

Note that it is legal to explicitly specify the class type as follows:

```
void fn(MyClass& mc) {
    mc.MyClass::data = 0;
    mc.MyClass::method();
};
```

This approach has the additional effect of forcing the function to call MyClass::method() even if method() were virtual and mc were a member of a subclass with a different method().

Static member functions have no `this` pointer

Borland:
- 'this' can only be used within a member function

Microsoft:
- C2671: 'staticFn': static member functions do not have 'this' pointer

related:
- C2355: this: can only be referenced inside nonstatic member function

Example:
```
MyClass *pMC;
class MyClass {
  public:
    static int data;
    static void staticFn() {
        aMethod();              //implicit reference to this
        pMC = this;             //explicit reference to this
    }
};
MyClass* oFn();
void fn() {
    //static members can be accessed without an object
    MyClass::data = 0;
    MyClass::staticFn();

    //static members can be accessed with an object, but
    //only the type of the object is used
    MyClass mc;
    mc.data = 0;
    mc.staticFn();
```

```
//even expressions are not evaluated; only the type
//of the expression
oFn()->data = 0;
}
```

Explanation: Static member functions are allocated on a per class basis. Thus, they may be invoked without an object as in the first two assignments. Even when an object is present, only its type is used to determine class. If the static member is referenced against an expression, only the type of the expression is used. Thus, in the final assignment, the function `oFn()` is not called.

Since a static member is not invoked with an object, it has no `this` pointer, hence the error messages. To access a non-static member from a static member function, an object must be explicitly provided.

Static member functions cannot be virtual

Borland: • Storage class virtual not allowed here

Microsoft: • C2576: 'method': virtual used for static member function

Example:
```
class MyClass {
 public:
     virtual static void method();
}
```

Explanation: Calls to virtual functions are resolved at run-time in a process known as late binding. To do this, an object is required. Static functions are invoked without objects, and therefore cannot be declared virtual.

Methods of different classes cannot be overloaded

Borland: • Too few parameters in call to 'Derived::aMethod(int)'
related: • Extra parameter in call to *function*
             • Too few parameters in call

- Type mismatch in parameter *n*
- Type mismatch in parameter *n* in call to *function*
- Type mismatch in parameter *parameter*
- Type mismatch in parameter *parameter* in call to *function*

Microsoft:
related:
- C2660: 'aMethod': function does not take 0 parameters
- C2664: *function*: cannot convert parameter 2 from 'class ::MyClass' to 'int'

Example:
```
class Base {
  public:
    void aMethod();
};
class Derived : public Base {
  public:
    void aMethod(int);   //this declaration hides
};                       //Base::aMethod()
void fn() {
    Derived d;
    d.aMethod();         //this is not okay
    d.aMethod(0);        //this is okay
};
```

Explanation: Two methods within the same class can be overloaded with different arguments; however, a method in one class cannot overload a method in a base class. This problem can be solved by calling the base class method from an overloaded method in the subclass. Declaring the subclass method in-line avoids any overhead.

```
class Derived : public Base {
  public:
    void aMethod() { Base::aMethod();};
    void aMethod(int);
};
void fn(Derived& d) {
    d.aMethod();    //now refers to Derived::aMethod()
    d.aMethod(0);   //still refers to
};                  //Derived::aMethod(int)
```

Virtual functions must be declared identically

Borland:
- 'Derived::aMethod(unsigned int)' hides virtual function 'Base::aMethod(int)'

related:
- Virtual function *function* conflicts with base class *base*

Microsoft:
- no message generated

related:
- C2555: 'c1::f': overriding virtual function differs from 'c2::f' only by return type

Example:
```
#include "compat.h"
class Base {
  public:
    Base();
    virtual int aMethod(int);
};
class Derived : public Base {
  public:
    int aMethod(unsigned);
};
```

Explanation: Even though they are declared virtual, the two functions aMethod defined in the preceding example are not virtual with respect to one another because their parameter lists are not the same. Virtual functions must have identical argument lists.

Virtual functions also must have identical return types with the following possible exception. The ANSI C++ committee is considering and will likely accept the extension that a virtual function may return a derived class as in the following:

```
class Base {
  public:
    Base();
    virtual Base& aMethod(int);
};
class Derived : public Base {
  public:
```

```
    virtual Derived& aMethod(int);
};
```

Here `Derived::aMethod()` overrides `Base::aMethod()` with identical arguments, but returns a subclass of the class returned by `Base::aMethod()`.

Virtual function not declared virtual in base class

Borland: • no message generated

Microsoft: • no message generated

Example:
```
class Base {
  public:
     int aMethod();
};
class Derived : public Base {
  public:
     virtual int aMethod();
};
void fn(Base& b) {
     b.aMethod();
};
```

Explanation: The programmer must be very careful that this construction is correct. Since `aMethod()` is not declared virtual in the base class, the call `b.aMethod()` is not a virtual call. The fact that the method is declared virtual in the derived class is irrelevant.

The reverse is not true, of course. Were `aMethod()` declared virtual in the base class, it would be virtual in the derived class whether declared so or not.

Pure virtual function declarations improper

Borland:
- Cannot initialize a class member here
- Virtual can only be used with member functions
- Bad syntax for pure function definition
- Non-virtual function 'MyClass::fn2()' declared pure

Microsoft:
- C2252: 'i': pure specifier can only be specified for functions
- C2253: 'fn': pure specifier only applies to virtual function
- C2258: illegal pure syntax, must be '= 0'
- C2433: 'j': 'virtual' not permitted on data declaration

Example:
```
class MyClass {
  public:
    static  int i = 0;      //can't init static members
                            //this way
    virtual int j = 0;      //data members cannot be
                            //pure virtual
    virtual int fn2() = 1;//must be 0
            int fn2() = 0;//only virtual fns can be
                          //pure
};
```

Explanation: The syntax for declaring a pure virtual function is reminiscent of what one might expect for initialization of class members. However, this similarity is misleading. Static data members are initialized as follows:

```
class MyClass {
  public:
    static int i;
};
int MyClass::i = 0;
```

Non-static members are initalized in the constructor as follows:

```
class MyClass {
  public:
```

```
        int i1;
        int i2;
        MyClass() : i1(0) {          //this is legal
            i2 = 0;                  //so is this
        };
};
```

The value that follows a pure virtual function definition must be 0; no other value is allowed. This value is more a flag than an actual value.

A function does not have to be explicitly declared virtual to be virtual. In the following example, `Derived::fn()` is virtual because `Base::fn()` is declared virtual, so the pure designation is legal. If, however, the declaration of `Base::fn()` were changed in the future or if `Derived` were to no longer inherit from `Base`, the declaration would become illegal without any change to the declaration itself.

```
class Base {
  public:
    virtual int fn();
};
class Derived : public Base {
  public:
    int fn() = 0;
};
```

Cannot instance an abstract class

Borland: • Cannot create instances of abstract class 'Base'

Microsoft: • C2259: 'Base': illegal attempt to instantiate abstract class

Example:
```
class Base {
  public:
    virtual void fn() = 0;
};
Base b;
```

Explanation: An abstract class is a class that contains one or more pure virtual functions. Such a class cannot be instantiated with an object since the definition is incomplete. Abstract classes are useful, however, in defining conceptual groupings of classes.

Abstract classes can be inherited. Overloading the pure virtual functions with real functions completes the class definition and makes the derived class non-abstract. However, subclasses of abstract classes remain abstract as long as any pure virtual methods remain non-overloaded.

```
class Derived : public Base {
    virtual void fn();
};
```

Instances of Derived may now be created.

The most common cause for such an error is inheriting from a class provided by a third-party library without overloading all of the virtual functions. The solution is to overload any remaining pure virtual functions. If it is not known what the missing member should do or if it appears that the member is never called, overload it with a function that contains nothing but a call to abort().

In previous versions of C++, abstract classes could not be inherited without overloading every pure virtual function. This is no longer the case.

Operator with incorrect number of arguments

Borland: • 'MyClass::operator/()' must be declared with one parameter
related: • *function* must be declared with no parameters
              • *operator* must be declared with one or no parameters
              • *operator* must be declared with one or two parameters

Microsoft: • C2805: binary 'operator/' has too few parameters
related: • C2802: static member operator *o* has no formal parameters
               • C2803: operator *o* must have at least one formal parameter of class type
               • C2804: binary operator *o* has too many formal parameters
               • C2805: binary operator *o* has too few formal parameters
               • C2806: operator *o* has too many formal parameters

- C2808: unary operator *o* has too many formal parameters
- C2809: operator *o* has no formal parameters
- C2829: operator *o* cannot have a variable parameter list

Example:

```
class MyClass {
  public:
    float operator/();
};
float operator/(MyClass&);
```

Explanation: Overloading an operator cannot change its syntax, precedence, or binding. This would make the C++ parser too complicated and even further reduce its ability to detect input errors with little benefit.

In this example, `operator/` is a binary operator and, therefore, cannot be defined with only a single argument. (The two definitions of `operator/` in the preceding are almost equivalent — in the case of the member operator, the left-hand argument is the `this` object, and `this` counts as one of the parameters.)

```
class MyClass {
  public:
    float operator/(float denominator);
};
float operator/(MyClass& numerator, float denominator);
```

The `++` and `--` operators can take either one or two arguments, the form `operator++(MyClass&)` refers to the prefix form, while `operator++(MyClass&, int)` refers to the postfix form. In addition, the operators `-`, `+`, and `*` have both one and two argument forms.

Operators cannot have default arguments

Borland:
- Operators may not have default argument values

Microsoft:
- C2831: 'operator=' may not have default parameters

Example:
```
class MyClass {
  public:
    int operator+=(int val = 0);
};
```

Explanation: Providing a default argument would change the syntax of the operator (see the previous error). For example, if the preceding definition were legal, statements such as the following would have to be accepted.

```
void fn() {
    MyClass mc;
    mc+=;
}
```

Operator new declared improperly

Borland:
- 'operator new' must be declared with one parameter
- operator new must have an initial parameter of type size_t

Microsoft:
- C2802: static member 'operator new' has no formal parameters
- C2821: first formal parameter to 'operator new' must be 'unsigned int'

related:
- C2271: operator: new/delete cannot have formal list modifiers

Example:
```
#include <stddef.h>
class MyClass {
  public:
    void* operator new(char*);
};
void* operator new();
```

Explanation: The `operator new()` may be overloaded. Overloading `::operator new()` affects all `new` operations. Overloading `MyClass::operator new()` affects only allocations of objects of class `MyClass`.

The overloaded `operator new()` must return an object of type `void*` and its first argument must be of type `size_t` defined in `stddef.h` This argument specifies the size in bytes of the block to be allocated off the heap.

`operator new()` can be overloaded by other arguments after the `size_t` argument as in the following:

```
#include <stddef.h>
class MyClass {
  public:
    void* operator new(size_t sz);        //#1
    void* operator new(size_t sz, char*);//#2
};
void fn(char* pS) {
    MyClass *pMC1 = new MyClass();        //use #1
    MyClass *pMC2 = new(pS) MyClass();   //use #2
}
```

Neither `new` nor `delete` can be declared to have a different memory model than the class.

Operator new must return void*

Borland: • operator new must return an object of type void*

Microsoft: • C2824: return type for 'operator new' must be 'void*'

Example:
```
#include <stddef.h>
class MyClass {
  public:
    MyClass* operator new(size_t size);
};
```

Explanation: Although it is tempting to assume that an `operator new()` defined for a specific class will return a pointer to an object of that class, this is not true. `operator new()` always returns `void*`.

Operator delete declared improperly

Borland: • Declare operator delete(void*) or (void*, size_t)
related: • operator delete must return void

Microsoft: • C2815: first actual parameter for based form of 'operator delete' must be '__segment'
related: • C2810: second formal parameter for operator delete must be unsigned int
• C2816: alternative form of operator delete must be a member
• C2817: return type for operator delete must be void

Example:
```
#include <stddef.h>
class MyClass {
  public:
     void operator delete(MyClass*);
};
```

Explanation: The delete operator may be declared `void operator delete(void *pB)` in which `pB` points to the block to be returned or `void operator delete (void *pB, size_t sz)` in which case `sz` is the length of the block pointed at by `pB`. No other form is allowed. Under the Borland compiler, `size_t` is defined in the include file `stddef.h`, which must be included. Under the Microsoft compiler `size_t` is actually type `unsigned int`.

Operators new and delete have no `this` pointer

Borland: • Member cannot be used without an object

Microsoft: • C2597: 'MyClass::d': does not specify an object
related: • C2672: *f*: *new/delete* member functions do not have this pointer

Example:
```
#include <stddef.h>
class MyClass {
  public:
```

```
        int d;

        void* operator new(size_t);
};
void* MyClass::operator new(size_t sz) {
    d = sz;          //this is not legal
    return new char[sz];
};
```

Explanation: A `MyClass` object has not been constructed when `MyClass::operator new()` is invoked to allocate the space for it. Similarly, the object has been destroyed by the time `operator delete()` is invoked to return the memory. Therefore, both operators are static — that is, invoked without an object — and have no access to other non-static members of the class.

Operators new and delete may not be declared virtual

Borland: • no message generated

Microsoft: • C2650: 'new': cannot be declared virtual

Example:
```
#include <stddef.h>
class MyClass {
  public:
    virtual void* operator new(size_t);
    virtual void operator delete(void*);
};
```

Explanation: The new and delete operators are invoked before an object has been constructed and after it has been destructed, respectively. Therefore, no object of the correct type exists at the time these functions are called. Since a virtual function requires an object with which to perform late binding, new and delete are automatically static and cannot be virtual.

   The Microsoft compiler correctly generates an error message — the Borland compiler appears to ignore the declaration.

Must include `stddef.h` when overloading new or delete

Borland:
- 'size_t' cannot start a parameter declaration
- operator new must have an initial parameter of type size_t

Microsoft:
- no error message

Example:
```
class MyClass {
  public:
    void* operator new(size_t sz);
    void operator delete(void*, size_t sz);
};
```

Explanation: The *C++ Annotated Reference Manual* says that the argument `sz` in the preceding example should be of type `size_t`, which is "an implementation-dependent integral type defined in the standard header `stddef.h`." Under the Microsoft compiler, the type of `sz` is `unsigned int`. Under the Borland compiler, however, `sz` must be of type `size_t`. Since `size_t` is defined in `stddef.h`, if the programmer forgets to include this file, the compiler is told that it can't use `size_t` and must use `size_t` at the same time.

Overloadable operator expected

Borland:
- Overloadable operator expected

Microsoft:
related:
- C2800: 'operator.' cannot be overloaded
  - C2833: operator *o* is not a recognized operator or type

Example:
```
class MyClass {
  public:
    MyClass* operator.();
};
```

Explanation: Not all operators can be overloaded. Specifically ., .*, .->, ::, and ?: cannot be overloaded.

Overloaded operator must operate on a class type

Borland: • 'operator+(int,int)' must be a member function or have a parameter of class type

Microsoft: • C2803: 'operator +' must have at least one formal parameter of class type

Example: `int operator+(int,int);`

Explanation: Operators can only be overloaded for class types. That is, at least one of the arguments to an overloaded operator must be of a class type. Overloading intrinsic functions is not allowed.

Overloaded operator must be a member function

Borland: • 'operator=(MyClass&, MyClass&)' must be a member function

Microsoft: • C2801: 'operator=' must be a member
related: • C2581: id: static operator= function is illegal

Example:
```
class MyClass {
  public:
};
MyClass& operator=(MyClass&, MyClass&);
```

Explanation: Most operators may be declared either as members of the class or as global operators. When declared as members, the left-hand parameter is `this`. Consider the following:

```
class MyClass {
  public:
    int d;
    int operator+(MyClass& right) {
        return d + right.d;
    };
};
int operator*(MyClass& left, MyClass& right) {
    return left.d * right.d;
}
void fn(MyClass a, MyClass b) {
    a + b;          //called like: a.operator+(b)
    a * b;          //             operator*(a,b)
}
```

However, some operators may only be declared as members. These are as follows:

- operator=()
- operator->()
- operator()()
- operator <type>

Return type or arguments provided for cast operator

Borland: • Conversion operator cannot have a return type specification

Microsoft: • C2549: user-defined conversion cannot specify a return type
related: • C2835: user-defined conversion type takes no formal parameters

Example:
```
class MyClass {
  public:
    int operator int();
};
```

Explanation: Type conversion operators are specified without return types. The type is inferred from the operator itself — for example, `operator int()` is assumed to return an `int`.

```
class MyClass {
  public:
    operator int();
};
```

In addition, conversion operators may not have arguments.

Improper return type for operator->

Borland: • operator-> must return a pointer or a class

Microsoft: • C2818: incorrect return type for 'operator->'

Example:
```
class MyClass {
  public:
    int operator->();
};
```

Explanation: The indirection operator is applied recursively. That is, `mc->y` is interpreted as `(mc.operator->())->y`. Thus, `operator->()` must return either a pointer to an object containing a member `y` or the object of a class for which `operator->()` is defined, thereby starting the cycle over again.

   The intent of overloading this operator is to provide "smart pointers" as the following corrected example shows.

```
MyClass* MyClass::operator->() {
    return pMC;
}
```

In this case, `operator->()` returns nothing more than a pointer to an object of class `MyClass`; however, it could do much more. For example, if `MyClass` objects were persistent, that is, stored on disk,

`MCPtr::operator->()` could read the MyClass object off the disk and into a RAM cache.

The illusion of smart pointers is incomplete since the . operator cannot be overloaded. (Remember, `p->d` can be written as `(*p).d`.) The ANSI C++ committee has discussed proposals to allow `operator.()` to be overloaded. The problem with this idea is avoiding infinite recursions within the class for so basic an operation as `operator.()`.

Improper return type for operator-> (Part 2)

Borland: • Out of memory

Microsoft: • C2819: recursive return type for 'operator->'

Example:
```
class MyClass {
  public:
     int d;
};
class MCPtr {
  public:
     MyClass *pMC;

     MCPtr(MyClass& mc) {
         pMC = &mc;
     }
     MCPtr& operator->(); {
         return *this;
     }
};

void fn() {
    MyClass mc;
    MCPtr pMC(mc);
    pMC->d = 0;                     //may be infinite loop
}
```

Explanation: The expression `pMC->d` is interpreted as `(pMC.operator->())->d` (see the previous error explanation). If the return type of `MCPtr::oper-ator->()` is an object of class `MCPtr`, then the operator invokes itself recursively.

Operator++() provided without a postfix form

Borland: • Overloaded prefix 'operator++' used as a postfix operator
related: • Last parameter of operator must have type int

Microsoft: • C4620: no postfix form of operator++ found for type 'Complex', using prefix form
related: • C2807: second formal parameter to postfix operator *o* must be int

Example:
```
class Complex {
    public:
        int real, imag;
        Complex& operator++() {
            real++;
            return *this;
        };
};
void fn() {
    Complex c;
    c++;
}
```

Explanation: Early drafts of the C++ standard did not define a method for overloading `++c` and `c++` separately, since they both appeared as `operator++()`. The current specification uses the not very pleasing but functional convention that `operator++()` refers to the prefix operator, `++c`, and `opera-tor++(int)` refers to the postfix operator, `c++`. To maintain compatibility with older C++ programs in the absence of a definition for the postfix operator, most compilers will use the prefix definition. A warning is generated to alert the programmer, however. If there is to be no difference between the prefix and postfix operators, the following addition may be made to this class to remove the warning.

```
class Complex {
  public:
    int real, imag;
    Complex();
    Complex& operator++();
    Complex& operator++(int) {return ++(*this);};
};
```

Nonmember functions cannot be constant or volatile

Borland: • Only member functions may be 'const' or 'volatile'

Microsoft: • C2270: 'f2': modifiers not allowed on nonmember functions

Example:
```
class MyClass {
  public:
    volatile int m1();
    int m2() volatile;
};
volatile int f1();
int f2() volatile;  //only illegal declaration
```

Explanation: The declaration of `f2()` is the only one that is illegal. The functions `m1()` and `f1()` are normal functions that return a `volatile int`. The method `m2()`, however, is a volatile method that can be applied against a volatile object. The syntax for `const` methods is identical.

Cannot invoke non-const method with a const object

Borland: • Non-const function MyClass::m() called for const object

Microsoft: • C2662: 'm': cannot convert 'this' pointer from 'const class ::MyClass *' to 'class ::MyClass *const'

Example:
```
class MyClass {
    public:
        MyClass();
        int m();
};
void fn() {
    const MyClass mc;
    mc.m();
}
```

Explanation: Declaring a method constant means that it can be applied against a constant object. A constant object may not be passed to a non-constant method. The method m may be declared constant as follows:

```
class MyClass {
  public:
    MyClass();
    int m() const;
};
```

Constant method cannot change its object

Borland: • Cannot modify a const object

Microsoft: • C2166: lvalue specifies const object

Example:
```
class MyClass {
    public:
        int d;

        MyClass();
        int m() const {
            d = 0;
```

```
        return 0;
    };
};
```

Explanation: A constant method may not change any of its data members. (This is why a constant object may be passed to a constant member — a constant member cannot change the object.)

Cannot invoke non-volatile method with volatile object

Borland:
- Non-volatile function MyClass::m() called for volatile object

Microsoft:
- C2662: 'm': cannot convert 'this' pointer from 'volatile class ::MyClass *' to 'class ::MyClass * const'

Example:
```
class MyClass {
  public:
     int m();
};
void fn() {
     volatile MyClass mc;
     mc.m();
}
```

Explanation: Declaring a member volatile means that it can be applied against a volatile object. A volatile object cannot be passed to a non-volatile method. The method may be declared volatile as follows:

```
class MyClass {
  public:
     int m() volatile;
};
```

Occasionally objects are declared volatile to avoid some compiler optimization that is causing problems within a loop. Since volatile objects may be invoked only with volatile methods, this can cause other problems. The best solution is to define a volatile pointer to the object that will be used only during the loop, as follows:

```
void fn() {
    MyClass mc;
    //...other code
    //declare volatile object just for the loop
    volatile MyClass *pMC = &mc;
    while (pMC->dataMember) ; //loop until flag cleared

    //...function continues, using mc and not pMC
}
```

Local name not fully qualified

Borland: • Use qualified name to access nested type 'MyClass::MyType'

Microsoft: • C2065: 'MyType': undeclared identifier

Example:
```
class MyClass {
  public:
    enum MyType {mt1, mt2, mt3};
    MyType m();
};
void fn(MyClass& mc) {
    MyType mt;
    mt = mc.m();
}
```

Explanation: In earlier definitions of C++, types (such as a class or enumerated type) declared within a class had global scope. Thus, MyType was known globally even though defined in MyClass. In newer versions of C++, such types still have global scope, but they must be fully qualified with the parent class. Thus, outside of MyClass, the enumerated type is known as MyClass::MyType. Under the Microsoft compiler, this is an error. Under the Borland compiler, this message is only a warning, as it continues to accept the anachronistic form.

```
void fn(MyClass& mc) {
    MyClass::MyType mt;

    mt = mc.m();
}
```

Local class cannot have a non-inline function

Borland:
- Cannot have a non-inline function in a local class
- Type qualifier 'LocalClass' must be a struct or class name

Microsoft:
- C2653: 'LocalClass': is not a class name

related:
- C2601: functions cannot be defined in local classes

Example:
```
void fn() {
    class LocalClass {
      public:
        int m();
    };
};
int LocalClass::m() {
    return 0;
}
```

Explanation: The scope of a local class is limited to fn() in which it is defined. No syntax exists for defining a method of a local class. All the methods of a local class should be defined with the class itself.

```
void fn() {
    class LocalClass {
      public:
        int m() {
            return 0;
        }
    };
};
```

The Microsoft compiler does not allow local classes to have methods at all.

Local class cannot have a static data member

Borland: • Cannot have a static data member in a local class

Microsoft: • C2246: 'si': illegal static data member in locally defined class

Example:
```
void fn() {
    class LocalClass {
      public:
        static int si;
    };
};
```

Explanation: Static members are defined on a class basis — that is, a single static member is shared by all instances of the class. However, the scope of a locally defined class is limited to the function in which it is defined. To be shared by every instance of `LocalClass`, the member `si` would need to be defined outside the function. On the other hand, one could view each instance of `LocalClass` as a separate class, much like a class template, in which case `si` would need to be stored on the stack like an auto variable local to `fn()`. To avoid such decisions, local classes are barred from containing static members.

Base class or member initialized more than once

Borland: • Base class 'Base' is initialized more than once
         • Member 'm' is initialized more than once

Microsoft: • C2437: 'Base' already initialized
         • C2437: 'm' already initialized

Example:
```
class Base {
  public:
```

```
      Base(int);
};
class Derived : public Base {
  private:
    int m;

  public:
    Derived(int x, int y) : Base(x), m(y), Base(x) {};
    Derived(int x) : Base(x), m(0), m(0){};
};
```

Explanation: Neither a base class nor a member may be initialized more than once in the initializer list.

```
class Derived : public Base {
  private:
    int m;

  public:
    Derived(int x, int y) : Base(x), m(y) {};
    Derived(int x) : Base(x), m(0) {};
};
```

Base initialization without class name obsolete

Borland: • Base initialization without class name obsolete

Microsoft: • C2351: obsolete C++ constructor initialization syntax

Example:
```
class Base {
  public:
    Base(int);
};
class Derived : public Base {
  public:
    Derived(int x) : (x) {};
};
```

Explanation: Here the constructor `Derived(int)` invokes the constructor `Base(int)` to construct the base class portion. In older versions of C++ specifying the name of the base class was not necessary (or even allowed). Since C++ did not support multiple inheritance, there could be only one (or no) base class anyway.

Now that C++ supports multiple inheritance, a single class can have multiple parent classes and the constructor should specify which constructors to invoke with which arguments.

```
class Derived : public Base {
  public:
    Derived(int x) : Base(x) {};
};
```

This is a warning under the Borland compiler and an error under the Microsoft compiler.

No base class to initialize

Borland: • No base class to initialize

Microsoft: • C2351: obsolete C++ constructor initialization syntax

Example:
```
class Derived {
  public:
    Derived(int x) : (x) {};
};
```

Explanation: Under the obsolete declaration syntax it was possible to attempt to invoke the constructor for a base class without specifying it. If there was no base class, this was an error.

Cannot call the constructor for a non-base class

Borland: • 'Based' is not a base class of 'Derived'

Microsoft: • C2614: 'Derived': illegal member initialization: 'Based' is not a base or member

Example:
```
class Base {
  public:
    Base();
    Base(int);
};
class Derived : public Base {
  public:
    Derived(int x) : Based(x) {};
};
```

Explanation: Here the programmer attempted to call the constructor `Base(int)` but misspelled it. Only the constructors for base classes and data members can be invoked in this way.

```
class Derived : public Base {
  private:
    MyClass mc;

  public:
    Derived(int x) : Base(x), mc(0) {};
};
```

Multiple base classes require explicit class names

Borland: • Multiple base classes require explicit class names

Microsoft: • C2351: obsolete C++ constructor initialization syntax

Example:
```
class Base1 {
  public:
    Base1();
    Base1(int);
};
```

```
class Base2 {
  public:
    Base2();
};
class Derived : public Base1, public Base2 {
  public:
    Derived(int x) : (x), Base2() {};
};
```

Explanation: This message resembles the message "Base initialization without classname obsolete" except that now, in the presence of multiple base classes, the Borland compiler cannot hope to decide to which base class (x) refers. Unlike the earlier warning, this message is an error. Microsoft generates the same error in the presence of the obsolete form whether multiple base classes are present or not.

Multiple conversion paths

Borland: • Ambiguity between 'Real::operator Complex()' and 'Complex::Complex(Real&)'

Microsoft: • C2658: multiple conversions: Complex(Real) and Real::operator Complex()

Example:
```
class Real;
class Complex {
  public:
    Complex();
    Complex(Real&);
};
class Real {
  public:
    Real();
    operator Complex();
};
```

```
void fn() {
    Real r;
    Complex c;
    c = Complex(r);              //conversion ambiguous
}
```

Explanation: The cast `Complex(r)` is ambiguous since there is more than one way to get from a `Real` to a `Complex`. The cast operator is normally used to cast from the current class to another type over which the programmer has no control, such as `int`; however, the target class can be a user-defined class as well. A single argument constructor provides a conversion path from another type to the current class. When both are provided, the result can be ambiguous. This error can be frustrating, especially when the two conversions are functionally identical. The solution is to decide on one conversion operator (usually the constructor) and remove the other.

Members ambiguous between base classes

Borland: • Member is ambiguous: 'Base1::d' and 'Base2::d'

Microsoft: • C2385: 'Derived::d' is ambiguous
  • C4385: could be the 'd' in class 'Base1' of class 'Derived'
  • C4385: or the 'd' in base 'Base2' of class 'Derived'

related: • C2585: explicit conversion to type is ambiguous

Example:
```
class Base1 {
  public:
    int d;
};
class Base2 {
  public:
    int d;
};
class Derived : public Base1, public Base2 {};
void fn() {
    Derived d;
```

```
        d.d = 0;
}
```

Explanation: A derived class inherits the members of all of its base classes. If a member of one base class has the same name as a member of another base class, then either member can be accessed only from the derived class by specifying its base class.

```
class Base1 {
  public:
    int d;
};
class Base2 {
  public:
    int d;
};
class Derived : public Base1, public Base2 {};
void fn(Derived& d) {
    d.Base1::d = 0;
}
```

No error is generated if the ambiguous member is not accessed. The fact that a d exists in both Base1 and Base2 is not an error. The ambiguous reference d.d is the error.

Ambiguous inheritance

Borland:
- Member is ambiguous: 'Class1::fn()' and 'Class2::fn()'

Microsoft:
- C2250: 'Derived': ambiguous inheritance of 'Class1::fn()'
- C2250: 'Derived': ambiguous inheritance of 'Class2::fn()'
- C2385: 'Derived::fn()' is ambiguous

related
- C2506: 'Class1::fn()': ambiguous

Example:
```
class Base {
  public:
    int fn();
```

```
};
struct Class1 : public Base{ };
struct Class2 : public Base{ };
class Derived : public Class1, public Class2{};
void fn() {
    Derived d;
    d.fn();
}
```

Explanation: The same class is inherited twice. Since the inheritance is not virtual, two distinct copies of Base are retained in the class Derived. When referring to members of Base, it is impossible to determine which Base the programmer intends.

Such references can be resolved by specifying the full path to the member or at least enough of the path to relieve the ambiguity as in the following:

```
void fn() {
    Derived d;
    d.Class1::fn();
}
```

The member fn() is no longer ambiguous when viewed from Class1.

This error can also arise when the programmer intended to inherit the Base class virtually. Inheriting a class virtually guarantees that only one copy of the class is retained in the derived class, even if inherited through different paths. Consider the following:

```
class Person {//...};
class Student : virtual public Person {//...};
class Teacher : virtual public Person {//...};
class StudentTeacher : public Student, public Teacher {
    //...
};
```

In this case, since a StudentTeacher is not two people, the Person information need not be duplicated. Inheriting class Person virtually ensures that `StudentTeacher` ends up with only a single copy of this information and no ambiguity exists.

Base class inherited more than once

Borland: • Base class 'Amplifier' is included more than once

Microsoft: • C2500: 'Stereo': 'Amplifier' is already a direct base class

Example:
```
class Amplifier {
   public:
      int volume;
};
class Stereo : public Amplifier, public Amplifier {};
Stereo s;
```

Explanation: The same class cannot be inherited directly more than once since every member of the base class would be ambiguous in the subclass with no way of relieving the ambiguity. For example, does `s.volume` refer to the left or right volume? (See error 'Ambiguous inheritance'.)

One way to address the problem is to use a "has a" relationship. That is, say that a stereo has two amplifiers as follows:

```
class Stereo {
   Amplifier left;
   Amplifier right;
};
Stereo s;
```

Now the left volume is `s.left.volume`. The problem with this solution is that `Stereo` is no longer a subclass of `Amplifier` — a `Stereo` could not be used in place of an `Amplifier`.

A more accurate solution would be to allow `Stereo` to inherit from `Amplifier` through two intermediate classes. These intermediate classes can be used to resolve the ambiguities.

```
class Amplifier {
  public:
    int volume;
};
class LeftChannel : public Amplifier {};
class RightChannel: public Amplifier {};
class Stereo : public LeftChannel,
               public RightChannel {};
Stereo s;
```

Now the left-hand volume is `s.LeftChannel::volume`. In this solution, `Stereo` is a subclass of `Amplifier`. However, a pointer to `Stereo` still cannot be cast directly into a pointer to `Amplifier` — the programmer will need to specify which `Amplifier`.

```
void setVolume(Amplifier *pA, int v);
void silence(Stereo *pS) {
    setVolume(pS, 0);    //this is an error - which amp?
    setVolume((LeftChannel*)pS, 0);//this is okay
    setVolume((RightChannel*)pS, 0);
};
```

(See the 'Ambiguous inheritance' error for further discussion.)

Indirect class hidden by direct class

Borland: • Base class 'Base' is inaccessible because also in 'Class1'

Microsoft: • C2584: 'Derived': direct base 'Base' is inaccessible; already a base of 'Class1'

Example:
```
class Base {};
class Class1 : public Base {};
class Derived : public Base, public Class1 {};
```

Explanation: Unlike the previous error, one of the classes is inherited directly while the other is inherited indirectly through an intermediary class. The directly inherited class takes precedence. Under the Borland compiler this is only a warning.

Private members not accessible by nonmembers

Borland: • 'MyClass::data' is not accessible
related: • Storage class 'friend' is not allowed here

Microsoft: • C2248: 'data': cannot access 'private' member declared in class 'MyClass'
related: • C2241: *id*: member access is restricted
              • C2255: fn: a friend function can only be declared in a class
              • C2508: id: access denied

Example:
```
class MyClass {
      int data;
    public:
      MyClass();
};

void fn() {
    MyClass mc;
    mc.data = 10;
}
```

Explanation: A private member of a class is only accessible to member functions of the class and any publicly derived classes. Thus, the member data is not accessible from the function fn(). The default for class is private. The programmer can declare the function fn() to be a friend of MyClass, thereby granting it access to private members, as follows:

```
class MyClass {
    friend void fn();     //friend decl must be in class
    //...as before
```

Only a class can declare another function or class to be a friend. A function or class cannot grant itself access privileges. Alternatively, the programmer can provide the class with an access method for data, as follows:

```
#include "compat.h"

class MyClass {
  private:
    int d;
  public:
    MyClass();
    int data() { return d;};
    int data(int v) {
        d = v;
        return d;
    };
};

void fn() {
    MyClass mc;
    int i = mc.data();          //retrieve value of data
    mc.data(10);                //change the value of data
}
```

See the next error description as well.

The members of a class inherited privately are private

Borland: • 'Base::d' is not accessible

Microsoft: • C2248: 'd': cannot access 'public' member declared in class 'Base'
related: • C2247: *id* not accessible because *c1* uses *specifier* to inherit from *c2*
• C2249: *id*: no accessible path to *specifier* member declared in virtual base *c*

Example:
```
class Base {
    public:
```

```
        int d;
};
class Derived : Base {
};
void fn() {
    Derived dObj;
    dObj.d = 0;
}
```

Explanation: The members of a privately inherited class default to private in the derived
class even if they are public in the base class. The default inheritance type
is private; thus, the foregoing is the same as

```
class Derived : private Base {
};
```

Individual members may be declared public in a privately derived class
as follows:

```
class Base {
  public:
    int d;
};
class Derived : Base {
  public:
    Base::d;                        //restore access to public
};
void fn() {
    Derived dObj;
    dObj.d = 0;
}
```

However, a member's accessibility may not be increased in the derived
class beyond what it enjoys in the base class.

A private member may not be redeclared public in derived class

Borland: • Attempt to grant or reduce access to 'Base::d'

Microsoft: • C2604: cannot declare public access to private member '::Base::d'

Example:
```
class Base {
   private:
      int d;
};
class Derived : private Base {
   public:
      Base::d;          //cannot grant access to d since
                        //its private in the base class
};
void fn() {
   Derived dObj;
   dObj.d = 0;     //member not accesssible
}
```

Explanation: The accessibility of an inherited member can be changed from the default that it derives from the inheritance type. However, a derived class may not grant itself access to a member that is declared private in the base class.

A public member may not be redeclared private in a subclass

Borland: • Access can only be changed to public or protected

Microsoft: • C2606: '::Base::d': illegal private access declaration

Example:
```
class Base {
   public:
      int d;
};
class Derived : public Base {
```

```
    private:
      Base::d;
};
```

Explanation: A publicly derived class, also known as a subclass, must retain access to all of the public members of the base class. Otherwise, an instance of the subclass could not be used in lieu of a member of the base class.

Cannot derive a subclass of different storage class

Borland:
related:
- Trying to derive a far class from the near base class 'Base'
  - Cannot have a near class member in a far class
  - Trying to derive a far class from the huge base class *base*
  - Trying to derive a huge class from the far base class *base*
  - Trying to derive a huge class from the near base class *base*
  - Trying to derive a near class from the far base class *base*
  - Trying to derive a near class from the huge base class *base*

Microsoft:
related:
- C4149: 'Derived': different ambient model than base class 'Base'
  - C2269: id: different ambient model than base class *c*

Example:
```
#include "compat.h"
class near Base {};
class far Derived : public Base {};
```

Explanation: The member functions of a near class expect a near `this` pointer, those of a huge class expect a huge `this`, and those of a far class expect a far `this`. Since a subclass inherits the members of a base class, if the base class and subclass are of different memory models, the subclass will end up with member functions of different models as well. The Borland compiler does not allow this, but the Microsoft compiler does. However, having a base class and subclass of different memory models is not a good idea, as a near method cannot invoke a far method or huge method.

Pointer to member declared improperly

Borland: • Cannot convert 'int MyClass::*' to 'int*'

Microsoft: • C2446: '=': no conversion between 'int*' and 'int MyClass::*'

Example:
```
class MyClass {
    public:
        int  d;
};
void fn() {
    int *pMCMember;
    pMCMember = &MyClass::d;
}
```

Explanation: To take the address of a data member of a particular object the function should appear as follows.

```
void fn() {
    int *pMCMember;
    MyClass mc;

    pMCMember = &mc.d;
}
```

Applying the & operator to a member of a class creates a pointer to a member. The pointer is not compatible with a simple pointer, because the class object has not been specified yet. The class object must be specified when used. Declare a pointer to a member as follows.

```
void fn() {
    int MyClass::*pMCMember;//declare pointer to member
    pMCMember = &MyClass::d;//specify which member...
                           //...but not which object
    MyClass mc;
    mc.*pMCMember = 0;    //supply the object when used
}
```

Pointer to member declared improperly (Part 2)

Borland: • Conflicting type modifiers

Microsoft: • C2638: 'pMCMember': memory-model modifier illegal on pointer to data member

related: • C2637: id: cannot modify pointers to data members

Example:
```
class MyClass {};
void fn() {
   int far MyClass::*pMCMember;
}
```

Explanation: Since a pointer to a member is actually an offset within the class, normal pointer modifiers — such as near, far, cdecl, and pascal — do not apply. The object to which the pointer to member is applied may have these properties.

Pointer to member function declared improperly

Borland: • Cannot convert 'void (MyClass::*)()' to 'int (*)()'
             • Use :: to take the address of a member function

Microsoft: • C2446: '=': no conversion between 'int (*)(void)' and 'void (MyClass::*)(void) __near'

Example:
```
class MyClass {
  public:
     void m();
};

void fn() {
    int (*pMCMethod)();
    pMCMethod = &MyClass::m;   //incorrect
```

```
            MyClass mc;
            pMCMethod = &mc.m;          //also incorrect
        }
```

Explanation: This case is similar to the previous example. The result of applying the & operator to a member function is a pointer to a member function, which is not compatible with a pointer to a function because the object is missing.

Notice that supplying the object as in assignment 2 is still not sufficient. A member function expects to be called with the object upon which the function is to operate — this object is referred by the `this` pointer within the function. Although `&mc.mc` has sufficient information to specify the unique address of the function, `pMCMethod` has no place in which to store the object address.

Pointers to member functions are declared as follows. Notice the placement of the parentheses.

```
void fn() {
    int (MyClass::*pMCMethod)();
    pMCMethod = &MyClass::m;

    MyClass mc;
    (mc.*pMCMethod)();
}
```

The following declaration is for a conventional function `pMCMethod` that returns a pointer to an integer member of `MyClass`.

```
int MyClass::*pMCMethod();
```

Incorrect syntax using pointers to members

Borland:
- Member d cannot be used without an object
- Use . or -> to call 'MyClass::m()', or & to take its address
- 'pMCMember' is not a member of 'MyClass'

Microsoft:
- C2039: 'pMCMember': is not a member of 'MyClass'
- C2171: '*': illegal operand

- C2597: 'MyClass::d': does not specify an object

Example:
```
class MyClass {
  public:
    int   d;
    void m();
};
void fn() {
    MyClass mc;
    int MyClass::*pMCMember;
    void (MyClass::*pMCMethod)();

    pMCMember = MyClass::d;//this is incorrect

    pMCMethod = MyClass::m;//Borland doesn't like this

    *pMCMember = 0;          //these are both incorrect
    pMCMethod();
    mc.pMCMember = 0;        //as are these
    mc.pMCMethod();
}
```

Explanation: The first two assignments are missing an &. Use the & operator to take the address of a class member. In keeping with the C rule that a function name without a following () evaluates to the address of the function, the & is optional for member functions under the Microsoft compiler. It is required for member data under both compilers.

Pointers to members cannot be referenced without an object, hence the error on the next two statements. Use the .* or ->* operators as shown.

Finally, pointers to members are not members of the classes to which they point. Again, use the .* or ->* operators.

```
void fn() {
    MyClass mc;
    MyClass *pMC = &mc;
    int MyClass::*pMCMember;
    void (MyClass::*pMCMethod)();
```

```
            pMCMember = &MyClass::d;//take the member address
            pMCMethod = &MyClass::m;
            mc.*pMCMember = 0;          //now use member address
            (mc.*pMCMethod)();
            pMC->*pMCMember = 0;
            (pMC->*pMCMethod)();
    }
```

Don't take member address with an object

Borland:
- Cannot convert 'int*' to 'int MyClass::*'
- Member function must be called or its address taken

Microsoft:
- C2446: '=': no conversion between 'int MyClass::*' and 'int'

Example:
```
class MyClass {
   public:
      int   d;
      void m();
};
void fn() {
    MyClass mc;
    int MyClass::*pMCMember;
    void (MyClass::*pMCMethod)();

    pMCMember = &mc.d;      //this is illegal
    pMCMethod = mc.m;       //Borland does not like this
}
```

Explanation: To take a member address, apply the & operator against the full member name, including class. Applying the & operator against the member of an individual object returns a simple pointer, not the pointer to a member.

Microsoft does not generate an error on the second assignment, because a function name not followed by () is assumed to refer to its address, and the class is inferred from the object's class. This is not proper syntax, however, and should be avoided.

```
class MyClass {
  public:
    int  d;
    void m();
};
void fn() {
    MyClass mc;
    int MyClass::*pMCMember;
    void (MyClass::*pMCMethod)();

    pMCMember = &MyClass::d;
    pMCMethod = &MyClass::m;
}
```

Pointer to member is not compatible with a simple pointer

Borland: • Cannot convert 'int MyClass::*' to 'int *'
Cannot convert 'void (MyClass::*)()' to 'void (*)()'

Microsoft: • C2446: '=': no conversion between 'int *' and 'int MyClass::*'
• C2446: '=': no conversion between 'void (*)(void)' and 'void (MyClass::*)(void) __near'

related: • C2643: illegal cast from pointer to member

Example:
```
class MyClass {
  public:
    int d;
    MyClass();
    void aMethod();
};

void fn() {
    int *pI;
    void (*pF)();
    MyClass mc;

    pI = &MyClass::d;   //next two assignments incorrect
```

```
        pF = &MyClass::aMethod;
}
```

Explanation: A member pointer is not compatible with a regular pointer and cannot be made so. Member pointers have meaning only when applied to an object as in the following:

```
int MyClass::*pMI = &MyClass::d;
MyClass mc;
mc::*pMI = 0;
```

This assigns `pMI` to point to the member `d` of the class `MyClass`. The statement `mc::*pMI` then refers to the `int` member pointed at by `pMI` of the `MyClass` object `mc`. The member pointer may be viewed as an offset within the object of the member.

In the case of pointers to member functions, the member pointer must also include information used to adjust the `this` pointer to indicate the beginning of the base class.

The address of a data member of a particular object may be assigned to a simple pointer, however, as in the following:

```
MyClass mc;
int *pI = &mc.d;
```

Since `mc` has an address, `mc.d` has an address apart from its class. Its type is `int`. However, the address of a member function cannot be taken in this fashion.

Cannot access static member from a pointer to member

Borland: • Cannot convert 'int*' to 'int MyClass::*'
• Cannot convert 'void (*)()' to 'int (MyClass::*)()'

Microsoft: • C2446: '=': no conversion between 'int MyClass::*' and 'int*'
• C2446: '=': no conversion between 'int (MyClass::*)(void)__near' and 'void (*)(void)'

Example:
```
class MyClass {
  public:
    static int  d;
    static void m();
};

void fn() {
    int (MyClass::*pMCMember);
    int (MyClass::*pMCMethod)();
    pMCMember = &MyClass::d;
    pMCMethod = &MyClass::m;
}
```

Explanation: Static members are allocated on a class basis — all objects use the same static member. Thus, no object is required to use the returned address. In other words, `&MyClass::d` is of type `int*` when `d` is a static member.

```
void fn() {
    int *pMCStaticMember;
    int (*pMCStaticMethod)();
    pMCStaticMember = &MyClass::d;
    pMCStaticMethod = &MyClass::m;
}
```

Cannot access virtual base class from a pointer to member

Borland: • Conversion to 'int Base::*' will fail for members of virtual base 'Base'
related: • *base* is an indirect virtual base class of *class*

Microsoft: • C2641: illegal pointer to member cast across virtual inheritance path
related: • C2639: cannot use pointer to member expression &*c*::*m* - base *c* is inherited as virtual
                       • C2640: cannot convert a pointer to member across a virtual inheritance path

Example:
```
#include "compat.h"
class Base {};
```

```
class Derived : virtual public Base {};

void fn() {
    int Derived::*pMDerived;
    int Base::*pMBase;
    pMBase = (int Base::*)pMDerived;
}
```

Explanation: A virtual base class is included in a derived class only once, even if it is inherited through multiple paths. Subclasses of Base may inherit subclasses in different orders — space for Base is allocated once at the end of all other base classes. This makes the offset of a virtual base class within the object different when viewed from different inheritance paths. The net effect is that calculating a simple member pointer to a member inherited from a virtual base class is impossible.

Defining a template class or function improperly

Borland: • < expected

Microsoft: • C++ 7.0 does not support templates

Example:
```
template T min(T x, T y) {
    return (x > y) ? y : x;
}

template
class Array {
  private:
    T *pT;
    int size;

  public:
    Array(int s);
    ~Array();
};
```

Explanation: A list of class name placeholders must follow the keyword `template`. The placeholder will be replaced with an actual class name when the function or class is invoked, as follows:

```
#include "compat.h"

template <class T> T min(T x, T y) {
    return (x > y) ? y : x;
}

template <class T>
class Array {
  private:
    T *pT;
    int size;

  public:
    Array(int s);
    ~Array();
};

void fn() {

    int min(int, int);    //instance min with a T of int
    Array <float> arrayOfFloats(100); //here with floats
}
```

A template function can also be invoked implicitly by use as in the following:

```
void fn(int a, int b) {
    int i = min(a, b);
    //...
}
```

Here the template class `T min(T, T)` is invoked as `int min(int,int)` so that it can be used to compare `a` and `b`.

Instancing template class improperly

Borland: • Invalid use of template 'Array'

Microsoft: • C++ 7.0 does not support templates

Example:
```
template <class T>
class Array {
  private:
    T *pT;
    int size;

  public:
    Array(int s);
    ~Array();
};

void fn() {
    Array arrayOfInts(100);
}
```

Explanation: To invoke a template class, each of the template types must be provided. In the preceding example, the type of T must be specified. The proper declaration is as follows:

```
void fn() {
    Array <int> arrayOfInts(100);
}
```

Instancing template function improperly

Borland: • Could not find a match for 'min(int,float)'

Microsoft: • C++ 7.0 does not support templates

Example:
```
template <class T> T min(T x, T y) {
    return (x > y) ? y : x;
}


void fn(int a, float b) {
    float x = min(a, b);
}
```

Explanation: C++ can automatically promote an `int` to a `float` in order to call an existing function `min(float, float)`; however, it will not change the type of an argument to match a function template.

There are several solutions to this problem. The most straightforward is to divorce the class of the first argument from that of the second.

```
template <class T1, class T2> T1 min(T1 x, T2 y) {
    return (x > y) ? y : x;
}


void fn(int a, float b) {
    float x = min(a, b);
}
```

The problem with this approach is that `min(int, float)` differs only incrementally from `min(float, float)`. Given the large number of possible argument combinations, memory is consumed with little or no gain. In addition, since the return type was declared as the class of the left-hand argument, `min(a, b)` returns a value different from `min(b, a)`. This is probably unexpected behavior.

A better solution would be either to promote `a` explicitly or instance the class before use, as in the following;

```
template <class T> T min(T x, T y) {
    return (x > y) ? y : x;
}


void fn(int a, float b) {
    float x = min(float(a), b);
}
```

```
OR
void fn(int a, float b) {
    float min(float, float);
    float x = min(a, b);
}
```

Different instances of the same template are different

Borland: • Cannot convert 'MyClass<float>*' to 'MyClass<int>*'

Microsoft: • C++ 7.0 does not support templates

Example:
```
template <class T>
class MyClass {
  private:
    T data;

  public:
    MyClass(T d);
};

void fn(int a, float b) {
    MyClass <int> intMC(a);
    MyClass <float> fltMC(b);
    MyClass <int> *pMCI;

    pMCI = &intMC;          //this is okay
    pMCI = &fltMC;          //this is not
}
```

Explanation: This creates two classes, `MyClass<int>` and `MyClass<float>`, and instances each with a single object. Notice how `pMCI` is declared a pointer to `MyClass<int>`. The `<int>` is part of the type. As such, `pMCI` is assignment-compatible with `&intMC`, but not with `&fltMC`.

All template arguments not used

Borland: • Template function argument 'T2' not used in argument types

Microsoft: • C++ 7.0 does not support templates

Example:
```
template <class T1, class T2>
    T1 min(T1 a, T1 b) {
        return (a > b) b : a;
    };
```

Explanation: Here a template has been defined with two arguments, T1 and T2. However, only T1 is actually used within the template function. It will not be possible to differentiate between two instances of the template that differ only in T2.

Bibliography

Basili, Victor, and Musa, John. "The Future Engineering of Software: A Management Perspective." *Computer*, IEEE, September 1991.

Beck, Kent. "Think Like an Object." *UNIX Review*, October 1991.

Beizer, Boris. *Software Testing Techniques*, 2nd edition, New York: Van Nostrand Reinhold, 1990.

Bersoff, Edward H., and Davis, Alan M. *Impacts of Life Cycle Models on Software Configuration Management*, Communications of the ACM, August 1991.

Binder, Robert. *Application Debugging*. New York: Prentice Hall, 1985.

Boehm, Barry. *Software Engineering Economics*. New York: Prentice Hall, 1981.

Booch, Grady. *Object-Oriented Design with Applications*. Redwood City, CA: Benjamin/Cummings, 1991.

Chidamber, Shyam R., and Kemerer, Chris F. *Towards a Metrics Suite for Object-Oriented Design, Proceedings of the 1991 Conference on Object-Oriented Programming Systems, Languages and Applications*. New York: ACM Press, 1991.

Cox, Brad J., and Novobilski, Andrew J. *Object-Oriented Programming: An Evolutionary Approach*. Reading, MA: Addison-Wesley, 1991.

Crosby, P. B. *Quality is Free, The Art of Making Quality Certain*. New York: Mentor, New American Library, 1979.

Davis, S. R. *Hands-On Turbo C++*, Reading, MA: Addison-Wesley, 1990.

Davis, S. R. "Objects Which Change Their Type." *Journal of Object-Oriented Programming*, July 1992.

Davis, S. R. *Turbo C: The Art of Advanced Program Design, Optimization and Debugging*. Redwood City, CA: M&T Books, 1987.

Dunn, Robert H. *Software Defect Removal*. New York: McGraw-Hill, 1984.

Ellis, Margaret, and Stroustrup, Bjarne. *The Annotated C++ Reference Manual*. Reading, MA: Addison-Wesley, 1990.

Ezzell, Ben. *Using Turbo Debugger and Tools 2.0*. Reading, MA: Addison-Wesley, 1990.

Freedman, D., and Weinberg, G. *Handbook of Walkthroughs, Inspections and Technical Reviews, Evaluating Programs, Projects and Products*. 3rd edition. Boston: Little, Brown & Co., 1982.

Hetzel, Bill. *The Complete Guide to Software Testing*. 2nd edition. Wellesley, MA: QED Information Sciences, 1988.

Humphries, Watts. *Managing the Software Process*, Reading, MA: Addison-Wesley, 1989.

Jacky, Jonathan. *Inside Risks*. Communications of the ACM, December 1990.

"Focus on Analysis and Design." *Journal of Object-Oriented Programming*, 1991.

Koenig, Andrew. *C Traps and Pitfalls*. Reading, MA: Addison-Wesley, 1989.

Lientz, B., and Swanson, E. *Software Maintenance Management*, Reading, MA: Addison-Wesley, 1980.

Lieberherr, Karl. "Theory of Object-Oriented Design and Its Application to C++," class presented by Northeastern University and the National Technological University, May 17, 1991.

Manel, Denis, and Havanas William. "A Study of the Impact of C++ on Software Maintenance." *IEEE*, May 1990.

Markham, McCall, and Walters. "Software Metrics Application Techniques." *IEEE Conference Proceedings*, 1981.

McCabe, Thomas J. "A Complexity Measure." *IEEE Transactions on Software Engineering*, December 1976.

McMahon, William. "A Generic Command-Line Switch." *C User's Journal*, October 1991.

Mody, R. P. "C in Education and Software Engineering." *SIGCSE Bulletin*, September 1991.

Myers, Glenford J. *Reliable Software Through Composite Design*. Mason/Charter Publishers, 1975.

Myers, Glenford J. *The Art of Software Testing*. New York: John Wiley & Sons, 1979.

Miller, G. "The Magical Number Seven, Plus or Minus Two: Some Limits on Our Capacity for Processing Information." *The Psychological Review*, March 1956.

Myer, Bertrand. *Object-Oriented Software Construction*. Series in Computer Science. New York: Prentice Hall International, 1988.

Petzold, Charles. *Programming Windows*. 3rd edition. Redwood, WA: Microsoft Press, 1990.

Rains, Ernie. "Function Points in an Ada Object-Oriented Design." *OOPs Messenger*, October 1991.

Riedl, T. R. et al. "Applications of a Knowledge Elicitation Method to Software Debugging Expertise," paper presented to the Fifth Conference on Software Engineering Education, October 1991.

Sakkinen, Markku. *SIGPLAN Notices*. Volume 32, Number 12, New York: ACM Press, 1989.

PC-Metric(TM) tool documentation from Set Laboratories, Inc., P.O. Box 868, Mulino, OR 97042.

Stroustrup, Bjarne. *The C++ Programming Language*. Reading, MA: Addison-Wesley, 1991.

Swanson, E. Burton, and Beath, Cynthia Mathis. *Maintaining Information Systems in Organizations*. New York: John Wiley & Sons, 1989.

Tanenbaum, Andrew S. *Operating Systems Design and Implementation*. New York: Prentice Hall, 1987.

Proceedings of the USENIX C++ Conference, The USENIX Association, 1990.

Walsh, T. J. "A software reliability study using a complexity measure." Proceedings of the 1979 National Computer Conference, Montvale, N.J., Reston, VA: AFIPS Press, 1979.

Walker, M. G. *Managing Software Reliability, The Paradigmatic Approach*. New York: Elsevier North-Holland, 1981.

Ward, Robert. "Debugging Instrumentation Wrappers for Heap Functions." *The C Users Journal*, October 1991.

Yourdon, E. *Structured Walkthroughs*, 2nd edition. Englewood Cliffs, NJ: Prentice Hall, 1979.

Index